ALSO BY ROBIN CODY

Ricochet River

Voyage of a Summer Sun

VOYAGE *of a* SUMMER SUN

CANOEING THE COLUMBIA RIVER

Robin Cody

Alfred A. Knopf NEW YORK 1995

This Is a Borzoi Book
Published by Alfred A. Knopf, Inc.

Copyright © 1995 by Robin Cody
Maps and illustrations copyright © 1995 by Heidi Cody

Grateful acknowledgment is made to TRO–The Richmond Organization for permission to reprint excerpts from "Goodnight, Irene," words and music by Huddie Ledbetter and John A. Lomax, TRO–copyright © 1936 (renewed), 1950 (renewed) by Ludlow Music, Inc.; excerpts from "Roll on, Columbia," words by Woody Guthrie, music based on "Goodnight, Irene" by Huddie Ledbetter and John A. Lomax, TRO–copyright © 1936 (renewed), 1957 (renewed), 1963 (renewed) by Ludlow Music, Inc., New York, NY. Used by permission.

Library of Congress Cataloging-in-Publication Data
Cody, Robin.
    Voyage of a summer sun: canoeing the Columbia River / Robin Cody.
    —1st ed.
        p.   cm.
    ISBN 0-679-41768-0
    1. Columbia River—Description and travel.   2. Columbia River Valley—Description and travel.   I. Title.
F853.C63   1995
917.9704′43—dc20
                                                        94-15527
                                                        CIP

Manufactured in the United States of America
First Edition

To Donna, who put up with it

CONTENTS

Voyage of a Summer Sun

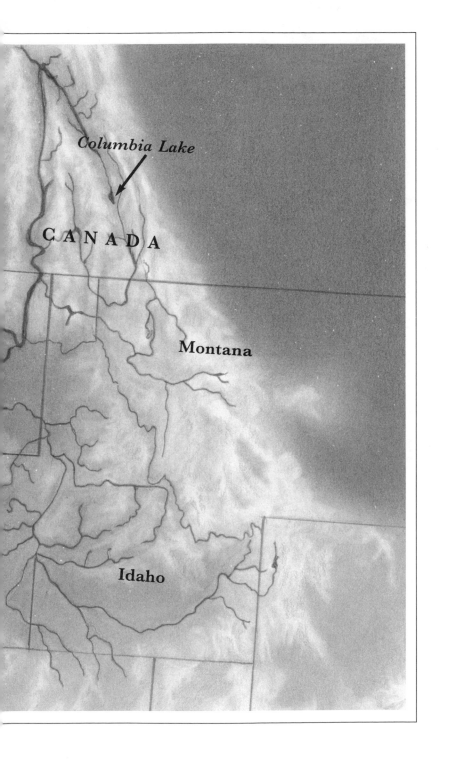

Columbia Lake

CANADA

Montana

Idaho

Prologue

WHERE THINGS COME FROM

A water skipper skates a shallow pool on six little pads of surface tension, and you have to remember that what you're seeing is not the water skipper but the shadow of the water skipper on the pebbled bottom of the pool. With each jerk and drift, water and sun conspire to make more of the water skipper than he is. For that moment, at that place, the world is a little different. But the water skipper is just a deflection, is all he is, of light through moving waters.

The story is the Columbia River, not the canoe and me, but I've learned that friends can't hear me tell about the river until they know why I was out there. This is not an adventure story, although some adventure was unavoidable, and I didn't set out to find myself if I could help it. Nor did I launch the trip with a large point to prove. It was a voyage of discovery, and its telling is the uncovering of surprise on a river I thought I knew. It is an attempt to put words on those occasional true chords that come when a man puts his ear to the river for a good long time. I can't say precisely where the idea of the solo canoe trip came from. I think now it may have been simmering for over forty years in a slow, slow cooker, and the heat rose from many different sources.

My mother is from Astoria, Oregon, Dad from a gyppo logging family that drifted up and down the river through the Depression in search of the next working sawmill. Their courtship revolved around picnics on lower Columbia islands near St. Helens. The episode that sent initial horror and lasting shock waves through her family, I understand, was a prenuptial overnighter: a wind came up, and Bob and Betty couldn't—or didn't—paddle their canoe back to St. Helens. The theme of the family album, then, was established well before I slipped into it.

Rivers. Rivers and beaches. This family photographed its firstborn gripping a clam shovel at Long Beach, Washington; smaller than Dad's chinook salmon at Ilwaco; recoiling from a crab at Netarts, Oregon. When I was five we moved from St. Helens to the Clackamas River, just an hour's drive or a day's float from Portland and the Columbia, still connected by waters. There, on the Clackamas, I learned without knowing I was learning how a paddle cuts water and causes movement, how river mud smells and feels between your toes, and how a flat stone will go skipping across smooth water.

The connectedness had a lot to do with the certainty that all moving water was on its way past St. Helens to Astoria, and the Pacific Ocean. The connectedness also had to do with the deep mystery of salmon and steelhead, who had been to the ocean and returned each season to the Clackamas, back to us.

Mom, for her part, thirsted for place. A teacher, she was curious about the flow of humanity that had put us here. It was she, with her maps spread on the Saturday morning table, who explained where we were going this time: to the Indian fishing grounds at Celilo Falls; to the Astoria Column and Fort Clatsop, where Lewis and Clark first wintered over; to Fort Vancouver, for the British chapter in Northwest history; to The Dalles via the Barlow Road, along which Americans finally spilled into the territory on the last leg of the Oregon Trail not so long ago. You could still see the rope burns on trees, where the pioneers lowered their wagons down Laurel Hill. From my mother came a strong sense that it mattered who came before us, and how they did it.

Dad loved and fought rivers all his life. While rivers and fish, to me, were interesting, to him they were an obsession. The Columbia took a piece of Dad early. In his youth, he dived from a pier into a swimming hole that the river had sand-shifted and shallowed overnight, and cracked a vertebra in his neck. As a result, he could tolerate no breeze from behind. We could never roll down a car window when he was driving. So the Columbia was always with us on Mother's hot history excursions, and on our visits to uncles and cousins at St. Helens, The Dalles, Longview. At gatherings of the larger family, his brothers celebrated Bob for his tendency to step into river holes while bank-fishing, and for his growing history of over-turned boats and lost-in-fog goofs, some of which I shared with him on the lower Columbia. It was said that Bob would die by water, and his brothers speculated on what never-yet-thought-of way he might drown.

I understood this as a rich family joke. The truth, I knew, was that rivers lit my dad up. Rivers made him funny. Rivers made him careless. In town, people knew Bob Cody as the school principal, a sober and responsible man, but what made him alive was rivers. On rivers he could forget, or remember, who he was. He fished the Clackamas nearly every day the salmon were running, before school if necessary, and at least once a year he went out to sea to get them.

Each year, in the two weeks before Labor Day, Dad was drawn by forces as large as life itself toward Astoria, to the river-mouth fishing village of Ilwaco. He put me on the bow of our fourteen-foot Birchcraft, for ballast, and we headed out in a heady mixture of salt air and gas fumes to cross the Columbia River bar, where salmon gathered offshore to await whatever mysterious signal called them back into the river. As the river surged to the sea, our open wooden boat corked atop the crests of greater and greater swells. Over and over again the water receded from beneath the bow and pitched the boat into the next trough. In my growing bones I felt the river pound the underside of the boat. I tasted salt spray breaking over the bow as this mighty river heaved out to sea. Before I knew anything of cubic feet per second or the bar's reputation as the Graveyard of Ships, Dad showed me the Columbia River as a terrifying, nourishing, soul-shaking thing.

The end of the Birchcraft came on the flooding Clackamas River, near home. Dad plucked friends from a rooftop but then lost control of the boat, which swept sideways into a fir and snapped in two. He and those he had rescued spent that December 1964 night clinging to high tree limbs, listening to boulders the size of Volkswagens tumble in the floodwaters below.

The end of Dad came some fifteen years later, in a larger boat. His bout with rivers reached a more or less happy conclusion—a no-decision—near Buoy 10 at the Columbia River's mouth. At age sixty-five he landed a bright fall chinook, leaned forward to tag it, and keeled over dead of a heart attack, all in one continuous act.

So family was steeped in river. I don't mean to say my father's river obsession rode some twisted gene down to me. Where the old man had an active, passionate, lifelong affair with the Columbia, my own has been passive, distant, unconstant.

Life's other currents took me away—East to college, to Germany with the army, and then ten years' teaching in France. Not until later in life did I feel the slow and almost accidental pull of rivers. Back in Portland, wanting to be a writer, I set about telling others' stories for magazines and newspapers. After a few years of this, I looked up to find the thread of rivers running through my work. I'd written about the outlaw Indian fisherman, David SoHappy; about Coast Guard search and rescue at the Columbia River mouth; about hog-line salmon fishermen in downtown Portland. My own forays onto the Columbia and its tributaries were limited to speedy shoots in an inflatable kayak down the Clackamas, down the Sandy, the Deschutes, small stuff that rekindled the excitement and reawakened the fear that comes with rivers.

Gathering, then, was a stream of readiness for the long solo canoe trip that had not yet suggested itself.

When my daughter approached college age, I cast about for better-paying freelance work and hooked the Bonneville Power Administration, the Portland-based outfit that sells electric power from federal dams on the Columbia. Writing BPA's public explanations, I began studying the river in ways I wouldn't otherwise have considered. I had to learn—and became more and more interested in—how the modern river works.

In the span of just two generations, my father's and my own, mankind has shackled this once-raging river and turned it all but completely to human use. Of the main-stem Columbia's 1,200 miles, 800 are now impounded behind a series of fourteen dams. These dams are not often celebrated today, but when they are it's for converting a clean and renewable fuel—falling water—into electric power. Cheap electricity heats and lights Northwest homes, and it fuels electricity-intensive industries that go about their business without smokestacks or air pollution. The dams also divert Columbia River water for irrigation, greening vast expanses of formerly brown desert. Through their locks pass barges carrying crops on a river highway from inland Idaho, and the dams tamed floods that once ravaged low-lying cities downstream.

With change, of course, came incalculable damage to the river system. We're only now tallying up—beginning to figure—the consequences. In the process of harnessing the big river, Euro-Americans wiped out the native way of living in relative harmony with nature's cycles. Dams and their reservoirs flooded huge tracts of wildlife habitat. The fishery suffered not just from dams but also from clear-cut logging, pesticide farming, dredge mining, and streamside grazing. Cities, roads, and industry polluted the drainage system. The river still supports a fishery of Pacific salmon and steelhead, but the wild ones—the natives, with their irreplaceable genetic diversity—are reeling toward extinction as they are replaced by hatchery-bred substitutes. And along the upper shores lurks the malignancy of the nation's largest radioactive waste dump.

It's possible to see clearly both the civilizing benefits of the river and the damage we have inflicted on it, and still be blind to the whole thing. You can know in your bones that Northwest Man and the Columbia River are now and forever braided together in mutual dependency, without knowing how it works. That's where I was before the canoe trip. Missing was the whole sense of it: how energy flows through the Columbia and its systems, both natural and man-made, and how those systems play off one another.

The Columbia River, like the idea for my canoe trip, springs from no single source. The river gathers from glacial drip into brawling mountain streams all along the west slope of the Rocky Mountains, from British Columbia, Idaho, Montana, Wyoming. Before the Columbia becomes the border between Washington and Oregon and knifes through its cliff-guarded gorge in the Cascade Range, it has already traced Canadian rainforest and high desert. Green ferns and tall spruce are replaced by sagebrush and dry wheat, salamanders give way to rattlesnakes, loggers to cowboys, snow-capped peaks to dry-baked hills. After gathering itself from Canada, seven Western states, and two time zones, the Columbia slides from the desert into another dripping rainforest and heaves more water into the Pacific than any other river in North or South America, more than ten times what the Colorado sends through the Grand Canyon, twice the flow of the fabled Nile.

The idea of a single source for all this says more about how we think, our need for clean labels, than about how a river works. Traced backward from the Pacific, the Columbia splits into the Willamette, the Snake, the Pend Oreille, the Kootenay—all major rivers that broccoli into tributaries of their own. What we call the Columbia River is but one branch, the one that carries the most water at each river confluence. Other branches start at higher elevations. The Snake is longer. So why isn't the Snake called the Columbia?

It is because in 1811, David Thompson, the British explorer and mapmaker, used the most-volume idea to first chart the Columbia. He pinned "the source" of the mighty river to a tiny lake high in the Canadian Rockies, a place called Columbia Lake.

Columbia Lake is not wilderness.

I'd known the lake was "up in Canada," a phrase that led me to picture it as nearly inaccessible, its surroundings savage and vertical. The surprise was that I could drive a city car right to it, in winter, and Columbia Lake wasn't even the end of the road. Bonneville Power had asked me to write a short piece for school kids on how the river works, and where it comes from.

This was February, and Columbia Lake wore a cap of gray-blue ice, its surface frozen into white, wind-sculpted waves. Because springwater is warmer than ice, a small probe on the lake's southernmost reach was ice-free where a tinsel ribbon of springwater flowed into the lake. I followed the stream on foot. Crunching along flat frozen shoreline, I watched this silver stream become narrower—and shallower. Up close, the stream edged into aquamarine, deepening to rich blue holes at the bottom of which swirled flecks of loose gravel. Smaller holes, the size of cereal bowls, bared round lips of shoved-aside glacial till. I reached the spot in flat snow and ice where this stream stopped. Or began.

Percolating as springwater from the earth at my feet was the baby Columbia River, flowing north.

Untroubled by the idea that it has many different sources,

I straddled the Columbia River—left foot on the west bank, right foot the east—and breathed deeply of clean mountain air. At that moment, witnessing birth, I felt large and full of the world. Down at Astoria, where my first impressions of the river were formed, only a person nine miles tall could straddle the Columbia River. But bigness evaporated when I considered how little I knew about what lay in between the lower river and its source.

A guy could probably canoe it, I thought.

Because of the dams, the river now falls from this Rocky Mountain loft to the Pacific in a series of broad, flat steps. The Columbia runs free only at its beginning, at its end, and in two middle stretches of about fifty miles each. You'd have to portage around dams, put up with a lot of wind. It would take a long time. But *a guy could probably canoe it.* It was one of those ideas that gets filed away, and you forget which folder you put it in when you get back to the world.

Hunger pangs and the gathering February darkness drove me to the nearby village of Canal Flats. I stopped where the pickups were, at a frozen parking lot and a Quonset hut rink, where loggers on skates roughed each other up in ragged pursuit of a hockey puck. As the match swept and sliced to an end, I drifted with the skaters to the Columbia Inn, the only beer joint in town. The place was thumping to the beat of a country combo from Cranbrook. Two slim pine trees, modified with fake palm fronds, bracketed a hand-painted mural of a coconut-studded Caribbean island. It was "Beach Party Night" at the Columbia Inn. Mountain women in bikinis danced with hairy, white-legged mill hands in swim suits. A party from Radium Hot Springs carried a birthday-boy surfer overhead on his polystyrene board, which snapped in two and dumped him to the floor. A black-bearded logger stood on a corner table, waving a Kokanee beer bottle and blubbering a general challenge to fight. Headlights flashed in the window as a rig skidded across the parking lot and slammed into the east wall, unseating the band's drummer, who took his drums and a refrigerator-sized amplifier with him to the floor in a resounding, mountain-shaking crash.

A fight broke out and I ducked into the john.

And waited.

When the commotion died down, I tried to return to the bar. I couldn't. A body lay slumped against the base of the door. I cracked the door open enough to see the empty bar-room. The fight and its spectators had slid outside.

I pushed against the john door to get out, and something else happened. Maybe it came from having found and strad-dled the river's source. Maybe I had been traveling toward the big river for a long time and was just ready. Much on my mind that day had been thoughts of activity and passivity, of fathers and sons, of a wild river now dammed and tamed. Maybe it was because my own life was moving along so comfortably, without test or danger. I could use some danger, and here I'd just ducked a barroom brawl.

Bubbling like springwater into my pool of shame came a resolve to engage the Columbia River. I would take on the Columbia River.

Resolve, for me, usually cures itself with a good night's sleep. Not this time. Back in Portland I threw together the children's pamphlet for BPA—they wanted it in three weeks. In thinking it and writing it, resolve grew to bursting and filled me with unnatural energy. Scouting, planning, canoe-testing, and provisioning took another three months. On June 17, 1990, I was back at Columbia Lake with the canoe on top of the car.

I owe thanks to many good people at BPA but especially to Lynn Baker, who tossed free-lance writing assignments my way and sparked my interest in how the river works. And to Jack Hart, a close friend and fierce critic. Sam McKinney, the riverman and historian, made the supreme sacrifice of giving me the title he'd been saving for his own Columbia River book. I am also indebted to people I don't even know—Wallace Stegner, Annie Dillard, Loren Eiseley, Ivan Doig, and Jonathan Raban, to mention only a few of the best—whose writing made me think in fresh ways about waters and the West. Rosalie Siegel found the right publisher, and Ash Green and Jenny McPhee at Knopf were correct to insist that shorter is better. And to the many helpful folks I met along the river but whose stories and names are missing from the text, I'd like to say it's entirely the editors' fault.

I

HEADWATERS TO GOLDEN

The River Awakening

Summer comes late to Columbia Lake. The headwaters lie 220 miles north of Spokane, Washington, on the other side of the Canadian Rockies from Calgary, higher on the globe than New Brunswick or Nova Scotia. Because the infant Columbia River flows another 200 miles north from Columbia Lake, the trip had to wait for the breakup of ice. If the start was the only consideration, I would also have waited for the annual June freshet to subside. But the trip would take three months, I figured, and I wanted to reach the Pacific Ocean before autumn storms rolled in. The more I pored over maps and studied weather, the clearer it became. Mid-June was the time to begin.

Thunder Hill Campground on June 17, 1990, was chilly, deadened, and colorless. From the campground, carved into the foothills near Canal Flats, British Columbia, I looked down on a lake reflecting the uniform gray of low cloud cover. A north breeze roughed the surface. My wife, Donna, was with me, and we took an evening paddle into the narrow springwater source of Columbia Lake. Each of us, in turn, stood astride the Columbia River and snapped the other's picture. But the joy I'd known here five months earlier was lost in the fold between anticipation and start. Foreboding, not promise, was the mood. You never know about a river, how it will take to a long solo canoe trip.

Solo. Donna is not a water-person. Her role in all this—and she was touchy about it—was to drive the car back to Portland. To juice up the idea of her taking this long, scenic drive to Canada and returning home alone, I'd tried to talk her into joining me for the first week of canoeing. Just the first week. The first hundred miles, through two natural lakes and into the slow, easygoing waters of the awakening Columbia, might be the calmest and most beautiful of all.

"No rapids," I told her. "Lots of wildlife. You'll love it."

Donna hadn't yet said no. But here at camp she'd begun referring to herself as Your Lackey, a near-truth that was beginning to grate on me.

My nerves were about shot anyway. The last couple of days we'd poked about the upper Columbia, scouting, and had failed to get a good look at Redgrave Canyon, a bad stretch downstream from Golden. And here on the easy part, we found a river at flood stage. Runoff from a heavy winter's snowpack had swollen the river to thick chocolate. Swift current swirled woody debris against the legs of logging bridges, and we watched the Columbia carve new banks at its S-curves. At Fairmont Bridge, near the outlet of Columbia Lake, a nasty roil of whitewater licked at riverbank boulders.

"River's as high as it's been in eight years," said the locals. "River's late rising."

Also, we had read the cautionary signs at Thunder Hill—signs posted about the campground, including one inside the john where you could sit and think about it: YOU'RE IN BEAR COUNTRY. Store food in the car, not in the tent. Secure garbage can lids. Burn food scraps and tins.

"Your Lackey has decided," said Donna, on her return from the john, "to drive to Lake Louise."

That became the plan. She would leave me to the river and

cross the Canadian Rockies to Lake Louise. Maybe she would drive on to Banff. Then Donna would check in on me at Golden, less than a week down the river. We might need the car to scout that mystery stretch past Golden, or perhaps for portage.

I woke up before Donna at Thunder Hill and built a good fire. Morning light slanted through pines as the sun capped a jagged ridge of Rocky Mountain foothills across Columbia Lake. There was no wind. The lake lay still and waiting, deep blue. White sandstone cuts answered their own reflections at the far shore. Coffee water boiled sooner than I expected, a reminder that Columbia Lake lay half a mile higher on the continent than Astoria.

Waters, from here at Canal Flats, can go either way, north or south, to reach Astoria and the Pacific Ocean. Columbia Lake is a small depression within the much larger Rocky Mountain Trench, a broad rut more than a thousand miles long, from Montana toward the Yukon. Less than a mile from where the Columbia bubbles north into Columbia Lake, the Kootenay—already a full-grown river, too wide to throw a rock across—dives into the trench and flows south. The strangeness is that the Kootenay, flowing south, and the Columbia, leaking north, are branches of the same river. The two will come together a month later in my trip. They make an island, essentially, of a land mass the size of England.

While I was packing my gear into waterproof bags, Donna came out of the tent and eyed my stacks of food—a small pile for the canoe, a big pile for the car until we met again at Golden.

"Okay, now let's think," she said. "Five days to Golden?"

Four to six days. My strategy was to save the good wilderness fare for later. After Golden, resupply would be impossible for a hundred miles, maybe more. But here, from Columbia

Lake to Golden, I might pass a country store or two. It would be a shame to use up cooking gas and freeze-dried meals before I had to.

"I thought you were camping," she said.

For crying out loud. After twenty-four years of marriage you'd think she'd know I wasn't going to dig roots and gather berries, or kindle my fire from cedar shavings. I was camping. If the canoe came to a hamburger joint, why not stop in? But like I say, I was on edge.

After breakfast we drove the canoe and gear to the marshy edge of Columbia Lake. I wedged truck-tire inner tubes into the canoe, fore and aft. Toward the bow fit the gray waterproof bag with food, the WhisperLite camping stove and gas canisters, hatchet, fishing tackle, and dry kindling. In front rode a two-gallon water jug. In the stern I put the big black waterproof bag that held the tent, sleeping bag, self-inflating air mattress, and dry goods, mostly clothes and blankets and tarps. I latched to the thwart a smaller bag full of stuff I might need at a reach—camera, apples and cheese, emergency flares, Swiss Army knife, Bic pens, and a Rite-in-the-Rain spiral notebook.

I jammed the spare paddle beneath the rear inner tube and tied the whole business down. Before we said our good-byes, Donna helped me push the canoe through tall lakeshore grass. Mud sucked at our feet.

Columbia Lake is fifteen miles long, an easy half-day paddle if the wind doesn't act up. Because it's natural, not a man-made reservoir, the lake holds at a constant elevation. The more water in, the more pours out. Water and shore have come to agreeable terms with each other, and vegetation knows just how far lakeward it can go. Shore pebbles arrange themselves in tiny half-moon beaches, one after the other, like the lacy edge of a doily. No town has settled on the lake.

A light breeze came from the south, bending lake reeds in the direction I wanted to go, up the west shore. Across the narrow lake, timber furred the slope. On top, snowcapped pinnacles of Rockies appeared only in the bare-rock gaps between nearer mountains. On my side of the lake, sheer sandstone cliffs leveled off to a high bench of hay fields and horse pasture. The highway rode the bench, out of sight and sound. Columbia Lake was all mine. I saw no other person, no other boat, all morning. From holes in white sandstone, blue-backed swallows dived at the canoe and veered away. Puffed clouds bunched at peaks east and west, but the sky above stayed blue and the lake took on a deep, Scope green close to shore.

An osprey rode the updraft into lazy figure-eights above the lake. Mosquitoes weren't out yet, but whenever I put ashore I attracted no-see-ums, big enough to see um. Pink wild roses were out. The world was awakening, fresh, as if this were the first warm day, and maybe it was. A pale yellow butterfly hitched a ride on the bow and flexed its wings in slow dry air.

Across the lake I saw movement on a sandstone cut. Crossing over, I came to a family of six mountain sheep—ram, ewe, and four yearlings—on a near-vertical slope. Their coats were mottled with tufts of tan winter wool shedding to brown. All six had horns—the youngsters' just spikes, but the ram's a fine scimitar curve to a backward point. The sheep stood with their white butts lakeward and watched me over their shoulders until I tired of wonder and moved on.

From south to north, the lake lost its springwater clarity and took on a murkier green. Dutch Creek carried suspended glacial flour into the mix like milk into green tea. Back in February I'd seen lake becoming river as a shallow trickle— twenty feet across and less than a foot deep. Now the whole northeast corner of Columbia Lake was spilling wide through brush and willows. Low saplings bent from their shins. From canoe-level, I could not easily see where I was. But the shore-line cattails aligned themselves to reveal the end of lake, the start of river, and I felt the first strong pull of current.

Follow me, said the river, and I leaned into it.

The baby Columbia swept the canoe into a series of broad,

swift turns. On the left, bullrushes combed the flooded shore. On the right bank stood chic summer bungalows on the outskirts of Fairmont Hot Springs. A trio of chestnut horses watched from behind a white fence. A cedar bent low over the stream, and Fairmont Bridge came into view. As the river narrowed toward the bridge, I heard the whitewater and felt a rush of adrenaline. The water's inverted vee led to a right-of-center chute. The canoe shot between boulders, slid beneath the bridge, and I swept into a wide turn that landed the canoe on the soft flooded fairway of the Fairmont Country Club's par-four fifth hole.

Kootenay Indians built the first wooden bins here to catch hot water rushing from the mountainside. Today the bins are gone, but steaming water, piped from the earth, arrives at city-style swimming pools where busloads of pink Germans roll and sweat. Farther up the mountain, past the resort hotel, ski slopes strip through timber.

The best of my hike up the hill was the view of Rocky Mountain Trench and the twisting, umbilical channel between Columbia and Windermere Lakes. The river wound tight as ribbon candy in the wide trough between the Purcell Mountains to the west and the Rockies at my back. Shores separated river not from land but from more water—sloughs, lagoons, and marshes. Geese and swans stop here as they migrate along the Pacific Flyway, from the Arctic to Baja, California, and back. In all of western Canada, there's nothing like it—a long and contiguous wetland habitat left relatively undeveloped. Yet this is not a park, not a wildlife preserve. Ownership is a patchwork of private and Crown lands, the latter in control of the province but still up for sale. The upper Columbia marshland has survived, so far, because it isn't worth much in human terms. You can't farm it. It doesn't grow marketable timber. It's too spongy to live there. And the upper river escaped damming because it's not appreciably moving, not falling. It pokes along too slowly to spin turbines and generate electricity.

I looked down on the river, silvering in late-afternoon sun.

A calm and river-hardened person might have called it a day here at Fairmont Hot Springs. The idea of sleeping at a resort was not, by itself, a bad one, but skies were fair and my blood was up. Also, I thought, it might be more in keeping with the whole paddle-the-Columbia idea if I spent the *first* night out on the river. Someone might ask about it later.

I walked back to the canoe and pushed off. The Columbia snaked through the golf course and past polite summer homes, and then it twisted away from human sights and sounds. A huge inverted-sombrero of an osprey nest, deep as a bathtub, topped a snag on the left.

One thing about the Columbia, I expected, was I could hardly get lost. Just go downstream. But here the distinction between river and lagoons waned, then vanished. The low strip of bank broke down, and I had choices. Color—muddy brown for channel, slate green for lagoon—showed me where current turned and curled back on itself. So tight were these river folds that I passed again the osprey nest I had seen half an hour ago, now on the right. Getting out to stretch, I walked twenty paces and, just for the idea of it, peed a mile upstream.

The river leaked into more of these swampy lagoons. A woodpecker tattooed a hollow cottonwood like jungle drums. The canoe glided spylike into a mushroomy world where water took on life shapes I didn't know, couldn't name. Three puffy little yellow-eyed creatures sat in the crotch of a snag, like targets at a carnival softball pitch. A fecund, musk-and-rot smell suggested that the world starts here. Great croaks and clicks and birdy racket issued from the backwaters, and I knew there was a lot of sex going on. Violence, too. Around a bend I startled a coyote, swimming from one bank to the other with a mallard drake between its jaws.

A beaver slapped and sounded in two distinct syllables—
cha-PLOO—like a fat kid cannonballing.

I hadn't seen the beaver before it sounded. Pulling myself
together, I thought of the question asked by many of the locals
while I was planning and scouting this trip. *Will you be carrying
a gun?* Mostly the issue came up in the context of bear stories.

No, I wasn't carrying a gun. I didn't want to kill a bear. I
didn't want to enrage, without killing, a bear. I could imagine
firing the gun accidentally or otherwise badly, shooting my toe
off or piercing the canoe. But you never know. It was the way
they asked it: *You're going alone, and you're not carrying a gun?*

The Columbia gave me hours more of easting and westing
before the marshes opened up and I needled the canoe north
through mats of broken reeds onto Windermere Lake. The sun
had slid behind the Purcells, and a chill breeze raced down the
lake. On the right bank I found firm dry ground for camp, and
slept hard.

On Windermere Lake the next morning, sun vaulted the Rockies and flooded the far shore—wooded, rising to far snow-
capped peaks—with rich early light that inspired a huge
laziness I hadn't known since I was little. There was a lot to see,
and not much to do about it. The beach at Windermere village
had strange little upright sheds on skids, which I discovered
were not outhouses but ice-fishing shelters, recently hauled
ashore. A row of pine bungalows waited for summer like toads
on the lakeshore. Two pale college-age women on a blanket
slathered themselves with Coppertone 12 and tried to remember how a picnic goes.

Farther down the lake, at a quiet crescent of shore, I
watched a first-grade class of mergansers and their teacher.
The adult, regal with auburn top-notch, showed her charges
how to fish. She deployed twenty-seven youngsters on the
water at evenly spaced intervals. They formed a half-circle, all
of them facing shore. At some signal I did not perceive, the

half-circle closed in, suddenly, toward shore. With great splash and abandon, they drove minnows and polliwogs to shallower water, for lunch.

After this pincer movement, the class moved on to another crescent of shore, and repeated it. This time a tiny merganser came up with a big fish, a four-incher, longer than its captor. At this amazing success, he broke ranks and paddled for open water, his catch squiggling in his beak. The teacher, upset, took chase. She overtook the little rascal, dunked him, snatched the fish from his beak, and swallowed it whole.

The class then headed on up the shore and resumed cooperative fishing.

The canoe, a sixteen-foot Traveler by Mad River, was new to me, and I wasn't yet sure I had chosen the right vessel. I'd settled on a canoe, rather than a kayak, because it carries more gear and you can change positions. And I just liked the old-fashioned, sit-upright feel of it. Most of the Columbia would be big open water. Wind on reservoirs would be the chief torment. The Traveler is narrow and low, the better to cut chop and catch less wind. Made of Kevlar, a tough space-age material, the canoe is light enough—forty-seven pounds, unloaded—to shoulder around dams. But it's tippy, and it won't slalom on tight turns.

On Windermere Lake it tracked well through shifting wind and light chop. The canoe loved a straight line. On the river curves that came next, it also wanted to slice straight ahead. It went for the outside of bends, where trouble lurked in the form of swift water, newly cut banks, and toppled trees—sweepers—that draped the water. The trick was to hug the inside of each bend, and then watch for a far-side eddy that wouldn't jerk the bow. Aside from a scare at a railroad bridge, where floodwater lifted me far too close to steel, the river gave me room to maneuver. The only equipment problem was the bailer I had top-sliced from a milk jug; it was too clumsy and ugly. I needed a jumbo sponge. With that from the Radium grocery store, and a fresh load of fruit, I pushed off for three days' paddle that left civilization behind.

The river was easy, and I had great blocks of time in which to only watch and think. I was cast off, set adrift. I followed slow current, dodged weather, lost track. In a canoe you sneak back on life. On the lower Columbia, where I live, dams have throttled the river and humans moved in for good. Other species adapted to us. Without much thinking about it, we put the river to work; the other creatures with whom we share it have little to say to us. Or us to them, except, *Move over, boys. Here we come.* But I paddled here as visitor, not master. In bear country, I wasn't even the unrivaled head of the food chain.

At a low, hard-packed mud bench, one of the few dry places, I aimed for shore and eddied in, thinking to peel an orange and stretch. On the bench a fat black bull snake sat sunning himself. He saw my approach but didn't budge. I stayed in the canoe. We looked at each other. It's hard to tell, with a snake, whether he's inert with spring torpor or intends to wrestle it out for his territory.

With the paddle, I splashed cold water on the snake. He didn't twitch. He didn't blink.

All right, I thought. *You got here first.*

Loggers have been here, miners have been here, but they only scraped the slopes and poked holes in the hills, leaving the river to recover itself. Now the trench is green with second-growth timber, the mine tailings grown over. Dots on the map—Briscoe, Spillimacheen, Parson, McMurdo—are not towns but, at most, a gas station and grocery store sharing the same small building. Abandoned sawmills. The river was once the highway, its bed dredged and widened for log booms and small steamers. Now beavers are the engineers, the dammers and loggers, the changers of landscape. Their great limb-and-stick lodges stopper the flow and shape the lagoons. No tree here is of too great a size for a beaver to fell. Beavers own this place.

On my first night past Radium, I stopped to camp on a low bench the shape of an airplane wing but smaller. The resident beaver began harassing me as soon as I put ashore. Back and forth he swam, patrolling in an ever-contracting semicircle. He sounded—*cha-PLOO*—to scare me away. I was not intimidated. He swam closer. This beaver was reddish brown, four feet long, half tail. He had tiny black ears and blond eyes. Behind his square snout and a disapproving brow, he trailed a vee of river back and forth.

My paddling had been interrupted by off-and-on thundershowers all day, and I hurried to pitch the tent and rig a rain fly before the next downpour. Hurry and ineptitude, with the beaver watching, led to my erecting a lopsided tent over nasty stubs of wild rose, topped with North America's ugliest rain fly. I tried to fix it. Another beaver joined my tormentor, and together they went berserk. They showed their teeth and dove—*cha-PLOO, cha-PLOO*—perhaps to exchange low fives beneath the water and summon their friends to come look. I could have saved face by departing. I could have said it was all just an exercise, and I had no intention of staying the night. As I struggled to improve my rain fly—and made it worse—the skies cleared. Evidently it would not rain tonight—or tomorrow night, or ever—on a camp so badly built.

I awoke in fading daylight, thinking it was dawn. When I stepped outside, I felt no dew on the tent flap. My watch, dug from a pack, said 10:40. June 20, this far north on the tilted globe, you get a lot of daylight.

I put myself back in the tent and wished for an interviewer. *Well, Ted, it's a long river, and I'm going to take it just one day at a time.*

The river, still rising, meandered across the broad valley floor. Even while flooding, the Columbia here was a small thing, with

no channel more than three canoe-lengths across. It had no
hurry, no idea it was to become a great river. It split for low
islands, forked for mud spits, and leaked into blind sloughs. As
a rule I opted for each western-most branch, to remove myself
from the paralleling highway.

Spring and summer started and stopped, double-clutched,
slid into and out of one another. Air shaded by scudding clouds
was hugely different from air touched by high sun. When it
rained, it poured, the harsh cold rain of spring. And then that
was over. Putting ashore after a downpour to dump the canoe
of water, I felt summer's hot sun on my shoulder. This was
clean stuff, pure sun, tweezing wildflowers straight from steamy
black earth. And now again rain. The weather played like
twiddling a radio dial across the band, volume on loud.

Elk had left the river for higher browsings, but soon after
breaking camp one morning I heard something crashing about
in a right-bank lagoon and looked up at a bull moose, his
massive antlers poking above cattails. He was straight into the
glare of early-morning sun, and I saw only his head and rack.
Deer were all over, and always spied me before I saw them.
Only one raised her white tail to flee in alarm. Others eyed me
warily, frozen except for head movement and intelligent brown
eyes that followed the canoe. No doubt whole committees of
white-tail deer, hidden in shadowy foliage, saw me pass without
my seeing them.

The whine of jet skis shattered the thin air. Two grown men,
their wetsuits filled to capacity, throttled past and unzipped the
river. I rocked in their wake. I smelled their fuel and heard
them round the bend. Waiting for birdcall to come back to the
river, I reflected on the whole idea of jet skiers and why we
should let them live.

*   *   *

Past the Spillimacheen bridge, I poked through right-bank sloughs looking for Mary Yadernuk's place. I'd heard about Yadernuk from some trappers at Golden. I gathered she was a trapper of the old school, somehow too complicated for a stranger to grasp, so of course I was curious. Nobody had said, "Tell Mary I gave you her name." She didn't have a phone, so all I could do was drop in on her. Across the tracks and the highway, I found her double-gabled brown house with barn and outbuildings. Geese, sheep, goats, rabbits, a hog, and two donkeys saw no distinction between pasture and yard. Yadernuk was hanging her wash. The washline had slipped off its pulley, and it was a tough reach for her, a short old lady. By way of manly introduction, I offered to help.

"I do things alone," she growled.

In profile, Yadernuk's face was a relief map of basin and range, her hair a fright of white wires. Wearing a gold Golden High School football jersey (88) and navy sweatpants, she yanked at the pulley. She wasn't going to turn a visitor away, but she wasn't about to look at him either. As she worked, she talked. Yadernuk had good reason, beyond my visit, to be crabby. Vandals stole the motor from her boat. Coyotes got into her sheep. Three of her cows were missing. The game warden had confiscated a whole line of her traps.

Yadernuk consulted her watch. I followed her into the house. She plugged in the TV and adjusted rabbit ears for a game show called "Talk About." She futzed at the stove. She bawled out the TV set. "Oh come on!" she said. "That's the same repeat as yesterday! They're in the bonus thing now, and this couple wins $5,600."

When her show ended, Yadernuk shoved a cup of tea my way and broke open a package of store-bought crumpets. Now she was willing to be visited. Against the doorjamb leaned a shotgun. Above the wood stove floated a gauzy portrait of Queen Elizabeth as a young woman. Yellowing stacks of papers and magazines covered the living room floor, and a bull moose had rammed the wall and stuck above the fireplace. Yadernuk told me her husband died in a 1953 mine explosion, and her only brother drowned young in the Columbia River. Now seventy-three, she lives here alone and works the land.

"In the bad years," she said, "we trapped out of season. Everybody did. The only way we knew it was a Depression was when a man walked up from the road and offered to work if we'd give him supper. That kept happening. We had lots to eat. We were never poor."

The game warden took your traps?

"A misunderstanding. I was using modified paw traps. I never break the law," she said, perhaps meaning she didn't know the law. Paw traps are illegal—too cruel.

Yadernuk's trap line has been in her family for over eighty years. She has exclusive rights to trap both sides of the Columbia, its sloughs, and adjoining slopes for a fifteen-mile stretch bracketing the mouth of the Spillimacheen River. Sometimes a man from the Canadian Pacific Railroad will stop by.

"The CPR men come to me when they have a nuisance beaver. Say a beaver blocks a culvert under the railroad tracks. I trap the beaver, and sell its pelt."

On the Yadernuk scale of beaver behavior, worse than a nuisance beaver is a problem beaver.

"I worked two and a half years on a problem beaver," she said. "Three miles south of here, around a CPR culvert. That beaver was ee-lusive. Good land. Every trap I set, she made a detour. Put a trap on the bank, the beaver made a channel around it. Put a trap in the water, she went back on the bank. The CPR men were laughing at me. 'How's your beaver, Yadernuk? Catch that beaver yet?' I went down there one night, stayed up all night and watched. This beaver put a stick in the trap and sprang it. Then she piled brush over the trap. She buried the trap! I knew it was a female. No male would do that much work. And then, guess what."

What?

"When I finally did catch her, I had her in *two* traps: a leg-hold and a body trap. The most beautiful dark female. So big I couldn't lift her."

Yadernuk refilled our teacups and noted that social pressures have ruined the market for beaver and muskrat pelts.

"Ten years ago, a trapper could make some money. But now, these twenty-one beaver I got, I'll clear two hundred dollars if I'm lucky. Can't make a living. You have commissions, postage, royalties."

At the mention of royalties, she nodded to Queen Elizabeth, above the stove. When I caught up with her train of thought, Yadernuk was talking about picking cones for the B.C. Ministry of Forestry. Forestry uses spruce and fir cones for replanting clear-cuts. "I started cone-picking on my sixtieth birthday," she said. "Mostly it's young people. This new money. People won't go where I go. I picked three and a half bushels the first day. Guess how much I made."

How much?

"*A hundred and twenty dollars.* Good land! That's the best money project outside 'Talk About.' "

Yadernuk limped out the back door. I followed. A clutch of geese, including a pair of wild ones, joined us in the yard. When she picked up a wooden stepladder, I offered to help. But Mary Yadernuk does things alone.

Why the limp?

"Butchering hogs last year," she said. "I pulled a muscle. Then I hiked too far after huckleberries because I heard there was a grizzly to see up there. I slipped on a spruce and had a hell of a time getting out."

After the Spillimacheen River joined in, the Columbia picked up and moved right along. Wolf Creek, Tenmile Creek, and others came tumbling into the trench, and the flow quickened, widened, and browned. Like a child that's going to turn out all right, the river began making its own choices. It found direction, sensed purpose, began to feel like the heart of something.

Now the canoe needed little steering. Cottonwood fluff rode the surface pull of current, and my canoe was no more, no less. I swung the bow to the left, let it go, and the world revealed itself in a slow, 360-degree turn. Ahead and behind, north and south, the trench lay low as far as I could see. East and west, a berm of false shore separated river from wide lagoons. Beyond the lagoons lay a true shore of black-green woods rising to white crags of Rockies on one side, Purcells on the other. The mountains reached for sky and sent more and more river off their melting skirts.

The daily challenge was to find a camping spot. Trees lacked visible trunks, along the flooded shore, and their low limbs writhed and shivered in the current. Whenever shore came close, I searched for a landing flat enough to hold a tent. Late on the day after Mary Yadernuk, I came to a spot where the left bank had broken down. I paddled from swift brown river into pea-green lagoon. Along the shore was a thin linear clearing high enough to be dry, a piece of abandoned logging road.

The road had been long-enough unused that I could push tent stakes into its bed without using my hatchet, which I used anyway to make noise. *Bears won't bother you if they know you're there.* I pitched the tent and rattled the stove and clanged pots in fixing turkey tetrazzini, a freeze-dried feast that I thought fit for this magnificent setting. Across the river rose the multiple turrets of Castle Mountain, white against late blue sky. Black flies buzzed but didn't bite, and bees were more intent on buttercups than on me.

Standing, the better to let blood flow through canoe-cramped knees, I heard a loud splashing. The commotion came from a dense thicket in the lagoon, a hundred yards away. A small black-hooded, ducklike bird—a coot?—flapped erratically along the water, not flying. It dived and came up flapping again, as if winged, maybe feigning injury to draw attention away from its nest.

A moose came from the same thicket, in clumsy pursuit of the coot. Belly deep in lagoon, the moose plodded toward the near shore. Giving up on the frantic coot, she reached shallower water, stood knee deep and flapped her big brown ears. She snorted to drive off bugs. A moose is really strange. A moose is a life form I never would have thought of. She came galoshing ashore, her hooves sucking at mud and snapping driftwood, and disappeared into shoreline brush.

She hadn't seen me. Evidently moose are nearsighted, or not very observant. The old roadway followed a crescent curve of shore. If I just walked up the overgrown road, here, I might get another look.

I took only a step or two, readying my camera, when something spooked the moose. Had she heard me? Smelled me? There's nothing subtle about a moose in rapid movement. It sounded as if she were felling whole trees in her path. Her crashing organized itself into heavy gallops, and the galloping grew louder.

I froze. Would I get trampled by a spooked moose? Would she overrun my tent?

The moose came snorting into view, less than twenty yards away, her massive overbite pointed straight at me. I dropped the camera, waved my arms, and hollered. "HEY!!!" The moose, terrified, went into a skid. All knock-knees and saliva and then rear flanks, she finished her Bullwinkle slide and peeled out to the right and up the hill, leaving me breathing heavily as she tore a receding hole in the woods.

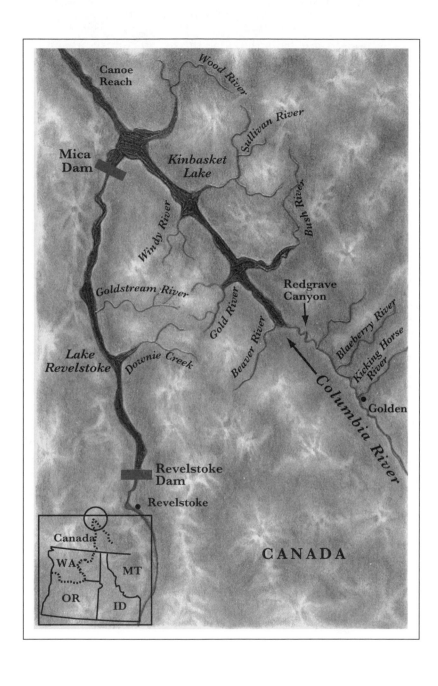

2

GOLDEN TO REDGRAVE CANYON

Bear-Scare and Water-Fright

The river ran high and swift and mud-green to Golden. Glad
for my life on the Columbia so far, I wheeled into a man-made
lagoon by the airstrip and pulled the canoe ashore. Donna was
going to meet me here Saturday, but I'd arrived Friday. Rather
than lug the gear or hitch a ride the half-mile to town, I pitched
the tent in short trees near the spit that separated the Columbia
from the Kicking Horse River. I thought I had picked an
out-of-the-way spot, but the dike separating the two rivers from
the airport was a walkway for evening strollers and a bikeway
for kids who need to throw rocks at the river. I ordered two
beers from three muscled studs on dirt bikes, and they roared
to town and brought them back.

After I'd cooked and eaten dinner, an Einstein-haired man
in lederhosen, accompanied by his wife, stopped to chat. They
planned to go to the States on vacation next month, to Ilwaco.
(Ill-WAY-co, he said.) I told him Ilwaco is where *I* was headed.
He didn't get it.

The river comes out there.

"You mean this river?"

The Columbia River. It finishes at Astoria, Oregon; at
Ilwaco, Washington. The river's last place.

He eyed me skeptically. His wife batted a blackfly off her white leg. These people had lived in Golden nine years, and they didn't know where the river goes. I thought less of them until I remembered that I, living on the lower Columbia, had had little idea where the river comes from. The man said he was a poet. From memory he recited lines about still waters and a beaver breaking the glassy surface. He had known beaver without the beaver anger, and his poetry sounded odd and good to me.

"I go to a quiet lagoon when I feel nature in trouble," he said. "There I can think. Maybe later, I can write."

I tried to remember, after the riot of nature I'd paddled through, that nature could be in trouble anywhere on earth. A foolish urge came over me to dance with these strangers, laughing, over the surface of darkening river, and to whisper to them of Mary Yadernuk, the gnarly trapper. But they wandered off. I lit mosquito coils and drank the second beer and listened to the rush of river, wondering if my tent was on high-enough ground. The Columbia, I knew from having stabbed a stick at the water line each night, was rising four inches every ten hours.

Donna arrived before noon on Saturday. We loaded the canoe and gear and set up at the municipal campground, where the Kicking Horse River split a stark gorge and came bucking into Golden. The Kicking Horse strained at its banks and carried limbs and planks and a cartwheeling stump off the slope of the Rockies. The water, turgid with glacial flour, ran the color of pear meat. Heat, not rain, generated all this runoff. The town shimmered under a white sun as we hiked in shirtsleeves to the Laundromat, bought film and groceries, and looked around.

Golden felt bigger than its population of four thousand. Vacation rigs with out-of-province license plates gassed up on their way to somewhere else, and mud-spattered pickups drove in from the hills to resupply. Golden's original purpose had been to supply miners. In 1884 the Canadian Pacific Railroad made Golden the base for construction crews punching the tracks from Kicking Horse Pass, east, into Rogers Pass, west. Until 1927 you couldn't drive here. When the Rogers Pass section of the Trans-Canada Highway was completed in the 1960s, a string of motels and gas stations sprang up on the shoulder of town. The Husky sign rose a hundred feet high, its dollars-per-litre numbers taller than a man. Golden had a railroad switchyard and a big sawmill, with log trucks coming and going, but the new money was on tourism. The visitors' center was all about whitewater rafting on the Kicking Horse River, helicopter skiing in the Purcells, hang gliding off the dogtooth peak of Mount Seven, snowmobiling and cross-country skiing.

At every stop in town, I asked about Redgrave Canyon. Ahead of me on the Columbia lay a half-day paddle on flat water to Donald Bridge. And then a mystery drop into the canyon. How was all this angry water—and my canoe with it—going to fit through the narrow S-curves of Redgrave Canyon?

Nobody I met had seen the canyon for himself. That didn't stop folks from describing it, but much of what they said was contradictory.

"River's high," said one. "It'll shoot you right through."

"It butts into a cliff," said another. "Whirlpools cough up logs like toothpicks."

"No problem, eh? Friend of mine did it. It's flat."

"Two dandy French in their kayaks stopped at the Donald mill for water. CPR crew picked 'em up the next day, all busted up. Lost one kayak, the other one smashed. Flagged a train and rode it straight back to Montreal."

Asking about the river, Donna and I heard a lot of bear stories. Bear stories in Golden are the accepted way of welcoming strangers. Tina Buchanon, the manager of the natural history museum, said she'd surprised a black bear inside her camper Tuesday.

"Right behind the museum," she said. "The dog chased the bear out of the camper. I called the game warden. The RCMP came out, too. 'We've heard about this bear,' they said. 'He's been around town. We'll shoot that little son-of-a-bitch.' Well, this bear from my camper wasn't a little one. It was a six-footer, I told them. But they don't believe a woman. They went into the bush, looking for the bear. Pretty soon I heard shots. They dragged a bear out. I said, 'That's not the bear that was in my camper.' They were disappointed. They said, 'This is not the bear *we* were looking for either.' "

At the Mad Trapper, from an elk hunter: "She was a teacher from Victoria, and I think she'd been disappointed at love. Anyway, she took off in her Volkswagen and got stuck in the mud where a logging road crosses Wolf Creek. When we found her, she'd been stuck for eight days. She had a blanket over her head. Scared of bears. I tried to talk to her, but she was disoriented. She wouldn't get out of the car. She'd written her final words and put a note on the seat. That lady was so scared of bears she'd starve before she'd walk for help. Eight days with a blanket over her head. I get a card from her every year, every Christmas."

What I knew about Redgrave Canyon came from books.

M. J. Lorraine was a civil engineer from California who, in 1921, navigated the entire Columbia River in a rowboat, and wrote it up. In *The Columbia Unveiled*, now a rare book, Lorraine gives a no-nonsense account of the rapids he saw along the way. He arrived at the head of Redgrave Canyon in early June that year, and he, too, found the river at flood stage. Lorraine holed up for a week at Waitabit Creek, waiting for the river to drop.

A deep swirling hole lay just downstream from a foaming narrow chute. "I knew that if I would get into the maelstrom, it would mean curtains for me." When Lorraine pushed off and his boat touched rushing current, the left-hand oarlock flew upward out of its socket. While Lorraine recovered his oar, his boat somehow skirted the maelstrom and he tied up to collect himself at Redgrave station. A railroad watchman, posted on Calamity Curves, helped Lorraine line his boat through a washboard of standing waves called Kitchen Rapids, farther downstream.

Earl Roberge, the author-photographer of a handsome picture book about the Columbia, shot the canyon in 1978. With Don Hodel, then head of the Bonneville Power Administration and later Secretary of the Interior, Roberge took the rapids in a two-man kayak. Misled at Golden about what to expect, they rounded a placid bend and were suddenly drenched in spray. "Huge waves broke over our bow and slammed us around like puppets on a string. . . . Boiling crosscurrents tugged at our craft and tossed us about until I began to wonder if it were any use at all to paddle so frantically."

So Redgrave Canyon was trouble.

Donna and I scouted what we could. On the drive up here, we had taken a dirt road down to Beavermouth to see that the reservoir, though rising, was not backed into the canyon. Then we had followed a logging road downstream from Donald Bridge and watched the Columbia bend ominously into the narrow cliffs. Now, having narrowed the bracket of mystery from twelve river miles to about five, we bounced down a CPR maintenance road for a glimpse of the middle. At the bottom of a long series of hairpin turns, the railroad tracks rode a bench on a westering bend of the river. Branches and skinned trees rode the water around the bend. Small pieces, not whole logs, slid beneath the surface to pop up again downstream. The Columbia ran sudsy with brown foam, a sure sign that what we could see from the tracks was not the worst part. Downstream, the CPR tracks cut the corner and disappeared into a hard-rock tunnel. There would be no exit, no way to recover a wreck but to ride the river to Beavermouth.

We drove back to Golden and ate at the Mad Trapper. Unless I could find someone with the skills and proper vessel to go with me, portage seemed unavoidable.

On the other hand . . . If I didn't do it, I would carry the burden of timidity, of not quite having done the whole river.

I was so worked up that when a bearded stranger entered the Mad Trapper and called out my name, I knocked over a beer in the act of greeting him. I introduced Donna and we began an animated conversation before it came to me I had no idea who this guy was. He was a florid Scot with a curled whiskbroom beard, thick torso, and a baseball cap. Wayne Houlbrook had heard about me from his son. I then recalled having met the boy when Donna and I first looked at the airport lagoon. He saw the canoe on our car and said his dad was a wilderness guide. No, his old man hadn't done Redgrave Canyon, but the boy had heard him wonder about it.

So you've never done Redgrave Canyon?

"Did it yesterday," Houlbrook said.

Did it yesterday! Donna snagged a waitress for a towel and a round of beers. Houlbrook and his daughter's boyfriend had taken Redgrave Canyon in a twelve-foot aluminum boat with a 6-horse Evinrude. He'd always wanted to do it, he said.

So you'll take me down the river?

"Nope," he said. "Just dropped by to warn you. You got six-foot standing waves in there, mate. Suckholes and whirlpools, eh? That river'll swallow a canoe whole. Later in the summer you could do it," he said. "But not now. I'm not goin' in there again."

Thunder pealed off the walls of Kicking Horse canyon, the backdrop to our Golden campsite, the next morning. Bursts of windblown rain peppered the tent. Between squalls I brewed coffee, liberated a handful of granola bars from the car, and ducked back into the warmth of tent, carrying room service to Your Lackey.

I had planned to use this Sunday to float the short—sixteen miles or so—stretch of flat Columbia River between Golden and Donald Bridge. By late morning the thunder passed high into the Rockies. Showers became less frequent, less severe, and finally petered out altogether. Sun drew steam off the tent. No sooner had we latched the canoe to the car roof than Houlbrook drove up in a black four-wheel-drive Suzuki Samurai with *his* canoe on top. His paying customer, a birdwatcher from Edmonton, had failed to show up this morning.

Seeing what I was up to, he asked to go along. This was awkward. I didn't want him to confuse me with a paying customer on this easy run to Donald Bridge. Yet he already had scouted Redgrave Canyon for me. Did I owe him something?

"No, no," he said. "No charge. I got nothing better to do."

We took Houlbrook's canoe, a yellow fiberglass sixteen-footer, because it was built for two, and launched it at the airport lagoon. The surging river ran flat and wide, and we moved fast in the company of woody scrap and corkscrewing logs.

A faint hissing sound rose from the canoe, and then faded. Both of us heard it, and neither of us knew what it was. It sounded like air escaping from an inner tube. The hissing came from inside the canoe, yet we carried nothing that could make such a sound. No more than a few drips of water lay at our feet. Houlbrook said the canoe's two flotation compartments, fore and aft, were filled with foam, not air.

The hissing faded and then came on again, very strong, as we passed the influx of a glacial-white stream to starboard. And then it dawned on me. Glacier-ground rock, suspended in fast water, was playing the canoe like a long fiberglass instrument. Here was the sound of pulverized Rocky Mountains on their way to flat white beaches that flank the mouth of the Columbia River, up and down the coast. We were listening in on geological time. A river's riddle had unfolded into a fresh view of the planet, and I was pleased beyond all reason as we rode nature's slow machinery at the forming of landscape.

And Houlbrook was vastly relieved we hadn't sprung a leak.

Two strangers in a canoe must test one another. You have to listen for the other paddler's river knowledge, and subtly display your own. Watch for canoeing skills, for physical strength, for judgment at the edges of danger, for a sense of humor.

No doubt I, too, came up short on a number of these scales. But Houlbrook didn't strike me as your ideal wilderness guide. Before launching at the airport lagoon, he'd estimated Donna should pick us up at Donald Bridge in six hours. Six hours? I guessed three hours, at the rate the river was flowing, and he readily revised his guess to four. And he was not interested in maps. On the river, now, he missed the cutoff to a back-channel slough he wanted me to see. Paddling aft, he U-turned the canoe and powered us through a particularly dangerous maneuver, I thought, slicing swift current to enter the slough against the grain.

With probing I learned that Houlbrook was *hoping to become* a wilderness guide. He had a business card and had selected the pictures he would use in a color brochure—Kinbasket Adventures—to lure tourists off the Trans-Canada Highway. He'd led birdwatching trips on the upper river and hoped to find hunters who would pay for a guide. A welder by trade, an odd-jobber, he dreamed of making money at what he loved to do. The bird-watcher from Edmonton this morning would have been one of his first paying customers.

Yet there was a lot to like about Houlbrook. He was strong at the paddle, and he took to the river with unfeigned enthusiasm—"a rush," he called it—at spying on wildlife along the banks. He was invariably the first of us to spot the critters, leaving me to wonder how much I had missed on the river until now. Anyone could have seen the deer that scampered from our passing canoe, but Houlbrook also pointed out their wiser cousins who held ground, turning only a well-camouflaged head to watch us.

We passed wooden platforms on stilts, for geese to nest on. "The rod and gun club put up these gander landers," he explained. "The trouble is, eh? They work. Too many geese grow up and come back." He told me about a place I'd passed upstream where geese had taken over a heron rookery. "And I saw a goose this year in an osprey nest! The herons and ospreys were out of business. Moved out."

When moose didn't appear where Houlbrook expected them, we put ashore to lunch and walk around. He heard the snap of a branch and set to work calling moose. His high-pitched groaning whistle was so agonizing, so pleading, I couldn't help but think it authentic, although the moose did not show.

The Blaeberry River came rollicking into the Columbia the color of piña colada. Howse Pass, up the Blaeberry, is where David Thompson, the astronomer and mapmaker and scout for the Crown's fur trade, crossed the Continental Divide in 1807. Thompson was looking for the Columbia and assumed he hadn't found it yet. This river flowed north. He built a trading post that winter on the shores of Lake Windermere.

In his journal, Thompson mentions asking the Indians how far he was from the Pacific Ocean. Thompson wrote: "After drawing a Chart of their Country . . . they assured me that from this House to the sea a[nd] back again was only the Voyage of a Summer Moon."

I suspect confusion. I picture language problems: the Indians pointing down the river, gesturing toward the sky, drawing stick marks in sand. Before dams it might have been possible to get from here to the sea in one moon, one month, although portages on the wild river were long and difficult. *And back again?* No. Thompson, who set up more trading posts and waited four years to find Astoria, didn't complete the journey in anywhere near a month. Maybe the Indians were putting him on. Still, I like the scene. I like the idea of it. The voyage of a summer moon.

The river drew near the highway, and we closed ground on a scruffy young coyote loping the bank, going our way. He was up to no good. The coyote glanced at the canoe and gave a start, confirming his guilt, and hurried to stay ahead of us. We continued this way for a good long spell, two men and their coyote going down the river. The coyote paused only to look over his shoulder and to see that it was true, we were still on his yellow tail. He disappeared into brush a time or two, then appeared farther downstream. Houlbrook feared we were driving him from his range, too far from home.

"Just hold your ground, young fellah," he said. "We'll pass on by."

Before we could, the river bent left and away from road. The coyote darted into the bush and was gone.

I think maybe what happens is the river, like alcohol, can blur differences between people who have shared it and make them more trustful of one another. More dangerously, it can lead them to think a questionable joint venture is not only possible but also the suddenly obvious and correct thing to do. Houlbrook and I sat on a log beneath Donald Bridge, waiting for Donna to pick us up. The full flat river disappeared around a bend toward the siren call of Redgrave Canyon.

"What a guy could do . . ." Houlbrook began. He, too, had

been thinking about the canyon. "I could get a big whitewater raft, eh? Friend of mine has one. Can't sink those suckers. I have a couple of survival suits, the kind they use for river rescue."

Houlbrook guided Donna and me to his house that evening and we met Pat Howard, his mate. She pan-fried a mound of elk steak and moose sausage, and the two of them ("Tell 'em about that grizzly, Pat") made us feel at home. They'd built their log house themselves, or were still building it, south of Golden and up a winding pavement that turned to gravel and then to a quarter-mile dirt-and-rock driveway to a hillside view across the Columbia River valley, no other house in sight. Still testing, I was glad to see that the plumbing and electricity worked. Doors closed with a Swiss heft and fit.

At the table Houlbrook was telling *his* bear story. "We were new here, building the house, living in a tent. And bears don't see so good, eh? This grizzly stalked up the path toward the tent, and alls I had was the boy's BB gun. I laid real still at the flap. When he got close I plinked him on the nose with a BB, and he took off down the hill like a raped ape. It helped us get to know our neighbors, eh? They'd say, 'Are you the guy who shot the grizzly with a BB gun?' "

Also, I liked his photo album. Close-ups of big game proved he could call wild animals to his camera. And to his rifle, I recalled, with a moose-sausage burp. He talked of each animal in the album with a familiar pride—"This guy here," or "That old girl"—like a family member. I settled with Houlbrook on a fee, and we agreed where to meet the next day to ride a whitewater raft through Redgrave Canyon. We discussed how to shuttle vehicles and vessels between Donald Bridge and Beavermouth, a story problem that only Donna was able to think through.

Donna and I drove back to our campground. The night sky was star-punctured and still, but not black dark. When we got in the tent I lay wide awake, full of moose sausage and bear stories, racked with brain-race and river-fear. The Kicking Horse roared past camp, and my stomach wrenched itself taut as rope.

Now, if I were writing fiction, I'd cut this part. Truth, sometimes, is unbelievable. But what happened was I was lost in that netherland between dream and sleep, past midnight, when something sudden and powerful crashed into our tent. I sat bolt upright, half out of my sleeping bag. My scream was a snake-in-the-sleeping-bag kind of scream, an extended yowl that could never be practiced or taught. Donna had a hand on my shoulder and was whispering things before she saw for herself that our tent was half down. One end lay collapsed at the foot of our sleeping bags. Not yet aware of where she was, Donna pulled on a sweatshirt and moved to step outside. In the time it took me to catch her, I realized that screaming was not an adult response to our situation.

I found the flashlight and turned it on. Something had, in fact, collapsed the tent. I flicked the light off.

We lay there, breathing.

I banged the flashlight against the hatchet blade.

Manlike, now, when the whatever-it-was did not return, I stepped outside with the flashlight to look around. The campground slept. There was no wind. Stars were out, and no branch had fallen on the tent. Spooked, I half restaked the tent and returned inside, where Donna lay bordering on delirium. And I, quickly and unaccountably, fell into a deep and seamless sleep.

We can't be sure it was a bear. Nobody, least of all Donna and I, saw it.

Surveying the damage in morning light, I discovered that whatever hit the tent had uprooted six of the fourteen tent stakes from good solid ground, and bent the tent pole. One stake landed fifty feet away, behind the car. But there were no claw marks on the tent. We'd heard no woofing, no growl. And our camp neighbors had heard nothing at all, not even my screams, over the rush of Kicking Horse River.

Houlbrook, when he drove up, was more amused than respectful. "Not getting much sleep, eh?" He didn't think it was a bear. "Probably a vandal. Kids have been raiding coolers around this campground."

Oh, sure. It was a bear, all right. No doubt I had saved our lives by scaring the beast into the night with my screaming. Bears hate that.

Houlbrook had come to the campground not with a white-water raft but with his twelve-foot aluminum dinghy strapped to the roof of his rig. He'd had some problem getting the raft, or judging its condition, and anyway, "I did the canyon in this boat," he said. "I guess we could do it again." The boat was dented and used, obviously loved. But rapids-worthy? And a 6-horse Evinrude isn't much.

At Donald Bridge we slipped into yellow survival suits that covered body, arms, and legs. They would keep us afloat and ward off hypothermia if the boat swamped. I wore neoprene boots, leather gloves, and a red stocking cap. We launched the boat and waved good-bye to Donna, hoping to see her again at Beavermouth, and gave ourselves over to wild brown river.

We passed under the railroad bridge and turned the corner at Marl Creek into a roiling quarter-mile-wide eddy where the Bluewater River joins the Columbia. High water had sliced a new bank, and toppled hemlocks raked the water at the only place we could have bailed out before dropping into Redgrave Canyon. Cliffs shouldered in. The river stood on edge, gathered speed, and I wanted to grab a fir tree to keep from flying off the planet as it rolled.

We plunged into a sheer-walled chute that led to the first

series of curves, the river climbing against the outside of turns and leaving the inside bends to lower suckholes and boils around jutting rocks. I clamped a death grip on the left gunnel and hooked my right hand under the bow, bracing elbow on knee to wedge myself into the heaving boat, and Houlbrook shouted DON'T SHIFT YOUR WEIGHT over the roar of river and the whine of engine. He steered us close to river center, lining up curves on the outside to get a view of what loomed ahead, and then skated to the inside just short of the tallest breakers. River smacked the boat and threw icy spray over the bow as we corked among whole trees and lesser debris through the next chute and toward a towering straight-ahead cliff, where huge scissoring waves kicked out from the wall. On the left was the sworling maw of Lorraine's maelstrom, and we rode the slope of its vortex before the river slung us forward, spit us out.

We knifed through the curve by the railroad tracks, nudging the waterbillow of a mid-river boulder and slam-dancing another, and then into a series of standing waves—Kitchen Rapids. The river narrowed, and we blasted these breakers head-on. The boat rose high on the crest of each wave and then pitched down to smack the next one. Angry water broke across the bow, over which I registered nothing but sky, water, sky, water, in rapid sequence. Houlbrook, keying on a naked boulder that had been here just two days ago and was now gone—the river had changed on him—missed a turn. We slid backward, then sideways, into a suckhole. It wasn't a big one, not the maelstrom, but the whine of the Evinrude, pathetic against the roar of river, drew us deeper into the hole. I felt the river grip at thin aluminum and watched a straining row of rivets at my feet. The river, in the voice of God, said, *You're mine.* And our little craft answered, *No, we're not.* The Columbia River barreled past. I left my body for a while to watch this from a neutral tree branch, just to see how it would all come out, but the suckhole reversed itself into a rising pillow, as a suckhole will, and tossed us forward. We sliced downstream into a final set of curves, where Houlbrook maneuvered the boat as if it were an extension of his central nervous system, making no mistakes, and we glided out into the calm open headwaters of Kinbasket Lake.

3

KINBASKET LAKE

He Saw What Was Coming

The story they tell about Kinbasket Lake, the reservoir behind Mica Dam, has these innocent fishermen trolling the lake when a tree busts loose from the lake bed. A whole tree, with no warning, comes whooshing from the bottom of the lake, splits the water surface, and leaps skyward like a Poseidon missile.

Because the reservoir wasn't logged before it filled, a forest lies under the lake. Picture this. A 150-foot fir, rooted 400 feet deep, has died but it hasn't decomposed. Its wood aches to rise. Roots hold the tree down. The roots stiffen over time and lose their grip on forest floor until finally—next week? six years from now? today?—the tree tears itself loose. It rises from the bed of the lake, picking up speed. Brittle upper branches snap off. Clean as a javelin, now—*What's that noise?*—the tree spears anything in its path.

Nature blasts from man-made lake. Everyone who knows Kinbasket Lake has heard this story, and most have told it: Revenge of the Flooded Trees.

No paved road reaches the shores of Kinbasket Lake, but you can take a dusty logging road from the Trans-Canada Highway down three and a half miles of switchbacks to Big Lake Resort, a brave huddle of camping sites and cedar shake cabins at Beavermouth (population two). The Beaver River comes in here. When Houlbrook and I emerged from Redgrave Canyon, Donna was waiting with the canoe on the car, and we had a heroic wienie roast with Dave and Reta Wurzer, the owners of Big Lake Resort. The Wurzers can reach the world, if necessary, by radio phone, and their electricity comes from a propane generator. We were in advance of the tourist season, but when they come they come mostly from Germany. "The Bavarians have mountains," Reta said, "but I guess it's not wild. Not like this. The other day I went to put the dog out, and there was a bear with his paws up on the railing, like 'Can Duke come out to play?' The bear got so friendly we had to put him down."

Donna and I stayed the night in a cabin. After a thumping good breakfast of sausage and eggs the next morning, she and the Wurzers pushed me out onto the big lake, Kinbasket Lake. The railroad tracks took a sweeping left turn up the Beaver Valley into Rogers Pass toward Revelstoke, only two hours away by train. My own route from Beavermouth to Revelstoke would take two weeks. The Big Bend. The Columbia probes much farther north before it remembers it is the Great River of the West, turns sharply around, and returns on the other side of the Selkirk Mountains.

Now I paddled on man-made waters. The chief strangeness was I had passed from all-out flooding to empty-looking reservoir. The vertical gap between lake and the high-water mark was 40 feet, about the height of the left-field wall at Fenway Park. The reservoir looked empty to me, but it wasn't. In fact, Kinbasket Lake was nearly full. When it's all the way down, the gap to the high-water mark is 155 feet, twice the height of the *roof* at Fenway Park.

Kinbasket Lake is the reservoir backed up by Mica Dam, North America's tallest earth-filled dam. In 1973 it plugged a natural drain and backed the waters of the Canoe and Co-

lumbia Rivers into opposite reaches of the Rocky Mountain
Trench. So Kinbasket Lake is long and narrow, seldom more
than two miles wide. Though smaller on its surface than Lake
Roosevelt, behind Grand Coulee Dam, Kinbasket is the Columbia River's deepest and most capacious, with 20 million
acre-feet of stored water. If you had a pool one mile square, six
miles deep, you could fill it with the water from Kinbasket
Lake.

Mica Dam's primary purpose is not to generate electricity
but to control floods and hold back energy potential for populations far removed, in the U.S. Pacific Northwest. It's a storage
dam. In combination with three other big storage dams on the
upper Columbia and its branches, Mica evens out the river's
flow. Otherwise the Columbia would send more water rushing
seaward in spring and early summer than anybody can use.
Anybody, that is, except young salmon and steelhead, who ride
seasonal high flows toward the ocean. These upriver storage
dams give the Northwest a steady, year-round supply of hydro-
electric power. In years of heavy snowpack and generous runoff
(an infrequent occurrence of late, but 1990 was one of those
years), federal dams on the lower Columbia will generate more
power than the Northwest states can use. The Bonneville
Power Administration then sells the excess to California over its
federal power lines.

Canada, for its part in the Columbia River Treaty, signed
in 1964, got the money to build the dams. And more. British
Columbia also sold its half of the downstream power benefits
(thirty years' worth) to U.S. utilities for a onetime payment of
$273 million. That part of the treaty is up for renegotiation in
the late 1990s.

From the low perspective of a canoe, Kinbasket Lake goes and
goes and goes. I spied a house-shaped object floating in the far,
far-ahead distance. It slowly rose from the water until I saw—
after blinking, looking away, then concentrating anew—that it

was a house. The barge it rode on, and the tugboat that pushed it over the curve of the earth, became visible three hours later.

A big storage dam grips nature by the belt and stands it on its head. Mica Dam stoppers the river and releases water at the "wrong" time of year. In winter, when the high country is locked in ice and mountain rivers run lowest, you want Kinbasket Lake full. And for that to happen, the lake must be drawn down in May, to capture all the spring-summer runoff. Kinbasket Lake is high in the dry season, low in the wet season.

Debris is a problem. Because the province was in such a hurry to collect on treaty terms, B.C. Hydro filled the reservoir without logging its bed. Loggers skinned the periphery, clearcutting only deep enough that treetops wouldn't show at low water. And the reservoir also filled faster, in 1973 and 1974, than it would have in average water years. Thick snowpack and heavy runoff floated slash piles onto the lake before they could be burned. At the same time, Mica Dam blocked the Columbia River's natural ability to cleanse itself.

Woody debris that had tumbled through Redgrave Canyon with me was matched now by the loads of other rivers—the Beaver, the Gold, the Bush, the Sullivan—which spilled into Kinbasket Lake like multiple spigots into a massive tub. The newly arriving trash bobbed on the surface of the rising lake. Shoreline was a sloping brown scar, littered with tangled driftwood from other years. Stumps, lacking soil that once wrapped their roots, stood on grotesque stilts. And because the "tide" here is not daily but annual, the young lakeshore had not yet established its angle of repose. Whole trees, their roots undercut, lay where they had toppled lakeward, some with their needles still green. The mouths of creeks entering the lake were choked with logs and limbs.

Stop a big river, reverse its annual pulse, and you stop a lot of things. My first day on Kinbasket Lake I saw only one deer—a skittish doe. She was the last cloven-hooved animal I would spot for the next five days' paddle. After the teeming, buzzing, chirping banks of marshy upper river, I had passed into dead-wall, barren-shore silence. The distant whine of a chainsaw was all that found my ear.

Among the flotsam on Kinbasket Lake were these strange small green islands. Inspecting, I saw they were sections of former forest floor that had risen intact to the surface. Peat islands. Peat, slow to disintegrate and two feet thick, had come to the surface in great, low-floating blocks. The largest peat island I saw was the size of a softball infield. Three leafy birches, taller than my canoe is long, had grown up among the grass and ferns, sailing the island from one lakeside notch to another as winds shifted.

When a peat island adjoins shore, it looks like a low shelf of land. A logger told me that moose, when the lake first rose and moose still lived here, would come looking for meadows and step onto a peat island. Their hooves punched through the peat, trapping the moose for coyotes to clean up.

In the British Columbian way of naming waters, a "reach" has "arms," instead of the other way around. As I paddled the west bank of Columbia Reach, the lakeshore jogged to meet each small creek tumbling in. The bigger the creek, the sharper the leftward notch. A big tributary, the Gold River, had carved its own sideward canyon that is now flooded and is called Gold Arm.

These arms are the most beautiful and the most treacherous places on Kinbasket Lake. Houlbrook and others had warned me that twisted winds come shrieking to and from their canyons, and can do so quite suddenly. If the wind shifts outward from the arm, great rafts of debris can loose themselves lakeward and swamp a canoe. A locally famous swath of such wind caught Boy Scouts in canoes crossing Sullivan Arm in

August 1982. Three canoes capsized. Four boys, all age thirteen, and two adults died of hypothermia. Their bodies, wrapped in orange life jackets, blew across Kinbasket Lake, where searchers picked them up days later.

My own strategy was to paddle within a stroke or two of shore, ready to beach the canoe at the first rush of wind. This would add tens of miles, maybe a day or two, to the straight-line route to Mica Dam. But what was the hurry? If shore detoured, so would I.

Toward late afternoon, I bent left with the shoreline into Gold Arm. I turned the corner and saluted the stiff white pinnacle of Mount Sir Sanford, whose glacier sloped in light-jade crevasses toward the Gold River. As I paddled into it, Gold Arm narrowed to a mile wide, half a mile wide, a quarter mile wide. Across the arm, I saw a grassy flat that looked like a good campsite. The safe way to get there was to keep paddling along the left shore until the arm narrowed to a finger, and then return along the right bank. This would take an hour or so more than cutting across the arm.

It had been a long day. The good campsite, so close, fired the wrong synapses, melted gray matter, and cocked my finish-hammer. I broke my own rule and cut across the arm. And *just like they tell you,* the wind slammed into the canoe with no warning. No sooner had I committed to crossing than the wind howled off the lake and wrapped the canoe in whitecaps. Lucky for me the waves came inward, from open lake, but the squall hit so suddenly I couldn't turn the canoe around. Paddling hard, on the left side only, I quartered into the waves and dropped to my knees to lower the center of gravity. Waves pounded the right side of the canoe, but the canoe tracked well in this first tough test. It stayed quartered. I surfed to the opposite shore and landed in rocks and stumps much farther into Gold Arm than the flat grassy campsite I had aimed for.

By the time I pounded the last tent stake into crooked, stump-guarded ground, the wind had died. Gold Arm lay smooth as olive oil, inviting me to paddle up the shoreline to the better campsite. I sct up the camp stove and boiled water, thinking it over. Across the wide lake, high above Bush Arm, thunderheads purpled and blanched, gathered and dispersed, as if a two-day sequence of weather were wound onto a two-minute reel.

I stayed where the weather had put me for the night, crooked ground or not.

The next day no animal called. No movement caught my eye. When a chipmunk twitched across a fallen cedar, it jump-started my heart and put a hitch in my stroke. Wildlife! The chipmunk, in his own isolation and surprise, stood upright and bent his wrists in front of his chest, as if holding an invisible sign: WILL WORK FOR FOOD.

M. J. Lorraine, the old boy who navigated and wrote about the Columbia River before dams, came along on my trip as Xeroxed pages in a Ziploc bag. A good dead friend and useful companion, he didn't intrude unless I asked him to tell me what the river used to be.

The Columbia River, before 1973, had a Kinbasket Lake of its own. The original was a twelve-mile pause in the river's tumble northward, like Windermere Lake only narrower. For Lorraine, Kinbasket Lake was a flat platform to set up his camera and photograph the magnificent white peaks that ripped the sky. Mountains had been there all along, but he, on his low and tree-crowded river, hadn't seen them. Upstream from the old Kinbasket Lake, he'd lined his rowboat around Surprise Rapids, and again at 23-Mile Rapids, a sequence of unrelieved white-water that took him a full week of wading and lining from canyonside rock to rock. The Columbia dropped four hundred feet in the sixty miles between Beavermouth and the bend.

*   *   *

When skies cleared, which was often for an hour or two, Kinbasket Lake basked in a setting as grand as any I've seen. Across the water, green-black conifers rolled the view past timberline to the white sawtooth spine of North America. High in that thin blue air to the east lay the Columbia Icefield, a rumpled and frozen blanket 60 miles long and up to 350 yards deep. On its far side, the icefield gives birth to the Saskatchewan River, which wends across Canada toward Hudson Bay. And at another corner, so huge is the icecap, it drips into the McKenzie River, eastward and then north to find the Arctic Ocean. I couldn't actually see the three-way Continental Divide. It was just the idea of being here, where so much begins. This lake on the roof of the world had a silent and climactic beauty, which was all the more disturbing because of the trash in the foreground. I couldn't breathe long of Kinbasket Lake's far vistas without choking on the nearer view. Massive clear-cuts reached all the way to the trashed shoreline, and it was impossible to ignore the debris-strewn lake.

I was surprised at my own anger. Having grown up in an Oregon logging town, I have a wide tolerance for woodsmen and what they do. The logger I stopped to talk to at lakeside hooked thumbs in his suspenders and demanded: "Are you one of those en-vi-ern-mentalists?" I returned his gaze in good conscience and said no. Not me. Hoo boy. Not one of those. I just came here to see how this river works.

Yet on Kinbasket Lake I saw some extreme logging. Across the lake, a crew skinned a new clear-cut by skidding logs to a landing right at lakeside. The loader, culling logs, piled good ones onto a waiting truck and kicked the garbage off the landing and straight into the lake. I guess I was used to U.S. rules, where you can't do this anymore. Hiking up into another recent clear-cut, I followed logging-road spurs that lacked culverts. Chocolate runoff washed the roadbed and browned the lake.

*   *   *

Kinbasket Lake beauty.

Kinbasket Lake trash.

Rainbow trout live in the top ten to twenty feet of a lake. They hunker in shade close to shore, waiting for bugs and maggots to drop from trees and brush. Paradise, for rainbow trout, is a reservoir filling. When it does, the trout grow like mad. Trout feast at anthills and explore woodpeckers' holes. They pig out on slash piles teeming with bugs, maggots, and worms. Fishermen can rarely interest a trout in anything on the end of a line, and the rainbows that do find a hook have small heads and huge bodies—that is, their normal-sized heads are attached to finned blimps. These are great big trout. Six-pound trout. Trout freaks.

Nobody catches rainbow trout at Kinbasket Lake anymore. Fishermen at Mica Dam have given up and switched their attention to kokanee, transplanted to the lake. The prize-fish photos at Big Lake Resort are of Dolly Varden trout, not rainbows. Squawfish—a spiny, worthless, slow-water fish—are thriving.

As I paddled, I thought, *Where are the rainbows?* For one thing, this reservoir hasn't filled in four years. Because of thin snowpack in recent years, along with a booming economy and high demand for electricity in the Pacific Northwest, Kinbasket Lake has risen no higher than within twenty feet of its high-water mark. Slope translates twenty vertical feet to a lot of wasted shore between trout and trout food. Trees and brush are nowhere near the water, and they haven't been for four years.

For another thing, incoming streams now meet the Columbia at a much steeper angle than nature would have arranged. Missing are the delta gravels where mountain streams probed the river for a long time. Rainbow trout spawn in these shallow, swift-water places, which the reservoir has drowned.

A final clue: changes in water level here are dramatic, and they occur at unnatural times. Rainbow trout spawn in the fall. Their eggs hatch the next spring, in high water. But at Kinbasket Lake, nature's hydrology is reversed. Eggs planted in high-water fall will be high, dry, and dead as raisins come low-water spring.

I am not a scientist. I offer clues rather than conclusions because that's the way the river came to me. I saw things, and sometimes they added up. If they didn't, I asked a fisherman, a logger, a bargeman, somebody on the river. I had read in the Seattle *Post-Intelligencer* that Mica Dam killed an estimated 2,000 moose and 3,000 black bear. The province's own study, commissioned in 1973, said the Mica reservoir led to losses of 1,600 moose, 2,100 black bear, 1,600 mink, and a near-total displacement of migratory birds and wetland wildlife.

The numbers are guesswork. And they're just numbers.

Back in Golden, I'd talked to people who knew this valley before the flooding. Tom Sime, a brush-cut stick figure with excited blue eyes, is a trapper. Carl Wilson, a burly Cat-skinner in a red flannel shirt, logged and built roads in the valley for forty years. Larry Webber, a trucker in a bulging white T-shirt, is the son of Sid Webber, who was the bull moose of all trappers in the old Kinbasket Lake area. Larry Webber worked his CB radio and called in other truck drivers to the coffee shop nearest the mill in Golden.

"Dad had his cabin at Middle River," Webber said. "When I was thirteen I went out with him. We snowshoed out in November. All it was was a trail. He'd power out and then stop for a smoke, and I'd catch up. Out all winter. Back in March."

Others had their say:

"Sid was a big man. Powerful man. Smoked those fat woolies, roll-your-own in wheat germ papers. Run out of tobacco, he'd smoke dried moose shit. Sid found a dead man at the Falls Creek cabin. I wish he was here, you could hear him tell it. He put the stiff on the woodpile and slept in the dead man's fart sack. Stayed long enough to smoke the dead man's butts and eat his grub."

"Beaver so thick, the dog used to run them down the Sullivan at him. Him and that weimaraner."

"After the road went in, I stopped at his cabin. 'Want some supper?' he says. The beans hit that tin plate like shot. Bread you could stretch. Coffee, the closest thing to battery acid I ever tasted."

" 'First woman I ever had,' he told me, 'my very first piece of ass, was up on the Columbia Icefield. Of course that was before I knew your mother.' "

"Coming up Bush River one time, Sid run out of gas, eh? He beaches the boat, walks to the logging road, gets gas, and walks back. This grizzly humps out of the river, and Sid's gun is in the boat. He's got three shells in his pocket, a gallon of gas, his woolies, and matches. The grizzly stops, eh? Stands up. The dog's shakin' there with his tail between his legs. Sid rolls a cigarette, pours a lid of gas, and gets his matches out. The grizzly comes at him. Sid says to the grizzly, Sid says, 'Keep right a-comin', Big Fella, we'll have us a big ol' bonfire.' The bear saunters off, and Sid walks on down to the boat and his gun."

"When a bear went for a beaver in his trap, that's what really pissed him off."

"The lake practically finished the moose in the Wood River area. Herds of elk in the Bush and Gold."

"Kept the road open with a rotary shovel on the old Autocar. Snowbanks eight feet high, both sides. Narrow. Moose got in there and couldn't get out. Chase 'em down the road ahead of the truck. A truck comes the other way, chase 'em back. I got a moose up on the hood of my truck. Plywood cab. Put both front hooves through the hood. After that I put a cowcatcher on the front. A moose put his head down and ran right into it, put his antlers through the radiator."

"Mosquitoes, summertime, were big enough to spring a leg-hold trap, eh? The only way to eat lunch was to sit in front of that hot sonofabitchin' blower on the Cat."

"A little growler, a black bear, used to sit up and eat on the bank. Watch the trucks go by. He was a real gentleman, ate one fish at a time."

"You'd get to know them, eh?"

"It was a beautiful valley."

"They wrecked it."

"Millions of board feet of spruce. [B.C. Hydro] didn't want our log trucks interfering with their earth movers. They cut it and left it. D-8s pushed it into piles. Water came up and the wind blew it to hell and gone. Slash and all."

"It's beyond me how they can do what they do. Hydro said they were going to clean it up. There's been no real effort. They haven't been pushed."

"It's you Americans."

"It's politics. Politicians. When the Americans say shit, our guys squat and strain."

"Hydro is God."

"They were. It's changing now. It's getting better."

"Pretty hit-and-miss with Hydro. They clean up Revelstoke because people see that lake. In high water, here, the wind blows debris to the flats. When the water goes down, they'll go in and pile it. Burn it. There's twenty acres boomed off above Beavermouth."

"Take your moose, they used the low country for winter and spring. The meadows and swamps, that's what's gone. Dad took pictures. He saw what was coming. There's a whole album full of grizzlies."

"It must've been a grizzly that got him."

"We'll never know."

"Larry kept askin' me, 'Seen the old man?' I was haulin' out of there, and Sid was due in. Spring. June. He never showed and never showed."

"A grizzly must've chased that weimaraner back to him. That old open-sight rifle of his, and his eyes were going bad."

"Dad had his favorite spot. Up the Middle River, toward the Columbia Icefield. He used to say, 'You know, when I get to be a detriment to anybody. There's a tree, you'll find me.'"

"Tom and Ron know that tree. At the tree they found his hatchet. A cache. He was out there poachin'."

"They searched by air. Nine guys with boats. All they found was Sid's boat, eh? No motor. No gun."

"He *planted* that stuff, so we'd think he drowned. He saw what was coming. He'll turn up on the Columbia Icefield."

"We never will find out."

I scanned every shore and clear-cut for deer or bear. Or anything. A woodpecker. Not even mosquitoes were out.

Earlier in the trip I'd slapped enough mosquitoes to know I was pushing the start of their season. And M. J. Lorraine, when he came through here, met the worst mosquitoes he'd ever seen. "They come at their victims in clouds, and no sooner alight than their drills begin puncturing the skin. . . . You become almost frantic. I was compelled to admit myself defeated by the Columbia River valley mosquito." Heading north into mosquito hell at the same season Lorraine had, I carried bug juices, mosquito coils, mosquito netting. So where were the mosquitoes?

I didn't know much about mosquitoes except they hatch in still water. When you think about it, though, they'll come out after the first warm rains. The water rises, and when it falls it collects in the ponds and marshes where mosquitoes breed. Here on Kinbasket Lake, the water level will keep rising all summer. Any stillwater ponding will come much later, and will quickly ice.

Good God. Like a blow to the knees, it came to me that mosquitoes, here, are finished. That's why I was hearing no birdcall, seeing no animals. We've reversed the river, broken the food chain, and wiped out an entire ecosystem. Ideas like this have always stayed abstract for me. I can read about ozone depletion and global warming and acid rain, and I think, *Oh, that's terrible*. But the river still runs. Rain still falls. My habits change in small ways, but I am not a new person for what I can fathom only in the abstract. On Kinbasket Lake, now, the big stuff reached out and grabbed me by the throat.

Even the weather, I began to suspect, might be an unnatural phenomenon.

A dark horizontal line formed on the lake ahead. The water surface turned an eerie translucent green, then feathered, then swelled. In the three strokes it took me to reach shore and haul the canoe to safety, whitecaps were up and a quick, compact rainstorm barreled down the Rocky Mountain Trench like a hippo on skates. I rigged a rain fly in the lee of a cedar stump and settled in among the roots. Before I finished peeling and eating an orange, the squall was over. The rain stopped. Blue sky broke through, and the wind was pushing waves the other way. Is this natural? Is this nature?

Maybe it is.

Or maybe a lake this size makes its own weather. A flat, slick, wide-open surface has replaced wooded slopes, greasing the chute for a harsh new Arctic wind straight to Golden. The trees far below used to brush the snarls from the wind and capture more gently the rain that now finds me in erratic, short, stinging bursts. Maybe the reservoir, like a small ocean, holds heat and accelerates the pressure differentials that build and quickly extinguish "a storm."

Power managers at BPA complain that four consecutive years of drought have shackled the Columbia River hydro system. They're just not getting the water these storage dams were designed for. Could it be that climate has changed *because* of dams and huge reservoirs?

From the truckers at Golden: "We don't get the snow we used to get. You'd have a D-8 Cat bulldozing the main street of Golden. And we never used to get this wind. You'd see snow piled high on a fence post."

"But there's screwy weather all over. The Okanogan, too. How are you gonna know?"

Nobody knows.

It will take years to separate the reservoir-made weather, if any, from what could simply be random ups and downs—the "noise"—of climate. A native memory of snow accumulating on a Golden fence post is a powerful image, but it doesn't prove anything. It does, however, change the way I think. What if weather in the Columbia River basin is not the huge and independent force I always thought it was? And if I *think* we have changed climate, a whole set of ideas about nature, and my place in it, begins to unravel.

Time, as I paddled the endless left shore of Kinbasket Lake, was only the long slow loop of sun, the crawl of cold light down one mountain range and up the other. Daylight began well before I woke up each morning and finished long after I conked out, somewhere else, inside the bright blue tent. My wristwatch lay deep in the waterproof bag, undisturbed. It was the tool of a prior world, of no use here.

Place, on the other hand, took on exaggerated weight. I found foolish comfort in my maps. Excitement was the unfolding of a new small rectangle of map and sliding it just so into a clear plastic sheaf on the thwart. *Here's where I am now. Right here.* I wallowed in contour lines and hugged to my chest the names of remote creeks, towering peaks, and the gashes between them. At rest stops, if it wasn't raining, I unfolded the larger laminated map, already softened and crumpled like the blanket of a preschooler, to confirm where I was on the globe. Three days from Beavermouth, I was more than halfway to Mica Dam. And that, come to think of it, was time. Time was my slow measured movement from one known place to another.

I thought often and with growing wonder of David Thompson, the first to map this country. After crossing the Rockies and wintering at Lake Windermere, Thompson followed the Kootenay River from Canal Flats to where it empties into the Columbia, and charted the river on to Astoria. Retracing the lower river and finding a new route back, he filled in the blanks and mapped the Columbia River from mouth to source. Star Man, the Indians called him. They watched Thompson aim his brass sextant and scribble his marks on parchment. Thompson's map was the one he drew as he went. Star Man. What large spirit must drive a man who is scrolling back the edges of the known world?

For me, it mattered a great deal where I was. Aloneness had not been a factor in my life for years and years, maybe ever. Aloneness was not bad. It was not loneliness. Aloneness was not too heavy, and it breathed evenly. I wanted to name this feeling, this liberating despair, of being a very small thing in a very large place.

The valley below Kinbasket Lake never hosted a settlement large enough to call a town. In the mid-nineteenth century the valley did have Boat Encampment, a Hudson's Bay Company post near the confluence of the Wood and Columbia Rivers. Voyageurs of the fur brigades funneled their trade through Boat Encampment and down the Columbia River toward Fort Vancouver. By the time M. J. Lorraine came along, he met only a single trapper, a forest ranger, and a crew surveying Surprise Rapids for a dam that was going to power electric trains through Rogers Pass. The dam was never built. The valley lay still. The Big Bend remained a remote wilderness for small nature-busters like Sid Webber and his sons and allies, who couldn't put much of a dent in it.

Today nobody lives where the damage is, and logging camps are the only settlement on the shores I passed. Beyond the reach of logging roads on Kinbasket Lake, they barge logs, or tow them in bales, from clear-cuts to Bush Arm. To do this in summer, the landing has to be far below the high-water mark.

On my next-to-last night on the lake, at Goosegrass Creek,

I pitched my tent on an abandoned log landing, the only flat spot for miles around. Heaped around the landing was an enormous slash pile, big as a grade school, entirely below the high-water mark. Lakewater lapped at its base. At the rate the reservoir was rising, I figured, the whole pile would join the debris on Kinbasket Lake no later than August first.

In this I was nearly correct. Kinbasket Lake topped up on August 3, 1990, five weeks after I was on it. For the first time in four years, power managers at BPA, in Portland, were assured of meeting the demand for cheap, nonpolluting hydropower in the U.S. Pacific Northwest for the winter months ahead. Even while I was on the lake, they were exporting power to California at a rate of over a million dollars a day.

After hearing over and over the story of the tree blasting skyward from Kinbasket Lake, I thought it must have happened often and been seen by several witnesses. Although nobody I talked to had seen a tree breach the surface, many knew somebody who knew somebody else who had. I got suspicious. I took phone numbers. I gave my address to people who would get back to me.

Nobody did.

Unable to verify the tree-missile story, I finally, reluctantly, came to see it as a modern-day myth. Warren Ward, owner-operator of the house-carrying barge, has spent as much time on Kinbasket Lake as any man, and he's never seen such a thing. He doubts a tree could launch itself straight up. After years under water, the tree would be waterlogged. If not, Ward reasons, the buoyancy of thick trunk would tip the lower part toward the surface faster than the top. Trees rise from the lakebed, no doubt about that, but not missilelike.

Revenge of the trees—nature strikes back—is an idea I hate to give up. The notion of death from below, more random than reverse lightning, seems fair enough. But it's an outdated idea. Nature may well strike back, but it's not going to pick us off one at a time. The last moose has lowered its antlers into the last oncoming truck. We've changed all that. To believe in a mysterious and all-powerful Nature is to recall the absence of snow on a Golden fence post and to wonder—nobody knows— what the consequences of Kinbasket Lake will be.

4

MICA TO REVELSTOKE

Loon, Rain, and Oompah Music

The shore kept curving left, and I turned the Big Bend—the Columbia River's northernmost probe—on Friday, June 29. To my right lay wide-open water. Deep below rested the site of the fur traders' Boat Encampment, at the former junction of the Wood and Columbia Rivers. Kinbasket Lake behind me lay blue and untroubled, reflecting Mount Dainard and lesser snowcapped peaks marching down to their own images on the water. After all the turbulence I'd seen on the lake, I had a morning here of welcome calm—no wind, easy paddling, mild sun—and I passed this famous turning point with a great swell of relief.

Potlatch Campground, just short of Mica Dam, had only a pair of pit toilets and three picnic tables, but I'd arrived at the start of Canada Day weekend, and the camp was full of pickups and empty trailers. Everybody was out fishing, and I thought maybe I'd take a nap. But a boat came off the lake, and its fishermen carried plastic shopping bags full of kokanee. Inspired, I unpacked and assembled my rod and began sorting dry flies. One of the fishermen, eyeing me pitifully, gave me a silver-and-red spinner with treble hooks that was called, he said, a Dik-Nite.

"Can't miss with this," he said. "No sinker. Troll it near the surface."

I launched the canoe and headed for a small inlet where other boats had massed. Paddling with one hand in a slow arc, I let out line and trolled the Dik-Nite for kokanee.

Kokanee, planted here, are landlocked salmon. Genetically they are indistinguishable from sockeye salmon, which are in danger of extinction on the lower river. But kokanee don't go out to sea. They lay thousands of eggs at a single spawning, to compensate for the low odds of getting out to the ocean and back. And because they don't make the trip, they multiply like rabbits in captivity. These kokanee at Kinbasket Lake were a fishery manager's dream, a foot long and perfectly uniform one fish to another, plump and silvery. They had lost all instinct for avoiding predation. The water boiled with kokanee in a suicidal frenzy.

Fish, one after another, attacked the Dik-Nite with a no-doubt-about-it charge. But each time I set the hook I felt the line go limp.

After I'd hooked four fish and landed none, I paddled close to the boat of an elderly couple serenely hauling them in. Just above the man's leader and swivel was a rubber strip—a tiny, bungeelike band—that stretched and gave with the fish's bite. Kokanee have tender mouths, he explained. You can't set the hook as you would on a normal fish.

Disgusted at having trolled about maiming kokanee, and half-blaming it on them—these soft, backward-evolving fish—I accepted the fisherman's offer of a rubberized extender and paddled back toward camp. On the way I caught a kokanee and coaxed it into the canoe. Cooking it up, I noted that the kokanee smelled like fish. It also tasted good, and then I felt better.

Mica Dam rises 650 feet above where the river was, higher than Seattle's Space Needle. Take the elevator from top to bottom, and your ears pop three times. The dam is 3,000 feet thick at its base and stretches half a mile from bank to bank at the top. After the river was diverted into tunnels, in 1967, mammoth bottom-dump trucks began filling the canyon with 42 million cubic yards of sand, rock, and glacial till, borrowed from sites upstream. The dam was finished six years later, on March 29, 1973, two days ahead of the deadline set by the Columbia River Treaty.

The treaty called for a reservoir with 7 million acre-feet of live storage (releasable water). To capitalize on the enormous power potential of the site, however, the British Columbia premier, W. A. C. Bennett, had much bigger plans. B.C. Hydro, his new province-owned superutility, built Mica Dam to capture nearly twice as much live storage as the treaty called for. According to the brochure at the Mica Dam Visitor Centre, "Many logs were left where they were cut, to float for easier salvage as the reservoir filled because it was impractical to remove them by other means. Salvage crews will be working for several more years to remove the debris. When the clearing operation is completed, Kinbasket Lake will provide access to a vast wilderness area of spectacular beauty."

Here at Mica, that promise was almost credible. I stood atop the dam and saw the broad blue lake reflect the last I would see of the Canadian Rockies. The Monashee Mountains cleaved the northwest horizon, and the snow-clad Selkirks loomed over my right shoulder. The paved road stopped at the dam. Visitors would venture no farther than Potlatch Campground, and they wouldn't see the damage at all.

Marg Sproat, the perky blond guide, gave me an extended tour of the dam after a clutch of tourists, less interested than I, had seen the film, heard her spiel, and wandered off. Our ear-popping elevator descent to the bowels of the dam led to a powerhouse carved out of solid rock on the west bank. The cavern was 240 meters long and 12 stories high. It had room for six generators, but only four were installed. The service bay, clean as a kitchen, was an earth-humming place that smelled of hot oil and excited electrons and marine paint.

Carrying a flashlight, Sproat crawled into a turbine that was down for repairs. She beckoned me inside. Only a closed intake gate, far above, kept a column of Kinbasket Lake from blasting down on us through a 22-foot-in-diameter penstock. Our voices echoed inside the turbine. When it's working, water falls down the penstock and hits the turbine blades at an angle that forces the turbine into a horizontal spin at 128 revolutions a minute. The turbine is joined by a shaft to the underside of a generator, above where Sproat and I stood. The generator rotates magnets past coils of copper wire to put out 435,000 kilowatts of electricity. The moving parts of this single machine weigh 800 tons.

We checked in with Jim Sproat, Marg's husband and the chief machinist at Mica Dam. He explained how British Columbia didn't need the electricity when the dam went up, so B.C. Hydro didn't install generators right away. Nineteen seventy-three, as it happened, was the first of two straight years of huge snowpack above Mica. So Kinbasket Lake filled in three years, rather than the expected five. There was nowhere for the water to go, because the engineers hadn't expected to have to open the spillway gates so soon. Sproat was there. He saw the first spill: June 13, 1976.

When they raised the spillway gate, a column of lakewater crashed down the slope and slammed into the spillway's lower lip at 125 miles per hour, arched up at a twist and bit into the opposite bank, tossing up boulders big as cars. The spill wiped out a 30-foot bank and erased roads on both sides of the river. A maintenance shop on the right bank caved in. The shop's propane tank—the size of a railroad car—toppled, rolled, snapped off its safety valve, and went bobbing and hissing down the Columbia. The tank spun as it drifted, spewing propane. Fearing explosion, observers radioed to evacuate Mica Creek village, below the dam. They also called in a helicopter to follow the runaway tank until it finally expired and came to rest, to be salvaged weeks later.

I found it heartening that the river hadn't succumbed at Mica without a final thrashing of engineers, a last—*Remember me, boys?*—gasp. Yet the story was unsettling, too. The bigger the project, the more we assume that the engineers know what they're doing. Shouldn't they have anticipated an unlikely-but-possible event such as a quick-filling reservoir? That they hadn't is a reminder that these are young dams. They haven't yet withstood unlikely-but-possible natural events such as major earthquakes or massive slides.

I had imagined that I would shoulder my canoe and hike past each dam that didn't have a lock. With a return trek to get my gear, I figured I could portage any dam in a couple of hours.

In fact, most dams have at least a boat launch and usually a campground on the upriver side. People mill about. Pickups sit idle. And when you have a tent and *no motor vehicle,* people can't figure it out. They become extraordinarily curious and friendly. The morning I'd set for portage from Potlatch Campground, for example, dawned with a terrific thunder and lightning show. Tent-soaked and soggy, I accepted a neighbor's offer of coffee and eggs inside a warm camper. When the rain let up, we threw the canoe and gear into the pickup of a heavy-equipment operator from Salmon Arm whose name I didn't catch, and he lifted me and the canoe to below the dam.

The water of the next reservoir, Lake Revelstoke, backed all the way up to meet the tailrace from Mica Dam, so it was less than an hour's easy paddle to Mica Creek village. When the dam was going up, three thousand souls lived at Mica Creek. But now only seven, including the Sproats and their son, are permanent residents. I put ashore at the dock and talked my way into the dam workers' dormitory to shower, to spread and dry my gear, and—a surprise I hadn't counted on—to eat at the cafeteria. I wolfed down pork chops. Fruit! Ice cream. I did a load of laundry, then patched a sagging inner tube and found an air compressor to reflate it.

Lake Revelstoke is a run-of-the-river reservoir, as opposed to a storage reservoir. Instead of reversing whole seasons' worth of

Columbia River runoff, Revelstoke Dam captures only enough water to produce a day's worth of electricity. The lake rises and falls only a foot or two, holding back water overnight to be run through turbines the next morning when people are switching on lights, running hair dryers, cooking breakfast.

Revelstoke Dam is the Columbia's newest, completed in 1984. Because it's so young, I expected it to be as unsettled as Kinbasket Lake. But it was much cleaner. Lake Revelstoke's milder swings in elevation make it less prone to the freeze-and-thaw sloughing of raw banks. Fewer and lesser tributaries come in, and its bed was logged before the reservoir filled.

The Selkirk Mountains, now on my left, blocked moisture that had blown in from the Aleutians. Thick gray clouds thumped against the mountains and hung there, chilling, dripping rain as if from low dark sponges. I had turned the corner into rainforest. The trees rose taller and thicker—hemlock and cedar now mixed with the fir and spruce—and the undergrowth was lush with moss, sword fern, and skunk cabbage. As recently as 1921, M. J. Lorraine reported the forest here as "virgin, knowing nothing of the axe except in the hands of hunter, trapper and fire warden." Others, before Lorraine, had tried to portray the vast and apparently inexhaustible Pacific rainforest by noting that a squirrel could go from here to San Francisco without touching the ground.

For me, a fringe of trees lined the reservoir between water and the road, on the east bank, and the power-line right-of-way cut a wide parallel swath farther up the slope. On the far shore of the lake, a patchwork quilt of clear-cuts spread in shades of green to brown. Trees that remained standing were not old growth, of course. Timber closest to the river went first, the easier to float logs to mills. What I saw was second growth, trees that had come back more numerous, smaller, less majestic than the originals, which I deduced from their mossy and decaying stumps.

Cloud cover broke seldom, but when it did it revealed the white pinnacle of Frenchman Cap—or Cat Peak, or Park Glacier—as if a dark curtain were drawn from a brilliant stage.

These dazzling spires, upthrust from the earth's furnace, had been planed and shaped by centuries of ice on the move. Now their glacier tails feed icewater creeks that tumble from creases on both sides of the lake.

Although the road paralleled my course, I heard it more than I saw it. Lightly traveled but new, it carried half a dozen log trucks an hour and the odd vacation rig. In four days, except at Downie Creek, I saw not a single human being who wasn't inside a container: truck, car, or boat. Boats on the lake fished within a mile of a campground, as if tethered. On the entire eighty-five miles of Lake Revelstoke, I passed only one private home.

On the second day below Mica Creek, the wind kicked up before I could reach a good landing spot. I spent four midday hours clinging to stump roots on a steep bank. This was maddening, but not life-threatening. I could have scaled the bank to flag a log truck if necessary, but there was no place to put the canoe. I stayed in the canoe, buffering it against the port-side stump and fending off starboard waves. Forgetting I was in a different climate, I expected this squall to blow over.

When it got worse, I feared the canoe might swamp if I tried to get out.

Four hours is a long time when your hands and legs are busy keeping a canoe right-side up. Hunger came on. Food lay within arm's reach but unreachable. An itch, unscratchable. The rain was cold. The urge to pee became excruciating. I let it flow, warm in the leg of my wetsuit, and tried to remember why I ever thought canoeing the Columbia River would be a good idea.

The old Columbia would have been raging high toward Death Rapids and Priest Rapids. But because Mica Dam throttles the new river, Lake Revelstoke was not flooding.

Once a day or so I passed provincial campgrounds. I camped instead at raw places where an incoming creek had built up a bench of glacial till flat enough for my tent. At Bigmouth Creek, ferns and skunk cabbage lay trampled to form a clear trail from the woods. In the sand, I saw heavy-hoof tracks of moose. Remembering my run-in with the nearsighted moose cow on the upper river, I pitched my tent off to the side.

On the river the next day I passed more animals and animal sign than I had on Kinbasket Lake. Two mule deer, a forked horn and a doe, looked up from their grazing at alder sprouts on a steep cut-grade to watch me pass.

A beaver didn't see me coming. He swam near shore with his ears flat, unalert, against his shiny brown head. 'Beaver!' I called out, just to be a jerk. He sounded—*cha-PLOO*—in terror. Beavers on Lake Revelstoke lack confidence, but then what can they do? Not much on a reservoir. They can fell alder saplings near a creek mouth to fortify a small corner of territory. They can engineer a waterbreak so the waves build up a small sand point. But they can't do anything about water levels, and they know it. Beavers do not own this place.

Most of the time nothing happened. Nature, in real time, is not a dependable entertainment. In rereading my journal I am struck by how observation-filled these long days on Lake Revelstoke seem to have been. But long stretches of river gave rise to nothing at all to think about, nothing to fire a neural synapse, just the slow and repetitive paddle dipping water and sending ripples up the side of mirrored shore.

A merganser cruised by, trailing a wedge of water.

Hours later a helicopter passed overhead, ferrying cedar blocks toward Revelstoke.

Nor was my canoe as fast as I thought it would be. I checked the map and saw I had paddled only twenty-five kilometers—about fifteen miles—in six hours. Three miles an hour is about walking speed. I can paddle that fast, but I averaged

less with no current. I stopped to poke around. I daydreamed
in the canoe and forgot to paddle.

A loon surfaced—*ploop*—ahead of the canoe. Surprised to see
me, she tipped her butt feathers skyward and disappeared to
whatever loons do under water. When she surfaced again, still
ahead, she paddled about, and I could admire the clean silver
band on her stretched black neck. The stripes along her wings
were broken, as if viewed through Venetian blinds. This loon was
quite sure of herself, which made it all the more startling when she
issued the famous loon call, an agonizing climb and fall through
discord, sad beyond sad, as if mourning the death of twins.

Northwest Indians have a story about how the loon lost her
voice:

When the world was young, the story goes, Loon had the most
beautiful voice of all the people. They came from all around to
hear her sing. But the evil spirits showed up and stole daylight.
The world grew cold. Trees lost their leaves. The river froze over
and the sky got black dark. Evil spirits kept daylight in a cedar box
behind a wall of ice, and things looked dire. Raven, the boss,
called a conference of all the people to see what they could do.

Osprey tried to reach daylight by soaring high above the ice
wall, but the evil spirits threw shrill winds at her and she came
back shaggy of feather and defeated. That wasn't the way to do it.
Deer tried to burst through the ice wall with his antlers, but he
returned minus his antlers, head bloodied. That wasn't the way
to do it either. Bear, against Raven's advice, challenged the evil
spirits to a wrestling match. But the evil spirits cleaned his clock.
Bear staggered back, crawled into a cave, and slept.

Violence, Raven told the people, wasn't the way. They
would have to be clever.

Loon had an idea. Mole, with his sharp claws, could tunnel
under the ice wall and make a hole big enough for Loon to slip
through. Mole couldn't see far and had to be led by Loon to
the spot, but they did it. Loon reached the box that held

daylight. She lifted the lid. Daylight escaped, which alerted the evil spirits, who recaptured daylight and then grabbed Loon by the beak and threw her over the wall, stretching her neck.

Loon's tactic, however, proved sound. Raven herself tunneled beneath the ice wall and opened the cedar box. Sheltering daylight under a broad black wing, she put it back in the world. The world warmed up. The ice wall melted into the river. Seeds stirred in the earth, and the trees began to bud. Daylight was back, and all the people were happy.

"Sing us your song," the people said to Loon. "It's time to celebrate."

Loon began to sing, but it was a most horrid and embarrassing sound. Her neck and voice box, stretched, were damaged beyond repair. The people looked away, pretending not to hear. But Loon told them the loss of her voice was a small price to pay for helping bring daylight back to the world. The people soon saw it her way, and Loon became a great hero. Today, whenever darkness nears, Loon remembers the time the evil spirits stole daylight, and you can hear her haunting call across the water.

I read one version of this Loon story in a children's book by Anne Cameron, as told to her by Klopinum, an Indian woman. I'd heard another version of it from my mother, who liked Indian stories, when I was young—too young. What I remember about Indian stories is how dim the natives must have been. No Indian kids *I* knew believed this stuff. The stories were just too obviously not true. And if it was entertainment you were after, Indian stories were no match for television, the new thing, with talking bears and road runners and coyotes capable of wondrous and hilarious feats.

Plus, I think, my culture drew any youngster with a curiosity about nature to books—not to nature but to nature books. Science replaced observation. I'm not grousing, just trying to recall how it happened, how I, raised on the river, took nearly all of my nature instruction from books. Nature itself only served to confirm, in accidental observations, what I knew from books to be true.

There's a loss here I can't quite put my finger on. Bill McKibben, a smart world-observer and nature writer, blames television and especially nature shows for blunting our powers of observation. After the gore and chase of television nature programs, a live loon is pretty dull. "Vital knowledge that human beings have always possessed about who we are and where we live seems beyond our reach," McKibben writes. "A source of information that once spoke clearly to us, now hardly even whispers."

If that's true, and I think it is, it helps explain how a story I once had dismissed as childish came full circle to lie at the very core of what the river had to say. Here on Lake Revelstoke and farther down the Columbia—all the way to Wenatchee, off and on—I saw loon. I imagined these were all the same loon. This was irrational, impossible, and easy to believe. Each time a loon surfaced—*ploop*—I was reminded of the loon story and what a universal thing story is, sometimes truer than science.

July 2: rained all day.

Thick clouds hunkered down to the river. Steady rain blurred the border between water and atmosphere, muffled sound, and cut off vistas. Cold was no problem at first, because I kept moving inside my wetsuit, coaxing warm blood to fingers and toes. I had an easy, dreamlike morning of paddling. The trouble was, it had rained from the very start. Instead of rolling up the tent and stuffing it into its sheath, I had draped it across the bow, thinking it would dry later in the day. But the rain did not let up, and my sleeping bag and tent were soaked. I kept paddling in the hope of finding dry shelter. The map showed a campground at Downie Creek.

Six hours of paddling is enough for one day. Eight is too much. The twelve hours it took me to reach Downie Creek brought home a river's slow lesson, a lesson I still had not mastered. *Take what the river gives you. Don't push it.*

A dreamlike morning gave way to a late afternoon of numbed senses, of addled brain. You'd think when I mistook a riverside moose for a horse I would have recognized my confusion as a danger sign. A horse? But instead of calling it a day I reveled in my own muddle, thinking how funny it is to be stupid.

I paddled on, through cold rain.

I think what happens is that the river, like alcohol, can slow you down and seem life-enhancing. Yet more is not always better. It made perfect sense at the time to keep going, even when I got numb at the edges. I staggered ashore at Downie Creek a drunkard. My stone-cold fingers wouldn't flex to rope the canoe to a tree. Heavy of footfall, chilled to the bone, I swayed to the store and gas pumps that looked to be the hub of the Downie RV Resort and asked the lady about the cabin.

Yes, she said, the log cabin was unoccupied. But also unheated. She could let me have it for eighteen dollars.

I fumbled for the right-colored bills in my wallet. In the cabin I spread the tent to dry. To brew coffee, I fired up my camp stove indoors—a terrible decision that luckily didn't blow up on me—and fell asleep in the dry bed before drinking the coffee.

Downie used to be a town. Trappers and miners gathered here to prepare for, or to recover from, portage around Death Rapids, just upstream.

Death Rapids, which I had passed as a squeezing of flat river between perpendicular cliffs, once trembled with the force of Columbia pounding through a one-hundred-foot-wide chute and down a series of riverbed faults where the river buckled with cascades and devouring holes. Even the French voyageurs, those intrepid rivermen, portaged their fur-laden bateaux around Death Rapids. There is no record of anyone having entered Les Dalles du Mort and emerged alive.

On the heels of trappers came miners. Gold was discovered

in 1865, and the stampede was on. The frenzy centered on the Goldstream River and spread through the upper Columbia's creeks and hillsides. Frenchtown, with its hotels and dance halls, was more populous than present-day Golden. Another town of three thousand boomed at the mouth of Kirbyville Creek, now under water. When gold played out, the hills swarmed with copper miners. Big mineral companies moved in but didn't stay, and the Chinese reworked the mine tailings. By the time M. J. Lorraine passed through, only a few diehard grubstakers remained. He saw abandoned placer diggings, old flumes, and deserted cabins at riverside. Today, this evidence has melted back into the earth, and the Goldstream is unpopulated except for lone prospectors with gold fever.

"Somebody's always got a scheme to make it pay off," said Fred Munk.

Munk, with his wife, Margaret, owns and runs Downie RV Resort. *Resort* is a term used loosely up here. Munk and I were sharing a pot of coffee in the store, which doubled as the front room of the Munks' house. On the shelves were candy bars, nuts, and dusty fishing lures. An ancient top-lift icebox in the corner held soda pop. Somewhere a generator hummed, and Margaret was thumping my tennis shoes and sleeping bag through the dryer in a room nearby. Outside the window, two five-hundred-kilovolt power lines spanned the river, carrying the Columbia's power from Mica Dam to somewhere else. The resort had been in Margaret's family since 1946. Their son, Donald, now in his thirties, had come back to help them upgrade.

"We have flush toilets and hot showers," Munk said. His white hair was swept straight back, as if he'd been a long time going upwind. He had a gnomelike smile, even when talking about problems—and there *were* problems. No RVs had happened by today, and the campground huddled, windy, cold, and empty, in the first week of July.

"Someday this place will start breaking even," Munk said. His eyes misted. "It's the nicest spot on the lake."

* * *

I headed south on Lake Revelstoke with growing disappointment that I had not yet seen a bear. Bear stories, and even the tent-bashing at Golden, were no substitute. In three weeks on the river I'd had many false sightings. Hyperalert, I "saw" bear everywhere. Scanning a hillside clear-cut from the canoe, I saw a charred stump and registered—*bear!* I saw the black round opening of culvert—*bear!* A dark hole in foliage—*bear!* I converted every woods-breaking shadow to ursine lurk. So when I finally did see a bear, the image flashed to a tiny switchbox behind my optic nerve and registered—stump.

But it wasn't a stump. It moved. This was a medium-sized bear, I suppose, which looked small to me. He browsed just two hundred feet ahead of my canoe on a steep, wooded bank. He hadn't seen me. The bear sat beanbagged, his bulk all sunk to his rump, enjoying a salad of salmonberry greens. He stripped limbs between his claws and stuffed the results beneath his snout. This was a left-handed bear with a matted dark coat. His hump was brownish, his snout lighter than his fur. A black bear.

Keeping some river as a moat between us, I paddled closer. His triangle ears twitched upright, and he stopped eating. Puzzled, he stood to watch me. Then he woofed and bolted up the bank with startling big grace, like a cat-quick sofa. His power rippled in loose waves of fur. He stopped, rose on his hind legs, and turned to ponder the canoe some more. The bear then shifted his gaze toward the treetops, as if searching for something to explain it all.

Within six miles of Revelstoke Dam, on a sparkling warm day with a light breeze in my favor, I reached the campground at Martha Creek and laid up, although it was only a little past noon. I dried the gear in sunlight and cooked pot after pot of thick vegetable beef soup. The campground was neat as lawn. My tent was the only one in it, and I walked about barefoot, warm grass between my toes. Only a young mother, exercising preschoolers, used the wide sandy beach. The river lay deserted on a perfect blue day. In late afternoon two fishermen, separately, launched small boats and putted onto the river. I thought of fishing, but I was overcome by laziness. The trouble with fishing is you might catch one, and then what? Then you'd have to clean it, cook it, eat it, wash the pan and plate.

After my nap, life in the campground picked up. Two couples unpacked heaps of camping gear from a Ford van with California plates and rode shiny mountain bikes from campsite 6 to campsite 34 and back. Summer-job teenagers in a Provincial Parks pickup hurled green mill-ends at the firewood bin. Germans arrived in four identical Southwind campers they'd rented in Vancouver and were driving to Calgary. Three young CPR trainmen muscled into the campground in a gleaming black Camaro Z-28, radio throbbing, looking for love and settling for a purple sunset over the Columbia.

The three amigos leaned against their Z-28 and shared their beer and confessed to great wonder about how the Columbia River gets from Beavermouth to Revelstoke. I filled them in. And they, in turn, told mountain-slide and avalanche stories about how the railroad cuts through Rogers Pass. One of them wanted to take the canoe out, and I said okay if I could drive the Z-28, and he said okay, but we never got around to it. The green mill-ends, bubbling with pitch, made a snap-crackling fire. Flames leaped to the night sky.

After the Z-28 thunderboxed away, I lay in the tent wide awake. The Germans turned up the amplifier on a sound system, which sent oompah music thumping across the campground and echoing off the far bank of the river. One of the Californians rapped on the camper door and shouted. But oompah music over the Columbia sounded *wunderbar* to me. Just right. It answered the strangeness of the world and filled me with an unnatural joy that all this could fit, and I was sorry when the music died.

5

ARROW LAKE

This Is Why You Do It

The Columbia River flowed swift but without rapids below
Revelstoke Dam and swirled into a big eddy called Big Eddy,
half a mile in diameter, before it spun out, eastward, and
coursed under a pair of bridges—the CPR tracks and the
Trans-Canada Highway—at Revelstoke. I cached my gear on
a reed-capped island below the bluff. Then I paddled ashore,
hid my canoe in the brush, and clambered up the steep bank
onto the shelf of town. From the bluff I looked back to see that
my gear and the canoe were well hidden, and lugged a laundry
bag toward the nearest motel.

I showered and put on my town jeans and was surprised
they had so much room in them. I'd paddled my butt off. The
shirt, though, seemed familiar, and I set out for a walk about
town. Revelstoke, population 8,500, is a lumber milling community and a switchyard for trains that split the Selkirks
through Rogers Pass. The town faces across the river toward
triple-peaked Mount Begbie and huddles against the foothills of
Mount Revelstoke National Park. The rollicking Illecillewaet
(Ill-a-SILL-a-way-et) River caroms from its canyon to feed the
Columbia just south of town.

A measure of prosperity in the West these days is how well

a town can recall its frontier past. Forward-looking Revelstoke featured cast-iron lampposts, a red-roofed bandshell, brick sidewalks, and a town clock. Limestone and granite buildings anchored the center of things, and grand Victorian homes lined MacKenzie Avenue. Roofs were unnaturally steep and capped with sheet metal to shed snow. At the entrance to Grizzly Plaza, the town center, three life-size cast-bronze bears stood on pedestals. A lot of people looked as if they didn't live here, and I gathered that tourism was scratching for a toehold in an economy long based on extraction—of furs, of minerals, of trees.

I spent the morning between the museum and the Laundromat, and then followed the exotic smell of a deep-fat broiler toward lunch. Afterwards, shopping, I couldn't find the freeze-dried foods I'd hoped to resupply in Revelstoke, so I loaded up on bags of nuts and twigs, candy bars, and dried fruits.

The river here flows 1,100 feet lower than at Columbia Lake, its headwaters. After paddling a quarter of the river's length, I had passed over 40 percent of its drop. Of the 1,100-foot drop, about 950 came in my two portages around Mica and Revelstoke Dams. The rest was in Redgrave Canyon.

What sets the Columbia River apart as North America's champion power system is its fast and continuous drop from the mountains to the sea. The Mississippi River system is longer, for example, but Pittsburgh is only 715 feet higher than New Orleans. That river system lacks the rush and tumble a dam can translate into hydropower. The Columbia keeps falling, keeps building power potential, keeps kicking the flywheels that put the Northwest in economic motion. The biggest electric power-producer of them all, Grand Coulee Dam, is far downstream from here, and Bonneville Dam is only 140 miles from the ocean.

The building of Revelstoke Dam was a big boost to the local economy, and the change in the Columbia wasn't supposed to cause any trouble. The next dam, far away, only made the river here a little wider and slower, forming Arrow Lake. But change a big river, and you change a lot of things. Nobody had anticipated dust storms.

When Arrow Lake is down, as it is in early summer to catch snowmelt, the flat former farmland south of Revelstoke lies bare. Wind whips up the valley and kicks up terrific dust storms. Airborne grit can swirl so thick into Revelstoke that streetlights switch on at midday. Walk the wrong way, they say, and you have to turn your face and cover one ear. Dust storms have worsened recently because the reservoir, like Kinbasket Lake—and partially *because* of Kinbasket Lake—hasn't filled in four years.

"Come look at this," said a guy at the pub at the Regent Inn. He led me out to look at his 1988 Ford pickup. It was just two years old, and its blue paint showed sand-blasted bare spots.

B.C. Hydro is studying the dust problem. A possible solution is to reseed the bare shores. But that won't work if the water tops up every year, like it's supposed to. Another possibility, expensive, is to build a weir across the river below Revelstoke to keep the water up year-round. In the meantime, in the windy season, people caulk their windows against the dust and grit their teeth in anger.

Arrow Lake used to be Arrow Lakes, plural. The river calmed itself here into two natural and very long pools, Upper Arrow and Lower Arrow, separated only at midpoint by mild rapids. The lakes stretched as a deep-blue ribbon of inland sea between the Selkirks to the east and the Monashees to the west. The Columbia's fury dissolved into a quiet, leisurely, and glorious pause. Fur-bearing voyageurs welcomed the slow pace of Arrow Lakes and celebrated its grandeur in song that echoed to the peaks, two syllables to the beat, two beats to the oar-stroke. Later, great steamships—white, double-decked, wood-burning sternwheelers—plowed Arrow Lakes from Castlegar to Revelstoke.

Seasonal flooding, since the Ice Age, has deposited layer after layer of rich sediment in the trough of Arrow Lakes, and the flat shores were excellent for fruit farming. In spite of the short growing season, apples and pears and cherries burst plump from low orchards. Small towns came to the shores. Today, Arrow Lake is every bit as beautiful, but the towns are gone, or moved to higher ground, because Hugh Keenleyside Dam blocked the river in 1968 and made one big storage reservoir of the two former lakes. B.C. Hydro bought out the lowland farmers before flooding their orchards.

Keenleyside is not a tall dam—just 80 feet high—but the trough behind it holds a reservoir 140 miles long, a distance it took me a week to paddle. It was early July, and I saw no dust storms. This year's heavy runoff was catching up with me. Arrow Lake was within 12 feet of its high-water mark, and rising fast. The flats that were still exposed hadn't been submerged in four years, so they were covered with grass that held the silt in place.

A squadron of tundra swans cruised low above the lake in a diamond formation, headed north with great purpose. And geese, hundreds upon hundreds of Canada geese, clogged the lake. Honkers, we used to call them. In the Willamette Valley we seldom saw them, just heard them, passing high and ghost-like above the clouds. Remote and mysterious, geese were on their way to somewhere else, and I had always credited them with great dignity and high-mindedness, for knowing when and where to go.

Here I saw Canada geese up close and in crowds. I came upon huge floating rafts of geese, not at all graceful on the water, and tone-deaf. Honkers. Small-brained birds, the geese scattered and regrouped ahead of the canoe instead of taking to the air and wheeling around behind me or across the wide lake. I pushed great gathering hordes of geese down Arrow

Lake and had to put up with their heckling, as if it were my fault.

The osprey, unlike the goose, is not a flocker. She will shriek—a high-pitched repetition of the letter Q—but she has the native wit to gauge my direction. She stays put, or, if she leaves her high nest, will go behind me. But these geese . . . As many lined the shores as floated on the lake—and they, too, goose-stepped south to stay ahead of my advancing canoe. The little ones, already rolling fat, the size of mallards, followed in silly single file behind a mother goose down the beach until she tired of it and waddled into the woods, not into the lake. The little ones dutifully followed. Maybe they weren't flyers yet, I thought.

I found out later that none of them were flyers. Adult geese lose their flight feathers soon after the goslings hatch in spring. The adults can't fly until the little guys can, which is nature's way of keeping the family together.

The part of a reservoir farthest removed from a dam has the most "natural" slope of shoreline, because water level is near the river's original banks. The closer you get to a dam, the steeper the banks, the deeper the former riverbed below the surface. On the upper end of Arrow Lake, below Revelstoke, creeks wandered into the river where their alluvial fans were still visible. Rich former farmland was of mild slope, bleached and sandy, covered with grass. Accustomed to camping at the first flat spot after mid-afternoon, I now got picky. Did the site have a windbreak of trees? Would the sun hit it in the morning? Did it have a view?

One west-bank spit had all of these advantages, plus a tangle of silver driftwood waiting for, calling for, a bonfire. No roads disturbed the dark band of forest across the lake. Trees stretched to timberline, and the late shadow of sun crawled up the snowy Selkirks. Tall grass cushioned the tarp I spread for dinner. A windbreak of alders sheltered me from a light breeze, which pushed the grass into green waves near shore. As the sun dropped, the Selkirks coppered, then pinked, then purpled with alpenglow.

The next morning, when the sun had not yet peeked over the Selkirks, I stood over my camp stove waiting for coffee water to boil. I heard a rustling in the alders that formed a backdrop to my camp.

In bear country, it takes nerves of steel—or an empty cranium—to freeze, waiting to see what will emerge from the undergrowth. I froze. Whatever it was, not careful of foot, was coming from the woods.

A coyote nosed out of the trees just twelve paces from where I stood. Blurry-eyed, scruffy, not yet focused, this coyote looked as if he'd had a bad night. He paused between me and my tent, not yet aware of either, on his way to the river. He pawed a flat slab of driftwood and raised his leg to pee. Sniffing around, now, he spied me and leaped skyward, wizzing all over himself. When he came down, legs churning, his claws spun driftwood and he was OUT of there, like Wile E. Coyote surprised by Road Runner.

Gill T. Coyote.

On the flat dry spits of Arrow Lake, stumps rose high above sandy loam. River had eroded the soil below their former seat on land, so the stumps danced high on the tiptoes of their roots. The roots were a weathered silver, twisting around empty cores. Stumps, as I paddled past, took on powerful movement and deathly grace to the fugue of reservoir life. I saw leaping stumps. I watched stump ballet.

*   *   *

Dancing stumps.

Without much trying, I learned to forecast weather. A steady trailing breeze meant skies would be clear all day. A wind in my face, from the south, indicated that rain with bluster was on its way. A mare's tail cloud lacing westward peaks was ominous, and a vapor ring around the sun even more so. Soon the water would turn from blue to gun-metal gray, its surface choppy, and then an eerie swimming pool green. Unlike on Kinbasket Lake, the squalls here provided warning. I stepped aside and gave them sway with no hard feelings. I took what the river gave me.

On Arrow Lake, for a change, I thought less about danger than about scale. I no longer doubted I could handle any given quarter mile from here to the Pacific Ocean, but how long would it take? Stroke after stroke after stroke. Day after day. In theory, nothing stood between one stroke of the paddle and the next, all the way to Astoria. But the idea of it . . . This was the fourth week of probably a three-month trip. Looking back, over my shoulder, I saw the same mountain peak that had loomed ahead two breakfasts ago.

Singing was a curious boost. Since the birds didn't think me foolish for it—and no one else was around—I often sang. The song that came up, unselected, was "Good Night, Irene." I knew the words to only one verse, and it was this one:

> Sometimes I live in the country,
> Sometimes I live in the town;
> Sometimes I have a great notion
> To jump into the river . . . an' drown.

The strangeness was that these brooding lyrics and melancholy chorus had a powerful lift to them. The song was not a sad one, and I sang it over and over and over.

On the roadless shores of Arrow Lake, I was surprised to come across a colony of bright-colored tents on the pebbled shore. Scattered among them were temporary dwellings made of cardboard, driftwood, and plastic sheeting. I put ashore and hallooed, but got no answer. In the distance, I heard scratchy music. It was spooky, otherworldly, and I didn't stay. The music gained volume as I paddled on. Around the next bend I came abreast of a sheltered cove. Lank-haired men and women cavorted on the beach with their children and dogs. Some were nude, and rock-and-roll music blasted from a boom box. Three of them were erratically swimming, possibly stoned. It was Sunday, I remembered, and I didn't want to disturb their sylvan rites. I gave them a wide berth and, as far as I know, passed by unnoticed.

The ferry crossing at Shelter Bay was a break in my isolation, in my gathering weightlessness. Reentering the world, I boarded the free ferry for a chug across the three-mile-wide river and back. I'd hoped for a mid-river panorama of peaks flanking the valley, but clouds wreathed the mountaintops. The ferry was full. A long line of campers and cars and trucks, many more than the ferry could handle, waited on the west shore. A gloomy trucker told me the delay was overlong because a mud slide had blocked a road, sending more traffic this way. Vacationers were cross, their children cranky, everyone thrown off schedule.

I remembered what *that* was like.

Me, I had no schedule. I had nowhere to be. After Shelter Bay, my only schedulelike challenge was to find a campsite along a shore that had turned rocky and severe. I paddled into early evening, looking for a spot, but never found it. I came to a baled load of logs that had washed ashore. Over one long log at the top of the bale, I draped the rain fly. Then I suspended, rather than staked, the tent over broken ground and secured the ropes to rocks. It was ugly. It was uncomfortable.

Stroke after stroke after stroke, the next day. Will there be a million strokes? I figured in my head, 1,200 miles times 5,000 + feet in a mile equals over 6 million feet, from Canal Flats to the Pacific. Say half a canoe length—8 feet—per stroke. So 6 million divided by 8. The rough answer was no, I would not do a million paddle strokes on this trip.

But a million is a lot.

One time when I was little we were clamming with the Hallmarks at Long Beach, on the stretch north of the Columbia River's mouth known as the World's Longest Beach. You can drive a car on hard-packed sand for miles and miles. We were razorback-clamming. Billy Hallmark—an older boy, smart, wore glasses—asked me how far I could count. I could count all the way, and I told him so. I could count to a hundred. I knew my numbers. I could count to a million.

Billy Hallmark adjusted his glasses. "Do it," he said.

The early numbers rolled out easy. We clammed as I counted. He was the shoveler and I was the groper-grabber. Maybe I got all the way up into the two hundreds before the first symptoms of cottonmouth came on. But we clammed and I counted. My dad, the only one in either family who could spot clam spouts in low surf and dig them there, came by to see if we had our limits.

"Robin's counting to a million," Billy Hallmark told my dad.

"You boys are smashing clam shells," Dad said. "Start your dig farther from the hole." His bag of razorbacks had no broken shells at all. He hip-booted off into low surf.

We clammed and I counted. Despair rolled in like fog off the Pacific. How much was a million? Was it the number of drops of water I could see in the Pacific Ocean? Would the grains of sand in the World's Longest Beach be a million? Each number, as I said it, exposed heaps of larger and larger numbers that lay ahead, no end in sight.

Stroke after stroke after stroke. Day after day.

One of the best things is how surface water accepts the reach and pull of a paddle stroke with no visible shift, and then sweeps behind the canoe in tight swirls, spinning reflected clouds. I looked back to see the waterswirls widening, spaced one from another to mark my progress down the river. The waterswirls were clockwise, no matter if I paddled on the right side of the canoe or the left. I suppose if I were paddling the Amazon, the swirls would be counterclockwise. It made me wonder about some overarching Plan . . . but Who would have bothered at so small a detail? And to what mysterious purpose?

When the water is good you want to stroke a half-dozen or so times on the left, then switch to paddling on the right. For variety I sometimes paddled kneeling instead of seated, but that grew old in a hurry. Or I lay on my back for a spell, on the waterproof bag, and worked the paddle like a single oar. But then I couldn't see where I was going.

A tall rock promontory—Cape Horn—came into view, and I crossed the wide lake to follow the eastern shore. Wood smoke rose from the slash burner at Nakusp and wafted a blue haze across the wide valley. In the three hours it took me to reach Nakusp, I was drawn back to human scale. It was a welcome pull, the world having grown too large for me. Here came town. Here came language, a respite from untethered thought.

I gave the canoe one last stroke, and the bow sliced onto fine white sand of Nakusp beach. The river was boomed off for swimming, but no one swam. On the beach, small children shaped sand in the warm late-afternoon sun. Apart from the others, on a blanket, lay a young woman in a black tank top with slender brown legs and bright black hair. Her beer can was propped up in the sand, and she was smoking a cigarette.

Drinking beer and smoking cigarettes, as it happens, are two of my own favorite activities. "What an amazing coincidence," I told her. I hadn't had a cigarette since Columbia Lake, but now I couldn't remember why. Beth was her name. We drank beer and smoked cigarettes. She had a little-girl giggle that made me funny, perhaps delirious. No doubt she felt safe, knowing I must be twice her age.

A strapping young construction worker came stalking across the beach toward us. This was Beth's husband, Vladimir, just off work and carrying a six-pack of Kokanee. Once Vladimir thawed, and I cooled, the three of us sat on the beach and watched the sun fall. Vladimir was a landed immigrant. He'd escaped Czechoslovakia on foot—over razor-wire fences, past ferocious dogs, howling sirens. Beth and Vladimir's van broke down here in Nakusp a year ago. He carpenters when he feels like it, and they gather pine mushrooms from the forest across the river. There's good money in mushrooms, they said.

I also learned from Beth and Vladimir that the sabbath hippies I'd passed the other day must have been tree planters. They reseed the Crown's forest clear-cuts. In nomad tribes, they follow the planting season from Vancouver Island to higher elevations. They may hire out to brush and weed. They thin growing stands of trees when it's time. I wished I had stopped to visit.

After we polished off the beer, I tied my canoe for the night against Vladimir's boat at the moorage and checked into the Hotel Leonard, a hundred-year-old hostel that creaked and sagged as I walked up the stairs. The hotel housed many other young souls in addition to Beth and Vladimir, all looking semi-displaced. A bunch of us shared a meal, and then I could have joined a sweet-smelling gathering on the fire escape, but I declined, feeling more and more out of my age group.

Back in my room, I drew a steaming bath in the lion's-claw tub and stepped in. When I shut my eyes to shampoo, the tub rocked and pitched so canoelike I had to grasp both sides of it to steady myself.

Too much beer? Too much river.

I paddled the next morning toward The Narrows, which formerly separated the two Arrow Lakes with easy rapids. Although the surface lay flat for me, Arrow Lake still pinched to a thin waist as it jogged around Tomahawk Mountain. Current, which I hadn't noticed for days, constricted at The Narrows to form eddies along broken shore. And the wind, confused by this mini-gorge, gusted crazily instead of settling on any clear purpose. I put ashore for a rest at the left-bank terminus of Arrow Park Ferry. The ferry, two lanes wide with a pilot house in the divider, was long enough for two loaded log trucks. It pulled itself along a sunken cable from one side of the river to the other, not regularly but whenever traffic happened by.

When I paddled out of The Narrows, the river turned south and the wind whistled out of Mosquito Canyon, behind me, straight down Arrow Lake. Trailing waves kicked up. Relative to surface water I moved backward as I paddled forward. But in reference to shore, I swept right along and came to a boat-launch and campground on a scabby point. A dot on the map showed Burton, a mile up the road. But a dot on the map doesn't guarantee commercial activity, so I asked at the launch if I could find a store at Burton. I could, they said, but the store would close in twenty minutes, at 6:00 p.m. Thinking it was worth a brisk walk, I set out for the store.

I passed a white farmhouse with lush garden and a sign at the driveway: LOST VALLEY FARM. On my way back, I stopped and hollered toward the backyard. A grandfolksy couple re-clined in aluminum lawn chairs on thick grass among shade trees, as if they had died and gone to Eden. The man, Oliver Buerge, was shirtless and wore cut-off jeans and a flowing white beard. He unlatched the deer fence and led me into the garden. The Buerges once owned 130 acres of low farmland next to the river. B.C. Hydro bought them off, and they retired to this farmhouse, on higher ground. Of the two, the talker was Helen Buerge, a feisty-eyed and sharp-tongued farm frau.

"We got $35,000," she said, "but we had to take them to court. It was hard on Oliver. We fought them for six years on it, and Oliver's health deteriorated. We won, in theory," she said, "but we lost three-quarters of a mile of waterfront. It was like a big park," she said. "Corn grew like magic, and we kept cattle on it. High-bush cranberries grew wild. Bears loved it. Deer. It wasn't the money. We would have moved if they'd found us land."

"Two giant cedars," Oliver said. "So thick they cut through them and they wouldn't fall. Cattle had their babies there."

"Hydro wanted us to move to Fauquier," she said. "They burnt city hall and our credit union, so people would have to move. 'Move to Fauquier,' they said. 'We're going to have a beauty parlor at Fauquier.' Oh boy."

"The dirt smelled. It had a beautiful black-earth smell."

"The real estate guy, that little assessor, he had no idea. They were so mad at us for fighting them. They ran down our character. They said we sold bad meat. This is Hydro, yes. It got so you hated to see those little blue cars drive up. They were horrid people."

"Fellow wrote a book on it."

Helen Buerge marched into the house and emerged with a book called *Land Grab: Oliver Buerge vs. the Authority*. She said B.C. Hydro is a Crown Corporation and the government appoints everybody. "There's nothing you can do about it. We're just people in the way. The water's down because the Americans want it. One year it was too low for the kids' swimming lessons, all mud flats and stumps. That year we drove down to Spokane and stopped by Grand Coulee, and their water was up. I said, 'Look at that!' What gets my goat," she said, "is [Keenleyside Dam] doesn't even generate electricity. For nothing, we lost this place. It's just a concrete slab with spillways, to regulate water for the United States."

"Maybe this man would like some iced tea, Helen."

"Spring, early summer, we get these dust storms," she said. She talked quite a bit about dust storms, which I'd already heard about. "Oliver has to take off in the motor home. He can't breathe."

"One good thing," said Oliver, running fingers through his beard. "They got rid of our mosquitoes. We had terrible mosquitoes here."

"We're not getting the winters we used to. We used to get four feet of snow, and ice on the river. It's been mild now, like the coast. Is that the greenhouse effect?"

Who knows?

"I kind of like it," she said, "but it's scary."

Paddling down Arrow Lake, I moved into drier and warmer climate, a change that was natural and had nothing to do with dams. The last of the snowcapped crags withdrew after Nakusp. Mountains sloped to rounded crests, with trees all the way to the sky, and the timber included lodgepole pine and ponderosa. Shoreline changed, too. Gentle farmland lay deeper beneath my canoe, and the banks were faced with tough, heat-forged rock.

I came to Fauquier, B.C. Hydro's model town. The locals call it *FOKE-yer* when they're being polite. Curious, I beached the canoe past a set of sturdy new docks, unused, then stepped across a neat little nine-hole golf course with sand greens, also empty except for geese. Frontage Road, downtown Fauquier, had only a gas/grocery store, a defunct Laundromat, the Arrow Lake Motel, and a windowless community hall (closed). But the road had suburban curbing, tall modern streetlights, and concrete sidewalks. Yellow fire hydrants and gray electrical hookup boxes stood waiting on vacant lots.

I bought food and filled the water jug at the store. And because I expected to reach Keenleyside Dam in another three days, I phoned ahead to see if the locks would be working on a Saturday.

"If not," said a phone voice of gravelly good cheer, "somebody will be here to throw you over the dam."

Toward evening I reached a sheltered cove at the mouth of Eagle Creek, close to Edgewood, and my canoe headed for a large picnic cooler on the beach. The keepers of this cooler were the husky-voiced Linda Smith and her thin, loopy, platinum-haired friend Cuzzy. The women shepherded more children on the sandy slope than could possibly have been their own. Smith and Cuzzy's account of Edgewood, which B.C. Hydro had moved to sufficient elevation, was that it had been a haven for draft dodgers during the Vietnam War. Edgewood was (still is) two and a half hours removed from an officer of the law, and the law would have to cross the lake on a ferry. Sharp rural tensions divided the hippies and the loggers. With U.S. amnesty, most of the hippies left, but some stayed. Now they teach school, run the credit union, and are the better-educated and leading lights of town, which Smith called "Edgeworld."

I pitched my tent at Eagle Creek and walked toward town. Less than a mile up the road I saw trim yards and small houses. Smoke from wood stoves curled up into the trees, and pickups and boats rested in driveways. The Edgewood General Store was closed for the day, but I stopped and read notes posted on the bulletin board.

DR. LEA WILL BE VISITING THURSDAY, JULY 19.

3 CHAINSAWS ALL IN EXCELLENT CONDITION.

PLEASE RETURN MY WHEELBARROW!!!

A sandy-haired kid on a dirt bike said he could get somebody to open up the store if I wanted. He told me about a cafe, on the road out of town, that was probably still open. He rode ahead to see, or to alert them that a customer was coming.

At the cafe I ate fried chicken with mashed potatoes under thick white gravy, thinking what a fine thing a small woods town can be. I asked the cafe owner, who was also waitress and cook, what time she would be open for breakfast.

"What time do you *want* breakfast?" she said.

At the cafe the next morning I loaded up on cherry pie and ice cream. Over the radio, on a Castlegar station, I heard that a thunderstorm was coming. The front had hit Kelowna, just sixty miles over the Monashees and west.

I delayed my departure from camp for an hour, gauging wind and low clouds. When conditions did not worsen, I pushed the canoe onto the river. The wind was unstable, shifting the surface, but soon the clouds lifted, then scattered, and gave way to blue. The wind calmed, and the river settled. It was a beautiful warm day on the Columbia. I thought of radios and the modern tools of weather forecasting—wrong in this case—

and congratulated myself for reading the river instead of waiting at Edgewood for this alleged thunderstorm. That day I saw no people, no sign of settlement. No roads marred the forested banks.

A gold eagle nailed a kokanee and took to the sky with him in great, air-threshing flaps.

The water lay still and the sky was high over the river; *This is why you do it*, I thought. River slid out from the side of the canoe and set a mirrored world to a slow, upside-down dance. The only sound was the drip from paddle rising, nearly no sound at all when it's right.

A white mountain goat stepped from the woods to drink of the river. His sharp hooves clipped the rocky-block shore, so I saw him before he noticed me. Pony-size, he wore a white but not brilliant coat, thick and shaggy at the neck and belly. Small black horns, reverse carrots, rose from his skull as he lapped at the river. When I fumbled for the camera, he glanced up and saw me, only three canoe lengths away. He didn't bolt. I froze, hand on the camera but not lifting it. Drift carried me closer, slowly closer. His beady black eyes, curiouser and curiouser, met mine as he stood now within a stroke of my canoe, moving only his head to watch me pass.

I registered an emotion very near despair, like young love, at the breathtaking beauty of this scene, this animal, this day on the river.

At a right-bank inlet, a narrow bay answered the influx of Bowman Creek from a slit in the Monashees. I found sandy soil among the rocks and pitched the tent. Wading into the river, I lathered up with soap and dived forward to twist and rinse. The water, though bracing, was not as cold as I'd expected.

Walking back toward the tent, I heard a mammoth clap and rumble, and looked up to see thunderheads rolling down Bowman Creek canyon. By the time I'd toweled off and collected the gear, the advancing western sky was the color of plum. Darkness fell as I ducked into the tent and the first drops of rain, wide as pennies, splatted against the wall. A splash of lightning lit up the tent like a blue flashbulb, and then a crack and roll of thunder shook the earth. As the intervals between lightning-flash and thunderclap shortened, the intensity increased, and now one peal of thunder lasted a full six seconds. The wind howled through the treetops and roared down Bowman Creek canyon like a runaway train.

After my tent withstood the initial blast, I poked my head out to check the canoe. It had rolled across the beach but was still with me, propped against a stump. I sprinted into the gale and lashed it down.

Returning, drenched, to the tent, I changed clothes and waited out the deluge, thinking myself a foolish and lucky man. If this storm had banged in a few hours earlier and caught me where I couldn't have exited the river, it could have erased me from the Columbia without a trace. I read later, in *The Trail Times*, that its winds had reached 70 kilometers per hour and dropped 5.6 millimeters of rain in two hours, felling trees and knocking out power lines. Lightning sparked forest fires from Castlegar to Nakusp.

6

FREE-FLOWING RIVER
Keep the Wet Side Down

After Bowman Creek, I came from wilderness back into the world. A lawn mower wafted a smell of fresh-cut grass from a spread of new homes at Deer Park. Over the hills, tanker-planes droned in wide circles and strafed smoke from last night's lightning strikes. Fishing boats bobbed on the river. Half a dozen teenagers waved from a bluff, the girls adjusting bikini tops and admiring the boys, cliff-divers, who cannonballed my passing canoe. The wind slowed me as I approached Syringa Creek Provincial Park, where I hoped to find a hot shower, but didn't, and all the campsites were taken. So I pitched my tent on a gravel beach and washed in the lake.

In the morning I set out early for Keenleyside Dam. White-caps were up by the time I crossed to the right bank. Arrow Lake ends in a dogleg left. Nearing the dam, I squinted into a white glare of morning sun off the river. It wasn't clear where the lock was, or how to approach it. On my right floated booms of baled logs. Ahead, a small hyperactive tug rodeoed log booms toward the dam. The whole business, with whitecaps up, looked confused and hectic. I put ashore through a gap in log booms and walked to the dam to find out what to do.

Inside a concrete tower topped with an observation deck

and tinted windows, I walked upstairs to the control room. Leslie Godberson, running the dam, had just flushed a tug downstream through the lock. The tug would return soon, Godberson said, and I could ride with the tug on its next trip down.

Godberson sat at a bank of computerized control panels. One set of consoles was to move the dam's four floodgates up and down. At the moment, fifty thousand cubic feet of water per second boiled through, white and angry, foaming with rainbowed spray below the sluiceways. I struggled with scale. This dam I knew to be "small" was gigantic. Painters, painting blue, crawled about a suspended floodgate like fleas on a washboard. I imagined that if Godberson were to shut the gates suddenly he could tilt the earth a degree or two off its axis, maybe correct for global warming if he got it right. Even as this much water passed downstream, he was holding enough back that Arrow Lake was rising four feet a week.

"We expect to fill it this year," he said. "Another eight or nine feet to go. Couple weeks. Maybe three."

As the tug neared the dam from downstream, Godberson radioed for permission to piggyback a canoe through the lock. Then he pointed to a long J-shaped extension of dam, a low arm of concrete into Arrow Lake. "Paddle out there," he said, "and wait. It'll take him an hour to load up."

Noncanoers have no idea how scary it is to cut whitecaps at their own level, how easy it is to get blown off course. And with fifty thousand cubic feet of river per second crashing through the spillway . . . But since Godberson was so amiable— and there was no time to waste—I hiked back to the canoe and did it. I reached the appointed spot and tied up to wait.

Bruce Hocal, tug captain, has a job any kid with a driver's license would die for. A V-8 engine powered his green minitug, a pug-nosed riverbobber with a kitchen-sized cabin. He spun a wooden helm the size of a giant pizza and hot-rodded booms of logs into place. Pushing and pulling, he nudged booms toward the J-tip of concrete where I waited. His hefty blond mate, Louie Gritchen, danced about the logs with a big sheep-eating grin on his face, shouldering the peavey and coupling chains.

Louie and I lifted the loaded canoe onto a boom and lashed it down. Then we crossed the logs and stepped onto the tug. Hocal towed the load into a long, steel-walled, rectangular chamber—the lock—open only on the upriver side. Once we were tucked inside, Godberson closed the gate behind us, blocking off Arrow Lake. Then he pulled the plug, and the lock slowly drained. We sank down, farther down. We dropped seventy-two feet, with no water turmoil, in twelve minutes. High steel walls blocked the noon sun from the bottom of the pit.

And then the front gate rose, to reveal sunlight and the new river level. Hocal gunned the tug. He pulled his unfolding booms of logs into the grip of current, from sluiceways on the left. Ten fast minutes later, Hocal curled his load against a tall bundle of right-bank pilings at the Westar mill. Gritchen

Canoe and log boom in Keenleyside Lock before it drains.

helped me lift the canoe back into the river. The two of them waved me off, and the canoe picked up the big river with startling, exhilarating, speed.

Ahead lay forty-five miles of undammed, free-flowing Columbia. From Castlegar, B.C., to Northport, Washington, the river has no big drop or harrowing rapids, or it *would* have been dammed. Yet the river still loses seventy feet of elevation in these forty-five miles, and I expected technical difficulties. Tin Cup Rapids, Rock Island Rapids, and The Little Dalles were three I worried about. I'd driven this stretch in February to see that the rapids were navigable. But that was February. Far more water filled the Columbia now, and I needed to scout the river again. No doubt Hocal or Gritchen would have taken me for a drive after work, had it occurred to them. But you hate to ask.

It was Saturday, early afternoon.

Close to the right bank, I swept past orange alps of wood chips between the sawmill and the Celgar paper mill. Then came an abandoned ferry landing at the upriver edge of Castlegar. A man on the bank threw a stick at the river. His dog charged from the bank to retrieve it, floating swiftly downstream. This was a big young hound, maybe part black Lab. When I floated into his territory the dog came swimming for my canoe, nearly drowning in his fury as I beat him off with a paddle.

The dog's owner, calling "Gus!," waded in and got a grip on the beast. I put ashore and Gus settled down as soon as he saw that his master and I were fast friends. Although I'd never met him before, Garry McAdam is one of those people who, when he learned my destination, didn't have to ask why. Some people just get it. McAdam had see-through, Jesus-blue eyes and wore a soiled red baseball cap, slightly askew. Today he had come to the river before tackling a nasty linoleum-laying job, but that could wait. Immediately grasping my need to scout the river, he had nothing in the world more pressing to do.

I stashed my canoe in the bushes. We slid into his battered Dodge van and took off. At his shop we traded the van for a brown '79 Ford pickup, because he'd rebuilt the engine and wanted to put some miles on it. Gus and I crowded into the front seat with him, and we crossed the Castlegar bridge to a bluff overlooking the confluence of the Columbia and Kootenay Rivers.

McAdam had only the vaguest idea where these two rivers came from, but he was curious. I told him about Canal Flats, the capital of weird geography: how the Kootenay River turns its back on Columbia Lake without quite touching it and flows south from the Rocky Mountain Trench. The Kootenay (spelled Kootenai in the United States) drains the glaciers of Montana before turning north again to cross the panhandle of Idaho and come back to Canada here at Castlegar. I told him about David Thompson, the first white guy to figure it out and ·map the whole river. I probably didn't tell him, though this was the place to think about it, that two big dams on the Kootenay also came with the Columbia River Treaty. Duncan Dam—no power, all storage—has its reservoir in British Columbia. Libby Dam, in Montana, backs Lake Koocanusa forty-two miles into Canada.

Where the Kootenay and Columbia joined, below our bluff, lay Tin Cup Rapids. The rivers mixed and billowed, but the surface never broke into whitewater. High water made the river flatter than it had been in February. No problem. We recrossed the bridge and followed the high-shelf road down the Columbia toward the smelting town of Trail, stopping here and there to study the river.

McAdam had been a horse logger, a long-distance trucker, and a backhoe operator. These days he drove a cement truck and took odd jobs. Ageless, maybe early forties, he was lax and loose, and if he'd had a volume knob I would have turned him up.

"A couple years ago I blew out a heart valve," he said. "I woke up three weeks later in a hospital. When you've already died," he said, "there's no hurry."

Approaching Trail, he pointed to the leafy hillsides as if they were a green miracle. "These hills used to be completely bare," he said. "No trees at all. In town you couldn't grow a garden or grass. Nothing grew. I was twenty before I knew snow was white. In Trail, it was black."

I'd heard of Trail, but only vaguely. I was surprised now to learn that it's the second-largest industrial center on the Columbia, after the Portland-Vancouver-Longview area. Gold and copper strikes in the nearby Rossland district gave rise in the 1890s to the Consolidated Mining and Smelting Company of Canada, Ltd. (Cominco, for short) at Trail. Lead, zinc, and silver took over when gold and copper played out, and the Cominco works became a colossus, the biggest lead and zinc refinery in the world. Trail prospered, but paid the price. Sulfurous emissions threw a pall and stench about the valley that peeled paint, closed schools on windless days, and withered plant life.

"Dad worked at Cominco," McAdam said. "He died young. Life expectancy was about fifty, and he didn't make it. He used to say the inspectors were in Cominco's pocket. Cominco blew the lead up the stacks at night, when people slept. I forgot one night and left the dog out, and she died."

The road into Trail passed the Cominco plant, a mile long and towering above the river like a medieval castle. Smokestacks rose breathless against a blue sky. Knots of workers, on strike, sat in folding chairs at roadside. Some played cards, their picket signs propped at rest. "They get eighteen an hour," said McAdam, with a shake of the head that suggested this wasn't enough. "But nowadays they have the baghouses and tighter pollution laws."

Baghouses?

"To filter out the bad stuff. They catch it in a kind of

gunnysack material before the stacks. Make fertilizer out of it. The air's a lot better."

Heaps of coffin-shaped slag lined the road, which dove into switchbacks and dropped to the center of town. At the river I watched the high Columbia smack the bridge pillars, raising three-foot waves on the upriver side and sending a frothy white vee downstream.

On the left bank, two miles downstream, we stopped to scout Rock Island Rapids and to give Gus a run. Then we followed a narrow riverside road to the border. No town here. The U.S. inspector, in a cinderblock shanty and having nothing else to do, asked to see Gus's papers. Did the dog have his shots? For Chrissake, we were just going to Northport and back, to scout the river. The inspector studied McAdam and his Jesus-blue eyes. He scanned McAdam's bearded passenger and this big black fur ball of a dog, now growling as McAdam tensed. The border guard refused to let this mess into America.

McAdam U-turned cursingly from the border, and it occurred to me he might have had some earlier, unpleasant dealings with the law. But within a mile or two he recovered his easy-does-it self. Back in Castlegar, we loaded my canoe into his pickup for safekeeping overnight, and he dropped me off at a cheap hotel. He hadn't let me buy gas. He wouldn't let me pay for dinner. The next morning he and I returned, Gus-less, to scout the rest of the free-flowing Columbia.

So on Sunday afternoon I saddled up the canoe and spurred it into the current from the ferry landing. Tin Cup Rapids, along the Castlegar bend, rolled over bumps in the riverbed and bucked the canoe more than I'd expected. I dug my knees into the gunnels and paddled only for direction, to point the canoe forward. The river did the rest. I sailed beneath the Castlegar bridge like a hero and shot between the narrowing granite walls of canyon chute. Riverside bouldering trailed whitewater, but the middle coursed deep and flat. When the river bent, it also widened, and I had plenty of room to avoid trouble.

My own effortless speed brought home the river's power, its tremendous and still-gathering force. Summer snowmelt had caught up with me. The Columbia here was a big horse, but young and coltish, and you had to keep your eye on it. Nobody ever called the Columbia Ol' Man River.

Nearing Trail at sensational canoe-speed—I'd come twenty miles in two and a half hours—I aimed right-of-center to miss the bridge pillars. Then I focused on how to stop, because the shore at Trail is a tall rock seawall. Just downstream from the bridge lay the landing, an L-shaped dock with its short arm attached to the bank and the open end downstream. The dock drew its own backcurrent of rushing surface water. If I missed that opening, I wouldn't be staying the night in Trail. But I hit it just right, and eddied into the protected side of the dock.

I checked into the Hotel Arlington, an ancient rock structure newly fixed up, and spent the rest of the day poking about town. Trail Creek wandered under town in a concrete conduit, and narrow houses shouldered one another on the steep hillside for a look at the Columbia. A roofed wooden stairway zigzagged up to the smelter on its bluff above town. People I met confirmed McAdam's horror stories about the air in old Trail, and I learned that the local hockey team, which won the world championship in 1939, is called the Smoke Eaters. But now the air was better. Flowers flourished, and trees leaved.

Neat elderly women shuffled to Sunday-evening church, one woman at a time. I passed a pair of old ladies in flower-print dresses and sensible black shoes. Where were the men?

"Dad died young," McAdam had said. "Life expectancy was about fifty."

Knowing how quickly the river would push me from Trail to Northport, I slept late, ate a big slow breakfast, wrote postcards, and called home.

Near noon, I pushed off on the river again.

First up was a nasty clutter and tumble called Rock Island Rapids. Its main feature, a rock island the size of a bandstand, humped to the left of river center and split the current into green-white waves that scissored around lesser boulders on both sides. With McAdam and Gus, I'd scouted the island from the left bank. The suckholes looked more dangerous on the left, the narrower channel. On the right, the bank was of gentle slope, and the river reversed itself downstream into a wide eddy. The idea was to reach that eddy without getting drawn into the crushing mid-river current.

I hugged the right bank, back-ferrying. Back-ferrying is a defensive maneuver in which you point the canoe's bow in the direction you don't want to go, in this case left, and stroke backwards. Onrushing current catches the canoe at an angle that pushes it to the right. In big water, if you point the canoe in the direction you want to go, even if you paddle forward, current overpowers the canoe and pushes it the other way. M.J. Lorraine, for example, took Rock Island and other rapids stern first, not only to see what lay ahead but also to steer his descent by angling his rowboat cross-wise to current. In a canoe, stern first is not the ticket. But the same hydraulics are at work.

The river picked up speed above the rapids, and I heard the low rumble of water across rocks. Adrenaline kicked in, and I braced against the paddle to fight the river's rush toward middle, where everything wanted to go. In less time than it takes to say a long sentence, the island raced upstream on my left, and I skipped past deep green whorls in the island's wake and slid toward the broad, upstreaming eddy. I wheeled the canoe and sliced across the seam, leaning upstream to counter the kick. The eddy spun the canoe into a wide circle against the right shore for a slow, looping view of the river turmoil I'd just passed.

Pretty good. But on rivers, as a rule, it's not what you're scared of that will get you.

Now the river threw up a wind that gusted straight up the valley from the south. Aspens bent to the wind, their leaves spinning like quarters. The water below Rock Island pillowed and swirled, recovering itself. Head-on wind wanted to swing the bow, and I sped downstream without full control. Just upstream from the border station, on the left, a strong gust pushed me to the right bank—the side I didn't want.

I exited on rounded-rock shore to sit under a thin alder and wait for the wind to die down.

Here on the border, waiting, I pictured the bold straight line on maps that separates Canada from the western United States. Nothing on the land respected that division. The river didn't know the difference. Nor did the rounded, forested hills. Nor the mule deer doe that wandered up the shore and, seeing me, detoured up the cutbank and continued on her way. No sign marked the border on my wild side of the Columbia, no fence or clear-cut swath.

The border cuts maps at the 49th Parallel, a line marking the standoff in 1846 between the Americans and the British. For three decades, from 1813 to 1846, the Crown's Hudson's Bay Company had a stranglehold on the Columbia River's fur-trading traffic. The British fended off the ragged Yanks until overland wagon trains flooded the raw country with American settlers. President James Polk ("Fifty-four Forty or Fight") campaigned to annex the Oregon Country all the way from the 42nd Parallel to 54 degrees 40 minutes north latitude, which included the entire Columbia River watershed. But once elected, Polk and the U.S. Senate got caught up with the more pressing prizes of California and Texas, and opted for compromise here at the 49th Parallel.

Today the division seems arbitrary, almost quaint. British Columbia and the U.S. Northwest have far more in common with each other than with, respectively, Ottawa and Washington, D.C. If politicoeconomic upheaval were to force a new look at the national bonds we now take for granted, a redrawing of borders could make a strong union of Columbiana, the new nation that would have the water in a drying and warming world.

Mention this idea to a British Columbian, and he'll bite your ear off.

Across the river from where I waited, the Pend Oreille River entered the Columbia just a hundred yards upstream from the border checkpoint. The Pend Oreille is another branch that can arguably be called the Columbia's true source. It's longer, for example, than either the Columbia or the Kootenay. The Pend Oreille starts high in the Montana Rockies, where it is called Clark's Fork, and empties into a large natural lake near Coeur d'Alene, Idaho. It pokes north into Canada only for its last fifteen miles. Although it's longer, the Pend Oreille carries much less water than the now-combined Columbia and Kootenay Rivers. Its confluence with the main stream didn't look like a hazard from where I sat and waited.

And waited.

It was late afternoon, and the wind still gusted. I spread the life jacket for a nap, but I couldn't sleep. A cardtable-sized metal sheet, an airplane warning device, hung from a power line over the river and blew horizontal with each gust of wind.

I'd blown ashore on a low shelf that had wide oval depressions among the rounded rocks. I chose to believe these depressions were man-made, and maybe they were. Indians used to gather here, not in tepees but in pit houses dug into the ground. They piled brush on top, poked a smoke hole in the roof, and dropped a ladder down. After 1846 and the border compromise, the Hudson's Bay Company put Fort Shepherd up on the plateau here to catch French and Indian furs before they slipped down the river to America.

With nowhere to go I thought about the French, so active on the early river as voyageurs and trappers. A lot of Frenchmen took Indian wives and blended into the mountain gene pool, leaving the British and the Americans to squabble over sovereignty. From the names the French stuck on the Columbia's places and people, I picture them obsessed with body parts—Pend Oreille, Nez Percé, Coeur d'Alene, Grand Tetons. But they also survive in how we name river-related things. We say glacier instead of icefield, source instead of headwaters. *Les rapides, sur face, le courant* and *le banc, le port* and *le portage, le voyage, les cascades, les dalles,* and *des chutes.*

I had to cross the river because the border checkpoint was on the left side. Like a good American, I would obey the law and show my passport. I also wanted the inside of a left bend, just downstream, where Waneta Rapids laced the right shore. I could have set up *le camp* here and pitched *la tente.* But some people in Northport knew I was coming, and I could imagine their launching an embarrassing river search.

Finally my wind indicator hung at near-rest.

I pointed the bow upstream and powered into current at an angle that pushed me rapidly toward the far shore. Then I swung the bow and eyed the Pend Oreille River rushing in on my left. I tried to slice the seam where the two rivers met, but the seam had a powerful grip. I lost control. The river took the canoe, and I went swerving downstream in riled water. A whorl snagged the bow and jerked it to the right, while momentum took me to the left.

There's a moment beyond truth when time defies physics and you hover above calamity with sudden but slow surprise. *Aha! I am no longer seated in my canoe.* In this expanded time zone, a mere split-second, a good canoeist will swing his paddle and whap the flat surface where he's falling, in an effort to check his fall and rebalance the whole business. I'd done it before, and it works. But you have to *do* it.

I was already in the water.

The canoe, ahead of me, rolled and plooped upright.

Buoyed by its inner tubes and the waterproof bags, all tied in, the canoe floated low and half-swamped in the swirling current. With a couple of quick kicks I caught up with it, grabbed a gunnel and wedged the paddle inside. The border checkpoint raced upstream on the left, and I passed an ashen-faced fisherman on shore. I crossed the border clinging to the canoe, now a heavy, river-obeying object. I could only hang on, like a flag to a log, as the river took us to the outside of the bend and into its roller of Waneta Rapids. Which was really interesting. You spend so much time anticipating danger, avoiding it, and when it comes you just kind of relax and take it. It was sexual, is what it was, this change from on it to in it. The river had her own ideas. The waves came rounded and voluptuous, powerful and soft, and if there were rocks to miss I couldn't see them past the leading canoe.

It was over too soon. As the rapids played themselves out, I maneuvered the canoe into a back-ferrying angle. Grabbing the bow rope with one hand, I kicked and one-arm swam, which brought me to rounded-rock footing against the left shore, a quarter mile below the border. I hauled the canoe ashore after me.

The pale fisherman who had watched my spill now appeared on the cutbank above. I hoped he would just take a look and leave me to my private excitement and shame. But no. He advanced with a step-slide down the bank.

"Hoe's the water?" he said.

Warm, I told him. In fact I wouldn't have needed a wetsuit, although I was wearing one.

"Tippy sonsabitches, them canoes," he said.

He helped me roll the canoe, and we emptied it of water. The bags, water jug, and spare paddle were still in place, tied in. I'd lost only a red plastic drinking cup, a flannel shirt with a scratch pad and pen, and my blue Crooked River Round-Up cap. I was about to hike back to the border, but he said not to bother. "They shut 'er doan at five," he said. "Road's closed, eh? Nobody there."

So I unpacked a dry scratch pad and wrote a note for him to deposit at the checkpoint: "CROSSED BORDER BEHIND CANOE 7 PM MONDAY, JULY 16. NO FIREARMS OR DRUGS." Thanking the fisherman without thinking to jot down his name, I pushed off again.

Ever helpful, he called after me: "Keep the wet side doan."

The river ran fast, but wide and unbroken by rapids. Long shadows of ending day drew deer to the riverbank in pairs and threes. I passed a few houses, isolated farms. Blue herons patrolled the bank and unfolded themselves skyward in long, languid flaps. Having forgotten what a river smells like, I relaxed my paddling and breathed in the damp, sweet history of the world. Drifting close to shore I slapped at mosquitoes and kept my mouth shut. A hatch of mayflies hung in low hazy clouds upon the swift water, and fat rainbow trout leaped to feed.

The river bulged, then narrowed to a Z around a pair of rock promontories. This was a set of broken waters, far from the road, that McAdam and I had not scouted. Normally you want to cut the corners of a Z. Stay to the inside of each bend, because trouble and faster water will be on the outside. I should have stopped to walk the shore and take a look, but it was getting late. No back-ferrying here, I bent hard to the paddle to pick up full speed. The canoe sliced the inside of the first curve close enough to startle a banked turtle, who ducked inside his shell, and then I knifed across the surprised river toward the inside of the next bend. I taxied into a downstream eddy and then rode the river to a soft left-bank landing at Northport, USA.

The sun was down, but daylight lingered. I checked into the motel and took a walk around. Northport was once a smelting center to rival Trail, but it got left in the competitive slag heap by Cominco. Now a red-brick smokestack hulked above ruins of a smelter, overrun by blackberry vines. On

Columbia Avenue, the boarded-up Liberty Hotel and Kendrick Mercantile Co. stood where they had a hundred years ago, orphaned beside the tracks. History here hasn't been cuted up. You can squint and see the hotel still swarming with speculators, saloons running double shifts, and prospectors mobbing the music hall. At Kruk's Tavern, sagging steps led up the back to where the whores used to wait. Inside, I hoped to learn something about the river, but it was just a bunch of drunk Canadians who had come to Northport for gas and beer and cigarettes, all much cheaper than north of the border.

At Northport the Columbia widened and began slowing into Lake Roosevelt. But one more free-flow challenge remained. Five miles downstream lay The Little Dalles, a sudden narrowing and sharp drop in the riverbed. M. J. Lorraine had taken a look at this "gloomy gorge cut through limestone" and portaged around it, an effort that took him two days. The water level today can rise fifteen feet above what Lorraine saw, so The Little Dalles is a vastly changed place. When we were scouting it the other day, McAdam and I had driven through an orchard and private brush to a clifftop fifty feet above the chute. I threw chunks of deadwood upstream to see what the river would do with them. The Columbia moved swiftly, with swirls, but the channel had no vortex that could suck anything down. Wide green pillows rose and spread on the surface, and they did so at odd locations. There was no pattern to their rise and flat burst. Left of center, as we watched The Little Dalles perform, was the course most free of pillows.

"Piece of cake," McAdam had said. And I had agreed.

Yet now I awoke in Northport with a cold heart and a deep, unspecific dread. It didn't help that I'd scraped my knees raw against the gunnels while bracing against yesterday's river-tossings. When I put on jeans to walk to breakfast, strawberries rubbed the inside of my pants. My stride was stiff and old. At the cafe I remembered that scouting rapids from clifftop is not the same as seeing them at water level. In the Spokane paper I read that Lake Roosevelt was at 1,287.8 feet. Maximum elevation is 1,290, so The Little Dalles would be nearly as tame as it could ever be.

Half a short stack of hotcakes filled me to near-gag. As I was paying, I asked who knew the river.

"He just walked out the door," the waitress said. "Bob Weilep."

I hailed Weilep, a stout logger and deputy sheriff, as he backed his pickup from the gravel lot. He rolled down his window. I asked him about The Little Dalles and told him I was traveling by canoe.

Weilep stabbed at a back molar with his toothpick and regarded me with rich contempt. His wife, in the cab, stared out her window. Loggers and their wives have a pretty clear idea who the men are, and they aren't canoeists.

"Don't do it," he said.

I stuck with him, and Weilep poked his beefy elbow out the cab window and told me a story. He had led the rescue crew a couple years ago after some bonehead tourists found trouble at The Little Dalles. "Three canoes went in," he said, "and only two came out. Both of them empty." The people had life jackets and floated out. "Except one guy," said Weilep, "six-foot-four and strong. He reached shore and caught some vines. We had to lower a rope over the cliff to get him off a ledge."

Water was low?

Weilep's eyebrows went up. At least I knew *that* much. But his wife was anxious to leave. "My advice to you," he said, "is to skip it, and put back in at China Bend. If I told you it was okay, and something happened, I'd have to live with that."

He drove off.

Weilep was a deputy sheriff, probably just covering his ass, but my confidence was shot. Back at the motel, I delayed departure by talking with Bob Graham, a wise trout fisherman who owns most of Northport—the gas station, grocery store, and motel. I was scared of The Little Dalles, and he knew it.

"Tell you what," Graham said, and—thinking quickly—he spun a yarn about how he had to boat downstream anyway, something about checking the trash booms below The Little Dalles. "I'll go down and check it out. If it's not safe, I'll come back and stop you."

We shoved off from Northport, me in my canoe, he in a sixteen-foot outboard with a 50-horse Johnson. Graham sped away in a roostertail of wake, and disappeared down the river. Half an hour later, sooner than he expected me, I passed Graham visiting at Tom Wood's riverside cabin, his boat tied to the shore. The river bunched and narrowed. Current picked up my canoe and pulled it into the chute. Graham followed.

I paddled for the left-of-center channel, but I might as well have thrown the paddle skyward. A wide boil, like a foam mattress, unfolded from the deep and snapped open, throwing the canoe to the right and catawampus to the current. I slid to the right of center, the side I wanted to avoid, and from there I was on defense. Lesser pillows buffeted the canoe, which slithered forward and fishtailed downstream. I whacked at air, searching for the correct side to stroke on, and the gray stone canyon walls slashed by too close. I kept the wet side down, but it was ugly. The Columbia's last great swoop into Lake Roosevelt spit my canoe downstream like a watermelon seed between wet fingers.

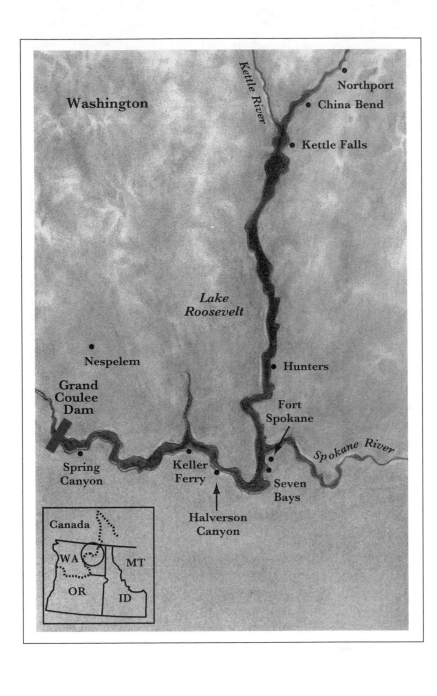

7

LAKE ROOSEVELT

We Were the People

Below the narrow slot of The Little Dalles, current was a mere echo of river expiring, with weaker and wider swirls into Lake Roosevelt. The river still moved, but it had to show me where it was. A light trailing breeze matched the current, so the part that was moving moved smooth as glass—*now here, over here*—into the gathering truth of lake. Near Snug Cove, a powerboat pulled four blond kids on ski-disks behind four tow ropes. An aluminum fishing boat on the far shore amplified a boom box of Chuck Berry.

The land, too, changed. Hills came rounded to shore, and trees spaced themselves on brown earth, no underbrush, as if the dry slopes had sucked in the firs and left only the lodgepole pine and tough juniper. Desert was coming. Summer was here. I'd lost my cap, so I cut a white T-shirt into strips, soaked them, and wrapped my head against the blazing sun. Giddy with triumph at having passed the last of the Columbia River's rapids, I watched my own color change in the two easy days it took to reach the National Park Service campground at Kettle Falls. I was hard as brown rock. My back and shoulder muscles were truck springs. Blue veins bulged and spread about my elbows and forearms, and when I snapped my fingers, triceps twitched. With a swell of lungs, I beached the canoe at the campground and tossed it effortlessly among the bushes.

Now I had to get to the town of Kettle Falls, four miles from lakeside. I was all dirty laundry and sweat, and the campground didn't have hot showers. Also I wanted to box my cold-weather gear—long johns and wool shirts, blankets and wetsuit—and mail it home. I phoned the H & H Motel, and a yellow Toyota pickup arrived to take me there.

After showering, I put on my town jeans and a clean shirt and walked through Kettle Falls. A vanilla ice-cream cone tasted incredibly delicious, as if I were rounding second on a triple to the left-centerfield gap. Language crowded about me. The commonplace became wondrous. At the hardware store I overheard a pair of young buds on vacation, one wearing lipstick for perhaps the first time in her life and the other in orange shorts, talking about someone else.

"The tall one with glasses?"

"The short one with brown eyes," said Lipstick.

"Yeah. That's the one," said Orange Shorts.

Like a man with something to do, I drew an umbrella from the rack and inspected it.

"Well, why don't you just call him?"

Lipstick sighed. "Because," she said.

I could have died. What a huge and separate gift it is, this language, that makes us different from the osprey and the fish. I left the store, my heart pounding, and reached the motel light-headed, dizzy.

I was suffering from river fatigue. River fatigue is a chemical imbalance that's not as bad as hypothermia or schizophrenia, though it's related to both. You don't know you have it until it's there, and it shows up as an exaggerated response to the good and the bad of a river. You're scared beyond reason of a danger, exhilarated beyond reason for having passed it. In rapid sequence, you can think yourself too little, then think you're too much. The world comes at you unfiltered, through the scared clear eyes of a child. You're suddenly tired.

A good night's sleep helps. It helps even more to lay up for a day. The river will be there tomorrow. Another cure for river fatigue is television. Watch CNN. Or listen to Tim McCarver call a Reds vs. Expos game, and it'll quash any thrill you ever had for language. The world comes at you in a familiar blur, and then you can go back to the river.

Ann Anderson, with her husband, owns the H & H Motel and the yellow Toyota pickup. She was driving me back to the canoe, and she wasn't happy about lake levels lately. "Up and down," she said. "We never know. Those idiots at Bonneville, they sell power to California cheaper than we get it here."

Lake Roosevelt is supposed to be full by the Fourth of July every summer, but for the last three years it hasn't been. Vacationers who come to a drawn-down reservoir aren't likely to come back. At Kettle Falls the shoreline gradient is very mild, so the lake dropping only a foot can expose a hundred yards of mud flats and orchard stumps. Then the mud bakes and cracks in the summer sun. Docks slump beached and crooked.

"Last year we had big sailboats here for the regatta," Anderson said. "They drew the water down at night, and the boats keeled over on the mud flats." She shook her head. "They didn't even bother to tell us. If they'd just tell us."

She took a back road toward the marina, and we passed neat orchards with roadside kiosks. Peaches, cherries, honey. She dropped me at the canoe, which I'd locked to a tree in the piney, needle-floored campground. The marina bustled with pleasure craft, and the smart river people wore iridescent oranges and greens. The water was up, and Lake Roosevelt glimmered blue under a strong morning sun.

*   *   *

From archaeological digs, we know people have lived at Kettle Falls for at least 9,000 years. And for at least 8,950 of those years they lived here because the Columbia River dropped 33 feet in less than a half mile. It broke over a pair of cataracts between close cliffs, and salmon squeezed into the narrows before they leaped Kettle Falls. Indians speared the salmon with stone-tipped spears, and they dipped hoop nets of spruce roots off long poles. In the pools, Indians caught salmon in cedar-bark baskets and trapped them in weirs. Salmon were the natives' chief food; they baked some and split and dried others, packing them away for winter.

Columbia River salmon are anadromous: They hatch in freshwater mountain streams, migrate to the Pacific, and spend three to five years in the ocean growing up. Then they return to their native streams to spawn. Unlike Atlantic salmon, Pacific salmon die in the act of spawning. The salmon returning to Kettle Falls had ranged as far as ten thousand miles out into the ocean, north off the tusk of Alaska and back, before homing back up the river.

The miracle of annual salmon runs spoke to the Indians of Creation. Salmon were a great people who lived in splendor at the faraway ocean. The Indians followed a solemn protocol each season at the arrival of the First Fish, an emissary from these ocean people. Once caught, He was shared in small pieces among the members of the tribe. At the longhouse they sang and prayed and danced before returning the First Fish's bones to the river. The bones floated downstream to show the salmon hordes it was okay—the First Fish had found proper respect—to come on up the river.

It worked. Salmon that passed Kettle Falls and went on up the Columbia were the fittest of all. They had to be. Salmon don't feed once they enter the river from the ocean. All the fuel for fighting upstream was packed in their own meat and grease. June hogs, they were called. My dad, as a youth, caught a 52-pounder that was not a freak. They ran that big. The freaks were 80, 90 pounds. There are photos. The record Columbia salmon is 110 pounds, big as my grown daughter.

Grand Coulee Dam blocked the river and flooded Kettle Falls in 1941. The government built the dam without a fish ladder, and that was the end of June hogs. When you block a river, it takes four or five years for a salmon run to obliterate itself. I picture the little ones that got out, June piglets, rushing downstream. They returned as great beasts from the ocean and found a concrete wall in their path. They didn't stop. I've seen it elsewhere, below dams. They die trying. The salmon's huge urge to continue, to spawn, drives them head-first against concrete.

The only memorial these days to Indian fishing at Kettle Falls is a powerful one. A sharpening stone has been lifted to a pine bluff above where the falls were. The stone, a river boulder the size of a small davenport, is scarred and grooved where Indians honed the rock points of their spears. You can stand at the sharpening stone and look down at Lake Roosevelt, where the river was, and think about how this place was once the hub of Northwest civilization. And about the thrust of genetic memory, lost forever, that drove June hogs.

Ahead of me lay a lot of lake. The shortest line you can draw from start to finish on Lake Roosevelt is 130 miles: two-thirds of it south, and then west to Grand Coulee Dam. Total shoreline is over 630 miles. If you lifted the shoreline off the map and stretched it straight, it would go from Portland to San Francisco. A big lake.

Now and again on the trip I had fiddled with ways to boost paddle power with wind power. Back on Arrow Lake, when the wind was right, I'd jerrybuilt a sail by draping the rain fly over my spare paddle, lashed vertical toward the bow. But the sail was stiff. In gusts, it wanted to tip the canoe. With time to think about it, I had tried some other arrangements too stupid to mention.

The latest scheme involved a sturdy green-and-yellow plaid umbrella and a pair of heavy orange-handled clamps, which I'd picked up at Kettle Falls. On the lake, now, with a trailing breeze and calm water, I put ashore and rigged up an umbrella sail. The clamps held the umbrella's shaft horizontal on the bow, where it could pivot with gusts of wind, and the umbrella, open and pointed forward, helped pull me down the lake. Paddle strokes came easier. The water surface felt greased, and I had no trouble steering. So satisfying was this arrangement that I thought I must have covered thirty miles, a new one-day flatwater record, that first day. I hadn't—it was closer to twenty—but that didn't dampen my enthusiasm for the umbrella. The *illusion* of harnessing wind power was as invigorating as the tiny pull of the sail. Often in the next week, whenever the wind blew favorably, I put out the umbrella sail.

On my right, all the way to Grand Coulee, lay the Colville Indian Reservation. Except for a touristy white tepee and some

Umbrella sail.

low houses at the Inchelium ferry landing, this side of the lake was deserted. The Indians had turned their back on Lake Roosevelt. Tribal headquarters for the Colville Confederated Tribes is at Nespelem, up in the dry hills, a dusty place where unemployment and alcoholism, as on other reservations, are the signs of despair. I'd been to Nespelem. A couple of years ago I had gone there to write about a new fish hatchery that the Bonneville Power Administration paid for and the Colvilles own and run. The hatchery—a trout hatchery—was a form of compensation for lost salmon runs. The Colvilles raise brook, rainbow, and cutthroat trout to plant in the reservation's lakes and streams.

Mike Someday, head of the tribal fish and wildlife committee, was the man I'd asked to see. A shy man in his forties, Someday wore a dress shirt with string tie and beads-around-turquoise clasp. He led me to a conference room and we sat under a glowing portrait of Chief Joseph of the Nez Percé, who lies buried in Nespelem. Someday was in a tight spot. He'd tried to avoid the interview, he confessed, but his assistant was off elk hunting. Someday didn't want to appear ungrateful to BPA: His people appreciate the hatchery, and BPA pays the young Indians who train and work there. Yet he didn't want to give the impression that power-money gestures like this were fair compensation for what his people lost. In his gentle way— Northwest Indians, as a rule, don't beat drums and raise hell— Someday fed me a careful line that would satisfy BPA and not shame his people.

"If we had our druthers," was the strongest he would state it, "there would be no dams. We'd rather have salmon than resident trout."

When I had enough to write up the hatchery, we dropped our formal roles and talked, as if we were just people, about Kettle Falls and how the Indians had been of the salmon culture.

"I'm not a doctor, not a nutritionist," he said, "but I think the dam caused this alcoholism and disease. The metabolism of Indians changed overnight. You take a fisher culture and make them farmers . . . It changed the diet, changed everything."

He filled me in on how the Colville Reservation used to be 2.8 million acres on both banks of the Columbia, from Kettle Falls to the grand coulee. After measles and smallpox eliminated the call for that much land, the Indians were pushed to the right bank only. Then came a gold strike near the Canadian border, and a northern swath got lopped off. Today the reservation is 1.3 million acres, most of it hardscrabble sage and rattlesnake country. Many Indian bands got lumped on the reservation—the Moses, the Lakes, the Chelan, the Entiat, the Palouse, the Okanogan, the Colvilles, and others.

Someday referred more than once to "the Nation," and I wasn't sure what he meant. The confederated tribes? His tribe? His band? What tribe was he?

"Tribe," he said, "is an idea you get from books. On the plains, maybe, you had tribes because the people had to defend a lot of land to find a living. On the river, here, a living came to us. There was plenty. We didn't call ourselves Colvilles or whatever. We were the people. My mother was what you'd call a Lake Indian. She came from Canada."

A sturgeon fisherman at a peninsula campground placed a twenty-pound weight—a cannonball—on the lakebed by rowing it out from shore and dropping it. Attached to the cannonball was a gaff-sized hook and a wad of fetid herring. "Anything will do," he said. "Moldy meat is good."

Sturgeon, ancient fishlike creatures, occupy a low limb of their own on the tree of life. They can live hundreds of years and grow twenty feet long, vacuuming the Columbia's floor for food. I followed the fisherman to the bank. He took up slack in his line, stabbed the stout rod into a holder and sat in a lawn chair to watch the cow bell at the tip of his pole.

For a fisherman, he was entirely disagreeable.

"They charge six dollars a night for this spot," he snarled. "Look at it." He'd parked his camper on caked brown earth next to a shabby picnic table and fire pit. Pit toilets. No shade, no water. "I'm not paying it," he said. "They're exporting power right now. They've drawn down the lake since this morning. We don't get a damn thing from this reservoir."

On Lake Roosevelt, people say "they" a lot to begin resentful sentences. "They" can be the Bonneville Power Administration, which markets and delivers the power from federal dams. BPA coordinates the hydro system and decides when and how much power to sell, and to whom. "They" can be the Bureau of Reclamation, which runs Grand Coulee Dam and draws water from the river to irrigate half a million acres of former desert. "They" can be the U.S. Army Corps of Engineers, which runs other Columbia dams and regulates flood control and downriver shipping, both of which influence water levels at Lake Roosevelt. A river is hard to split up and share. From here to the ocean it gets enormously complicated, and the "they" can be a useful construct. The U.S. Departments of the Interior, Energy, Agriculture, Defense, and Commerce all have an oar in the river, and they're not all pulling in the same direction. House Speaker Tom Foley, a Democrat from Spokane, issues the occasional thunderclap on behalf of his upriver constituents that echoes about the heads of federal agencies. But so does Senator Mark Hatfield, the Oregon Republican and white eagle of hydropower, BPA, and the status quo.

"They" do what they did last year, and the year before that, until crisis forces change. Low water, for four straight years, has accelerated the crisis that is now forcing change. There just isn't enough river to satisfy all the competing interests—for fish, electric power, irrigation, and barge traffic. In the meantime, upriver recreation draws the short stick.

"They cruise around in their new white cars," said the sturgeon fisherman, still grousing, vowing not to pay. "They" in this case is the National Park Service. "And you can't camp except in designated spots."

*   *   *

At a grocery store called Daisy: "They lower it when trout are spawning," said the elderly attendant. "Kill 'em off."

I was tiring of this theme. Before dams, the weather issued its flood years and droughts, and the river was uncertain, inconstant, for the Euro-American way of using it. The difference, it seemed to me, was that homesteaders had no choice but to take nature as it came. Now the Canadians can blame Americans. Americans have "them" to blame, and it's easy to suspect "them" of favoring other groups of people. The Indians certainly do have a complaint, but a guy selling gas and groceries at Lake Roosevelt? Part of my view of things, no doubt, was that the lake was sparkling full. People were catching fish. I thought it was a great place to be. I mentioned this to the storekeeper, and repeated it, before I realized the old buzzard was hard of hearing. When I finally got through to him, he said, "It's up, but it ain't plumb up."

If the lake wasn't plumb up it was within a foot of full, and shores of the upper lake were as friendly to canoe-camping as any on the entire river. Lake Roosevelt was different from the raw reservoirs I'd seen. It had been here fifty years, and it was mature. Sandstone cutbanks had sluffed to the high-water mark long ago, and they sloped to river with sandy bars. Sheltered coves, where the trees grew, lapped with Ice Age gravels in wide crescent beaches, with driftwood. Blond grasses softened the hills, and the sharp scent of sage and juniper spiced the air. It's true, the designated camping spots, except a green grove at Hunters, were sorry. At Barnaby Island, the lone picnic table lacked one bench, and nails poked from shrunken boards. Crows picked at a pile of popcorn someone before me had left, and there was no toilet. But few boats rode the upper lake, and I camped wherever I pleased.

A bald eagle soared from branch to snag as I put ashore past Inchelium, and glided on down the lake. I built a driftwood fire inside a circle of round rocks and roasted Polish dogs;

heat stayed on the river long into the evening. I awoke that night for no apparent reason and walked the beach. Stars poked the black sky so close I reached up to stir them. A dip in the calm river got me thinking about M. J. Lorraine and the fierce rapids he had descended from here to the grand coulee. I tossed small stones into Lake Roosevelt for him, and watched their ripples reflect the pinking eastern sky.

Two days below that quiet campsite the lake got crowded. I welcomed the choppy wakes and the sound of human laughter and the smell of gas fumes over water. It was Saturday morning, the start of a late-July weekend above the Columbia's elbow, where the Spokane River comes in. Powerboats, sleek as letter openers, sliced the lake. Their purpose was just to roar and go fast, which seemed like an interesting idea. A large cabin cruiser knifed up the lake straight at me. I stood in the canoe and waved a paddle. The cruiser veered to miss me, and I wheeled my bow into its wake as the captain lifted a cold one in happy salute.

At midday I turned the corner into the Spokane River and powered against wrong-way wind to a grassy park below a green steel bridge. At Wannamekas, an Indian snack bar, fry bread tacos and cold pop tasted really good. The cook, whose name was Juana—Wana? Wanna Meka?—said her specialty was the Pow Wow Burger, and I vowed to return for one that night. I took a cold outdoor shower at the beach rest rooms, lay out in the hot shade, and read the paper. Around me were families at picnic. Kids with lifesaver arm bands worked the beach with bright shovels and buckets.

The Spokane River, when I jumped in, ran clear and clean and startlingly warm, like the hot spigot into a tepid tub. The Spokane joins the Columbia after crossing high desert, and its dams slow the water to capture even more heat than it would have in the old days.

A big reason, in addition to its rapid and steady fall, for the Columbia River's huge power potential is that its different branches drain the Rocky Mountains at different times of year.

In May, when the far-north Columbia Icefields are still frozen, the Montana and Wyoming Rockies are already shedding snowpack. Storage dams on the Spokane, the Snake, and other southerly tributaries fill their reservoirs a good three months earlier than does Mica Dam. One branch of the system covers for another. In winter, when the Rockies are locked in ice all the way from British Columbia to Utah, the west slope of the Cascade Mountains enters *its* high-water season—with rain, not snowmelt. Lower-river tributaries run highest in December and January, filling the Willamette, the Santiam, the Clackamas, the Lewis, and many others.

So nature designed the system with a built-in constancy, which could be smoothed out even more with dams and reservoirs. The builders erected not just the fourteen mainstream dams but over two hundred on the whole system. The number won't increase much, if at all. All the major sites are filled with concrete, and remaining lesser sites are guarded to protect salmon runs. At the time, though, and it wasn't long ago, river-busting know-how combined with a growing thirst for power to overrun any caution about damage and land-change. Few people, and those disenfranchised, lived where the reservoirs would go. Dams displaced an occasional white settlement, but mostly it was Indians and fish who lost out.

High on a plateau above the confluence of the Spokane and Columbia Rivers, the army's Fort Spokane garrisoned cavalry regiments at the turn of the century. I walked up there to take a look.

A handful of the fort's fifty buildings still stood, and a gravel path led in a walking tour of the foundations of others. This post was founded in 1880, three years after the army captured Chief Joseph and when the Indian wars were already over, so the army busied itself keeping order among white settlers. In twenty years at Fort Spokane, no shot was fired in anger. By 1901 the army had pulled out and Fort Spokane housed an

Indian boarding school, where a chief complaint was that the Indian children's cultural patterns were hard to change. "The rewards of education," wrote the headmaster, "are not yet apparent to the Indians."

In 1914, an outbreak of tuberculosis wiped out 92 percent of the resident Indian population. The boarding school became a sanatorium, then closed for lack of patients.

The sign at the park said CAMPGROUND FULL, so I waited until dusk and then paddled a quarter mile west to a thin sandy beach, out of everybody's way, and pitched the tent. Then came the law. A green-shirted young woman, a park ranger with gapped front teeth, approached in a Boston Whaler with a 150-horse Evinrude, V-6, probably $20,000 worth of water-cruiser not counting the radio and electronic bullhorn and flashing blue lights.

"This is a no-camping area," she said.

The campground was full, I pointed out, and this beach wasn't posted. She didn't blink.

Where can I go?

That was my problem, not hers. Not here. I'd Van Winkled into her world from a very different one, and now I appealed for a waiver. I was polite. I explained where I'd been, where I was going. She didn't get it.

"Where's your car?" she said.

Portland, Oregon.

She took me for a smart-ass. "We have our rules," she said, and she ticked off some rules. No overnight tents except in designated spots. No campfires. Each boat must carry a U.S. Coast Guard–approved marine sanitation device (a chemical toilet). Now that I think back on it, these rules are sensible, and I endorse them for others on Lake Roosevelt. The world fills up, you have to have rules. But I was a brat. I was an exception, I thought. I didn't plan to build a fire. The designated spot was full, and there was no nearby alternative. I'd already used the rest rooms, and could do so again after my Pow Wow Burger. "It's a hundred-dollar fine," she said.

The flashing lights drew other boats near shore to see what was up. Finally the ranger remembered the campground wasn't *really* full. The CAMPGROUND FULL sign applied to motorized campers. A tents-only clearing back in the woods was always open, never full. I could go there.

Furious, I did. I paddled back upstream and set up camp by flashlight at a walk-in spot far off the river. I paid my six dollars and walked across the bridge for a Pow Wow Burger, but the Indian snack bar was closed.

The next morning I tied a fishing line to the stern of the canoe and drowned some worms on my way out of the Spokane River into wide Lake Roosevelt. No luck. It was probably too hot for fish. The Spokane paper had reported a heat wave—six days running in the high nineties—but it hadn't bothered me until I read about it in the paper. I'd picked up a straw hat at Kettle Falls, and now I wore a long-sleeved cotton shirt and slit a pair of sweat socks lengthwise to cover my thighs during the heat of the day. Shade was rare, and wherever it appeared I stopped.

Seven Bays Marina, a store and RV park with willows and sprinkler-cooled grass, had many small coves in the shape of a seven-leaf clover. This is where you rent houseboats and come in to refuel or buy food. The houseboats are white with blue trim, and *big*—fifty-two-footers that ride tall on the water—skippered by well-heeled vacationers who were not necessarily skilled at navigating anything, let alone a floating condominium. I watched as a dapper and terrified old man at the helm of a houseboat responded to vague hand signals from an Indian brave on the dock, and they brought 'er in, like a 747 into a country airstrip.

Colville Indians own the houseboat franchise here and at Keller Ferry. Their fleet of thirty-seven houseboats could be the biggest town on the lake, but mostly the boats scatter and find privacy in the many inlets and coves. A houseboat sleeps thirteen. The procedure is to gather multiple families. Bring your ski boat, too, and your rowboat or canoe, and tow these lesser craft about the lake like the tail on a fat kite.

As if I had so much money I didn't need to dress for it, I boarded a houseboat at Seven Bays Marina to look around. The back deck was a low platform for swimming or skiing. The vessel had a full galley with casket-sized ice chest, a bar, flush toilets, and mirror lighting in the head. It had a spacious middle for dining and playing cards, a shaded front deck, and a roof laid out for sun bathing. A water slide curled to the Columbia from the upper deck.

The lake took its wide bend west, into a roadless area of basalt bluffs and granite outcroppings. The wind gusted and shifted. Whitecaps pushed me to shore a time or two, but never for more than an hour. At one stop I thought I was alone, but a tumble of small rocks clattering down the slope told me otherwise. I looked up to see a doe and her fawn. The fawn, unsure yet of what it was to be a deer, took another inept step. More rockfall. The doe stared back at him—*Where did I fail?*—then down at me. If deer roll their eyes, she rolled her eyes.

Now I encountered the familiar pattern of finding sheer shoreline when approaching a dam. Places to camp, or even to exit and stretch the legs, were few. I reached a boat-access-only National Park Service campground called Halverson. It was deserted, and at first I wondered why. Halverson sat in a narrow slit of left-bank canyon with a view across the lake to stacked rocks. But the small shelf of beach lay broken down. A trail of cow pies led to a lone picnic table on a flat maybe big enough for three tents, if their sides touched. The privy was a single pit with a plywood stool—no cover, no toilet seat, no walls—astride the cow path up the hill. Flies swarmed. Yellow-jackets drove me off my cooking, so I ate granola bars in the hot zipped tent.

That night I awakened to cattle hoofing to lakeside, and the bawl of a calf who found my tent in his way.

Range cattle. National Forests and National Recreation Areas, like this one, can be grazed for profit. At Halverson the only inconvenience was to me, another life form that isn't native here. But elsewhere in the Columbia watershed, grazing on public lands has badly damaged the habitat salmon need for spawning. Cattle trample shoreline and graze on riverside greens that once threw shade. Mud covers gravels, and native creatures do poorly.

Cross and short on sleep, I left Halverson in the morning without coffee or cooking, swatting at bees. The river, too, was in a foul mood. We quarreled all day. Thunderheads rolled the western hills and seemed to plan something bad, but never got it organized. Wind was mostly against me, and strong. In late afternoon, less than four miles separated me from Keller Ferry, but those four miles included nasty cliffs on the left shore of the lake. No exit in sight. I pulled up short and waited for the wind to die down.

When a small sailboat turned the point from the direction I wanted to go, I pushed off in the canoe. At least someone would see me if I swamped. The sailboat and I closed distance before the wind picked up again. A man and a boy on the sailboat—a Force 5—began a tack that became a 360-degree pirouette. The sail spanked water as the wind whisked them to a surprise dunk. Good sailors, they recovered before I could reach them. We rounded the point together and pulled into Keller Ferry at dinner time.

Keller Ferry had a working ferry, from the left shore to the road north through the Indian reservation. The campground was a beauty, clean and watered. I pitched the tent and downed a pan of chili con carne before the storm, which had been flickering silent lightning, alit with full thunderclapped fury on Keller Ferry. At first it blew sand and swallows, the birds crazy with excitement. I lashed the canoe to a tree and jammed my stuff in the tent, dirty dishes and all. The wind blew tablecloths and towels through camp, and a little boy stood under a tree and jumped up and down. A boat broke loose from the dock, and nine of us chased into the water after it. There was great joy to all this, strangers thrown together, no real danger but the world flying around. Nature was loose, and all we could lose was *things*. What fun. Because I'd pitched my tent under a tree and lightning flashed close, I sat in the open flat and watched the rain blow in sheets across camp.

There was symmetry, too, in all this. Six hundred miles down, six hundred to go. It had taken me thirty-nine days to get to Keller Ferry, almost to Grand Coulee Dam. Monday, July 23. Halfway to the Pacific Ocean.

8

GRAND COULEE

A Man Has No Idea

There was nothing on earth to compare it to. Grand Coulee Dam was the biggest assault of man on nature in the then-history of the world. For seven thousand years the planet had spun unburdened by any man-made object larger than the Great Pyramid at Giza. Grand Coulee Dam was going to be three times that size. A flickering newsreel camera gazes down from D Street in Tent City, and the crackling voice of the narrator struggles for words. Colossal? Mammoth? Three thousand men on a shift, three shifts a day, men and their machinery as if God's footfall had lit on a gigantic termite mound. The narrator: "Enough concrete to pave a highway from Seattle to Texas! More steel than in the transcontinental railroad! Eight miles of tunnels within its bulk!"

Squads of federal publicists, in their zeal to find scale and to pump up a Depression-ridden nation, were inspired to overlook the Great Wall of China and perhaps the Panama Canal, depending on how you figure it. But let's not quibble. Grand Coulee Dam is still the most massive man-made structure in the United States, and the largest concrete thing in the world. Grand Coulee Dam captured—deserved to capture—men's souls.

They came from Astoria when the price of salmon fell to ten cents a pound and nobody could pay it, proud Scandy fishermen with the wife and three towheads and all they owned on a broken-down flatbed Ford. They came from Portland and Seattle, where the breadlines had never been longer and men sold small pyramids of apples from upturned crates. They came from the woods when the mills shut down, and they came from the parched plains of eastern Washington when their farms went belly up. They Joaded up from the Hoovervilles of California, and straight from the lost heartland of America.

September 1933: The government's first steel buttresses for the dam were a great magnet for iron-bodied but desperate men who needed work and couldn't find it. Jobs—thousands of jobs, at fifty cents an hour under the hot sun and choking dust—awaited those who would uproot themselves to harness the Great River of the West. As they came, they *be*came: blasters, mixers, crane operators, carpenters, electricians. Those who could read and figure were foremen. Workers sorted themselves into camps around the vast construction pit according to job and social rank. The big shots took the only shade, down in the willowed burg called Coulee Dam. Up the dry hills sprawled Mason City, Electric City, Tent City. Thirty thousand souls rushed to the high desert, including those who came to clothe, house, feed, swindle, and preach.

At Grand Coulee there was promise. There was hope.

The English language lacks a single common word for a steep-walled, trenchlike gulch cut by flash-flood rains or melting snow. The Spanish call it an *arroyo*, the French a *coulée*. The Columbia's grand coulee is an ancient riverbed where an Ice Age blockage shifted the river overflowing into lava-busting, terrain-carving floods. The coulee, today, is a high rimrock canyon without a river. Glacial melting has shifted the Columbia back into its even-more-ancient bed—its modern course—that bends north and west in search of an outlet to the Pacific. The riverless coulee lies 280 feet higher than the surface of Lake Roosevelt. What intrigued freethinkers and surveyors in the 1920s was the idea that *if you could just put some river back in the coulee,* simple gravity would feed that water toward the high desert. You could turn the brown land green.

From the upriver side, at canoe-level, the size of Grand Coulee Dam was not immediately apparent. Lake Roosevelt stopped at a low concrete wall across the river. No trees or houses gave the wall scale between its buff rock shoulders, themselves massive. But the dam's size snapped into perspective when I realized that the flyspeck creeping across it was a car. The dam is a mile across; on the far side is a spillway twice the height of Niagara Falls. But I couldn't see that.

What I could see was the big idea: *If you could just lift some river up into the coulee . . .* The landscape ahead of my canoe made a *Y.* The Columbia River valley split into two. The dam lay at the right branch of the *Y,* where the modern Columbia River flows. The left branch, elevated, was the stranded old riverbed, the coulee.

Twelve pipes crawled up the left bank, in parallel, and arched toward the coulee. I would have called them big pipes, and let it go at that, until I read their dimensions, later. Each pipe is big enough to drive a station wagon through. The pumps, at their base, can push eighteen supertankers' worth of water a day up into the coulee, to set in motion the biggest irrigation project in the Western Hemisphere.

I turned the canoe around and paddled back to Spring Canyon, a green wedge of campground where rangers were sweeping up debris from last night's gullywasher. Spring Canyon was the only place on the river, so far, where I'd arranged to be met by someone. Nick Carter, an umpire I work with in Portland, had told me about his grandparents, Ben and Ruth Seibold. The Seibolds had lived at Grand Coulee since the dam was going up, and Nick said they would be glad to put me up when I came through.

I'd phoned them from Fort Spokane, and again now from Spring Canyon.

"A brown Ford pickup will be there in twenty minutes," Ruth said. "Ben is slow."

Ben is eighty-four years old. He brought the pickup to the campground, and I waved him to the canoe. Square-shouldered but stooped, brush-cut, Ben had the large rough hands and untroubled brown eyes of a laborer. He let me load the canoe by myself, and he tied a red vest on the end that stuck out. Ben drove at fifteen miles per hour to a trim white house with a spinning weathervane and red potted geraniums on the dry bluff above town.

Inside, Ruth gave me an arthritic hand-touch from her corner recliner and then roused herself to heat up a vat of spaghetti and meatballs. When I opted for ice cream before dinner, she blossomed like a desert flower. And when I didn't object to her smoking—and shared her ashtray—Ruth opened her heart. She gave me the raspy dickens for not telephoning them after last night's storm. "Ben was frantic with worry," she said.

At the dining room table, we talked for a spell about the weather. Weather doesn't often happen here in late July, so they were wound up. And then we talked about the dam.

"I was a wood butcher on them doggone forms," Ben said. "For concrete pours. Three-eighths-inch plywood, plug the knotholes with pine. After a pour you'd have your shrinkage, and they sent us carpenters in to shore 'er up, tighten the she-bolts. Square 'em up. Terrible hot down there in the dust and grime. They run them quarter-inch pipes through the concrete with water to cool it. Later, you'd fill the pipes with grout."

Ben forked a wad of spaghetti, but he didn't raise it to his mouth. His eyes gleamed as he recalled the chaos and the glory of the work.

"A person has no idea," he said. "Trestles. Ship cranes and what have you. Them eight-yard buckets of concrete come swingin' in on a gondola. It took three stout men on a handle to pour. Trains and trucks comin' and goin', you'd look down in the hole at all that like a beehive. Conveyor belts. Eight thousand men, three shifts, around the clock. Floodlights at night and the dust. Whistles blowin' to tell you—a long-short-long was us wood butchers—where to go. They sucked the cement from big silos to the magic house, and them doggone inspectors, they weighed every pour. How many pounds of rock, gravel, sand, all washed and weighed, just so."

The magic house?

"The mixing plant," Ruth said.

"That's right," Ben said. "We had your colored, your Indians, everybody. They come from all over, but from Washington had preference. A lot of drifters."

"A lot *walked* into this town," said Ruth. "Riffraff. Scum."

"If you didn't put out," Ben said, "you didn't last long. Fired. Go to the end of the personnel line. But that guy and his walkie-talkie, he knew every man. He'd say, 'Where you from? Didn't I see you last week?' There was *some* good Indians," he said. "Even then they wouldn't work. It was in the contract, Indians had to be hired. Work a day or two, go tie on a drunk. You'd find them Indians sleeping in the shade."

"Now Ben."

"That's right."

The part that always gets me is what they do with the river while they build the dam. The idea of cofferdams, which shunt the channel to one side while construction proceeds on the other, was familiar to me. But at a site this wide, with this much river? Ben explained how they had to V the river around giant columns of concrete that began to rise in the middle. Then they diverted the river through cliffside tunnels when it was time to fuse the columns into a solid slab.

"I was a farmer," Ben said, "not a construction worker. I was afraid of heights. When they got 'er off the ground, I took the garbage franchise. You'd pick up four times a month for an individual, fifty cents. I had a '27 Chevy tank truck for septic and a '34 for haulin' garbage. Mornings. Oh, I seen some awful things on B Street. Them back alleys, hard to drive through, the drunks lyin' out there. They say eighty-nine men lost their lives building the dam, but most of that was on B Street. Fights and what have you. Cockroaches. Them fifty-gallon barrels of garbage and juice."

"B Street honky-tonks," Ruth explained. "Hookers upstairs. Taxi dancers charged ten cents a dance, and some were married women, all dolled up. They made out all right."

"I wanted to raise it to seventy-five cents a month," Ben said. "The city wouldn't go for it. I told 'em to shove it."

"We had a string of cabins," Ruth said.

"That's right. Unplaned lumber. Finished with fiberboard. Table and wood chairs, a chest of drawers. We got beds and this and that at a second-hand store in Seattle. You had twelve people under one roof. Plank walkways with a water tap every few feet, and outside toilets at the woodshed. All's we had was one shower for the whole deal. We kept the stove going and hot showers."

"Five dollars a week," Ruth said. "Our cabins were considered *up*town. Towels, bedding, dishes. We furnished fuel. Shack people would come visit and load up on wood at night."

"Them doggone kids put that cat down the toilet hole."

"Oh, we had a time."

Ben, overcome with it all, excused himself from the table. He lay down on the couch and closed his eyes, and Ruth and I ate our spaghetti.

"We had some desperate cases," she said. "The woman

with a goat, to feed her allergic baby, took my sewing machine. I saw her leave, but I felt sorry for her. You'd just cry. Flat broke. She had given me her engagement ring for rent, and I said, 'What are you going to eat?' She didn't know. She had a four-year-old and the allergic baby. The goat. I said, 'You take this engagement ring over to my uncle, owns the store.'"

Ruth remembered the dust boiling up from the excavation site. Grit worked its way into your shoes and ears, and she had the devil's own time keeping those cabins clean. She told me about more of her desperate cases. Their checks would bounce, no funds, and she'd find the renters had slipped away into the night.

"That motorcycle outfit took my curtains, even."

"That's right." I thought Ben had drifted off, but his head was up. "River used to cut right through here, them geologists say. I was drilling wells and I come across the old riverbed in the draw, where the Safeway is. A cedar tree, in a black layer of clay. You had them alder leaves, fir needles, and what have you."

"That's okay, Ben," Ruth said.

He put his head back down.

"You'd just cry," she continued. "They were good people. My land. They just needed work."

They just needed work. Because the people who lived the Great Depression are getting on, peeling off, we stand to lose a big part of the collective American memory. Folks my mother's age still carry with them the terror of having been decent, hard-working, and dirt-poor. Mom, as a high school senior in Astoria, lived in a shack insulated with mail packets when her father found work at the Astoria post office. When she graduated, she Sister Carried to Portland and spent a fifth year in high school because she couldn't find work. Dad, the youngest of seven siblings, six brothers and a sister, attended four high schools along the lower Columbia River—White Salmon to Stevenson to Clatskanie to St. Helens—as his father, a gyppo logger, kept packing up the family to sniff out the next working sawmill. Venison and blackberries were staples.

These were not your desperate cases. Each of my parents, separately, made their way to Oregon Normal School and earned teaching degrees, found jobs. Those of us in the next generation, who never wanted for shelter or food or a basic sense of participation and choice in the world, probably don't really get it.

The federal government landed with both feet on the Columbia River, building Grand Coulee Dam and Bonneville Dam at the same time. The idea was to prime the economic pump of this slow corner of the nation. If the government could put folks to work, Northwest electricity users, not taxpayers, would repay the people's investment in the Columbia River basin. Only the U.S. Treasury, with its money-printing presses, could have pulled it off. The immediate boost from Grand Coulee Dam was construction jobs, but supporters justified the dam in terms of irrigation, flood control, and electric power—in that order.

Irrigation was the big deal. No one doubted what this land, with water, could do. Homesteaders, arriving in years of good rainfall, had found a long growing season, rich and powdery soil, and easy rolling terrain. But the rain, ten inches in a good year, fell mostly in winter, not in the growing season. Some farmers kept trying against the high-desert sun, but most of them pulled up stakes and moved on to greener pastures.

The idea for a river diversion at the grand coulee had been around at least since 1908, when Billy Clapp, an Ephrata, Washington, lawyer, wondered why some of the Columbia River couldn't be siphoned toward the arid steppe. Clapp found an ally in Rufus Woods, publisher of the Wenatchee

World. Woods grabbed Clapp's idea and ran with it, whipping up Pacific Northwest enthusiasm for a big river-block at the grand coulee. Opposition was fierce. Private utilities and big holding companies wanted to enrich their stockholders by building other, lesser, dams. They dismissed Clapp and Woods as dreamers, cranks, subversives. A proposed grand canal to the desert from Clark's Fork had its own feverish supporters, and controversy over how to tame the Columbia fueled hot arguments about who would do it. Here was government landing in a field that Americans had long roped off for private enterprise. Many foresaw calamity. A massive federal irrigation and power project would quash capitalism, would rise as a monument to a new socialist era.

The part that glows in the dark, looking back on it, is that the question was not whether but how. If the government didn't harness the Columbia, private enterprise would. This was long before environmental impact statements, and no loud voices questioned the wisdom of river-change. We inundated Kettle Falls, undid an Indian culture, and lost June hogs without a second thought. The mountains of books, pamphlets, and congressional records about the genesis of Grand Coulee Dam are almost entirely political and economic. But that's the way our Euro-American culture advanced on this land, looking to bring nature to its knees.

Listen to Franklin Delano Roosevelt, stumping for the vice-presidency in 1920, speaking in Portland:

> When you cross the Mountain States and that portion of the Coast States that lies well back from the ocean, you are impressed by those great stretches of physical territory now practically unused but destined some day to contain the homes of thousands and hundreds of thousands of citizens like us, a territory to be developed by the Nation for the Nation. As we were coming down the river today, I could not help thinking, as everyone does, of all that water running unchecked down to the sea.

As everyone does. Wild was wasteful. Unquestioned, given, was man's duty to bend the river to his own will.

Roosevelt, of course, when he reached the White House in 1933, became the Big Daddy of the Columbia Basin Project. He collared the fractious Pacific Northwest delegation and pushed enabling legislation through Congress. Public power and publicly funded irrigation were cornerstones to Roosevelt's New Deal, and the desert bloomed. Today, 2 million acre-feet of Columbia River water leaves Lake Roosevelt each May to September and spreads via six thousand miles of canals, tunnels, and ditches. Corn and alfalfa, apples and peaches, potatoes and peppermint—there's hardly a crop you can think of that won't grow on the half-million acres of irrigated Columbia Basin.

Another reason for the big dam was flood control. For as long as humans have known the river, periodic flooding shifted the Columbia here and there to cut new corners, carving the bed and spreading plains. The earliest people knew better than to build on any but the highest of river-abutting ground, or they constructed dwellings they could pack up and move when the river turned angry. When Euro-American settlers reached the Northwest, only two hundred years ago, their towns and cities found the lower river—the closest places, by sea, to Boston and San Francisco. And because their civilizings were immobile, the idea of "the thirty-year flood" took hold. Once every thirty years or so, a whopper flood came smashing through.

Nineteen eleven was a terrible flood year. And in 1948, on Memorial Day, the Columbia blasted through a dike and wiped out Vanport, a shipyard housing area between Portland and Vancouver that had once been Oregon's second-largest city. Vanport flooded when Grand Coulee Dam was already in place, proving that one big block on the river couldn't stop it all. By 1972, the next thirty-year flood, more dams checked the river and prevented the estimated $200 million in damage that would have occurred if the water had slammed into Portland unchecked, at eighteen feet above flood stage.

Now all the big storage dams are in place: Grand Coulee, the four Canadian treaty dams, Dworshak Dam on the Clearwater, Brownlee Dam on the Snake, Hungry Horse Dam on the Flathead. You don't hear any more talk in these parts of the thirty-year flood. Like polio, flood ceases to threaten, and we forget what a crippler it once was.

Electricity, at the time, was the weak link in justifying Grand Coulee Dam. What could you electrify out here in the desert? Rural electrification did make sense, and that was part of the answer. You could bring electricity to farms and small towns, not just to population centers on the far side of the Cascades. But Bonneville Dam, rising downstream, could generate enough electricity to do it all. Who could possibly use the additional 8 million horsepower Grand Coulee Dam could put out?

The answer arose very soon. On December 7, 1941, the United States turned suddenly to war. Irrigation slid to the back burner at Grand Coulee, and electricity moved forward. Electric power would fuel the war machine. Shipyards. Airplane factories. Aluminum smelters. The challenge now was not how to use that much electricity but how to deliver it quickly. The Portland-Vancouver area became the nation's prime shipbuilding area. Where people had been desperate for work, now there was more work than people. And not just for men. Rosie the Riveter was America's answer to Tokyo Rose. By 1943 these shipyards rolled a new Liberty Ship down the ramp every three days. Riveting hammers and overhead cranes were fueled by electricity, as were the cauldrons of nearby steel mills. The Boeing Company on Puget Sound grew to be a city in itself, stamping out Flying Fortresses that droned to Europe and spearheaded the Allied drive. The aluminum came from new smelters along the Columbia River that sucked up huge amounts of electricity to zap the conversion of bauxite ore. The water rolled and the turbines spun and the factories and smelters ran all night.

And then, Grand Coulee began delivering massive blocks of power down the river to a mysterious War Department complex at Hanford. Only a few top scientists and engineers, sworn to secrecy, knew what for.

So the timing of Grand Coulee Dam could hardly have been better. Cheap materials and rock-bottom wages made the dam a bargain, and the dam, eight years in the building, was nearly done by the time the Japanese bombed Pearl Harbor. The initial bank of eighteen turbines, the world's largest, was in place. Electricity, which was seen only as a way to pay for irrigation and flood control, turned out to be a key in mobilizing the United States for war and jump-starting the economy. The Pacific Northwest became, as it is today, the most thoroughly electrified part of the country.

The original eighteen generators at Grand Coulee are still working, each fed by a penstock 18 feet in diameter and with 330 feet of head. Nine more generators came on in the 1950s. And when that still didn't exhaust the potential of the dam site, engineers gouged out the right-bank cliff and added a dogleg to the span, making room for the Third Powerhouse—another six generators, much larger, redoubling the dam's output to 20 billion kilowatt-hours a year. The electricity leaves the dam to link up with 14,000 miles of federal power lines in the Pacific Northwest. The Bonneville Power Administration delivers bulk power to public and private utilities, which in turn break it down into usable doses to factories, businesses, and homes. The federal power grid, if laid straight instead of crisscrossing the Northwest, would reach from Seattle to Miami and back— twice.

* * *

Ruth Seibold gave me the keys to her plum-colored 1964 Ford Fairlane and I drove south from Grand Coulee Dam through the grand coulee. I was hoping she or Ben might go along, but they weren't feeling up to it. After canoeing, driving at fifty-five miles an hour seemed like reckless abandon. What little traffic there was piled up in my rearview mirror, and I pulled over to let it pass.

Basalt walls of the coulee towered five hundred feet above, capped with sharp red rimrock, and I could see how the lava flows had piled layer upon layer of magma across the Columbia River basin and built the inland plateau. Then came floods of water and ice that scoured the lava, etching the battle scars between water and land that came to define this coulee. Rock fragments fell in skirts below the cliffs. Tufts of sage lined the road, and cattails grew at lakeside. Banks Lake, the reservoir in the coulee, was nearly full but it looked depleted in this grand setting, like the last inch of water in a long tub before it gurgles and drains.

The coulee, fifty miles long and up to three miles wide, ended at the headworks of the main irrigation canal. Just a couple of miles past that I stopped at a geologic exclamation point called Dry Falls.

I'd read in *Cataclysms on the Columbia*, by John Allen and Marjorie Burns, about how the Columbia came to be, and here I saw that story etched large upon the earth. The Bretz Floods occurred near the end of the Ice Age, a mere fifteen thousand years ago. When the floods blasted through, the Columbia carried ten times the flow of all the rivers on earth today. The floods had their birth behind an ice dam, half a mile high, that collected glacial melt and formed a huge inland sea called Lake Missoula. When the dam gave way, a four-hundred-foot wall of water and boulders and icebergs hurled through the breach. The wave face, moving seventy-five feet a second, amassed a destructive force far greater than the eruption of Mount St. Helens. The Columbia River hurtled from its bed and ground a new channel through the grand coulee and across

Dry Falls.

these Dry Falls. The torrent spread across the basin south of here and scoured the channeled scablands, vast moonscaped areas marked today with coulees and potholes where the earth lies exposed to bedrock. The Bretz Floods came time and again, at least forty times.

I took pictures of Dry Falls, but I knew the camera couldn't handle it. Three miles wide. About all you can do is look, look away, look again, and try to imagine the Columbia raging at forty times its current volume. Dry Falls, during the floods, was the largest waterfall ever to operate on the earth's surface.

Back at Grand Coulee Dam, I caught the 2:00 p.m. tour, the one that would take all afternoon and maybe scratch the surface of what goes on here.

The tour began with a movie. Historical clips about the construction were interspersed with rousing color evidence of

all the dam does today. The movie's musical score was by
Woody Guthrie. In one of the marvels of that anything-is-
possible era, BPA hired Guthrie in 1941 to chronicle the
heroism of dam-builders. Guthrie wrote twenty-six songs
in a month, and the best of them is called, without irony,
"Roll On, Columbia." I'm not what you'd call a sucker for
industrial ballads, but this one is really good. I heard the
words as if I were seeing that era through a window newly
cleaned.

As my tour group filed out, I stayed to watch the movie
again, and to write down Guthrie's lyrics. Just two verses:

> On up the river is Grand Coulee Dam
> Mightiest thing ever built by a man
> To run the great factories and water the land
> Roll on, Columbia, roll on.

> Roll on, Columbia, roll on
> Roll on, Columbia, roll on
> Your power is turning our darkness to dawn
> Roll on, Columbia, roll on.

> These mighty men labored by day and by night
> Matching their strength 'gainst the river's wild flight
> Through rapids and falls, they won the hard fight
> Roll on, Columbia, roll on.

> (Chorus)

Thinking to catch up with the tour at the Pump Station, I
got waylaid by scale. In the exhibition hall was a large empty
Plexiglas cube, to show how big one cubic yard is. A grown
man could sit and eat lunch in one cubic yard. In building
Grand Coulee Dam, they moved 37 million cubic yards of
earth and poured 13 million cubic yards of concrete. I tried to
imagine 13 million. At Dodger Stadium they draw 3 million,
say, in an eighty-two-game home season. If each of a whole
year's fans sat in a cube this size, you'd pile up a Grand

Coulee's worth in about four years. But I couldn't really picture
it. I'd had enough trouble with one million paddle strokes.

By this time I'd missed the Pump Station part of the tour.
Maybe I could catch up with the group at the Third Powerhouse. I fired up Ruth Seibold's Ford and drove across the
dam.

There, unguided, I found a bank of down-leading elevators and plunged to the depths. The descent left me not at a
viewing room but at a junction of green-walled labyrinths
with the familiar thrum and whiff of kilowatts, megawatts,
gigawatts. I walked a long sloping tunnel with sea-green tiles
and pink marble walls. I found a viewpoint but no tour. Reversing my search, I took another corridor that was leading,
perhaps, to Boise, Idaho. I felt unnatural winds and air pressures at the opening of doors. A corridor I thought I should
take was chained off, and I was lost in the dam. I met a
scrubbed and done-up family of four from Susanville, California, coming the other way. They, too, were lost—and not as
cheerfully as I. I offered to explore *this* corridor, if they would
explore *that* one. But the mother was beady-eyed claustro-
phobic and wanted only to find the *up* elevators without losing her children.

When they disappeared, I sat on the buffed stone floor and
cooled. It was just as well I'd missed the tour. I could stay
another day with the Seibolds and try it again tomorrow. The
words of Woody Guthrie echoed in my head, and I thought of
the dreamer Billy Clapp and the hounder Rufus Woods and
the visionary Franklin Roosevelt and workers like Ben and
Ruth Seibold. Nothing of this gargantuan scale had ever been
done before. They built it before anybody quite knew how
to—or what for. What the engineers learned, they applied at
other dams on the Columbia, and in the next forty years they
got it all. The most farsighted among them, who didn't worry
about what the electricity would be for, who said cheap electricity would *draw* clean industry to this far corner of the nation,

were right. And the doomsayers who predicted the onset of a new socialist era were at least partially right. Although Grand Coulee Dam didn't bring capitalism crashing to earth, it did rise as a monument to a new era: one of federal stewardship and control over nature.

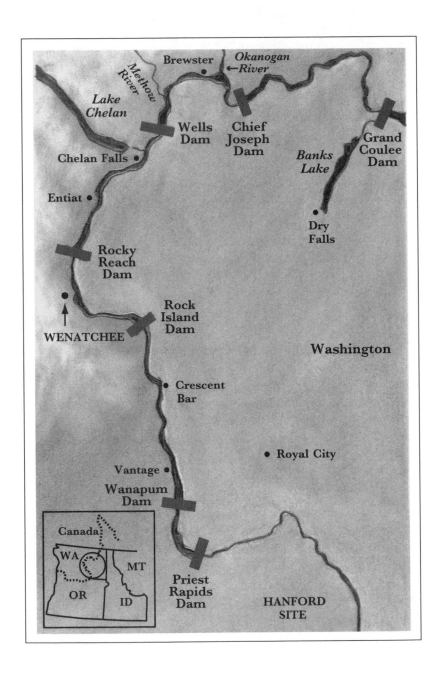

9

CHANGE A BIG RIVER

Rattlesnake, Milfoil, and Carp

It's impossible, not just illegal, to launch a canoe at the base of
Grand Coulee Dam. The river roils from the penstocks into a
narrow channel between steep rock banks. So Ben Seibold
drove me two miles downstream to a boat launch where the
river ran swift but flat. We shared a moment of awkwardness
when Ben wanted to see me safely onto the river, and I wanted
to see him safely turn the pickup around and head back. We
couldn't do both. Nor could I say, without insulting him, what
I was waiting for. So I pushed off on the Columbia, wheeled a
180 and waved him thankingly good-bye as the current took me
around the bend.

As the Columbia moved into Rufus Woods Lake, the
shoreline eased to rounded hills with blond bunchgrass. The
only green was at riverside, where roots of short trees tapped
the water. This was open range. Herefords and Black Angus
sought the shade near shore when the sun blazed highest in the
sky. A calf bawled and scampered away, but mostly the river
lay quiet. Only the isolated ranch and the hum of its irrigation
pump broke the silence. All three boats I saw that day were
idling, fishing, the kind of lost-to-the-world fishing you ac-
knowledge with a slow salute and pass by without words.

Sage grouse. Quail. A spotted sandpiper, on busy little stilts, skittered about the shore and poked its needle beak at mud-bugs and minnows.

Large boulders, rough and red—called "erratics" because they don't belong here—pocked the tan slopes as if they'd dropped at random from the sky. Glaciers left them behind after scraping the ancient riverbed and melting. These basalt stones were the active agent of prehistoric scouring, some as big as woodsheds but most the size of Yugos or smaller. Hillsides lay littered with this giant grit, which took on a time-shadowy beauty as I paddled past.

The current slackened but pulled me along. I dodged no hazards, met no traffic, felt no wind. Because shade was taken by cows, I ate my apples and sandwiches in the canoe and let the river-lake drift me at its own slow pace. No need to paddle. I splashed water on an inner tube to cool it, and leaned back on the tube. With the straw hat between my face and the sun, I drifted off—as well as down—the big river.

Sound goes a long way on a river. I awoke to conversation, as if the voices were inside my canoe. But I was alone, still in mid-river. After blinking and searching, I found the source of these voices. They issued from a pair of ranchers, half a mile downstream, setting irrigation pipe in a hay field.

The next day, early, I came across a fish farmer sowing food pellets into pens that floated on pontoons anchored to the left bank. The man was wiry and open-faced, wearing a green baseball cap, a flannel shirt, and tennis shoes. He'd parked his aluminum skiff with 115-horse Yamaha beside the four fish pens, each the size of a squash court. He introduced himself as Bill Tattersall and said he was raising Donaldson trout, a breed of rainbow. Swarms of three-inch youngsters rose to meet each spray of pellets he cast on the water.

"We're going to try Atlantic salmon next," Tattersall said. He was tending these pens for Seafarms of Washington, a private outfit based in Port Angeles.

"These fish are happy here," he said.

I thought that was an odd thing to say, so I tied up the canoe and he let me cast fistfuls of rice-sized pellets at flashing fingerlings. He had 25,000 young fish. I helped him adjust the nets, which hung over each pen to foil herons.

"Herons will sit on the nets," he said. "Their weight drops the net close to the water. They poke their beaks through and spear fish, but they can't get them out. That's what these dead ones are."

Life is hard in the West. Tattersall lifted the netting and scooped out some silver belly-uppers from one corner. We pulled the net tight and fastened it. Permit hassles had delayed Seafarms' scheme to raise Atlantic salmon here. And it was a bigger job than he thought to build the fish pens and anchor them against shifting water levels.

"Nothing is predictable," he said. "Since the fire at the John Day powerhouse, they compensate at Grand Coulee. We get big drops and rises, up to six feet a day."

Tattersall explained how four years ago he and his wife quit a straight life in Tacoma—he with Kaiser Aluminum, she with Safeco Insurance—to revive her dad's dying ranch here on the Columbia and try to make a vineyard of it. Fish farming is a sideline, a way to pay the bills while they grow grapes. It's been a struggle. The vines, on a mild slope toward the river, looked dwarfish and scraggly.

"Actually, they grow terrific," Tattersall said. "Bushy. Up to here." He put his hand to his chest. "But each year the deer get them."

Grape vines, to deer, are like fingerlings to herons. The fence around the vineyard was six feet tall, meshed with barbed wire, and electrified. "Fencing seems to work until October each year," he said. "Then the deer figure it out. One gets his head through, and after that the fence doesn't hurt him. They see one deer in, they all go in. This fence I'm using now is a new kind of fence."

Tattersall talked more about what grows here. He said he had killed five rattlesnakes on an evening drive.

"I wasn't even looking for dens," he said. "They go to the windrows along the fence, for shade. Kids come out from town, they kill dozens. But rattlesnakes don't bother you if you don't bother them."

The main thing about Tattersall, I saw, was that this stark land, this fickle river, this hard place, had not defeated him. He eyed the river and the low mountain crags across the way, and he saw no neighbor. He had no phone, no paved road. The mailbox was two miles distant.

"We'll be the first since the homesteaders," he said, "to make it here."

Early in the afternoon, before I was tired, I paddled past some flat spots with shade that would have made good campsites. Hours later, I was scanning the shores in vain for any patch of shade or mild slope, wondering why I didn't beach the canoe back up the river. I kept going, late into the day. Thunderheads bunched to the west, and lightning cracked the air. I pointed the canoe toward the Indian side, the right bank, to a narrow rock bench with bitterbrush and thistle. Because the idea of rattlesnakes sizzled in my head, I banged the side of my canoe with the paddle and made a ruckus setting up camp.

Gray rocks patterned the brown earth like diamondbacks.

A quarter mile upstream I'd passed a broken-down farmhouse in a stand of Russian olive trees. Now I saw telephone wires, so perhaps someone lived here. Should I walk to the farmhouse and get permission to tent? Maybe I should have, but I had the rattlesnake yips.

In the corner of my eye, a sage root moved.

But no, it didn't. Once I'd satisfied myself that no snakes coiled nearby, I cooked dinner and watched lightning splash the far evening sky. To keep rattlesnakes out, I laid a circle of five-eighths-inch rope around my tent. Everybody knows that rattlers won't crawl across rope; they hate that scratchy feeling on their bellies. But I wasn't sure whether my polyester river rope would work as well as good old-fashioned hemp rope.

The next morning I rustled the tent before stepping out. Rattlesnakes are known to seek body heat at night, and will find a sleeping bag to curl up to. But the old rope-around-the-tent trick had done it, or so I thought. For all I knew, there wasn't a snake within five miles, and my rope had been equally effective at keeping out tigers and woolly mammoths.

Pleased with my wilderness survival skills, I fired up the stove to boil coffee water and walked to the canoe for the life jacket to sit on. As I bent over the canoe, a *bunny*—a little jack rabbit—leaped out of it and scared me half to Astoria.

Chief Joseph Dam, the second-largest hydro plant in the United States, is the dam that backs up Rufus Woods Lake. The Army Corps of Engineers runs the dam, and the Bonneville Power Administration sells its power. As I came through, the dam was spinning out 1,118,000 kilowatts—enough to run Seattle all by itself. A digital recorder clicked off BPA revenues at six dollars a second. It's a measure of cheap federal hydro that this dam's $200 million per year of electricity would go for $843 million if Consolidated Edison had it in New York.

Chief Joseph Dam went up in two stages. In 1958, the Corps built the first part, with sixteen generators. Because no major tributaries enter its reservoir and Grand Coulee had already blocked salmon runs, the Corps didn't build any fish ladder here. The barrier to oceangoing fish slid another fifty-one miles downstream. In 1980, they raised the dam, put in eleven more turbines, and added ten feet of elevation to Rufus Woods Lake. When the lake rose, it drowned 550 more acres of wildlife habitat.

But the idea of compensation for fish and wildlife losses had taken hold by 1980, when Congress passed the Northwest Power Act. Some losses you just can't compensate for, but now any need for new power was supposed to be considered on an equal footing with the needs of fish and wildlife. Power money, by law, was to mitigate the damage caused by federal dams. Here on Rufus Woods Lake, for example, money from BPA power sales paid state wildlife agencies and the Colville Tribes to build islands, to erect raptor poles and nesting tubs, and to reserve some of the new shoreline for wildlife.

These wildlife sites along the river were abrupt and self-conscious, as if a billboard announced HABITAT. I paddled past a set of giant sprinklers mounted atop twenty-foot poles, watering an area the size of a high school. Under the sprinklers, plants grew thick and green, junglelike. The fence around the plot was designed to keep out livestock but to admit deer and other natives. Tall sunflowers rose brilliant gold in the green, and the busiest wildlife were canaries and songbirds. An owl hooted from deep in the leafy canopy. A beaver nosed from a burrow in the bank and worked the rooted shore.

And then it was over. I was in parched desert again, with no green living thing.

I saw no eagles, and only one osprey, who had figured out a raptor pole and chosen to perch there. The goose-nesting tubs—old metal tubs, the kind you'd use with a washboard for laundry—rested on stanchions above shallow water. The tubs sat vacant, this being the off season for geese. But I guess it all helps. Eagles, of course, would pay more attention to raptor poles if there were salmon in the river.

The only rattlesnake I saw on the whole trip was on the move, slithering under a concrete skirt that lines the boat launch at Bridgeport State Park. Just a little guy, a two-rattler, he was not looking for trouble. I camped at the state park, just short of Chief Joseph Dam. The tents-only section had yellow-bellied

marmots that stood on the berms above their holes and whistled, not in anger, not *at* anything, just to whistle.

I picked a nasty sliver from my foot and worried a bit when
I couldn't focus my eyes on it. Maybe river-glare was catching
up to me.

The next morning, a camper gave me a lift in his pickup
around Chief Joseph Dam to Bridgeport, a leafy oasis on the
left bank where everybody looked old or Mexican.

The Columbia past Bridgeport hooked a sharp right to
begin a long horseshoe bend northward and back. When the
river turned north, it pointed me into a stiff breeze gusting
down from the Okanogan Valley. The wind carried a blizzard
of cottonwood fluff, and I faced some tough head-down paddling to cut the chop. To settle the canoe lower in the river, I
loaded heavy chunks of driftwood into it, one fore and another
aft. Then the canoe caught less of the headwind and more of
the helping current.

At midday the wind settled down. Or else it lacked the
funneling effect of narrow shores as the river widened into Lake
Pateros. The surface lay flat, the water slow and shallow over
former farmland. Across the lake the Okanogan River emerged
south from its wide, fruit-famous valley. The Okanogan is the
northernmost branch the ocean-returning salmon and steelhead can take, up into Canada from here, and they do. Ospreys
and bald eagles occupied the raptor poles here. Along the shore
of Lake Pateros, apple and cherry orchards overlaid the land
with a crisp geometry of squares and rectangles. Tall poplars
lined the orchards to break the wind. Because water drawn off
the Columbia at Grand Coulee goes to the high inland plateau,
not to here, the irrigation I saw was local. Small pumps drew
water straight from the river to individual orchards.

At a riverside row of hospital-green cabins, like a budget
motel, the children spoke Spanish to each other, English to me.

But when I put ashore the kids read the alarm in their parents' eyes and wouldn't translate. I didn't learn much. The cherry season was past, and the apple harvest was still to come. No picking right now.

Down the river a piece I came across three kids messing about with sticks and crude fishing line. On an impulse I gave them my telescoping fishing rod, my ABU-Garcia reel, and the fishing tackle that wasn't buried deep in the waterproof bag. In just a minute or so, I had relieved myself of all the guilt and shame that had piled up from not fishing—or from not catching. I wished them well in broken Spanish and they looked at each other.

At Brewster I put ashore at a willowy town park with green lawn and a white sand beach. I might have landed at Vera Cruz, Mexico. Everybody spoke Spanish—on the soccer pitch, the baseball diamond, the basketball court, and playground. Young adults drove large, old, American-made cars, and I wished my Spanish were better. I walked the half mile to a grocery store for stronger sunglasses, camera batteries, and pop. When I got back to the park, a badly dyed blonde in a pink halter top lay on a beach towel, sunbathing. Thinking she might speak English, I offered her a cold 7-Up from my six-pack. Margaret was her name, and this was her day off from the apple-processing plant.

"Five sixty-five an hour," she said. "It's not hard, but it gets awful hot. And boring, on the belt. But we can talk. We switch posts, and it's not so bad. Right now we're packing from the CA shed."

CA?

"Controlled atmosphere," she said. "Cold, for storing apples out of season. And the air in the CA shed has low cee-oh-two. Or is it high cee-oh-two?"

She saw I had a copy of the local paper, *El Mundo*.

"The Mexicans *really* pour in in late August, for three

months of picking," she said. "Pickers live in the orchard cabins. Water. Electricity. The kids go to school. And it's mostly Mexicans at the plant. Everything's automated. Sorting. Packing in rows in big crates. Apples are about all there is here. And now the Alar scare."

It had been about a year since "60 Minutes" aired a feature about the alleged carcinogenic qualities of the pesticide Alar. Growers using Alar got clobbered. Washington's red-apple growers, claiming "reckless disregard for the truth," sued CBS, and Alar was still the lead story in *El Mundo*. Apple sales were down. A chart showed prices falling below cost of production.

"They're worried about the future of agriculture," she said.

Margaret rolled to change her angle to the sun. She talked for a while about a domestic problem I wasn't too interested in. What it boiled down to was she was glad she had a job.

"Five sixty-five an hour," she said. "You know, that's not bad."

I pushed off for Pateros. *El Mundo* had reported forest fires, no doubt sparked by the distant dry lightning I'd seen. But on the river I saw no smoke—no forests, for that matter. The Columbia crawled through rocky, sage-covered hills, and the only color was at low green strips of river-hugging orchards.

Milfoil, a grisly water weed, forced me farther from shore than I wanted to be. Once, in fact, the canoe squidged to a full stop on mats of milfoil.

Back on Rufus Wood Lake, too, I'd seen this ugly plant colonizing the shallows. Signs at boat launches warned boaters to hose down their boats and trailers, to prevent the spread of Eurasian milfoil. All it takes, the signs said, is a piece of the plant stuck to a propeller shaft or a trailer spring to transport the weed from one lake to another. If that's true, wouldn't it also spread on the feet of geese and ducks? All of the Columbia's reservoirs from Grand Coulee on down are contaminated, and here at Lake Pateros milfoil had spread like an epidemic. Milfoil roots in the shallows, and it likes slow warm water. Kelplike vines reach the surface to flower and twist into thick brown mats.

As if the milfoil weren't creepy enough, I got a weird *thump* on the underside of the canoe. Looking ahead, I saw a hump in the milfoil, like the blue-black arc of tire tread. When I got closer, the tread became fish scales. Carp. It exploded into a downward dive, startled by the canoe. Then, looking for them, I saw more carp in the milfoil. *Big* suckers. Big *suckers*. They cruised just below the surface, like slow rural cops. *Thump*, my canoe hit another one. Blind or plain stupid, they were big enough to give the canoe a jolt. As I continued down the lake, squads of carp rolled on the surface. They were feeding—pairs breeding—in the milfoil.

It was all kind of sickening. Exotic weeds and fat trash fish had found their niche, were right at home here, in the new slower and warmer Columbia River.

Wells Dam is the first in a series of five, coming up, that were built and are now run by local public utility districts (or PUDs), not by the federal government. Douglas County PUD owns and operates Wells Dam. Electricity from PUD dams is even cheaper than from the federal power system, mostly because the feds began financing nuclear power plants in the 1970s and are still paying for that fiasco. At the Douglas County PUD it's all hydro, and much more than can be used locally. They sell power to the Puget Sound area to help pay off the dam. For a rural, sparsely populated county, it's a good deal, better than levying taxes, to have a big dam of your own.

From Pateros, I'd called ahead to Wells Dam for advice on how to get around it. Now Tom Hook, supervisor of operations, met me at the powerhouse with a pickup and three linebackers who tossed the canoe into the truck without unloading it. They drove me across the dam and down to a river-rock launch site below.

Maybe I thanked them too much. Hook looked surprised. "We *have* to do this," he said. "It's the law. It's in the working agreement." Turns out the operators must do what they can, if the dam doesn't have a lock, to carry river traffic past the dam. Something about the Columbia River being an international navigable waterway.

"But we don't often get to do it," Hook said. "There was a canoe couple last summer, sent us their itinerary. They never showed up. That happens more often than we actually lift someone around."

Anyone doing the whole river, from source to mouth?

"Oh, yeah," Hook said. "I'd say, what, every third year or so?, somebody like you comes through. One wacko in a kayak was going *up* the river. I tell them to let me know when they get there," he said. "Nobody has. But that doesn't mean they didn't."

No doubt lots of people have.

"Could be."

Hook and his crew were in no hurry. I wasn't either, so I grabbed a couple of oranges and rode back with them to the powerhouse, leaving the canoe on the rocks. Hook dismissed his crew and led me to the control room. He introduced dispatchers and power controllers, good old boys, country-friendly, just a bunch of guys in jeans and short-sleeved shirts running a dam.

Wells Dam makes a seventy-foot differential in Columbia River water levels, above and below. Completed in 1967, it's a run-of-the-river dam. No storage. "We just work with the water that comes through," Hook explained. "We draft more water in the mornings. Breakfast. Businesses start up, and they need the power. On hot days, we'll keep drawing for air-conditioning. Then we push the lake back at night. We can make quite a difference in water level below the dam, where the river's narrow, but Lake Pateros is so wide it usually only goes up or down a foot or two."

At the lunchroom, broad windows faced downstream.

Hook and some others broke out their lunch sacks. I peeled an orange.

"This dam is a good design for fish passage," Hook said. By that he meant for young fish—young salmon and steelhead—on their way out to sea. The hazard at any dam is that juvenile fish can be sucked into the powerworks and get mashed up as they migrate downstream. "Each turbine has its own spill passage. We adjust the current to draw fish into the spillways and away from turbines."

I asked about milfoil, which I'd seen clogging the intake pipes at irrigation pumps above the dam. Wouldn't it foul the dam's powerworks, too?

"It does," Hook said. "The grates catch a lot of it, and that's an ongoing maintenance problem. To clear the intake. What gets through mostly gets chopped up in the turbines."

"A lady from Pateros called the other day," said Jesse Allen, one of the controllers. "Mrs. Whats'ername, has riverfront property, you know her. She called and she said, 'I've put up with this milfoil a long time,' she said, 'and I'm not a whiner. But I just saw a duck *walk* across my cove.' "

What can you do about milfoil?

"Nothing," Hook said.

"But you could," Allen said. "If it came to that, you could drain the reservoir every year and kill it. Milfoil only grows to about twelve feet deep. Out of water, it dies."

"But if you dropped the pool, it would screw up shore-spawning fish," Hook said. "And everything else you've got in the lake."

On my walk back to the canoe, I looked down upon a mile or so of tight-twisting concrete ditch on the right bank, just below the dam. The ditch was an artificial fish-spawning channel. Twenty feet wide and bottomed with gravel, it coiled like the large intestines from the right bank of the Columbia to a fish hatchery. All but a small part of the spawning channel was dry, baking in noonday sun. Probably, I thought, it was not the season for adult salmon to return.

I stopped at the hatchery. Six women in rubber aprons and surgeon's gloves sat on stools at stainless-steel drainboards next to an extended sink. They were clipping adipose fins off steelhead fry. One young woman, all business, dipped a strainer into a freshwater bucket of one-inch fish and transferred her catch to a plastic pan of anaesthetic. She covered the pan with netting until the baby fish settled into a stupor. Then she tweezed out one doped fish at a time, clipped its fin and released it into a trough of running water.

Steelhead are a breed of rainbow trout that, like salmon, migrate to the ocean and back. Unlike salmon, they can go out and back more than once. They don't always die in the act of spawning. The women clipping fins here were making it possible for fishermen, years from now, to distinguish hatchery steelhead from wild steelhead. If you catch an adult steelhead that has an adipose fin, it's a wild one. Release it.

I walked outside to the rearing pens. Mobs of young fish shifted collectively from my shadow, like dark clouds in the water.

Farther on, I came to adult fish in a holding pen. I was surprised to see, because the spawning channel was dry, adult salmon returning. Summer chinook. They had swum from the river through a shortcut of man-made stream to this holding pen, a fifteen-foot-square box enclosed on three sides by high plywood walls. Swift water flowed through the pen from a grate at the upstream end, and out over a two-foot waterfall on the lower end. These fish were beat. After ranging the ocean for three or four years, they'd come five hundred miles up the river and now were battered and gaunt, ranging in size from fifteen to twenty-five pounds. The males were darker than the reddish females, and some had blotchy white bruises on their flanks. They'd homed in on this freshwater flow that promised shallow riffles and spawning gravels farther upstream. Instead, the man-made stream ended at the holding pen.

Two more salmon leaped the low waterfall into the pen, which didn't have to be enclosed on its lower end because salmon won't go back. Confused, they nosed the forward wall. One big female took a run at the forward wall and leaped high, way up—five feet above the water surface—but short of the top. She slapped the wall with her tail and flank, leaving a dark wet imprint of her own shape on the blond plywood.

She fell back into the pool.

Salmon, even when they're close to spawning and death, can muster the leaping strength that would have, in the past, driven them far upstream from here and past obstacles such as Kettle Falls. But these ripe fish would go no farther. Wondering what would happen to them, and when, I went looking for a boss and found Steve Miller, the hatchery manager.

"These are summer chinook," Miller confirmed. "We draw them to the holding pen and sort the chinook from the steelhead, whose run is just beginning. After sorting, we put the chinook in longer pens. Come September, we'll pick up the salmon and get the eggs and milt. We do it by hand. Other hatcheries raise spring and fall chinook."

The return rate?

"Numbers are down from six or seven years ago," Miller said. "There are so many factors, we can't say why. There hasn't been as much water in the river, but it also depends on ocean conditions. It depends on harvest, predation, things nobody knows."

Wells Dam, like every dam downstream from here, has fish ladders. River water flows down a fish ladder like down a long staircase with switchbacks. The steps are low enough, the flat spots long enough, that returning adult fish can swim from below the dam to the reservoir above. Young hatchery fish can be *outplanted*—reared in hatcheries but released far upstream. When they come back as adults they will bypass the hatchery, take the fish ladder past Wells Dam, and home up into the Methow and Okanogan Rivers. Native salmon, too, will take the fish ladder.

Fish ladder at Wells Dam.

Simple? No, it's not. Miller got cloudy when I asked about native fish. The whole idea of wild salmon is no longer a clear one. Hatchery fish, successfully outplanted, interbreed with native spawners in their adopted streams.

"What you might call wild fish will take the east side fish ladder," he said, "because that's where the old river channel is. But we get some wild ones in here, and hatchery fish over there. It's just real complicated. I've been here twenty years," he said, "and I don't know how this all works. Nobody does, really."

What about this dry spawning channel?

"Oh, that." Miller blanched. "It was designed as a spawning channel, but it never worked. The river water that fed it was too warm. By the time the spawning channel was finished," he said, "they'd impounded all that water upstream. Canadian treaty dams. Fish wouldn't take to the warmer water. Now we use well water—fifty-three degrees—and run this like a conventional fish hatchery."

The advantage of hatcheries is that you get a much higher survival rate from eggs to releasable fingerlings, and plenty of them make it all the way out to the ocean and back. About 90 percent of the Columbia's salmon and steelhead runs today are hatchery fish. A big disadvantage is that they lack the genetic diversity of their wild progenitors. Hatchery fish come in large batches from the same mix of eggs and milt. Thousands are reared to fishhood in close proximity to one another. If something goes wrong—human error, disease—they die off in hordes.

"One crop of winter steelhead came up blind," Miller said. "We traced the problem to a breed of snail that moved into the rearing tanks. That whole crop of fish had to be buried."

The tailrace below Wells Dam carried me swiftly into what the map calls Entiat Lake but the locals, more accurately, refer to as the Columbia River. Current and close-to-natural shoreline gave the upper lake the look and feel of big river, although it was completely under human control.

I passed three bald eagles in twelve river miles. They were feeding. Now, if you've never seen your National Bird in live action, you haven't missed much. When an eagle is *waiting* for action, perched on a snag, he shows the fierce yellow eye that inspires the Postal Service emblem. But in fact eagles are shameless scavengers. The eagles at Entiat Lake were drawn to the stench and rot of summer chinook casualties—the not-quite-the-fittest, close-but-didn't-quite-get-there salmon—that rolled their white bellies up in shoreline pools. An eagle swooped to a carcass and clawed it to the nearest rock, there to gut and slurp.

But still. I passed eagles and ospreys, and tall blue herons stood guard duty along the bank.

Live current brought the canoe to the Chelan River, on the right, which flowed an otherworldly blue, so clear that a depth of six feet looked like two. I paddled into the Chelan and beached the canoe to take a swim. Stroking back to shore, I was surprised to see Jesse Allen, he of the duckwalk-on-milfoil story at Wells Dam, grinning on the bank.

"I thought you'd find this spot," he said. Allen, a dam worker with the distracted blue eyes of a poet, had driven here after work. "If you've got time," he said, "I'll show you one of the secret beauties of this area."

I stashed the canoe in bushes and we drove in his black Chevy Z-24 convertible to Lake Chelan, just three miles distant but four hundred feet above the river. He took a back road, a steep gravel strip that cut the cliffs of Chelan Falls gorge. Allen stopped the car and I stepped out to look. Rust-colored canyon walls guarded the blue Chelan River as it slalomed among white rocks far, far below. I was amazed. I'd never seen pictures of, never even *heard* of, this breathtaking short canyon.

"It's a piece of forgotten land," Allen said. "Nobody comes here."

The gorge, owned by Chelan County PUD, is off-limits to the public. "Danger is the convenient excuse," Allen said. He explained how the canyon will go dry for six months each year when runoff from Lake Chelan gets shunted into penstocks and falls to the antique powerhouse at the base of the gorge.

"They're still spilling, but they'll cut it off in a week or so," he said. "For just fifty-two megawatts, we lose this canyon. We've spent millions on hatcheries when we could open up this canyon for natural fish runs."

We drove on up to Chelan, a snazzy resort on the lake, and ate chicken under deck umbrellas at the Campbell House Cafe, where the smart set wore Lacoste shirts, rich tans, and designer sunglasses. Barefoot and bearded, in my cut-off jeans, I might have just parachuted to the Bavarian Forgensee from the berry patch. Pine chalets and geranium-draped balconies overlooked apple orchards and the deep blue dazzle of Lake Chelan. Friends of Allen came by. The talk was of property values, and I didn't know what to think.

Allen dropped me back at the canoe. A mile or so down the Columbia I found a flat spot in low bushes below the apple-packing plant. I pulled in, set up camp, and sat on a flat-rock promontory, watching the river go by. A little weather blew in with the darkening sky. Light rain, in big drops, snapped dry leaves. Again, I didn't know what to think. What got me was milfoil and carp colonizing the new river, and how man, playing God, is still groping to find how big a role that is. The world evolves so quickly, before we really know about the wild salmon and how they do it. But change a big river, is what I was thinking, and you've changed the world.

10

'ΠCHIAWANA, COLUMBIA

We Live in Two Worlds

It's easy to forget what you came for. Eighty-two days on a
river, the river shows you only what it is right now, right here.
If you're looking for a big thing, the best view is not always from
right on top of it. Looking for connectedness—what the river
is to what it was—I found instead these sharp and clean-in-
themselves fragments that rang clear as church bells on a cold
clear morning, and I couldn't even say why I liked them so
much.

At a riverside dock, two small boys angling in thick milfoil
were not about to tell me *all* their secrets, but they tipped
a bucket and showed me a salad-plate-sized, green-backed,
orange-bellied turtle they'd caught on a Korn Kurl. "Marshmallows work," said the taller of the two, "but we're out of
those."

At Daroga State Park, a shaded green peninsula that smelled
like alfalfa just after the cut, the only other outfit in the boats-
only campground was the Ellis family from Redmond, Washington: Bob and Rox and a pair of teenaged girls. The girls
were grumpy that a wind had come up and spoiled their water-

skiing. *There's nothing to DO here.* Ellis didn't worry about the girls. He didn't worry about his boat, which he'd tied so loosely to the dock it might blow to Chelan Falls any minute. The girls badgered Ellis into building a fire, and he didn't worry when sparks danced the night air toward the tent. We ate marshmallows and told campfire stories and I wondered which was braver—solo canoeing the Columbia River from source to mouth, or camping with teenaged girls.

Out on the river, far from shore on calm water, cobwebs drifted against my face. Now again, a cobweb. I stopped paddling and brushed away gossamer threads. There was nothing within a hundred yards that a cobweb could be attached to. And how could its spinner have spun it here?

I wanted the whole thing, while its parts drifted by unattached. And yet . . . And yet there were times, too, when the river was deeper and more mysterious than thought, and I got a big view I wasn't looking for. Maybe it rode the smell of a rotting salmon, or the clip of hooves on rock before a goat stooped to drink of the river. I'd catch just a whisper, as fleeting as it was thrilling, of the whole thing. A. B. Guthrie, in *Big Sky Country,* had the idea when he wrote: "Looking out over [the Missouri] from a rise, Boone felt he was everywhere on it, like the air or the light." But that feeling is hard to come by, and even harder to hold.

Back on the upper Columbia, my river song had been "Good Night, Irene." I paddled to it, sang it out loud, couldn't get it out of my head. "Sometimes I have a great notion / To jump into the river and drown."

After Grand Coulee, my river song was Woody Guthrie's "Roll On, Columbia." I paddled to it, sang it out loud, couldn't get it out of my head. "Your power is turning our darkness to dawn." The song grew of its own staying power into cloying, annoying, doggerel. My doppelgänger, my secret self, rode in the canoe with me, singing "Roll On, Columbia." If he sang that insipid song one more time, I was going to brain him with the paddle.

Maybe, I thought, I could drive him out by singing a better song. I concentrated hard and sang "Good Night, Irene." And you know what? It's the same tune! Same tune, different words. Try it: "Good Night, Irene, Good Night." "Roll On, Columbia, Roll On."

The whole river-singing idea of it seemed strange and strangely familiar, and the short hairs rose on the back of my neck.

Five dams in thirteen days.

In my river journal I took care to record how each dam is unique, but a week after I passed them they blended together as a mid-river unit. For the record, I'll list them. After Wells (Douglas County PUD) came Rocky Reach and Rock Island (Chelan County PUD), and then Wanapum and Priest Rapids (Grant County PUD).

Together, in five steps, these dams account for a 367-foot drop in Columbia River elevation. They pump out 4,230 megawatts of electricity, most of which is sold over federal power lines to the Seattle-Tacoma area. All five dams have fish ladders. All five lack locks. Once a decade or so the Army Corps of Engineers will remind mid-river citizens that the Corps could, by dredging the channel and inserting locks, bring barge traffic all the way to Wenatchee. But that won't happen, because salmon-spawning grounds in the channel below Priest Rapids Dam are now recognized for what they are: irreplaceable.

Rock Island Dam did stand out from the others. It's an antique, the first dam to span the mainstream Columbia. Built with private funds and first owned by Puget Sound Power & Light, Rock Island began spinning out power in 1933, when work on Grand Coulee had just started. But it's not that kind of colossal project, and most people think Bonneville and Grand Coulee Dams came first. The old powerhouse is a beauty—oak doors, brass fittings, polished rock floors, and carefully crafted details—in contrast to the new powerhouse on the right bank, just a concrete block.

After a calm morning and easy paddling past the mouth of the Entiat River, large swells rolled up the Columbia. The waves swept north like the wake of a faraway ocean liner, yet I saw no river traffic. No wind brushed my canoe. The surface humped glassy and smooth as a horizontal fun-house mirror. Something was up, but I didn't know what. I headed for the left shore, and just in time. The blue-green line of froth appeared, and then a howling wind blasted upstream.

I waited a couple of hours on shore too rocky for camping. When the wind didn't let up, I sliced whitecaps from cove to cove. I stiff-armed rocks and fended off shore with my left foot and the paddle until I reached a thin nail-clipping of beach at an apple orchard. Next to the pumphouse lay a canoe. This was a good sign. Anyone who owned a canoe on the Columbia would know I was in trouble. I hoisted mine from the wave-pounded beach onto a lip of orchard and decided to ask permission to camp.

Walking toward the house, I saw a preteen girl and her little brother playing in the garden corn rows. I shouted to them, but the wind swept my voice away.

I got closer, and called out again.

The girl heard me. She turned and saw me. She screamed, snatched up her little brother, and ran into the house.

I stayed where I was. Mom came to the window like a woman who's heard a wreck. So here I stood, a wild-bearded stranger in cutoffs, spooking children in her backyard. Would she call the cops? Where was Dad? I couldn't think what to do. She opened the screen door a crack, but stayed inside. I shouted, from a distance of fifty yards, that I was traveling by canoe and got blown off the river. Could I camp by the pumphouse?

You'd think river people would know child molesters and ax murderers do not, as a rule, travel by canoe. But here I was. Terrified, she said something I couldn't hear over the wind, and closed the door. Maybe she hadn't heard what I'd said either. I slunk back through the orchard and sat with my back against the wall of the pumphouse. Were they rounding up a posse? At the slightest lull in wind, I got back on the river and pounded through rough river chop. Within an hour I came to a vacant, tall-grass-and-sage piece of shore in the lee of Turtle Rock, and holed up for the night like a criminal.

The inner tubes, dry and cracked from exposure to sun, no longer held air. I wasn't in top shape myself. The sliver in my foot had festered. And now I came up with a sharp upper back pain, brought on by, of all things, a sneeze. The trip so far had been remarkably free of injury or ache, but now I seized up like an old engine. I put in at prosperous Wenatchee, "The Apple Capital of the World," and registered at a motel for not one night but two.

On my day off I bought a pair of new tubes, did laundry, drank a lot of liquids, and read the paper. The masthead of the Wenatchee *World* said the publisher was Wilfred R. Woods, so I limped over to the newspaper office to see if the paper was still in the family of the famous Rufus Woods. It was. But the lady said Wilfred Woods was too busy to just drop in on, and after the apple orchard setback, my confidence about forcing myself on strangers was at an all-river low. I was turning to leave when a Father Knows Best kind of guy with short stiff hair, bristly gray eyebrows, and eyes like a fox strode down the hall. Desk folks snapped to attention, and I didn't doubt who he was. I introduced myself and asked for a chat.

"Glad to, son," he said. "Glad to." He gave me a booster's

smile and a vise-grip handshake. Wearing a short-sleeved shirt and brown loafers, brisk of step, Woods led me upstairs to his office. One wall featured old photos and yellow news clips about the public relations campaign for Grand Coulee Dam. Rufus Woods, his father, founded the *World* in 1907. Wilfred took over when his dad died in 1950. And *his* son, Rufus G. Woods, is managing editor of the *World* and *El Mundo*.

Wilfred Woods talked about the economic development of Wenatchee, and how most of the water for irrigation here doesn't come from the mainstream Columbia. It arrives gravity-fed from higher streams and lakes. The water rejoins the river with only a 5 percent loss to seepage and evaporation.

"This Alar thing has been tough, very tough," he said. "And the year before that we had enormous overproduction. The largest apple crop in history. We put out 80 million bushels in the state, and ended up selling at less than cost. Another thing, we have too many Red Delicious," he said. "We're looking at new varieties. The Japanese Fuji. A New Zealand strain. The Gala is a striped apple, red and green."

He talked about the dams, and how the public utility district wrested control of Rock Island Dam from Puget Sound Power & Light in the early 1950s. "Alcoa came in with a big aluminum plant in 1951," he said, "for the Korean War. Then there's the silicon plant. The aluminum smelter employs 850, but right now the silicon plant is down."

One thing I'd noticed, arriving by canoe, is that Wenatchee has its back to the river. You can walk the city center and never know the Columbia runs nearby.

"The town never faced the Columbia," Woods said. "That river was a dangerous place. An unfriendly place. The original train bridge had a slot in the middle for dropping the town garbage."

He rose from his desk and guided me through the wall-mounted pictures of old Wenatchee.

"Did you know about our Clovis find?" he asked. "The earliest Americans, right over in East Wenatchee." The Clovis people, hunters of large mammals, are said to have followed their food supply across the Bering Land Bridge from Asia to the New World and were the first people here. "From the Ice Age, ten thousand years ago," Woods said. "Mastodons and woolly mammoths. Just last year they put in an irrigation line and dug up a ceremonial cache. Prehistoric graves. Big spear points. Now the Colville Indians and the state are trying to figure out what to do. The Indians say they are direct descendants of Clovis Man, and they don't want the state in there digging."

On Saturday, another scorcher below Rock Island Dam, I joined gathering boat traffic and kids racing jet skis around Crescent Bar, a public launch with upscale condominiums. The campground was full. The air-conditioned restaurant looked like a good place to be, but I wasn't dressed for it. So I paddled a quarter mile farther, to a slender island not yet developed. On the Columbia's left elbow, like bone chips, lay islands with white sand and a few earnest, hard-working shade trees. It was a sensational spot to camp, far enough from the hubbub and facing sheer basalt cliffs of raw, phenomenal beauty.

The river here had sliced five hundred vertical feet and left 7 million years of history stacked, exposed. Layers of basalt, tier upon tier, alternated with swaths of squeezed loess like the cross-section of a twelve-decker sandwich. Geologists say two hundred layers, in all, two miles thick, accumulated over a period from 16 million to 6 million years ago. Showing above the river were the top blankets of magma that issued from fissures east of here and covered eighty thousand square miles of what is now Washington, Idaho, and Oregon. As each layer cooled, the lava crystallized into fierce kaleidoscopic radiations, vertical columns, and pillow stacks. Petrified trees were frozen in time, as if the earth had set just yesterday and might be hot to the touch.

Fire and then ice. After the lava floods came the massive glaciers that, in their receding, carved the initial course of the Columbia. And then the ice dams blocked the river and sent it hurtling overland, through the grand coulee, across Dry Falls and over the channeled scablands back to here. The Bretz Floods made these cliffs waterfalls. On the other side of the river, hills were the floods' gravel bars, and the shore lay pocked with the erratics dropped by melting ice scrapers. When the icefloods finally played themselves out, the river returned to this older channel to keep carving, as it does today, ever deeper into time.

More than once on this canoe trip I had passed up the chance to contact people I knew, or friends of friends. It wasn't a rule, but I'd had good luck with random encounters, dropping in on strangers.

At Vantage, where Interstate 90 crosses the Columbia, I made an exception to this nonrule. My sister Betsy, much younger than I, a smart cookie with strong ideas, had told me to be sure to call on her friends the Verheys when I got to Vantage. Dan and Sheila Verhey were peach farmers in Royal City. Betsy doesn't make many demands on me, but she was firm about this, so I called the Verheys from a phone booth oven near the Wanapum Inn. All I needed to say was "Betsy's brother." Sheila Verhey told me to wait for a blue pickup with racks.

An hour later, here came the blue pickup and out tumbled two bruisers—blue-eyed Paul Verhey and his dad, Dan, a white-bearded Kenny Rogers lookalike. They sized up my canoe and me. They looked at each other. Maybe it was because I am not much like Betsy, who is young and beautiful.

"You drink beer?" Paul said.

So *that* was it. People think canoeists drink carrot juice and eat yogurt and wouldn't know how to drive a stick shift. We drank beer at the Wanapum Inn. Peach harvest was on, and harvest knows no Sunday, but their workday was done. Dan and Paul were in no hurry to get back to the farm. After a couple of beers we loaded the canoe onto the pickup rack. It was hot. Dan reached into a cooler of iced Miller Genuine Draft in the pickup bed, and we sat on the running board for another cold one.

Paul drove. Across the I-90 bridge, he turned south to follow the river. Dan spotted a white pickup parked on the river side of the road. We stopped. Mike and Spud Brown, cowboy brothers in sage-stomper boots and jeans, came up the bank. Dan rewarded them with a beer apiece. The Browns were trying to figure out what to do with their property.

"We could switch the winery concerts to the bluff here," Mike said. "We could run a paddlewheeler up to Crescent Bar, past the cliffs."

"Should develop this, before the Seattle guys get to it."

High on the raw cliffs flapped the remnants of a huge white banner, no longer legible. "That banner was seven hundred feet long," Spud Brown said. "It said NO TOXIC WASTE ON THIS RIVER."

The Brown brothers had been fighting off Rabanco, the big garbage company, which planned to put a toxic waste incinerator just two miles downstream.

"Of all places," Mike said.

"On the river!" Spud said.

"Greenpeace and Audubon Society and them had a big scene over at the state park. They released balloons."

"To show which way the wind blows. It blows straight up the river. This is no place to burn toxic waste."

Dan Verhey interrupted. He said, "This is Betsy Cody's brother."

"Betsy's brother!" Mike and Spud Brown stepped back and eyed me with huge new respect. "No fooling? Betsy was there!"

Paul Verhey liberated another round of Miller Genuine Draft from the ice chest. He passed the icy full bottles around and I put mine in the shade of a fender because I still had some.

"So anyway, Spud and I wanted to help. Across the river, Audubon and them released the balloons, and here at the Rabanco site we torched a pile of tires. Five semi loads of tires. The black smoke curled right up the river, low in the canyon."

"Just like Rabanco's smoke would do!"

"Cops came from everywhere. I never saw so many cop cars. Royal City. Othello. The state."

"We got arrested," said Spud Brown, beaming.

"They held us. They didn't know what to do with us. It cost me five grand," Mike said. "I had to sign a paper and swear never to vandalize the river again."

When we left the Browns, Paul drove us down the river and Dan explained how Mike Brown was a big landowner. Mint. Potatoes. Construction and processing, up on the flat. He could drop five grand like the pop machine didn't give his nickel back. Paul was sweating. "I have to jump in the river," he said. He turned off the road past the railroad bridge and dived into the Columbia. Dan and I sat on the bank and drank beer. "One time the wind blew a train off that bridge," Dan said. "We went diving for treasure, but all it was was stuff from China. Dolls and fans."

We drove away from the river, up Crab Creek coulee. Paul bumped the pickup off the road, through a lift-gate fence, and across cow-pied range toward Saddleback Mountain and a natural attraction Dan wanted me to see. It was an ice cave. It was a natural hole, now collapsed, at the base of the mountain. We hunched down and crept ten feet in. A chill breeze issued from deep inside the mountain to this rubble-rock cubbyhole where we sat and had a beer and smoked cigarettes and Dan talked about how the homesteaders used ice caves for year-round refrigeration. Like a man who knew something, I told them the way you get an ice cave is the rampaging ice floods must have piled gravel insulation over a part of the earth still huge and frozen, not so far away, and they believed it and so did I. We drove back to the road and on up Crab Creek. Irrigation runoff spewed back toward the Columbia through

Crab Creek and past the ranch of the cowboy poet Bud Stewart—"a good storyteller," Dan said—but he wasn't home. Up on the flat we stopped to look at a suspicious outflow pipe from a food-processing plant or something, somewhere, and by the time we got to Verheys' Peach Farm the Sunday-of-harvest spaghetti feed had cooled, and so had Sheila Verhey, waiting for lost boys.

We ate cold spaghetti and peach cobbler and they got me to a shower and to bed, dog-tired, very happy, maybe 10:00 p.m., Sunday, August 5.

If you drew a straight line across the map from Grand Coulee Dam to Verheys, the line would be seventy-five miles long. But the water pumped above the dam into the coulee and Banks Lake doesn't arrive here in a straight line. The canal jogs and zigs and branches. The canal that feeds the Royal Slope tunnels south through Frenchman Hills and takes a sharp left to skirt the north side of the Verheys' place. A weir feeds water into troughs that edge the orchards. The Verheys run siphon tubes from the troughs into shallow ditches between rows of peach trees or asparagus, their two crops.

When I came up for breakfast, Sheila called Dan in from the orchard. We sat down to a farm feast of bacon and eggs and hotcakes with apricot jam. Dan flipped hotcakes at the stove while Sheila and I ate. She and Dan are both from the Yakima Valley. They met in high school and went on to Washington State, where he was a football tackle, and tackles played both offense and defense.

"We bought this farm when it was just sage and rattlesnakes," Dan said. "Bone desert. But the irrigation canals were already in place."

"The house came on in stages," Sheila said.

The kitchen and dining room overlooked peach trees, and living space radiated from a massive flagstone fireplace. The Verheys have a daughter and six sons, one still at home, and

a never-ending need for guest rooms. Outside, the peach orchard was overrun with U-pickers. On a walk after breakfast,
I met a couple from Kansas who motor to Verheys' Peach
Farm every other year, and order by mail in the off years.
"These are the world's best peaches," the man said. Peaches
hung so thick the tree limbs had to be propped up with two-by-
fours. Hired help among the U-pickers boxed peaches to ship
to stores and distributors.

"We'll ship four thousand boxes," Dan said, "at seven-fifty
a box. U-pick is twenty-five cents a pound. We ship to Austria.
Connecticut. I'd show you the mailing list but I lost it on the
computer."

The Verheys pay less than twenty dollars per acre-foot for
the water that reaches here from Lake Roosevelt. Their basic
allotment is ninety-three acre-feet a year for their ninety-three-
acre farm, but not all of their land is irrigable. So they're using
more than a foot of water per acre per year. Irrigators here pay
only a fraction of what the Columbia Basin Project costs. The
government—BPA, with its revenues from power sales at federal dams—repays the U.S. Treasury for construction costs
that are deemed "beyond the ability of the irrigators to pay."

A dust-caked station wagon drove up and the driver asked
about work. Dan greeted the driver by name, Raul, and told
him to come back Tuesday. The Verheys pay six dollars an
hour, which is high. Workers don't call here unless they are
legal, with papers for health, liability, and unemployment. It's
a hassle, but all for the good, Dan thinks.

"Before amnesty, the immigration guys raided a camp
down the road a piece. They fired guns in the air and had kids
scattering, everybody diving into ditches. It was a sickening
thing to see. More and more," he said, "the Hispanics stay here
year-round. They learn English and send their kids to school.
Now there's a backlash. Many resent them. Soon the Mexicans
will be looking for jobs that pay more than fieldwork. They'll
want their share of the good life. Which is only fair. It's much
better this way."

At the weigh-in scales, someone reminded Dan he was short on boxes. After he switched truck batteries, we drove the propane truck forty miles to Moses Lake and loaded up two thousand flattened cardboard boxes, baled, for $1,300.

Along the way we crossed high plateau that was completely, endlessly, transformed by Columbia River water. Apricots. Corn. Onions. Mint. Apples. This was FDR's dream come true. Shades of green quilted the land where the soil is a mineral-rich and good-draining mix of volcanic dust and ash. Water splashed orchards, silvered between rows of an onion field, and sprayed from long pipes rotating from the pump hubs. Shallow lakes and marshes reminded me Grand Coulee Dam created, as well as destroyed, wildlife habitat. With water to the parched steppe came hundreds of small lakes with fish, an explosion of the Canada goose population, and new resident waterfowl. There was that, too, and it was part of the same equation that included extinct June hogs. The land out the truck window was all parceled off, sectioned out—this for people, that for wildlife. New and watery life forms had come here, but it wasn't nature. These flawless farms, this engineered green . . . It was hard for me, having paddled beneath 7 million years the day before, to trust it. Man, guiding the water, had assumed total control.

"No, you're right," Dan said. "Every drop is metered and accounted for. We have our water police. We have our weed police. It's kind of scary, all right, but I don't know how you'd do it any other way."

Back at the farm, blond and toasted-brown children— Paul's kids, Dan's and Sheila's grandkids—whooped and splashed in a ten-foot diameter tub filled with Columbia River water, far from the river. One of the little kids was named Robin. This was the first time she'd met someone else called Robin and she wasn't happy about it. Phone messages and peach orders had piled up for Dan, and he went inside the shed to answer them. The shed was open at both ends. At the far end, outside, I saw Danny—the Verheys' youngest son, a big gentle fourteen-year-old space cadet with a gold earring—stack used boxes too high in the burn barrel. Flames licked above the barrel. Sparks ignited the pale grass next to an ancient Ford pickup.

Dan, too, saw this. But he was on the phone.

Danny with a rake, and I with a water bucket, fought the fire. Dan talked on the phone. The fire reached the grass under the pickup. Tire rubber bubbled. Paint began to peel. Dan talked on the phone. Finally he hung up. He coupled hose enough to reach us, and we watered and stomped the fire out.

Maybe I gave him a look. "That was a big sale," he said. "You could have let this old pickup burn."

There had been no mention, all day, of the Verheys' returning me and my canoe to the river. Sheila disappeared into town, and Dan was busy with customers. Not that I had to leave. Life was an adventure here, and I was welcome. But there was no wind. And windlessness anywhere near the Columbia is a great and fleeting opportunity. When I mentioned I was ready for river, Dan reacted in surprise, as if one of the Mexicans had quit. But he switched batteries to the pickup and we strapped the canoe on and drove to the river.

On the way, Dan got real quiet.

"I'd like to be going with you," he said. Which was a nice thing to say, and I felt bad. He said, "Everybody needs an adventure."

The river was calm and beautiful that afternoon, and at night a bright moon came up. And this was not the first time the river was too much for me, too many rivers all the same one. I thought about those sun-toasted little kids splashing in the irrigation tub, and I ached for a piece of language that would answer this river-to-person-and-back whisper, would speak to the whole thing.

Maybe I was trying too hard.

One night, a long time ago, my friend Tom Curry and I

were out rowing on the Clackamas above River Mill Dam. The stars were out and we were small and we didn't know we were close to the mind of God. Tom thought the stars stopped at the dimmest one we could see. I didn't think so. Smart me, I even had a word for it: *infinity*. I told him about infinity, about things without end, and the more I explained it the more muddled I got. Infinity is hard, even when you have a word. As I struggled with it, Tom reversed his opinion and decided I was right. He liked the word.

"It's easy," Tom said. "Infinity is a box with no sides."

At Priest Rapids Dam, Grant County PUD dispatched two workers in a yellow GMC flatbed, big enough to haul a trawler. We strapped the canoe down and stopped on the dam for the driver to check in with the boss. The other guy, a quiet Indian, was Grant Wyena. He and I leaned against the spillway railing, as men do, waiting. We faced the wide reservoir on the up side of the dam. Wyena had stubby legs and a yellow hard hat and a light blue T-shirt that bulged at the belly. He declined a smoke and seemed to enjoy this break from whatever he does at the dam.

Was he a Wanapum?

"Yes," Wyena said.

Something about a quiet Indian, you expect him to be deep. I watched the river. What I knew about the Wanapum (Wana-Pum, or river people) was that they used to follow the seasonal pulse of the river to gather salmon and roots and berries. They validated their ties to the land in song, dance, drumming, and "the vision quest," in which a Wanapum youth set off alone in search of a guardian spirit. On this quest, the young Wanapum would look for his own spirit to reveal itself in a particular animal—or a tree, maybe, perhaps the wind.

Had Wyena known this water, this place, before the dam?

"Yes."

The sun spread high in the sky. A light wind feathered the

reservoir. Gulls swooped and screeched behind us, over the foaming tailrace. The Wanapum didn't fight in Indian wars, nor did they sign a peace treaty with the United States. Following their prophet Smowhala, in the late 1800s, the Wanapum refused to adopt white ways or to be herded onto reservations. So they didn't get title to any of their river lands.

I thought maybe Wyena had lapsed into a coma, but then he said, "My brother and I used to paddle out to the island." He nodded toward an island in the reservoir that only he could see. "We stole goose eggs and brought them home. The river was fast, and we weren't supposed to go. They put the canoe in the museum," he said. "You could go see it."

The driver returned. We took a chuckholed road past an Indian village of a dozen pastel houses on rock fill below the dam. Wyena pointed out the blue house as his, and I asked if I could come back after work. We could talk?

"Okay," he said.

When he didn't show up, kids in the village pointed me to the brown house. They said Virginia Wyena, Grant's sister, could help me out. Like a woman who wouldn't be surprised by much, she invited me in. She had finished dinner, and she cleared a place at the table. It was awkward at first, because I was a curiosity and too many kids shouldered into the house to see what it was all about. But she shooed them out, and once she got going she had a lot to say. Yes, she had lived on the river when she was young. Her parents had spoken only Indian, and they lived in a tule-mat house. It was a big one, not something you'd pack up and move away. "And it wasn't cold, like everybody thinks. We had blankets. We had a stove and a pipe up through the roof."

She was a handsome woman with a rippling laugh, warm brown eyes, and tiny hands. She wore a purple blouse and bright red bandana.

"People talk like it must have been very strange," she said, "but I was little and that's just how things were. Grandma took me to the cellars. The potatoes were there, and that's where we stored dishes when we were going to dig roots. There was a tall white man with a hat used to come around, and I was scared of him. We hid. He said, 'Hello? Hello?' We thought that was his name. We called him Hello, Hello. That was the man who wrote a book. My name when I was little was Lamaia. The lady on the sheep ranch gave us English names, and then I was Virginia."

I asked about the vision quest.

"No," she said, "that was way past. We went to the long-house on Sundays and it was like church. We prayed to one creator. Puck Hyah Toot was the last prophet. He never spoke English. He spoke Indian. People today, they try, but they can't get it the way he did. Grandma saw what was coming. She saw fast cars. Airplanes, before they came. 'Everything is moving so fast,' she said. 'Flick your finger, the day is gone.' She saw the dams. Lights. Faucets. Yes, all these things foreseen. She said you wouldn't have to walk to water. You'd have it right in the house. You could go to the bathroom in the same house you sleep in!"

She laughed, a good rich laugh. It *was* strange. Here was a woman little older than I . . . How old was she?

"I was born probably in 1935. I have seventeen grandkids."

Probably?

"Maybe 1936 or 1937. They guess from when you started school. We were over in Prosser. The first day of school, Mom did my older sisters' hair and sent them out to wait for the bus. I wanted my hair done. I wasn't supposed to go to school, but the bus driver saw me running. He stopped the bus and I got on. I had to have a birthday. They put my birthday as February 22. That was George Washington's birthday, so I changed it later to February 23."

Virginia Wyena told me she had liked school and the people there. She didn't think much about being an Indian until sixth grade, when her relatives called her snooty for eating lunch with nonfamily friends, and she noticed groups of boys being mean to one another. At graduation she had enough to pay for her pictures, but couldn't pay for anything else, and went back later for her GED.

"I worked for the Yakima Nation at Toppenish," she said. "For the agency on aging. I could talk to the older people there, and I didn't feel so lonesome. I learned things I'd forgotten. I started doing things I did as a little girl. Now I make moccasins. I weave." She went to another room and brought back a sturdy little woven basket, a bead necklace, some cornhusk pouches, and braid ties. "My cousin and I were going to get language classes together," she said, "but people are just not interested enough. The parents didn't show up. Just the kids. You can't do it that way. The language was never written, just spoken."

Like her brother, Wyena works for Grant County PUD. She's the Native American Specialist at the Wanapum Dam visitors' center. She talked about how the Wanapum were moved off the Hanford Plain, downstream, first during the Indian wars and then by homesteaders. "Smowhala and his group kept moving away. Up the river. Until they got here. Nobody cared about this land," she said. When Grant County PUD, building Priest Rapids Dam in 1958, looked for river people to compensate, it found only a handful of full-blood Wanapum. The Bucks. The Wyenas. "The Wanapum now are all kinds of mixture of Indians who lived on the river. People who told their children, who told their children."

I asked about Smowhala's prophecy: that if his followers remained true to native ways, white people would soon enough disappear. She took a long time at it, and when she answered she seemed to answer a different question.

"We live in two worlds," she said. She looked around the house. It was a new house, a double-wide mobile home she rents from the PUD. The TV was on, but it was on a snowy channel and it was on low. The air conditioner was louder. "We can still dig roots up on the firing center," she said. "They train the artillery up there. When they are not firing we can dig roots."

What about the canoe Grant had mentioned?

"Yes, it's at the center," she said. "The last canoe. It's huge, all of one log. I remember going out in the canoe. The water up close was dark and frightening. I had to lie down and not look at the river."

I asked her about the Indian word for the Columbia, which I understood to be *Che Wana*, for "big river." I'd seen it written like that or as *Chiawana*, with four syllables. Just upstream from Priest Rapids I'd passed a railroad siding called Schawana. Was that the same word?

"See? That's just it," she said. "Somebody writes it and then people say it wrong. The word is," she said, and it rolled from her soul off her tongue to fill the world. And for that brief moment I was everywhere on it, like the first time you ever put your ear to a seashell. The word had four syllables, like *Chiawana*, but it started with an *n*.

'Nchi-a-wah-na, maybe.

I asked her to say it again, and she did.

I tried to say the word. I couldn't say it, not the way she did. Like you see a white stone in clear deep water, but the act of reaching for it disturbs the water. Then you can't see the stone anymore. You can't find it down there.

I asked her, "How do you spell that?"

"We don't," she said.

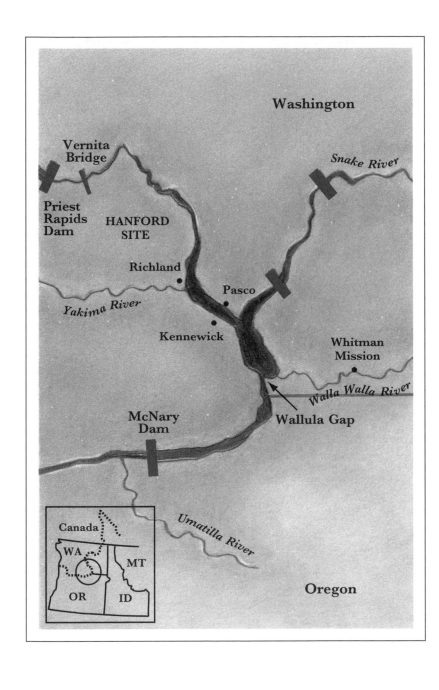

II

HANFORD

Nobody Knew What We Were Making

When a big river slams through narrow canyons, swift current flushes grit and gravel on through. Only the larger pieces— boulders and rock shelves—stay put, and you'll look long and hard for a quiet pool, a sandy beach. But when the river escapes its confining walls and spreads over a wider area, it loses velocity. The river yawns into lazy backwaters and eddies, and drops its sand and grit. That's where, on a smaller river, you'll find a sandy beach to spread a picnic and go for a swim. If the river is large, you'll find a broad flood plain, rich for farming. And if the river is the Columbia, downstream from the once-raging Wenatchee–to–Priest Rapids stretch, your sandy beach and broad flood plain cover a land mass half the size of Rhode Island.

This Hanford Plain is a raw, windswept, sun-blistered land of scant rainfall. The Wanapum lived across it, more than on it, in seasonal search of food. Gable Mountain was a sacred place to the Wanapum, and the land held their ancient burial sites. When the homesteaders arrived, they drew water from the Columbia, upstream, and gravity-fed it to fields of onions, potatoes, and fruit. M. J. Lorraine, in 1921, called it "the most intensively cultivated and charming section along the whole length of the Columbia River." But soon after Lorraine's passage, a ten-year drought drove all but the best-irrigated farmers to the wet side of the Cascades. By 1940 the Hanford Plain had few permanent residents.

It was, the U.S. War Department decided, the ideal site for a huge, secret experiment. Here was the place to brew plutonium for the world's first atomic bomb.

Hanford had everything the Manhattan Project needed. It had river water, for cooling and controlling the preparation of fissionable materials. Great blocks of electricity could be shunted here from Grand Coulee Dam. The railroad was already in. The army, for its exclusive use of 560 square miles, had to evacuate only two small towns and scattered farms. Hanford's isolation made it all the easier to keep a secret, or to cover the possibility of a Big Mistake. The bomb existed only in theory. Nobody knew for sure if a nuclear reaction could be packaged.

To the desert in 1943 came engineers and construction workers and Nobel Prize winners, and the Corps of Engineers built a complex that included 900 temporary buildings, 130 barracks, and 4,300 trailers. The population swelled to 51,000. In eight mess halls, they served up 80 tons of food a day to workers who had no idea what they were building. Through searing heat and bending against 30-mph winds, this army of unknowing workers led the race to build the first bomb.

It all happened so fast. June 1943: construction started on the B Reactor, the world's first plutonium-producing plant. September 1943: the B Reactor began operating. July 1945: the first atomic bomb exploded in tests at Alamogordo, New Mexico. August 6, 1945: Hiroshima. August 9, 1945: Nagasaki. August 14, 1945: Japan surrendered.

From a right-bank pool below Priest Rapids Dam, I paddled out into wide, swift river. Ahead lay forty-seven miles of free-flowing Columbia called the Hanford Reach. Riverbanks sped by on fast backward. The river sucked at the rocky right shore, where whorls could have eaten me up, but flat boils pancaked in the middle with no grip or darker purpose than to lift my canoe along. The river split for arrowhead islands of round stones and short alders, and narrow bars fanned downstream into washboard riffles. Fat trout darted from the shadow of my streaking canoe. It was early in August, and the fall chinook run had not yet arrived. In another month, Vernita Bar—not one bar but a series of small-island gravel-trailings—would be thick with spawning salmon. This is the only place left on the main-stream Columbia where salmon spawn naturally.

Because camping is verboten on the nuclear reservation, I stopped short of it, within sight of Vernita Bridge, and pitched the tent in the flat shade of alders. An eddying deep-water pool slowed the river here. I jumped in and soon found a place where I could put my full strength into a good long swim, and go nowhere.

They say wild horses roam the nuclear reservation, and elk. I didn't see any, but I counted twenty-six deer in the first hour past Vernita Bridge. It was a cool, overcast morning. Clouds dropped veils of moisture that never reached the ground. I hadn't spotted a coyote in three weeks, but here I saw four in a morning. A flock of geese fanned into the gray sky and let me pass, moving quickly on free-flowing river. Five white pelicans took flight from the left shore. White pelicans! I'd never seen one before. They flew close to the surface, and the slow flaps of their wings touched water.

Yellow, license-plate-sized metal signs guarded shore: "NO TRESPASSING. NO ACCESS FROM SHORELINE. Violators will be arrested and prosecuted." Both shores and even the islands were posted. Which seemed excessive. You can't go thirty-five miles in a canoe without getting out to piss and stretch. The Columbia River cuts the north and east quadrants of the Hanford Nuclear Reservation, which is known locally as the Hanford Site, or just The Site. The river ranged from a quarter to three quarters of a mile wide. Banks lay treeless and low, with dusty sage and tumbleweed. No roads came to shore, and no other boats plowed the river.

The boxy gray hulk of the B Reactor stood back from the bank, the size of a Safeway but eight stories high and flanked by a pair of water towers. From this building came the plutonium that triggered the atomic bomb dropped on Nagasaki. All was silent on the river, and the reactor's smokeless stack and lifeless bulk rode the desert as if from a separate world of triumph and horror.

A blue heron *grawked* and flapped from shore into flight.

Farther on, I passed twin plutonium factories on the right bank. In the 1950s and 1960s, the War Department had a total of nine plutonium reactors up and running at once, building the Cold War nuclear stockpile. All nine are obsolete, shut down. There's less demand for plutonium these days.

A huge reddish-black beaver slid from his den in a clay bunker and moved silently into the river.

The next reactor on the right bank was bigger, newer, and more complicated than the others. The N-Reactor. It, too, was shut down, but until recently it had a dual purpose. It captured steam, from Columbia River water that cooled the plutonium-making process, to generate electricity for peaceful purposes. The N-Reactor was the last of Hanford's plutonium factories to close. In 1988, an election year, the Chernobyl accident in the Soviet Union spooked U.S. politicians (as they explain it in Richland), and the government pulled the plug. Now the N-Reactor is in cold storage. I scanned the tinted green windows of the guard tower, but the whole complex, the size of a mall, was apparently unmanned. The reactor was surrounded by a tall fence topped with razor wire that coiled and glinted in the raking sun, which, without my noticing, had burned the overcast from the river.

Jackrabbits poked at the fence.

The overriding strangeness of paddling Hanford Reach lay not in these ominous buildings, these relics of the nuclear age.

N-Reactor at Hanford.

I'd expected those. What surprised me was all the animal life. Jackrabbits, like the deer and coyotes and geese and herons, love the nuclear reservation. In the last few weeks I'd grown accustomed to critter-free orchards and bugless evenings, where pesticides and herbicides held life in check. Not here. The huge irony of this passage was that the nation's most hazardous nuclear waste dump was teeming with wildlife.

Another strangeness was I had penetrated this far into the national secret without, to my knowledge, having been observed. I'd heard about a security force with gunboats, semiautomatic rifles, and nightscopes. With a born coward's respect for the law, I obeyed the never-ending NO TRESPASSING signs. But now, in early afternoon, heat waves radiated off the water and the air sizzled. Fatigue, curiosity, and a full bladder got the better of me, and when I saw the shell of a schoolhouse on the old Hanford townsite, with shade trees in rows, I aimed the canoe for the right bank.

No sooner had I stepped ashore and watered a tumbleweed than—through astounding coincidence or razor-sharp surveillance, I'll never know—I heard the *whump-a-whump-a-whump* of a lone helicopter wheeling a bend up the river. I scurried back to the canoe and backpaddled from shore. The helicopter circled and lowered overhead. As the canoe spun in a froth, I straightened up and offered a just-visiting, got-to-go-now salute. The chopper tilted and swooped away.

Downstream, I hugged the inside of Coyote Rapids and came around a wide bend into sandstone bluffs, white as eggshell, and then the Columbia rolled flat through wide, easy turns. Bald islands and bare shoreline scolded me for having used the term "desert" too loosely up to now. Here, however, was *desert*. Tall dunes flanked the shore, their rippled sands marked only by tracks of shore birds or a coyote whose passing the hot wind had not yet erased.

The coyote tracks reminded me I had read somewhere

Coyote tracks.

about coyote feces on the Hanford Site that a probing biologist had called "hummers." The turds were so radioactive they made his Geiger counter hum instead of click. Coyotes, he hypothesized, were using an open waste dump as a salt lick.

To the west, white plumes of vapor billowed from the Hanford's only active nuclear power plant, which was pumping 1,100 megawatts into the Northwest federal power grid, supplementing the river's own work.

The absence of NO TRESPASSING signs was the first clue I'd left the nuclear reservation. I stopped for a swim but there was no place to camp, no relief from pounding sun except in the river itself. Although thirty-five miles was twice my daily average, the river had done all the work. I paddled on. Short of Richland, the river widened and slowed into the next reservoir, Lake Wallula. On the left bank and across from the sprawling Westinghouse plant, I found a beach with puffy bushes, like the fringe of hair on a bald guy. A two-boat party of waterskiers had claimed the small beach, but they weren't set up to spend the night, so I slipped in to share their site.

Not everybody you meet on a river is friendly, or bright and talkative enough to be interesting. Some don't like canoes, or beards, or maybe just me. Soon after my landing, a hard-eyed young mother with a toddler in tow demanded, "Are you pro-nuclear or anti-nuclear?"

It was a line of questioning, not always so direct, I would get used to in the Richland area. *Are you Israeli or Palestinian?* It's not something to think about; it's something you are, on one side or the other. I told her I was just passing through, just seeing what I could see. This seemed to strike her as deeply disturbing, and she glanced at her husband like, *Can I smell one, or what?*

These folks soon packed up their skis and coolers and sped away. Perhaps they'd been about to leave the beach anyway.

In mid-July, back when I was on Lake Roosevelt, the Department of Energy's chief of nuclear safety, Steve Blush, had released a study that was sharply critical of nuclear waste storage on the Hanford Site. The Blush report lashed federal contractors and the DOE for lackadaisical management of radioactive storage tanks, for dumping contaminated fluids directly into the soil, and for failing to make public the hazards to human health. The report told of waste storage tanks that were beginning to leak. It cited poorly trained workers, bad record-keeping, broken equipment, and slap-dash repairs.

Over the last ten years, stories had surfaced about the horrors buried in the ground or released to the air at Hanford. The Spokane *Spokesman-Review*, for example, had worried that thyroid cancers in Franklin County might be linked to radiation that had fallen on farmers' fields. But until now, a cover of national security had prevailed over the Freedom of Information Act. In the summer of 1990, that cover flew off and Energy Secretary James Watkins admitted, "We do have to go back and look at what happened." The *Spokesman-Review*, which had led the campaign for disclosure, reacted with a mix of amazement and I-told-you-so glee. As I came paddling down the river, farmers in eastern Washington were picking up the paper, as I was, and learning that from 1944 to 1977 large amounts of radioactive material, including iodine 131, had been routinely released to the air from Hanford. Hot waste went into the Columbia River, too, most of it in the 1950s and 1960s, when all the plutonium reactors were running.

July 25, under the headline, PERSISTENCE FINALLY REVEALED THE HANFORD SECRET: "For 45 years the government consistently downplayed radiation risks and lied about the dangers of nuclear weapons plants."

July 29: TRUST REWARDED WITH LIES. "We were never warned, nor were we provided with adequate safeguards. Lies and denials became part of the coverup. Deception became routine policy."

August 2, in the Wenatchee *World:* TANKS DANGEROUS, PUBLIC MISLED. Because I thought the *World* had a high threshold of moral indignation on environmental matters, I read with large interest in that paper about the government "knowing for years that waste storage tanks could explode and spew radiation into the air."

The storage tanks in question contain liquid by-products from making atomic bombs. Strontium 90, technetium 99, and iodine 129 are among the isotopes swimming in the most toxic soup ever brewed on earth. The tanks—177 of them, some double-shelled but most single-shelled—are lined with steel and encased in concrete beneath the topsoil near Gable Mountain and within fifteen miles of the Columbia River. These tanks were meant to store the hottest of liquid nuclear debris—not forever but for twenty or thirty years, until a permanent storage site could be found. No such site has revealed itself, however, and the tanks are in bad shape. I learned new words to describe these tanks.

There are "burpers." A one-million-gallon tank, 101-SY, belches a potentially explosive mix of hydrogen, ammonia, and nitrous oxide through its venting system every two months or so. Below the gasses, inside the tank, lies a highly radioactive slurry. Hanford officials aren't sure of the chemical composition of this slurry, and would like to drill through the tank to find out. But the act of drilling, to sample the tank's contents, could spark an explosion. Nobody knows what to do about 101-SY.

There are "boilers." Tank 106-C is a 530,000-gallon, single-shell hull with high concentrations of strontium 90. The tank is four times as hot as any other and drinks 2,000 gallons of cooling water a week. If the tank were left to dry, officials fear, rising temperatures in its thick sludge could melt the hull. Where does all the cooling water go? They think it evaporates through the tank's vents. The DOE says it is confident the tank is not leaking radioactivity into the ground. But eventually the tank will leak; it's only a matter of time.

Tank 105-A has already ruptured. It split a seam and oozed at least 5,000 gallons of contaminated goo into surrounding soil. The DOE's estimate, as I paddled through, was that a total of 750,000 gallons of radioactive materials had leaked from storage tanks to the soil. This poison has "not yet" reached the groundwater or the Columbia River.

What *has* reached the Columbia River is seepage from waste dumped straight into Hanford earth. There wasn't room, in the 1950s and '60s, for all toxic wastes to be stored in tanks. Drain systems, using soil as the final filter, were supposed to take care of water laden with less toxic, but still radioactive, by-products. Some went into open trenches, to be bulldozed over. Now it emerges that these lower-level dumps may contain technetium 99, and that dirt under and around the open dumping sites could be a more long-lasting threat than the storage tanks. Technetium 99 will still retain half its present radioactivity in the year 214000.

In early evening, the wind died on the river and warm clouds of gnats descended on my camp. These were little brown gnats, not biters; the scarcity of green cover on the river had drawn them as well as me to this rare spot. Which seemed only fair. We could get along. The bushy fringe of beach droned and hummed with bugs as I prepared bug chili. Silver trout broke the river surface for a mouthful of protein-packed air, and a squad of sparrows looped the water, beaks open. A garter snake slithered from the brush and traced winglike tracks on a shaded apron of sand.

The sun spread across the river and dropped behind Gable Mountain, which slumped brown as a hibernating bear. A bat shadowed through camp and veered away. The planet rolled as it had for ages, and I pictured a radioactive underground plume creeping toward the Columbia, not yet here.

From the Verheys' peach farm I'd called home and was surprised to get my daughter Heidi on the phone instead of Donna. I'd thought Heidi was in Los Angeles. In this summer after her junior year in college, she'd landed an internship cataloguing old films. But she was in Portland with Donna. So they came to Richland and met me at the dock of the Shilo Rivershore Inn, where Donna had reserved two rooms and we caught up with things and later that day had a three-on-a-bed family conference about a huge crisis in Heidi's life. Her Hollywood internship had gone sour. They weren't using her right, and she had three more weeks to go but didn't want to return. Heidi needed advice, because in our family we don't quit without feeling terrible. "Just quit," I said. I was firm about it. I was full of river, and nothing mattered.

Who knows from what depths great wisdom flows? I had said the right thing. Now the master of all the earth, potent husband and understanding father, I terrorized my loved ones by driving us the wrong way up a one-way street and failing to notice a nasty divider in the parking lot of the restaurant, the Isla Bonita. But driving is a skill you never really lose, and after dinner I took us out on The Site as far as we could go without badges, and we counted deer in the headlights. Heidi, now expansive, narrated this romantic evening from the backseat as we parked and watched the nuclear power plant loft its vapors into lavender night sky, and I was very glad they had come to meet me here.

When I was Heidi's age, in 1963, President Kennedy's perfect hair blew wild in the desert wind here as he stood on a platform and dedicated the new Hanford N-Reactor: ". . . to strike a blow for peace and for a better life for our fellow citizens."

Nuclear energy, we knew, was clean. Nuclear power plants wouldn't pollute the air or the land. Nuclear energy would complement hydropower from dams and relieve pressure on fossil fuels—coal, gas, and oil—that were in finite supply and would otherwise be burned to generate electricity. Nuclear energy was safe. The idea of splitting atoms kind of gave you the willies, but we were told it wasn't really dangerous. These were power plants, not bomb factories. Don't be silly. They couldn't explode. And once the engineers got the hang of it, nuclear power would be cheap.

You could be well educated and alert to the world in the 1960s and believe all this. Government and big science— General Electric, Battelle, Westinghouse—would lead us out of the energy wilderness and into the nuclear age.

In the 1970s, power forecasters saw a huge energy deficit on the Northwest horizon. All the major dam sites were taken, and a vigorous economy would thirst for more power in the next twenty years. The forecast was wrong. In fact, a global petroleum squeeze forced a new look at energy conservation, and a long slump in the early 1980s squashed Northwest economic growth. We had a huge power surplus, not a deficit. But Congress had already authorized BPA to underwrite nonfederal power plants, including nuclear ones. Public utilities in the state of Washington banded together to form the Washington Public Power Supply System. WPPSS (known in Richland as "the Supply System" and elsewhere as "WOOPS") broke ground on five nuclear facilities: three at Hanford and two more west of the Cascades.

Design goofs, labor problems, and environmental lawsuits led to cost overruns that doomed WPPSS from the start. Only one of the five plants (WNP-2, here at Hanford) was completed. It was supposed to cost $394 million and take five years to build; instead it took twelve years and cost $2.5 billion. Of the others, two were partially constructed and then mothballed, and two more barely got off the ground. WPPSS stiffed its investors for $2.25 billion, the largest bond-issue default in U.S. history. BPA's investment raised power rates 50 percent and boosted the power supply only 5 percent. The unpaid bill, when I paddled by, stood at $6.6 billion. Payments on the debt run $580 million a year, more than five times what the agency spends on fish and wildlife projects.

Aside from the fact that it's not cheap, nuclear power is not clean. The part I don't remember hearing in the 1960s is that spent nuclear fuel is still radioactive, and you have to put it somewhere. Fuel rods from WNP-2 and elsewhere find retirement here at Hanford in sunken pools of water that cool but don't extinguish their radioactive glow. And when a nuclear submarine retires, the navy ships its hot midsection up the Columbia to Hanford for burial. The waste accumulates here, awaiting a permanent national storage site.

It was alumni weekend. Back at the Shilo Inn, the Richland High School class of 1970 had drawn a good crowd for its twentieth. At a poolside barbecue, hearty graduates pulled their stomachs in and checked reflecting windows. Classmates introduced the new wife or the baffled husband and pointed out a reluctant knot of kids and told who belonged to whom. Drinks flowed. It was just a high school reunion, might have been mine, might have been yours, except their alma mater is the Home of the Bombers. WELCOME BACK BOMBERS. On T-shirts and letterman jackets was the school logo: a field of green with a yellow-block *R*, issuing a white mushroom cloud.

In the morning, reading the Yellow Pages, I mentioned the Atomic Laundromat to the women and Heidi said that ought to do it. On the way we passed the Atomic Body & Towing Service and Atomic Foods. What I like about a place is when it has its own character, when you can't possibly mistake it for someplace else.

Richland is a modern, arrow-straight, well-watered city with crisp lawns and scrubbed sidewalks, the kind of place you might go to film a documentary on family values. With neighboring Pasco and Kennewick, Richland calls itself the Tri-Cities and boasts the highest concentration of Ph.D.s of any American city. Doctors of science gather here for research in nuclear medicine, power, defense, and space programs. The whiff of new money filled the desert air. Chic new developments, from Columbia Edgewater to Sagewood Summit, were selling their units fast, prices jacked up. At the gleaming Columbia Center Mall, the parking lot at Bon Marché teemed with late-model Hondas. Jane Fonda and Ted Turner were on hand for the Pan American Games hockey tournament, and Westinghouse Hanford Company was hiring.

The cause for optimism and surging property values was the money and time it will take to clean up Hanford. Recently signed was the Tri-Party Agreement—a pact among the state of Washington, the DOE, and the Environmental Protection Agency (EPA) to clean up nuclear waste. The government estimates it will take $50 billion and thirty years to restore waste sites and "to bring Hanford's ongoing operations into compliance with state and federal laws."

To an outsider it might seem odd that the state and two branches of the federal government were celebrating their intention to start obeying the law. But Richland is a complex culture. It's a kind of twilight zone in which very bright people can tell you "Really, it's safe," and then add "We're going to clean it up," and look at you like you're nuts if you see a contradiction.

When I was in town, Hanford officialdom was under siege from the national media about the Blush Report. A perimeter guard of hyperdefensive public relations hacks kept me at bay. *Who are you with? Do you have press credentials?* Lacking not only the credentials but also the patience to fight through this, I nabbed a copy of the Hanford Annual Report, and retreated.

I read about how science hopes to arrest the spread of nuclear waste. They're studying in-situ vitrification, for example: massive bolts of electricity would melt toxic gunk, which would then cool and harden into an inert obsidianlike log. In theory (its practice isn't expected before the turn of the century) you could vitrify Hanford's boiler and burper tanks and immobilize the radioactivity in glass. For larger, less-contaminated areas, perhaps they can mix contaminated soil with cement to form a grout that hardens like concrete and could be stored in vaults for centuries. The report didn't say where these vaults would be, nor did it worry that "for centuries" is not forever. The first challenge is to locate and sample all the lesser-contaminated dump sites, and to find out what's in the tanks.

To me, the uncertainty was the scariest part. Science is offering temporary solutions to a permanent problem of unknown dimensions. I doubt if nuclear waste is the worst of the Columbia's problems. My own guess is that it's not among the top five threats to the river and should rank well behind overpopulation, dams, logging, grazing, and nonnuclear chemical abuse. But nobody really knows how dangerous Hanford is, or how much time we have to clean it up. The possibility of nuclear accident, however remote, clearly exists at WNP-2 and the hot storage tanks. And even if we could excise Hanford's malignancy and put it somewhere else, the idea of storing nuclear waste is unnerving. The earth is changeable, home to cataclysmic events, and man-made storage vaults only underlie the assumption we don't expect to be here forever. A long time, maybe, but not forever.

At the Hanford Science Center, I picked up more of the rosy official view. I studied an exhibit dedicated to the truth that radioactivity occurs in nature and a little bit won't hurt you, and another that showed that Hanford no longer fouls the air. Radioactive seepage into the Columbia, I learned, is so diluted by river volume that it is far less than would be hazardous to human health. "Today the Columbia River is one of the cleanest in the United States." This, of course, is what I wanted to believe, but I had to remind myself that the Hanford Science Center is a product of the same sponsors who denied, for years, that there was anything at all to worry about here.

The best part of the Science Center was history. There was a good section about how the Hanford Engineering Works came to be, in wartime secrecy. In a copy of *The Villager*, then Richland's newspaper, I read about the satisfaction and jubilation—and evident surprise—that came when President Harry

Truman announced the Hiroshima drop. "IT'S ATOMIC BOMBS," screamed the headline. And then, just a week later: "PEACE!!! OUR BOMBS CLINCHED IT!"

"No, it's true," says Annette Heriford. "We didn't know what we were making. We knew it was a war effort. We were all so extremely patriotic."

Annette Heriford works part-time at the Science Center. It was her day off, but folks at the center said she was the one to talk to. So I phoned her at home, and Donna and Heidi and I followed her directions to a pink building with a view of the Columbia River. Heriford, a lady of manners with peach-blond hair, lived alone in an apartment with thick rugs and gilt-frame mirrors. Her whippet was uncomfortable with visitors. I sat in a Louis XVI chair and tried not to rattle my teacup against its saucer.

"My father homesteaded here in 1910," she said. "Just a one-room house at first, near White Bluffs. I came along in 1920. Our place was back from the river, and Dad sank a well. He hit an aquifer and it was ice-cold, unlimited supply. We had an apple orchard.

"When the army moved in," she said, "they moved fast. The letter came from Spokane. March 1, 1943. We had thirty days to evacuate. I came home from the University, and Dad showed me the papers. We had forty acres, and they offered ten dollars. Twenty-five cents an acre! If we didn't accept, we could go to court in Yakima. But it was wartime, and you had to have coupons for gas. We couldn't get to Yakima. It was the first I'd ever seen my father discouraged. 'We'll make a comeback,' he said. 'I'll get the gas.' He was disoriented. But we did get to Yakima, and the court gave us seventeen hundred dollars for our home, our well, our forty acres. There was nothing you could buy with the money, and I just wept. My folks had worked that place all their lives. Mother's shrubs and flowers."

Heriford said she knew how the Indians felt, because this land was hers too. She used to hike Gable Mountain and climb the white bluffs.

"One day I rode horseback to town," she said. "I cut through the desert and I saw Grandmother's house torn down. A red-brick floor in the kitchen was all that was left. The next day it was in a trailer camp, the largest trailer camp in the world. To see all this happening, I was in shock. But you adjust," she said. "I got a job at the youth center, and once I went to work I enjoyed it. You got caught up in it. The first theater was a huge tent. We had a Catholic church and bingo parties. They built an auditorium in eleven days, and we had prizefights and basketball games. Big bands—Tommy Dorsey, Benny Goodman. It was wild. I loved to dance, but there were so many more men than women. The mess halls stayed open all night. People weren't used to the heat. When the wind blew they called it a termination wind, because so many people quit. Nothing would grow. You'd see those ladies keeping house in trailers. For a yard they painted rocks and set the rocks in rows."

She rose from her chair and filled our teacups on an elegant tour around the living room.

"The gentleman I was with was a nuclear scientist," she said, "but I didn't know. He told me later they had trouble fissioning xenon, and Fermi went in and did the calculations and got it going. I delivered the blueprints."

You really didn't know?

"I never *wanted* to know," she said. "It was a war effort. It was a total surprise when we found out. It made everybody so proud."

I had read in the Tri-City *Herald* that "downwinders"—people who live downwind from, or east of, Hanford—had filed a lawsuit alleging radioactive fallout and claiming damages ranging from thyroid cancer to mental anguish and emotional distress. The point of the article—MEDIA HYPED

HANFORD DOSE REPORT—was that television and big-city papers had sensationalized the downwinders' claims. I asked Heriford what she thought.

" 'Downwinders' is a silly term," she said. "I'd live out there today, and wouldn't be afraid of the air or the water. But everybody's worked up. The media," she said, shaking her head. "I was at the museum the day they had an accident on The Site with americium. One man injured."

Americium?

"A by-product of plutonium. CBS called and wanted to know how big the crater was. The crater! We took newspeople out, and they wouldn't get out of the car without a Geiger counter."

Heriford didn't like the turn our conversation had taken. She paused and looked at my notepad, and nobody could think of anything to say.

"Look at me," she said, and she spread her arms.

She looked good.

"I'm seventy years old and I swam in that river all my life. We just had a reunion and all those people came back. We took a cruise on the river. People here haven't suffered. It makes you wonder."

12

TURNING FOR HOME

This Is Our Mother, This Country

The Columbia River leaves the Tri-Cities as if headed for
Texas, southeast, but then it sniffs the Pacific Ocean and starts
a slow fifty-mile bend toward Wallula Gap and into the Columbia River Gorge—Oregon on the left, Washington on the
right. More rivers—the Yakima, the Snake, the Walla Walla—
join east of the gap and braid themselves into the Columbia. In
August, now, these tributaries run low and tired. The mountains they drain lost their snowpack months ago, and water
reaching the Columbia has already visited crops—Yakima apples and pears, Idaho potatoes, Walla Walla onions. Long
before dams on the mainstream Columbia, farmers along these
feeder rivers built weirs, ditches, and canals that altered the
waterflow and killed off migrating salmon.

Soon after pushing off from the Richland Shilo and passing
the freeway bridge, on a calm Sunday morning, I poked the
canoe into the Yakima River, one of the most used and abused
of all the Columbia's tributaries. Wallula Lake had backed into
the Yakima's throat so there was no current and not much to
see, but a lot to think about. The Yakima has an Indian reservation along its now-diminished flow, and the native people
hold treaty rights to the fish that once swarmed here. Guilt-

soaked power money—over $1 billion in the 1980s—rains down from BPA on fish and wildlife projects throughout the Columbia River basin, and much of it pours into the Yakima. The tribes, the state, and a thicket of federal agencies are working to repair the river. New bypass systems at the irrigation works give adult salmon and steelhead a clearer path upstream, and give their offspring a fighting chance to get out. Screens at the heads of irrigation canals divert fish from dead-end flows. In 1989 a hatchery run of fall chinook returned to the Yakima River for the first time in living memory.

The emphasis in the 1980s was to boost the total number of fish returning to the Columbia River basin, and hatcheries were the quickest way to score. Numbers increased for many strains of salmon, but hatchery fish crowded the natives for food and habitat. And by putting more hatchery fish in the river we artificially respirated the sport- and commercial-fishing industries. A trawler in the Pacific or a gill netter at the mouth of the Columbia cannot avoid catching the endangered Snake River spring chinook along with the more plentiful hatchery salmon. Indiscriminate harvest—the effects of which are exaggerated by a series of low-water years and poor ocean conditions—now threatens the biological diversity and long-term health of the whole fishery.

After probing the mouth of the Yakima, I paddled on through the Tri-Cities. Columbia Park, on the right, held four shoreline miles of tall sycamores and tame geese and joggers and bikers. I passed under a blue steel bridge and then a white suspension bridge connecting Kennewick to Pasco. No wind. It was still early, Sunday. Sun dappled the river, and powerboats weren't out yet. A hard-to-break rule of Columbia paddling is when the wind is down you don't stop. But here on the left I approached the history-rich confluence of the Snake and the Columbia. I put ashore at Sacajawea State Park, a low green delta between the two rivers.

A small museum in the cottonwoods was open but empty, guarded by a firm young rule-keeper who said I couldn't go in eating an apple or shirtless or barefoot. I was about to walk back to the canoe when the guard, suddenly an ally, scanned the terrain for helicopter gunships and whispered he would admit me as is to his museum. But I wasn't wearing money either. At that, he drew the line. I walked back to the canoe and returned with two dollars, shoes, and shirt to visit the Lewis and Clark Museum.

In 1803 the United States concluded the Louisiana Purchase with France. Thomas Jefferson paid Napoleon $15 million—three cents an acre—and more than doubled the land area of the United States. The vast new territory was shaped like a New Orleans fire and all of its smoke, billowing north and west into the unknown. Jefferson wasn't sure what he'd bought. To find out, he dispatched his personal secretary, a proven army captain named Meriwether Lewis, who tapped another army man, the red-bearded William Clark, to help him map and explore this wild land and to note what lived and grew there.

Thirty men in the Lewis and Clark Expedition left St. Louis in May 1804, and poled flatboats up the Missouri to the Dakotas, where they wintered over. In spring they switched to dugout canoes and took along Toussaint Charbonneau, a French guide and cook. Charbonneau's wife, Sacajawea, a Shoshone Indian, was the better guide, not because she had traveled beyond the plains but because a woman and her papoose in the lead canoe proved to suspicious Indians that this queerly assorted group was not a war party. The expedition cached its canoes and proceeded on foot into the Rockies. Nearing starvation, the party was saved when Sacajawea, who'd been sold early in life as a slave, recognized a Blackfoot chief as her brother. The chief supplied horses that helped the party reach the Continental Divide.

By horse and canoe the party crossed several drainage areas—to the Salmon River, to the Bitterroot, to the Clearwater, to the Snake. Game was scarce, rations short, morale low. It began to snow. A steady diet of spawning-soft salmon brought on dysentery. "Captain Lewis verry sick," Clark wrote. "Nearly all Complaining of their bowells." The party bartered with Indians for dogs to eat.

Here at the Snake/Columbia River junction, Clark wrote, "The number of dead Salmon on the Shores & floating in the river is incredible to see—and at this season they have only to collect them." The Indians here were sincere in their friendship, monogamous, and respectful of elders, Clark noted, but the women "are more inclined to Corpulency than any we have yet seen." He blamed that and the Indians' sore eyes and bad teeth on their fishery culture—glare off the water and eating soft fish.

In 1811, just six years after Lewis and Clark, David Thompson made his way down the Kootenay and the Columbia. Here at the Snake, Thompson drove a post into the ground and claimed the entire drainage in the name of His British Majesty, by right of discovery. There followed thirty years of British and American rivalry on the Columbia, thirty years in which the Hudson's Bay Company held sway. Even before Thompson and the Lewis and Clark Expedition, trappers had brought whiskey and venereal disease to the country. Now measles, tuberculosis, and smallpox swept through Indian villages and laid flat whole populations. The newcomers, British and American, also carried new ideas about how the river and the land were to be owned and used.

Native culture gave way to immigrant culture like sand through an hourglass. Or like native salmon to hatchery fish.

Just three hundred miles to reach the Pacific, and now I was on a different river. After the Snake joined the Columbia, I paddled a river of commerce, a river that reminded me of one of those social studies maps with sheaths of grain, oil derricks, grain sacks. Except for Keenleyside Dam, back in Canada, none of the dams I'd passed had locks. From here on, all of them do. This river highway links the dry wheat country to oceangoing ships at Portland and Longview. Tall tugs, their wheelhouses four stories high, shoved barges up the slackwater Columbia and into the Snake on their way to Lewiston, Idaho. Up the river came petroleum fuels, chemicals, and fertilizers. Down the river went grains, wood chips, and frozen French fries.

Doug Cody, my cousin, is a tug captain. Back when I was planning the canoe trip, I'd promised to call Doug when I got to the Tri-Cities. He'd offered to carry me up the Snake to Lewiston if he was in the neighborhood. A side trip.

But I didn't phone him. Part of it was I wanted to keep going, without motorized interruption. Also, Doug had been skeptical I could do the Columbia River Gorge by canoe. Now I didn't want him to know where I was, or, worse, to have to rescue me. That's a family thing. A man thing. But there was more. Truth is, I liked being alone on the river. I belonged to the river, and this river belonged to him. It seemed almost incestuous. No, polygamous. Some other time I would go up the Snake with Doug. For now it was better to try for that other view, perhaps only possible on the paddle-dipped river, alone, where you have no closer relatives than everybody.

The Columbia, as Wallula Lake, widened. The sun arced into a nooning sky to match the river's slow bend—east to south—as if the sun pulled the bow of the canoe. Moving small on the big river, I paddled long into the day. On the left shore, a steamy green reserve had no visible wildlife, but later I passed hordes of nattering geese and dozing ducks on a mud island offshore from the Boise-Cascade box factory. Across the river rose the bald honey-baked rolls of Horse Heaven Hills.

The wind picked up. Wallula Gap came into view. Cliffs

rose on both sides of the river, ahead, to form a stark narrow slot in the sky. Looking for a campsite short of the slot, I hit shallow mudflats, and fat carp torpedoed away trailing clouds of mud. I backtracked into deeper water and fought whitecaps to the entrance of the Walla Walla River, a murky finger of jungle water where the air was humid and sticky.

In the brown water floated a jellyish lump like a human brain, but larger. A pair of elderly couples, bank-fishing, asked me what it was. I had no idea. It was translucent green. With the paddle I nudged the thing toward the bank, where one of the fishermen netted it. The glob filled his net and was hard to lift. He dumped it on the mud, and we watched it settle and spread inside a thin pale membrane. It was larval, alive, and it smelled like the history of the world. Nobody wanted to touch it. One of the fishermen said, "Some things you never know," which seemed about right, and we put it back in the water.

I camped on hard-packed black mud under a Russian olive tree, flanked by grass half as tall as the tent. All I wanted was to cook dinner and go to sleep, but I had visitors. A biker from Vancouver, B.C., blew off the road to rest and tell stories. When he roared off, a pair of tattooed middle-aged New Age recruiters stopped by. Then a cowboy father, bringing his daughter to his ex-wife in Walla Walla, was in no hurry to get there. With nightfall I escaped to the tent, but a pair of moaners parked nearby in a '53 Mercury and gave the seat springs a good workout. When that was over, an extended family of night fishermen came to the river waving lanterns, silencing frogs and crickets and shouting clues about who they were, including Uncle Charles, Cheryl the shrieker, and Big Mac, evidently a dog.

About all I remember of fourth grade is that one night Miss Rockhill took a select carload of us from Estacada to Salem, to see a play at Willamette University. I wore a long-sleeved shirt and felt proud to be chosen. It was my first play, other than nativity scenes at the Methodist church, and it made a searing impression on me.

The play was about Dr. Marcus Whitman and his beautiful blond wife, Narcissa, the first white woman to cross the plains by wagon. The Whitmans built a mission on the Walla Walla River and began ministering to Cayuse Indians, a shadowy lot who slipped on and off the stage like tall oiled salamanders. I sobbed with Narcissa Whitman when her two-year-old drowned in the Walla Walla River. I fretted with Marcus Whitman when the savages failed to grasp the idea of gardening, or of one God. Couldn't they see what was good for them? Measles broke out. The Indians decided that Dr. Whitman's medicine was *causing* the measles. No doubt I expected the play to have a happy ending. Instead, the Indians sneaked up behind Dr. Whitman, buried a tomahawk in his head, and set fire to the mission. I remember flames leaping, Indians whooping, missionaries wailing, as the Indians chased Narcissa off the stage.

It was a shameful, shocking, horrifying thing to see, this Whitman Massacre, and I absorbed the lesson well. The Whitmans were the highest examples of frontier bravery, an inspiration to us all. When you're in the fourth grade, everything is true. When you're in the fourth grade and the son of good Methodists in a small logging town, you absorb through your pores many such lessons about your own culture, and the stupidity and treachery of Indians.

The wind, next morning, roared in the trees above my tent, and alder trunks bent like catapults on the other side of the Walla Walla River.

Just up the road lay the ghosts of a truck-stop cafe and gas station, all boarded up, and four of the seven panels had blown out of a Join-the-Navy billboard. I started walking toward the Columbia, and a brown Dodge pickup stopped to pick me up. I was only going a couple miles down the road, for a look at

Wallula Gap. "Hop in," the driver said. When the highway reached the Columbia he was telling this season's Wallula Gap story, and he pulled off in loose gravel to finish it.

I'd heard this story many times, in several versions. The average of it was that in June the wind came up and swamped a twenty-four-foot cabin cruiser in high surf at Wallula Gap. Aboard were two elderly men with the daughter of one of them and her five-year-old. They stayed with the boat until waves crushed it against shoreline rocks. Grandpa wrapped his arms around the kid, but the kid's life jacket was too big and he slipped out. Both drowned. The other man, no doubt hypothermic, climbed the rocks to the railroad track. When he stood on the tracks to flag down the Burlington Northern, the train barreled over him and spread him down the tracks toward Richland. Three died in this train-boating catastrophe. The woman survived.

I thanked the driver for the ride, and got out. "Good luck," he said.

I stood beside the road, leaning west, and looked up at red cliffs, cut sheer at their river-facing edges. Between the road and the river, train tracks ran along a narrow bed of riprap. The wind, as it howled up the river, pounded high green rollers onto the rocks and threw up spray. This was a terrible place for a canoe. There was no exit for miles. The river here was only a quarter mile wide. Elsewhere on the Columbia, glaciers scoured the river's bed from a V-shape to a gentler U-shape. Wallula Gap was an I-shape. The Bretz Floods had burst through these basalt layerings like a chain saw through balsam, all at once. Those who study such things say when the ice dam burst, pent-up Lake Missoula smashed through as a thundering wall of ice, rock, mud, and water, five hundred feet high. They say it blasted the gap at the speed of a car on the freeway and carved the gorge we know today.

*   *   *

Others say Coyote did it.

An Indian legend holds that a long time ago, when the animals were people, a monster Beaver named Wishroosh had big waters. He had a whole ocean on the other side of the mountains. This Wishroosh was a bad one. He kept all the Fish to himself. Bear and Eagle and everybody were scared to do anything about it. Coyote said, "I'll take care of this. I'll kill that Wishroosh." Coyote didn't really have a plan, but now he had to do something. Coyote asked his Huckleberries how he was supposed to kill Wishroosh. The Huckleberries told him to make a big spear with an elkhorn tip, and tie a thong to the spear so he could haul Wishroosh in. "Ho," said Coyote. "That's what I was going to do."

Coyote went out and speared Wishroosh. The thong tied him to Wishroosh and they had a terrific struggle. They tore through the mountains and made the Columbia River gorge. The water rushed through, and Fish came up where everybody could get them. The fight was hard on Coyote, made him all nervous and scraggly. Coyote was so mad at his Huckleberries he threw them way up high in the mountains, where you can find them today.

Back at my Walla Walla River campsite, a yellow Datsun pickup with a canopy pulled off the road and stopped. The driver, Ed Meincke, drew a pruning staff from the canopy and used it to nab empty cans and bottles from the bushes. He had a wispy cinnamon-white beard, janitor jeans, and a key ring heavy enough to anchor a small boat. Seeing my tent, he gimped toward it and asked me what I had. "It's the labels I collect," he said. Meincke sorted through my canned goods and explained how Campbell's labels were good for the orphanage and Heinz labels were good for something else.

Sounds complicated.

"No, it ain't," he said.

For the label on my minestrone can, he gave me a full eight-ounce can of V-8 juice. "These were on sale," he said. He led me to the pickup and handed me a loaf of ice from his cooler. I carried it to the canoe, and he followed. He wanted to know how my camp stove worked, and I showed him. I told him about freeze-dried turkey tetrazzini.

"Well, what'll they think of next?" His bushy eyebrows lifted above child-blue eyes. "No, no, I ain't hungry. No, thanks."

Meincke was from Chicago. The family gave him up for dead years ago, but he went back for a stamp show in 1986 and looked up two brothers. "Surprised the hell out of 'em," he said. "I like it better out here than Chicago. I got a place in Walla Walla, and I get to the river about every day."

We sat on the bank and I fretted about the wind.

"What's the hurry?" he said. "You ain't goin' nowhere today. Maybe in the morning she won't blow so hard."

But she did blow hard. All the next day. Meincke dropped in with more ice and today's special—"Ocean Spray orange juice, six for a dollar at Safeway," he said. "Just what the doctor ordered." He put a six-pack with the ice in the canoe. "No, no, put that away," he said. "Your money ain't no good here."

If Indian culture gave way to immigrant culture like sand through an hourglass, the narrow middle of that hourglass is right up the Walla Walla River here. The Whitman Massacre in 1847 spurred the United States to take in Oregon and Washington (including Idaho) as U.S. Territories in 1848, and one of the first acts of the new government in Oregon City was to hang five Cayuse for their alleged part in the massacre. All across the territory, Indian battles flared. East of the Cascades, here, Indians raided wagon trains. Homesteaders and white vigilantes responded with hot furies of butchery called the Cayuse Indian Wars. To the Walla Walla Valley in May 1855 marched Isaac Stevens, governor of Washington Territory, and General Joel Palmer, Superintendent of Indian Affairs for Oregon. Guile, not warfare, was their strategy. They got the Indians to cede thirty thousand square miles—the best parts of the Columbia River basin east of the Cascades—in exchange for reservation land that was mostly rocky, dry, unproductive, the worst of the West. It was an astounding deal. Nearly all the land-change, all the river-change we know today, stems from the Treaty of 1855.

Meincke had nothing better to do, so we drove twenty miles up the river to Wai-i-lat-pu, "the place of the people of the rye grass." Here, where Mill Creek enters the Walla Walla, the Whitmans had their mission. We looked at monuments to the Whitmans and walked past foundations of the old buildings and saw where the baby drowned. The vee between the streams was sedge marsh and tall grass, rich lowland. Sycamores, now grown up, had been brought here as shade trees.

I was interested in the Treaty of 1855, how the Indians gave up the world, but there was nothing about that at Wai-i-lat-pu. Meincke said he thought there was a rock memorial about the treaty at Whitman College. So we drove another eight miles into Walla Walla—past fields of onion, garlic, and wheat—to the campus. We found a plaque on a boulder at the amphitheater, but it didn't say much.

Meincke left me at the college library, where I found "A True Copy of the Official Proceedings at the Council in the Walla Walla Valley." The Treaty of 1855. I guess what surprised me was it was so readable, in forty-eight single-spaced pages of typescript, and I had never read it. Nobody I know has actually read it.

Governor Stevens's and General Palmer's first challenge was to get the word out that they were convening a treaty conference. And then who would speak for the Indians? Stevens decided he was dealing with Nez Percé, Walla Walla, Cayuse, Yakima, and Umatilla, but the Indians, roaming the land in small bands, didn't think that way about their groupings. It was messy, confusing. The Nez Percé, for example, numbered some 2,500 and were by far the largest group. Their leadership was so scattered that Stevens brought along an eager young Nez Percé who liked school and had changed his name to Lawyer. Stevens called Lawyer a chief, and recognized him as spokesman for all the Nez Percé.

On Monday, May 21, the commissioners arrived at Walla Walla and waited—and waited—for Indians to appear. Seven days later, enough of them had. Stevens and Palmer delivered brief opening remarks. Lawyer gave a pep talk, citing advice from a Great Chief Ellis: "The Nez Percé are all going straight, yes! . . . Ellis's advice is to accept the white law."

The next day the Council opened before about 1,800 Indians. Stevens introduced the interpreters and asked if the Indians were satisfied with them. The Indians knew of no others. Over the next four days, Stevens and Palmer spoke at great length, addressing the chiefs as "My Children."

Stevens offered the carrot. Separate lands had been tried with great success on the plains, he said. The Great Father put Cherokee Indians across a great river into fine country where they have their own laws, their own schools, their own mills and shops. We should do that here, he said. "Then you the men will be farmers and mechanics, or you will be doctors and lawyers like white men. You will have your own teachers, your own farmers, blacksmiths, wheelwrights." Not only that, Stevens said, "but we must pay you for the land you give to the Great Father. . . . We will be friends forever."

General Palmer showed the stick. He spoke in a lengthy parable of Christopher Columbus, and of war and whiskey. "Thousands of Indians were killed and but few of our people were killed in the battles. . . . These Indians then began to see that they had acted very foolish. Their game was all killed.

They had nothing to eat." He reminded the Indians it had been just fifty years since Lewis and Clark came down the big river, followed by traders and missionaries. And now wagon trains of immigrants. "You cannot stop them. Our own Great Chief cannot stop them. Can you stop the waters of the Columbia River from flowing its course? Can you prevent the wind from blowing?"

At the end of each day, the Indians were invited to speak. They chose not to. Concluding the fourth day, Stevens said, "My Children: My brother and myself have opened our hearts to you. We want you to open your hearts to us."

Five Crows said, "We are tired."

Pee-o-pee-mox-a-mox said, "I know the value of your speech from having experienced the same in California, having seen treaties there. . . . You have spoken in a roundabout way. Speak plain to us. . . . We require time to think, quietly, slowly."

The Council took Sunday off.

On Monday, June 4, Lawyer told Governor Stevens, "If you will designate someone to speak first, he will speak. If you do not, they will sit here all day without speaking."

Stevens designated Lawyer to speak. Lawyer invoked the Supreme Being Our Maker and deferred to the wisdom of "the President who has made up his mind for us poor people." And then some of the other Indians began to open up.

We-at-tan-at-tee-me said, "My land it is for you and for me. It is not for ourselves here that we are talking, it is for those that come that we are speaking."

Pee-o-pee-mox-a-mox said, "My heart has to separate so. I do not know for what lands [the interpreters] have spoken. If they had mentioned particular lands, I should have understood them. . . . I like you Americans. . . . Although you have said the whites are like the wind. You cannot stop them."

The next day, Governor Stevens explained how rich and bountiful were the reservation lands proposed for the Indians. In addition to all the advantages of living on reservations, he said, "You will be allowed to go to the usual fishing places and fish in common with the whites, and to get roots and berries and to kill game on land not occupied by the whites; all this outside the reservation."

But he was not dealing with children. This was no beads-and-trinkets-for-Manhattan kind of deal.

Steachus said, "My friends . . . Interpret right for me . . . If your mothers were here in this country who gave you birth, and suckled you, and while you were suckling some person came and took away your mother, how would you feel then? This is our mother, this country."

Pee-o-pee-mox-a-mox said, "My heart cried very hard when you first spoke to me, the same as if I were a feather. I thought, What will I do? I cannot give you an answer. I do not know."

This went on for days and days. Nerves frayed.

General Palmer, losing patience, said, "We don't come here to steal your lands, we pay you more than it is worth." If the Council were to adjourn without agreement, he said, "we might have a great deal of trouble. Gold has been found in the country above yours. Our people are very fond of it. When our people hear of gold they will come here by hundreds. Among those will be some bad people, and those bad people will steal your houses and your cattle. You cannot prevent it. But if you are living in these reservations, we can protect you and your property. . . . Will you receive our talk or throw it behind you?"

Can-an-pello said, "How do you show your pity by sending me and my children to a land where there is nothing to eat but wood?"

How-lish-wan-pum said, "Your words since you came here have been crooked."

Palmer's reply was off the mark. Stevens came to his rescue, saying everybody was tired and they should adjourn until the following day.

The next day, in a surprising development, Pee-o-pee-mox-a-mox said he and General Palmer had had a talk. He had been promised a house at the mouth of the Yakima River. "Our hearts should not be otherwise than one," he said.

Joseph (father of the famous Chief Joseph) said, "It is a place for our good to live there. I am going without talking, and you don't know my talk."

On Saturday, June 9, Governor Stevens opened the Council with papers in hand. The Nez Percé would go on one reservation; the Walla Walla, Cayuse, and Umatilla on another; Yakima on a third. He outlined broad terms and read some small print. Promise to be friendly. Drink no whiskey. And that would have been it, except a Nez Percé named Looking Glass rode in and said Lawyer had no right to speak for his people. Looking Glass said his people would sign nothing until the President, first, approved all the promises in the treaty.

The Council was abuzz. General Palmer was hot. "We did not come here to talk like boys! If the Cayuses, the Walla Wallas, and the Umatillas are ready to do what they said they would, then the paper is ready for them to sign. Tonight they can get their goods and go home."

Everybody wanted to go home. Governor Stevens, so near to closing the circle, spoke calmly. "The Council will now adjourn till Monday morning, and I trust by that time Looking Glass will have thought the matter over and we will be able to agree."

Monday, June 11. Governor Stevens called on Indian leaders, one after another. And one after another, they agreed to terms. There followed lengthy valedictory speeches by Indians and commissioners, all of one heart.

Stevens said, "My brothers, the Treaties have now all been signed. All the speeches on both sides will be sent to the President. The President will see that you have acted like men. He won't find fault even with Looking Glass. . . . We have some few presents to give you which will be distributed upon your leaving the grounds. . . . Thenceforth you will have me for your Great Chief."

These twenty-two days of Council wrote the future of Columbiana. It took only one or two more taps on the hourglass to get all the grains in place. Just six months after the Council, Pee-o-pee-mox-a-mox was taken hostage in a skirmish with Oregon Volunteers and was slain trying to escape, but Governor Stevens and General Palmer earned places in Western history as men of wisdom and evenhandedness, a reading that leans heavily on the idea that the Indians might have fared much worse at the hands of others. They might have. Stevens, soon after the Council, was hounded out of office for being too soft on Indians, and the territorial newspaper, *The Oregonian*, consistently editorialized in the 1850s in favor of genocide.

The Nez Percé did get a big reservation, including the Wallowa Mountains and good land in the Grand Ronde Valley. But prospectors struck gold there in 1860. A few years later, the U.S. squeezed the Nez Percé reservation down to one-tenth its treaty size. The man we know as Chief Joseph, son of the treaty-signing Joseph, refused to go quietly. Joseph and his Wallowa band of the Nez Percé, mostly old people and children, embarrassed the U.S. Cavalry in a bloody flight across Idaho known as the Nez Percé War of 1877. Boxed into a Montana winter, Joseph gave up, saying: *"I am tired of fighting. Our chiefs are all killed. Looking Glass is dead. The children are crying for food and we have none to give. . . . Hear me, my Chiefs. My heart is sick and sad. From where the sun now stands, Joseph will fight no more forever."*

In the years of broken promises that followed the Walla Walla Treaty, the reservations turned out to be breeding grounds of lassitude and dependency. But more than that was something Isaac Stevens and Joel Palmer could not have anticipated. The land changed. The river changed. Dams, logging, farming, and mining rendered all but meaningless Stevens's assurances that these fish-dependent peoples could fish in common with whites "at the usual fishing places."

The places are gone.

13

EAST GORGE
Still in the Brown Country

On the third day at the Walla Walla River, the wind still howled and trees swayed. An eighty-one-year-old small-motor repairman brought his wheelchair to water's edge, caught and kept bluegills and threw back small perch. Meincke came by, bearing ice, and I visited with four retirees from Lewiston who were not catching channel catfish. Late in the afternoon, the wind eased. I struck camp, bagged the gear, and headed out of the Walla Walla estuary, prepared to turn back if open water was too rough.

It was not.

As I turned the corner into Wallula Gap, no whitecaps ripped the Columbia. The river lost its chop and lay calmer as I paddled on. It was a very fine thing, for a change, to reach for a bladeful of water, pull it back strong, and feel that jump-ahead glide of canoe over smooth water. Because I'd started late in the day, the sun was falling as Wallula Gap gave way to a widening Columbia. Ahead, the river lined up with a pile of pinking cotton clouds where I understood Mount Hood to be, and when the sun peeked around them it purpled harsh cliffs and threw deep warm shadows toward the river. Shirtless, wearing only cutoffs and the straw hat, I paddled into sundown like the end of a tearjerker movie. Camp, when it came, was a gentle slope of coarse black sand under cottonwoods. For the first time on the river—not the last—I pitched the tent by starlight and cooked in the dark. Campbell's mushroom soup and freeze-dried beef bourguignon. A shooting star scratched the eastern sky, and it was one of those evenings that make a river worth its trouble.

At daybreak a breeze stirred the cottonwoods. The wind huffed the flame to sputtering under my breakfast soup, and blew out the fire. I loaded up and put the canoe into a rising westerly and the staccato slap of water against the bow. The goal today was to reach McNary Dam and get through the locks, just twelve miles away, and hole up in Umatilla for resupply. I was down to my backup canister of cooking gas. Soup and granola bars were gone, and I was low on sandwich fixings. A restaurant meal and a motel in Umatilla, I thought, would do just fine.

But the gorge isn't a place for schedule. With the wind rising, I should have pulled off when a wide cove showed up on the shore. But the Northwest Guild of White Pelicans was convening there, and it would have been rude to barge in on them. When it became clear I would not make it to McNary Dam, I scaled down my expectations. Hat Rock State Park was just a couple miles farther on.

The *slap-slap-slap* against the bow changed to rolling swells. I placed stones in the canoe to settle it, but the stones shifted and the canoe took water. I put ashore and dumped the water, and the stones. When I got back on the river, wind caught the bow each time it swung more than a couple of degrees off head-on. Short, quick-and-heavy strokes on the paddle, always on the left, kept me off the rocks, but there was no glide, no rest. Whenever I could—not often—I dragged the canoe ashore and took a breather. In eight hours, I moved only three miles.

Close to where the map showed Hat Rock State Park, I

hiked up the rocks to scout: Was the park wind-protected and worth reaching? It was. Now I had to put the canoe on the river one more time and turn this last corner. Hunger, not courage, was the deciding factor as I timed the waves, pushed off, and surfed around the point into a narrow flat-water bay.

NO CAMPING, the sign said. DAY USE AREA. I walked a quarter mile up the road, looking for the camping area, before I decided this was too far to haul my stuff. Back at the canoe, cross and tired, I swept a willow flat free of goose poop. When I opened the food bag, the whiff of white gas knocked me back. I hadn't properly corked the gas canister that morning, and the gas soaked what was left of my food. I spread things to air, and soap-washed the eating tools in cold water. My freeze-dried meals were okay inside their packets, but now I had no gas for cooking and petro-stench was in my clothes, on my hands. The sandwich material was ruined.

If it were just bad luck—wind and delay—I might have hiked to the camping area and cadged food without shame. But misfortune weighs lighter than incompetence, and now I didn't want to face another human being. I found two Butterfingers and a pepperoni stick buried in the thwart-bag. These would have to fuel me to Umatilla.

Bad Day at Hat Rock was not just the day I got old. It was also my sixty-first day, August 16, the end of two full months on the Columbia.

Doubt crept in. I hadn't really questioned, since Redgrave Canyon, that I could canoe the whole river. With time, with patience, I could paddle it all. But now the river gorge was saying, *Don't bring that canoe in here.*

I'd misjudged, for one thing, how long the gorge is. When you live in Portland, you think the gorge is that spectacular stretch from the city to Hood River, but it actually starts way out east, here—at Wallula Gap. Now, too, the Columbia had collected all it would from the Rockies and turned huge toward the Cascades. My canoe was a small piece of work on this wide, windy water. And the gorge is bordered at waterline by highway or railroad. Shore is riprap—the unnaturally sharp rock filler supporting roadbed or track. Once you're on the water, it's hard to get off. More than once I thought of calling Cousin Doug for a tugboat ride through the gorge.

But a river can take hold of a man and make him stupid. I fought for every inch of shoreline on the way to McNary Dam. The river shouldered and slapped the canoe—*Get that small stuff out of here*—and I hammered back. Approaching the dam, I saw the locks on the right, on the far side. The only way to cross the river was to slip close to the dam, into the windbreaking lee of the spillway. I crossed the river. The locks swallowed 35 million gallons and dropped my canoe, like a thin sliver of soap, seventy-two feet to the river below. When the gate swung open, wind rushed in, and I fought it to a standstill, beaching the canoe on the rocky right shore just below the dam.

Umatilla—and food—now lay on the other side, across the river. Between me and Umatilla, the Columbia roiled through a quarter-mile-wide channel. In the channel bobbed fishing boats, anchored or motoring against the current. Gulls swooped and squawked.

The sensible thing would be to inch down the Washington shore for a couple of miles, past the bridge, and cross the river after current settled. But then I would have to paddle back upstream to Umatilla. Or I could leave the canoe on the rocks here and hike across the bridge. Eat. Rest. Resupply and carry stuff back. But Umatilla was right there, straight across the river.

I aimed the canoe at the dam, and pushed off. I thought it would be smart to paddle hard upstream and then quarter into current, so the river would translate my work into a quick push to the Oregon side. *Guess again,* said the river. As soon as I quartered, the Columbia snatched the bow and swung it three quarters. The world spun, and I took the deep breath for going down. But the canoe was still under me, the sky still on top. The river heaved, and fishing boats flashed by as I backpaddled, first for balance and then to clear the vortex of a bridge abutment racing upstream. Umatilla left. The river bucked and grabbed, but missed, and I caught an angle to slackening current that finally pushed me to the Oregon shore.

In Umatilla that noon, after paddling back to town, I attacked a big breakfast of hotcakes and bacon and eggs at Bo Jac's Landing. I couldn't finish it. I became nauseated. Recalling the decisions I'd made, and got away with, that morning, I grew smaller and smaller, stupider and stupider. By the time I laid tip-change on the counter, I could have sat on one of those dimes and dangled my little rubber legs off it free. Back at the canoe, I spread the tarp on a pebbled slope and fell into a deep, open-air sleep. When I woke up, the river lay flat. And when the river lies flat, it's time to go. I quick-shopped for provisions and rejoined the river.

The walls of the gorge fell away for a spell, and sky spread north and south as well as east and west. The Columbia's channel and barge traffic hugged the Washington shore, so I paddled the Oregon side. Sandy and brush-lined banks separated the river from flat chaparral plains where, in August, the only color was in green disks of cultivated land under rotating sprinkler pipes. Up the Umatilla River is Indian country—one of the three reservations set aside in the Walla Walla Treaty. Up the Umatilla is also cowboy country—the biggest rodeo in the land, the Pendleton Round-Up, where horsefolk stampede in a week-long September celebration of a wild west long ago fenced. Down the Umatilla, here where it meets the Columbia, I saw wheat country, fruit country. Grain silos were the tallest riverside structures. Barges pulled in to load up, and trucks groaned under loads of melons.

Irrigon—a string of fruit stands and truck stops—had a tidy green riverside park, with clean sand beach. Indian fishermen mended nets on the grass. Mexican parents barbecued chicken while their kids splashed and jabbered in cool blue river. It was Friday, early evening, and the air was sweet and rich. Happy farmers unloaded a truck and built a pyramid of thumper-luscious melons on the grass in preparation for the Irrigon Watermelon Festival. Starts tomorrow, they said. I joined the human chain passing melons, and soon dropped one. "Oops! It busted. Clumsy me." Spitting seeds and carrying my broken prize back toward the canoe, I hailed the tractor-mower guy and asked him about camping here at the park.

"No camping," he said, "but nobody cares. Down at the end, there. I'll set the sprinklers so they don't come on 'til eight in the morning. That be okay?"

Leaving Irrigon at daybreak, I surprised a family of mule deer grazing below the idle conveyor belt from a grain silo. Next came a wildlife preserve—more deer, raccoons, geese, and pelicans. A bald eagle. The wide sky darkened and gray clouds dropped veils of moisture that reached for, but failed to touch, dry earth.

Before the wind ripped the river too bad I reached Board-man, a gas-food-and-lodging kind of place with short trees and tall road signs on Interstate 84. Although dusty, Boardman looked new. The Army Corps of Engineers had moved the town from its lower elevation—now under water—when John Day Dam went up in 1968. At the Dodge City Inn I found the Longbranch Room and melded into a stool-row of real men with rough hands and baseball caps. The row of us drank cold draft beer. We ate beef. We ate chili-and-cheese potato skins and watched the ball game—Giants 3, Mets 2—and then switched to CNN for the Persian Gulf match, Bush calling up reserves, Saddam woofing, and the world seemed far far away, like a place you might want to visit someday.

You could drive from Boardman to Arlington in twenty minutes, but it took me two days. Two half-days. As a rule on the river, now, mornings were tough for wind, but not impossible. Afternoons were impossible.

You'd think the wind would blow itself out, but it renews itself each summer day as the jet stream pushes marine air off the Pacific, and cool air drifts inland. Portland will be ten degrees cooler than the gorge. The sun above cloudy Portland has already heated the flat skillet of high plains, east, and the temperature differential increases. Atmospheric pressure builds up. On a weather map, you'd see a big *H* off the coast, and a big *L* east of the Cascades. As high pressure seeks low, air rushes into the Columbia River gorge like through the neck of an expiring balloon.

I got an early start from Boardman, but soon the wind cranked up. Crow Butte State Park was on the wrong side—the Washington side—of the river. Whitecaps rolled up the river. Near shore, I put it in compound low and kept paddling. There arose the curious sensation I was stationary, and each stroke of the paddle simply pulled more river east. The only consolation for this tough going-nowhere was that my earlier calculations about how many strokes equal a river were way off. Over a million, for sure.

The first opportunity for exit was a good one. A string of small islands on the left protected a narrow lagoon. I ducked into a gap between islands and paddled the lagoon to a boat launch. Bob and Corina Neher, potters from Walla Walla, had come here with three hyperactive boys, the oldest about kindergarten age, to windsurf and camp. I didn't know where I was. Was this a place? Bob Neher told me I was at Threemile Canyon, the site made famous by the film *Hard Winds a-Blowin'*.

Surfers' luck rises in inverse proportion to canoers' luck, of course. The stiffening wind meant the Nehers could rig up their boards and go, while I looked after the kids. The two oldest could talk. They had seen two rattlesnakes this morning, they said, up by the stinker toilet. The boys wanted to go look again, but I collared them for a lesson in rock-throwing.

Two Indian women with children drove a plum-colored van down the gravel access road and parked at the boat launch, and the Neher boys played at lagoon-side with the children. It was hot. No shade. The women stayed in the van and kept the motor running for air-conditioning. They didn't get out until three Indian fishermen brought an open fiberglass boat into the lagoon.

I walked to the boat ramp and asked the men how they did.

Maybe they didn't hear me.

I asked again. Any luck?

One of them looked up from the net he was folding and regarded me with cold, silent anger. Maybe the fish box was empty, and he was mad at the first person who asked. Or perhaps the fish box wasn't empty and he thought I was the law. Non-Indians can't use nets on this part of the river, and Indian fishing is heavily regulated. The times Indians can fish, the gauge and placement of their nets, and the types and sizes of fish they can keep are all closely monitored. Even the purpose—for subsistence, for ceremony, or for sale—is watched, primarily by tribal fish-police but also, occasionally, by undercover cops from state and federal agencies. For all they knew, I might be a fish cop.

Just curious, I said, and excused myself.

When Corina Neher returned from surfing, an Indian woman got out of the van to talk to her. The Neher boys had shared Popsicles with the children, and now the woman offered to pay for them. I don't know if Corina was more surprised that her boys had shared or that the woman wanted to pay. Indian pride was at stake, and it met with confusion and embarrassment, thanks and no thanks. Money was wrong.

Bob Neher returned from surfing and wandered over to the fishermen, now with their boat on a trailer and ready to go. Neher asked if he could buy a fish. For dinner. The Indian group—men, women, and children—convened.

Nope. No fish.

Neher came back shaking his head at the curious ways of Indians. If they had no fish, why would they have to talk it over?

Soon after the van motored off, the oldest Neher boy screamed bloody murder near the boat ramp. "Come look!" There on the rocks, thrashing, still alive, was a white sturgeon—possibly illegal, maybe a little smaller than a forty-inch keeper—that the Indians had left us for dinner.

Bob Neher filleted and broiled the sturgeon. He served it with onions, beans, and wild rice. It was one of the best meals on the whole Columbia, brought short only when the wind died and black flies swarmed camp. The Nehers opted to head for Boardman rather than camp at Threemile Canyon. I was left alone to think about small kindnesses that loom large on the river. These Indian people had not spoken a word to me. They couldn't stay to share the meal they had provided, probably for fear of giving up their names.

Sunday, August 19, turned into a howler by mid-morning. Near Arlington, a carp jumped off starboard. The wind flipped him into a full-gainer, and he reentered the river tail first. It was all I could do to coax the canoe around the rocky hook into Arlington harbor and hole up for the day among freeway break-takers who looked, if possible, more frazzled and travel-numbed than I.

But the next day awoke gloriously calm, and stayed that way. The sun arced high over the wide blue river and somehow, somewhere, the big *H*s or big *L*s aligned in rare balance. Good thing, too, because shore was an endless wall of granite riprap on both banks. No exit. I paddled long and hard that day, anticipating wind that never came. When the water rippled in early afternoon I felt the breeze at my back, not in my face, and a light east wind pushed the canoe along. I passed up a green campground at the mouth of the John Day River and crossed the Columbia to be ready to enter locks the next morning.

On that wretched rock shore, however, I would have needed a sledgehammer to sink a tent stake. On a bench one hundred feet up was the smelter of Columbia Aluminum Company. There was no place to camp and it was only 3:00 p.m., so I put on shoes and a clean T-shirt, like going to town, and walked onto John Day Dam. At his control booth I found Jim Petersen, the lock operator, a narrow-faced scarecrow in jeans and plaid logger shirt, tennis shoes, and a brass Corps of Engineers belt buckle.

"Don't know if I can put you through today," Petersen said. He had a world-class squint. "Got a barge scheduled down the river at 2300 hours, but it's a hazardous load. Can't put you on it."

Hazardous?

"Petroleum barge. When the tanks are empty, you get fumes. Flammable."

Ordinarily he would put me through the lock alone, he said, if no piggybacker was due. But the lock was disabled and slow. There had been an accident. A week or so ago, a barge heading upriver had pulled too far forward. It rose beneath a lip on the upstream gate, smashing the ironworks. Now the Corps was using a floating bulkhead, manipulated by a tug with a crew of five, to plug the upstream opening with each lift and drop.

I suggested maybe someone could drive me around. A white Corps pickup was parked right there.

"This is the tallest single-drop lock in the world," Petersen said. Maybe he was lonely. Certainly he was friendly. He seemed to want to keep me here, and he had numbers. "It's 108 feet deep," he said. We peered down into the lock. "It takes 43 million gallons to drop a single load. That's enough to generate $2,400 worth of electricity, retail."

Canoe passage through a lock is a hold-your-breath experience even when the lock is working right. This one, the deepest in the world, was broken. Couldn't we save the people 43 million gallons by driving me around the dam?

Petersen didn't pick up on this. I couldn't think what to do, so I went for a walk.

John Day Dam had the glare of new white concrete. Its powerhouse was over on the Oregon side, a third of a mile from the lock. The wide river and the high sky dwarfed the size of the dam until I took a few puny steps across it and stopped at the fish ladder.

No fish came up as I watched, but this ladder is one of the best. The watery staircase is about twenty feet wide, with staple-shaped weirs that make resting pools for salmon on their way up a series of switchbacks. The outflow of water at the ladder's base attracts homebound adult salmon, and their climb is less demanding than falls in the river used to be. Paradoxically, the *ease* of man-made river, slow flow and higher temperatures, is more baffling to adult salmon than the physical barrier of the dam. If the fish get here, they can pass. It's not just the fittest who make it all the way back to spawn. Weaker and smaller salmon join the parade of unnatural selection, drumming new and ominous strains into the gene pool. We've changed what it takes to find home.

Fish ladders address only half of the fish-passage problem. The other half is downstream passage. The young ones arrive here from the swift and shallow streams where their parents spawned. About five inches long, silver with faint vertical black stripes, young salmon are called smolts while their inner-body workings are changing to adapt to salt water. As they approach the dam, some get sucked into the turbine blades and emerge stunned and belly-up below the dam, easy prey for squawfish and gulls. The rule of thumb is there's a 10 percent kill-rate at each dam for outbound fish, and the migration path can include as many as eight dams if the smolts are coming from the Snake River.

Before dams, spring floods flushed young salmon to the mouth of the Columbia in three weeks. Now the outbound journey can take three months. The delay can be deadly. It fouls up salmon's biological clock for adapting to the ocean, and it exposes them longer to predators in the reservoirs.

To speed things up during the out-migration period—mid-April through June—river managers send more water downstream than if power were the only consideration. Fish move faster—except when they don't. Some of the water still goes through turbines. Some of it bypasses the powerhouse and plunges through a dam's spillway. Spill can bubble nitrogen into the fish's blood, causing an affliction similar to what, in humans, is called the bends. Seagulls love spill. Power people hate it, because it doesn't generate electricity.

Another way to get smolts past the dams is to collect them far upstream, load them into tanker-barges or trucks, and carry them to a release point below Bonneville Dam. The Corps began barging fish in 1977 and keeps barging them today in the face of vigorous opposition by naturalists who insist that fish need to feel their way down the river in order to later find their way back home. Common sense is on the side of the naturalists. The numbers, depending on whose you use, can be read to support the Corps argument that artificial transportation is a useful supplement to natural fish passage. Barging, and the funding for it, continues.

A third way to get young fish down the river became visible as I walked across the dam. A rail-mounted gantry crane lifted a fish screen from its slot in the powerhouse. I was surprised at the size and complexity of this fish screen. If it were laid flat, you could park a Winnebago on it. It hung vertically, and had moving parts. An endless belt of tough nylon mesh scrolled around the frame, its rotation powered by a motor in the bowels of the dam.

A maintenance guy told me it takes three screens to block a single turbine intake. So there were forty-seven others in place at John Day Dam. The idea, he explained, is that the scrolling face of the screen diverts fish into a flume that carries them around the powerhouse and into a slippery-slide to the river below. Light, a powerful spotlight below each fish screen, helps attract young fish into the flume. The bypass system was installed here just a couple of years ago, its flume and screen-slots drilled into the dam at a cost of a million dollars per screen.

Does it work?

"They say it does," he said. He adjusted his hard hat, looked off, and gave me an I-just-work-here grunt. "See those wires?" He pointed to a set of fine steel wires off the face of the powerhouse, like a musical score without notes. "Those are to keep gulls off the tailrace," he said. "If the turbines weren't killing fish, we wouldn't need those wires. When fish come through, the seagulls still go nuts."

Man and the river. At the turn of this century, an estimated 16 million salmon and steelhead annually came up the Columbia River to spawn. Now about 3 million do, and about 90 percent of those are hatchery fish.

This was the summer of 1990. Later that year, Indian tribes and sport-fishing groups would petition the National Marine Fisheries Service to list wild runs of Snake River sockeye and chinook salmon under the Endangered Species Act. This hadn't happened yet, but word of it was on the river. Senator Mark Hatfield in the fall of 1990 would convene a "Salmon Summit," collaring all the usual suspects—power, irrigation, barging, logging, and commercial fishing—in an effort to find a regional solution that would avoid a federal fix. Special interest groups were hiring lawyers and biologists to put their own spin on the fish problem. Power blamed fish harvest. Commercial fishermen squared off against loggers and the Forest Service. Nearly everybody blamed dams, as the most obvious and visible cause of an enormously complex problem.

*   *   *

Word reached me through the maintenance guy's radio that Petersen was filling the lock. I jogged back across hot bright concrete, awakening leg muscles that hadn't been called upon all summer. A cabin cruiser, a pleasure boat, had radioed Petersen from below the dam. He was bringing it up. Which meant I could soon go back down. I went to the canoe, put the life jacket on, and watched the tug crew remove the floating bulkhead. The cruiser floated out at lake level. When the light flashed green, I paddled into the lock and waited for the bulkhead to float into place behind me.

Petersen told me to tie up to a mooring bitt. A mooring bitt rides a vertical groove on the lock wall, floating up and down as water level changes. But the bitt bobs and jerks a canoe. I'd learned that it's better to hang on, loose, than to tie up tight.

"Up to you," Petersen said.

He opened the downstream release valves. There came a great low rumbling as I rode the water down, slowly down, into the dank gloom of the lock. The creaks of the mooring bitt echoed off the far wall as shrieks, and small leaks of water sounded like waterfalls. A stress-pop in the steel bulkhead came to my ear as cannon fire. A drop that ordinarily takes twelve minutes consumed over half an hour, and I thought about Petersen up there with his knobs and switches, holding back the Columbia River. The lock smelled like a potato cellar, and then like the flu. Air temperature went from August to November. My sweat turned from clammy to chill, but I couldn't take my hands off the mooring bitt to put on a shirt.

Petersen shouted some garbled words down into the chamber, and I came to understand I was at river level. Hoping he was right, I waited for the front gate to swing open and expose the world. But this was a gate that rises, all of one piece. Petersen drew the gate up slowly, letting lock water meld into the river's new surface. By the time daylight appeared beneath the gate, all the water-boils died. I paddled from November back into August on smooth river, waved my hat in thanks to Petersen, and picked up strong current below the dam.

I was still in the brown country, east of the Cascades. Green Oregon, the Oregon of tall trees and rainy reputation, hadn't started yet. Rust-colored cliffs came to the river in tiers of long-ago lava flow, but the ages hadn't yet sanded the river's rough-cut. Weird rock sculpture angled from the cliffs. High above the rimrock sloped gold velvet hills never broken by plow, and reflecting it all was the big river. Strong current swept the canoe downstream toward a flattening orange sun. No wind. Without wind, I could look off the water. Without wind, the smell of chalky driftwood and what—peach?— wisped across flat water to the canoe. Birds called from low willows along shore, and the river, for all its problems, was alive.

Mount Hood, my home mountain, rose high in the near distance, its white cone floating on blue nothing.

The wonder was that the river could be so easy, after being so hard. So friendly, after being so mean. Here the current flowed and the large waters echoed that long-ago time when the mountains were people and Coyote prepared the earth for humans, and the river cradled all. Mother earth was not a metaphor but an expression of the proper order of things, and fish returned each season as affirmation and renewal. Collected, here on the moving Columbia, came all the river's springwater bubblings and glacial drip and the suspended grit of worn-away mountains, all of us borne along the slope of continent to the sea.

14

CELILO

She Who Watches

The wind shut me down early the next day. Between two fingers of brittle rock on the Washington shore, a sand beach rose into low dunes with waist-high snakegrass. Snakegrass, mashed under the tent floor, made a soft but noisy mattress, and I dug a fire pit and staked the rain fly against the canoe for a windbreak. After a swim, I stood at shoreline for the moment or two it took to blow-dry. Across the water, the Deschutes River came in through a crease in brown-pillow hills. Miller Island, a sacred site where the river people had their sweat lodges and burial grounds, rose downstream in the Columbia like a marooned piece of red-rock Utah. On my shore, posted signs warned not to remove Indian artifacts.

From the snakegrass camp, I walked down the train tracks for a look at where Celilo Falls used to be. The great falls in the river are gone now. Celilo village, too, the hub of Northwest civilization for thousands of years, was drowned when The Dalles Dam went up in 1957.

Not so long ago.

I was twelve, maybe thirteen, when my mother packed the family in the green Chevy and Dad drove us to Celilo Falls. We took the cliff-snaking old gorge highway out of the Willamette

Valley, past The Dalles, to this hard-baked treeless land where the Columbia thundered into rocky chutes and broken islands, cascading over crooked flat steps in the riverbed. The river frothed and boiled at the foot of each step, throwing spray to the sky.

The air was thick with smoke, too, and we walked down from the road into a knock-you-back smell of pink salmon on drying racks, salmon smoking, and piles of rotting fish heads, tails, and guts. Gulls screamed. It was chaotic. Dogs and brown kids had the run of the place, and the dwellings—made of scrap lumber, tar paper, plywood, corrugated tin—might have been thrown together only to last until spring flood. Truck and car parts littered the village, but the village was not poor. Many of the shacks had TV antennas, a new thing, and of the cars that were complete there were Cadillacs and Chryslers, caked with dust.

Rickety wood platforms reached over steps of the falls. Indian men, roped at the waist, stood on these platforms and dipped hoop nets on long wood poles. The best of the salmon leapers moved quickly and got through, taking ten-foot vertical jumps to the next-highest ledge of river. Catches were in the pools and on the rebound. A salmon jumped into the falls and then slipped backward, the force of falling water canceling his leap. The fish ended up tail first, thrashing, in the waiting net. The man swung the pole and its net to shore, where a woman, waiting, thunked the fish on the skull with a club. She dumped the salmon from the net and passed it to a row of other women, who sliced and gutted it on the rocks. The women had round brown faces and flat noses and muddy eyes. If one looked up, you took a step back.

On the bank below a platform, Indian boys my age threw harpoon-tipped spears, tethered with cord. I thought they were goofing around, but one speared a salmon square behind the gills. Two boys, struggling, bent to the tether and dragged a fall chinook onto the rocks.

We stayed and watched until the sun dropped and the

Indians quit the river. Mom knew Celilo was soon to be inundated, gone forever. That's why we were there. But I don't remember any discomfort in our family about the idea that Celilo Falls was soon to go, or any great sadness about it. Progress was the way of the world. We watched this famous fishing grounds the way you might feel privileged to see the last performance of a very good play. I knew I'd seen something huge, but I couldn't have said what it was.

At my snakegrass camp, the wind blew all day, all night. Wave-caps picked up a luminescent glow from a lop-sided moon. A lone silver cloud galloped across the night and disappeared into dry sky, east. Sleepless, I watched the world go by. Low black cliffs across the river framed the flow of Christmas-lit trucks on the freeway, and the bright white nose-light of a Union Pacific freight train moved past Celilo, up the far shore. Then the Burlington Northern thundered past, just fifty yards from my tent. In the dark sky, an airliner descended toward Portland International Airport.

For the Indian people displaced from Celilo Falls, one of the hardest parts was the absence of sound. The roar of the falls had been constant. When the falls no longer roared, they say, the people couldn't sleep.

From Snakegrass that night I could see another dark crease in the Oregon-shore hills, near Biggs, where the wagon-training pioneers broke off the high plateau of the Oregon Trail. They arrived here in the fall, behind oxen kicking up clouds of choking dust, and forded the Deschutes River toward The Dalles. Their wagons carried few possessions. The heavy stuff—bedboards, chests of drawers, plows—had long since been jettisoned on the two-thousand-mile trip from Independence, Missouri. Those who could walk did so to lighten the load. They were farmers, mostly, fleeing disease and failed crops and looking for a fresh start in the green promise of Oregon, the New Eden. This first look at the legendary Columbia River must have disappointed them mightily. Nothing green grew here, and the river was only another obstacle. At The Dalles, the pioneers faced two bad choices. Some took a steep and rough track south and then west, the Barlow Toll Road, around the far slope of Mount Hood, and crossed the Clackamas River into Oregon City. Others took the wheels off and loaded their wagons onto log rafts to shoot the cascades through the lower gorge. Those who made it made it just in time for the onset of winter rains, and their first task was to convert timber to shelter.

These plain white folks were not nature lovers, were not seeking beauty. Nature was the enemy. Beyond the Cascades lay lands to be conquered, vast forests to be felled. They found their purpose not in growing things but in cutting things down. It never dawned on them that nature was exhaustible, or could finally be subdued.

To the settlers, Columbia River fish runs were the source of fabulous natural wealth. They said when the salmon were running you could walk across the river on the backs of fish. Salmon were so big they spooked horses. Apparently self-replenishing, millions of salmon arrived from the ocean each season, here for the taking. And take them they did. Great fish wheels, like half-submerged Ferris wheels, scooped salmon from the Columbia, and nets stretched across the shallows near the river mouth. Gas engines and bigger boats pushed the fishery into the Pacific Ocean. Chinese coolies worked the fish-processing plants, and then the cannery operators installed new machinery, referred to as "iron Chinks," to vacuum-fill cans.

We caught too many fish, way too fast. And as more and more people filled the land, fish habitat got hammered. Early lumber mills took their first timber near water. Log rafts scoured out spawning grounds and jammed the narrows. Logging roads pushed deeper into the forest, where clear-cuts removed shade and fouled the gravelly shallows where salmon spawned. Cattle grazed at riverside and broke down the banks. Irrigators impounded small streams and returned the water, laden with silt, pesticides, and herbicides. Dredge mining tore up streambeds and added metallic poisons to the toxic runoff from cities and roads.

And then came dams, compounding the impact of overharvest, habitat loss, and pollution. The wonder of it is that there are any wild oceangoing fish left in the river at all. The record of humans and salmon elsewhere is not encouraging. Native runs of Atlantic salmon are gone from East Coast rivers, long gone from England and Japan. These may be the last wild salmon on the planet to sustain themselves in close company with humans.

If there's hope, here on the Columbia, it's only because we got here so late. The idea that nature can be used up and then it's gone has found at least a toehold in the Northwest ethos. Civilization has begun to back off. Loggers can't cut at streamside anymore, and some drainage areas are protected. The river is not the sink for toxic wastes it once was. Harvest is severely cut back. Fish passage at the dams has improved, and science is focused on improving hatcheries and controlling fish diseases so that the subdued river can accommodate both man and fish.

The harder idea, that we might actually have to loosen our grip on nature if we are to live here a long time, has not taken hold at all. The flow of river energy from nature's use to man's use is not well understood beyond the circles of those who profit from the way things are. We plug into the river in ways that are incredibly cheap for what they really cost. If it takes *a more natural river* to save the remaining wild salmon, nobody's prepared for that.

On my third day at Snakegrass, I hiked downwind along the tracks and watched a lone sturgeon fisherman row a small boat against the waves to place his cannonball weight twenty yards from shore. If he can do that, I thought, I can go. I walked back to the canoe, packed the gear and pushed off.

It was mid-afternoon. In the lee of Miller Island, I made steady progress through a narrow strait close to the Washington shore. Past the island, I had open river and angry water on my left. Green-white waves pounded shoreline rocks. A long row of boxcars on a siding hid the village of Wishram from view. Inching on down the river, I passed a rock quarry and bucked tougher and higher waves until I reached a small cove with a boat launch called Avery. Indian children fled from my landing. They scurried into a white camper under the only good shade tree. A battered fishing boat came off the river soon after I did, and the men coolly returned my nod of hello.

Camp here? I asked.

"Okay," one said, like it's a free country.

Avery is an "in-lieu site." In lieu, that is, of Indian fishing grounds lost to reservoirs. The Corps of Engineers has laid riprap parallel to the bank and filled in the difference with crushed rock to form a flat narrow campground. Grass won't grow here, but there were picnic tables, a unisex outhouse, and spindly locust trees in lieu of shade. The asphalt boat ramp had broken off several feet above water. The Burlington Northern shook the earth when it rumbled through, and trucks from the rock quarry broadcast a fine white dust with each passing.

Three pickups were parked around the Indian camper and a pair of adjoining tents. Another pickup pulled in at dinnertime, and the driver unloaded boxed pizzas. Even upwind, I could smell these pizzas.

I ate badly, alone.

Just before dark a Pace Arrow motor home with Arizona plates lumbered in and parked. Before I realized what he was up to, the driver lopped a limb off a locust tree to make room to extend his TV antenna.

I slept badly that night, alone in my tent between one group that shunned me and one that I despised.

*   *   *

In the morning the Arizonans were gone and the wind was up. Windsurfers descended on Avery in clean Chevy Blazers and Ford Broncos and Toyota Whatevers, roof-racks loaded. River access is rare on this part of the Columbia, and windsurfers swarm to the Indians' in-lieu sites.

Before noon, a slim young Indian emerged from the camper and failed to light a cigarette with the last of his matches. He came over and we stood shoulder to shoulder against the wind and got cigarettes lit. I traded him some aspirin for a glass of cold milk from the camper. Somebody Brown was his name, and he talked about his basketball team. "I'm five-six," he said, "and I used to dunk. We have great guards. David's brother was the center but he got killed in a car wreck. Now we're looking for a center. David," he said, "will be out pretty soon."

They were fishing for sturgeon, Brown said. "So we only have to check the nets every other day. Salmon are due, but they haven't come up the river yet. River's too warm," he said. "Seventy-three degrees yesterday at The Dalles."

We leaned into the hot wind and watched the river. Across and back, sailboarders shredded whitecaps, the best of them airborne between waves. Bursting with youth and health, they took to the river in neon-colored Spandex and Lycra, some without wetsuits, and the women took my breath away. But Brown was not happy.

"They'll go right into the nets," he said, shaking his head. "Tangle them up or slice a cork line. Lose a net, you've lost $600. Or they'll sail right in front of a barge. Barge man can't see 'em down there, and couldn't stop that big mother if he did."

Brown didn't like the wind either.

"Last week two boats went down," he said. "We almost went down, but David's a good driver. I think one of the boats, *something* real heavy, is in a net across the river. We gotta get more guys to lift it. If the wind lets up, you can help."

If the wind lets up, I'm out of here.

"Right," he said.

A clutch of children and Georgia, David's wife, spilled from the camper toward a rusty Ford pickup with its tailgate wired shut. The pickup wouldn't start. David and Brown raised the hood and jiggered the whatnots. It still wouldn't start. The men slammed the hood and looked about sadly. Georgia gave the starter one last twist, and the pickup coughed to life. She and the kids, all beaming, bumped off toward The Dalles.

Later in the day I talked to a windsurfer who was rerigging his board with a smaller sail, for bigger wind. John, a young chiropractor from the Midwest, had lived in The Dalles for a year and a half, long enough to have absorbed the local folk wisdom about Indians. "Some of these guys make $80,000 a year," he said. "They don't manage it well. You see how they live. They buy a new boat and strip it, scratch it up. The treaty limits them to their own-use fishing," John said. "They should follow the treaty, but they don't. One time I paid a guy twenty dollars for a fish. He liked that."

John saw something in my face and changed the subject. He talked about the gorge, a world-class place for windsurfing. Some say the wind on the North Atlantic, off The Netherlands, is better. Or in New Zealand. Some, like John, say the Columbia River Gorge has the best windsurfing in the world. "But the gorge is filling up," he said.

Filling up?

"With people. I could sell my house right now for a lot of money. Hood River has filled up, and now they're moving toward The Dalles. People like me, looking for an unspoiled place."

Tsagaglalal—She Who Watches—is the ancient petrograph guardian of the Columbia River Gorge. She was here before the first whites paddled down the Columbia. She watched over the pre-European people we call Indians. She was here before Coyote, even. Coyote was traveling up the river, they say, making the world ready for people, when he came to a village and found Tsagaglalal living among the rocks. She was a chieftain, and Coyote was not satisfied with her version of people. "Soon the world will change," Coyote told her, "and women will no longer be chiefs. You stay here and watch the people who are coming." Coyote spun Tsagaglalal around his head and flung her against the rimrock, to watch from there forever.

I knew this much about She Who Watches from Rick Rubin, the writer and Tsagaglalalogist. Searching for her, I beached the canoe at Horsethief Lake and crossed the train tracks. I ducked a barbed-wire fence and followed a well-worn path through patchy yellow grass up into rimrock, overlooking the river. Smooth rock held small samples of faint paint— whites, yellows, reds—ground into blood-black stone. I saw petrograph arrows, deer or goats, eyes with lashes, a fish.

Where was Tsagaglalal?

She saw me before I saw her, of course. Tsagaglalal's red-paint gaze found me from flat vertical basalt ten feet above my head. Her oval face was larger than I expected, about three feet wide. Tiny bear ears rose from her head. Her eyes were raccoon-ish concentric rings, and a queer exaggerated grin spread from a small square mouth. Like any image of face in two dimensions, but more so, her eyes followed my movement. She had the goods on me. Her rock face was weather-worn and pocked with bullet holes, but Tsagaglalal was still watching, just as she had when Celilo was the center of the world. She had seen the wagon trains creep down the other side of the river. She had watched the water rise to drown Celilo Falls, and she'd seen the power lines march up the brown slope from The Dalles Dam.

"She sees you as you come," the people said. "She sees you as you go."

*   *   *

She Who Watches.

My 1961 high school class and the class behind me at Estacada included three Indian boys. All three had lived in foster homes with white families since they were little. If they knew anything about the old ways, they didn't talk about them. The prevailing view—much changed today—was that the sooner Indian people abandoned native ways, the better. Assimilation was the way to go: best for the Indian children, best for America. The boys wore their hair short and laced their best store-bought shoes for church like everybody else.

One boy was clever, funny, prone to trouble, not school-smart. Another, shy except on the dance floor, was the best-dressed in the class. The third, Norman Riddle, was quicker-witted and a better natural athlete than I. When we were little, Norman knew where the crawdads were in Wade Creek, and we poked around on the Clackamas. One rainy day my mother accused us, before she thought, of running around the house "like wild Indians." As we got bigger, he had sure hands and a quick bat and we turned the double play. The coach called him Chief. Small-town rivalry crept in. I was the shortstop, he the second-baseman, if you know what that means. Although we had comparable gifts, I was the quarter-back. We grew more and more apart. On the first day of senior fall classes, Norman and I showed up wearing, coincidentally, identical Madras shirts. He gasped and said, "Now I'll have to burn my shirt."

It could have been funny, except his grin was gone. I was the smart guy headed for college. Norman was the smart aleck who could save a game for you if he attended school that day and was eligible, which happened less and less. Norman had girls and beer. Norman was cool. Big money—government compensation for lost Klamath lands—was waiting for him when he came of age. Why should he play my game?

It also had a lot to do with expectations. A small logging town knew what to expect of Indians. They would grow up to be lazy and briefly rich and drunk and shiftless. You couldn't count on an Indian. Not that this brutal caricature arose spontaneously, without examples, but it was so firmly rooted by that time that Norman could hardly beat it.

He got his compensation money and ripped through $40,000 worth of cars and booze before I finished college.

You could predict what would happen to these three Indians I grew up with. And you'd be wrong. All three are sober and alive today, which beats the demographic odds for any sample of Indian males born in 1943. And along the way they have woven bright threads through the human fabric. The clever one, Bob Crain, did some jail time for knifing a guy in a barroom brawl, but he settled down and now runs a small logging outfit. The shy one, Bill Ray, taught at Chemawa Indian School and stood tall for congressional action to restore the tribal status of the Klamaths; President Bush appointed Ray, still the best-dressed, to the planning board for the Christopher Columbus Quincentennial. Norman Riddle was in his late thirties before he whipped demon drink and gathered the shards of his life around native ways of thought and worship to find a way "the world could include me." Now he's a counselor to the abandoned, delivering health care to the homeless in Eugene, Oregon.

Change, on the river, would be easier to judge harshly if the people who changed it belonged to a different culture, if they spoke a foreign language, if they were stupid or knowingly greedy. But it's not that easy. Cody Logging and Construction Company is the outfit to which my dad's generation, and I growing up, pegged our idea of success.

Of six brothers and a sister, my dad was the youngest. Uncle Bill, the oldest, was the one who whipped the woods. He was the star of the Oregon Dream. Bill and his son, Billy Dean, based their logging operation at a place we called Camp, up from Wamic in thick pines on the foothills of Mount Hood. At Camp, where I learned early to shoot and to drive and to fold 'em with jacks and eights, there were a cookhouse and a bunkhouse and a fire engine and low houses for married loggers and foremen. Near the shop, on a Sunday, twenty-one yellow-and-black log trucks parked with grills in a perfect line. There were graders, dump trucks, loaders, rock crushers, Cats. Uncle Bill had a modest house at Camp but a better home in The Dalles. Billy Dean married a beauty queen and built a mansion near Camp with an ice dispenser on the refrigerator door and a swimming pool and a landing strip for his plane. Later, a helicopter. If you worked hard, over a lot of land, you had to fly. You could bid on trees in the Mount Hood National Forest and also contract to build the roads to reach them. The Bills solidified their empire by crushing rock and hauling it to the rising shopping mall and to the expanding aluminum plant in The Dalles.

Their dealings with Indians went way back to when times were tough and Uncle Bill and Aunt Daisy were just getting started with a one-horse logging outfit at Lyle. A riverman of the Dave family came to the door and asked Daisy if she had two dollars for a fish. She rummaged around and found two dollars and gave it to him. When he turned to go, she said, "Where's the fish?"

"Well," he said, "I haven't caught it yet."

Uncle Bill's view of Indians paralleled his view of the entire human race. "An Indian is either a hard worker or he ain't worth a shit," he said, and Cody Logging and Construction employed many of the former. Alex Henry and his sons. Ted Santeros. Family lore has it that the Bills kept on their payroll men who had served well and could no longer work, and that they were much loved by their employees. I don't know. Maybe we build our own story about who we are and how others view us. They say Louie Henry, a truck driver and the most senior of all of Uncle Bill's men, returned to Camp late one night after a toot at the All-Indian Rodeo and made it only to the couch. His wife stepped outside and returned in high alarm. "There's a white man," she said, "passed out in your pickup!"

Louie Henry roused himself for a look, and replied, "That's no white man. That's Billy Dean Cody."

Above The Dalles Dam, power lines crested a brown hill to the Celilo Converter Station, the north end of an 846-mile direct-current line that links the Northwest federal power grid to Los Angeles. The Bonneville Power Administration once hired me to explain to the home audience why it's a good idea, sometimes, to send Columbia River power to California. It was a tough writing assignment. The words I had to work with— *federal, electricity, agency*—combine to anesthetize thought, and the one word that is sure to strike terror in the soul of Northwest Man is *California*.

But that's part of the river now, and how things work. The federal intertie takes advantage of regional differences in how and when electricity is made, and how and when it is used.

First, supply. Most of the Northwest's electricity comes from dams, from falling water. In California, they generate power largely by burning fossil fuels: coal, oil, and natural gas. The supply of Northwest hydropower varies a lot. We have years of heavy snowpack and runoff, and years of low stream flows. For the power system to be reliable, BPA plans to meet its share of the Northwest's power needs even in the worst of water years. Which means that in a normal or better water year there is power left over to sell to the highest bidder.

Demand, too, has its differences north from south. On a day in September, for example, Angelenos use more juice in the heat of the day, for air-conditioning. On the same day, Portlanders' call for electricity peaks when they turn on the heat and fix breakfast, and again when they get home from work. So the exchange of power over the federal intertie— shooting south at midday, returning north for evening—cuts down on the emissions of greenhouse gasses from California plants, at no net loss of energy to the Northwest.

Seasonal power swaps are more important. In spring and early summer, snowmelt and rain in the Northwest send more water down the Columbia than can be saved or used for human purposes here. But outgoing salmon need those faster flows. In the process of flushing fish, the water flow generates excess power that goes to California just when air conditioners are cranking up and air pollution from fossil-fuel plants would otherwise be at its worst. The whole scheme can be good for fish, good for air quality, a relief to global warming.

That's the theory. In practice, there are some environmental benefits to the federal intertie, but only when they also ring the cash register. In a year of normally abundant water, BPA sells far more power to California than it accepts back. Money from the sale of surplus power helps keep Northwest power rates artificially low. Sales and exchanges of power have little to do with the environment-energy equation today except as an argument that things as they are would be hard, economically, to change.

It's not an overwhelming argument. The counter is that a gradual lifting of this region's power subsidy would encourage energy conservation, make power exports less attractive, and give more room for operating the river in favor of fish.

At a grassy riverfront park in The Dalles, windsurfers and picnickers were gathering for a Friday night rock concert. I was shot. I'd been two nights at Snakegrass, two more at Avery, and the wind fought me for every inch of shoreline. I locked the canoe to a tree in full view of the music lovers, hoping someone might steal it, and lugged the gear to a cheap motel.

The next day, out for a walk, I remembered why I like The Dalles so much. Lawn sprinklers stitched across green front yards, and willows swayed in the wind. Fine old churches and Victorian homes spoke to a rich history of river trade, and the whole proud business was anchored by a stone courthouse, brick warehouses, and stone banks. A billboard announced that the high school team, the Indians, would open its football season at home. Walking west, I came to the shopping center, McDonald's, Burger King, and stopped at Casa del Rio. While waiting in the lobby for a table, I stuck my thumb into a stress-reader machine and maxed it out.

After enchiladas verde, I carried a rich lump of cheese in my stomach back to the motel. The trouble was thinking. I could not walk The Dalles without thinking how life as we know it is tied to energy-conversion from the river. The biggest employer in town is Northwest Aluminum Company. The industry came to The Dalles, and stayed here, because of abundant and cheap hydro. Aluminum smelting uses huge jolts of electricity to zap the tight atomic bonds of alumina in bauxite ore, rearranging them to form liquid aluminum. In 1990, one-third of BPA's Northwest energy sales went to aluminum smelters.

The aluminum companies help stabilize BPA's electrical load, drawing large and steady amounts of power even while the rest of the world sleeps. And BPA has the right to interrupt that flow if it is needed elsewhere in the region. BPA, in turn, steadies the industry by lowering the price of electricity during hard times. The variable rate, it's called. When the aluminum market is soft, BPA's rate for electricity drops and the smelters can stay in business. When the market is flush, BPA's rate goes back up.

There are good arguments for government subsidy of aluminum plants. They put out the material for energy-efficient planes and cars, recyclable pop cans, and siding that relieves pressure on the woods. They do it without the smokestacks that usually accompany large industry. Northwest Aluminum doles out 20 percent of The Dalles's annual payroll. Other and much bigger—Kaiser, Reynolds, ALCOA—aluminum plants that run on Columbia River hydropower put ten thousand people to work.

Without the variable rate, the aluminum companies wouldn't be here. If the price of electricity were to approach its true cost, Northwest aluminum companies couldn't compete with modern, cheaper-labor smelters in Brazil and China.

Say the cost of electricity here did rise, more precipitously than it will anyway to pay for fish projects and conservation programs BPA has on the books. If the aluminum companies shut down tomorrow, the Northwest federal power system would have an extra three thousand megawatts on hand. BPA could then shut down The Dalles Dam and still have enough generating capacity to meet projected load growth ten years from now. Closing the Dalles Dam could bring back Celilo Falls. Give some of the river back. The river, without The Dalles Dam, would quickly scour this section clean, and the memory of what to do with Celilo Falls couldn't have passed from the salmon gene pool in fewer than seven generations. I don't know. The Dalles Dam has no flood control purpose, and it puts out less than 10 percent of BPA's total supply. If some larger intelligence could figure the environmental and spiritual costs of this dam that drowned Celilo, and weigh those costs against benefits . . . the dam could go?

But things are not that easy. The Dalles Dam is also part

of the transportation link. Remove one lock, restore Celilo Falls, and you'd wipe out barge traffic between Portland and the wheat country. Alternatives—the railroad, the freeway— are in place, but barging is cheaper for bulky loads that can go slow. Farmers ship their wheat from Lewiston to Portland for sixteen cents a bushel. It would cost thirty-two cents a bushel by train, more than that by truck. Raw economics, though, is not the only barrier to change. The real deal is political, ideological. The government has invested millions—$370 million just recently, to upgrade locks at Bonneville Dam. Could we recognize, now, that the whole idea of commercial river traffic isn't worth it? Not likely. Not soon.

I launched the canoe from The Dalles's riverside park early Sunday, August 26. Ahead lay the most wind-famous part of the Columbia River Gorge, the final cut through the Cascade Mountains. A light breeze licked the river at dawn. Strong current pushed me through the narrows west of town, and as the river widened, whitecaps appeared. I began eyeing, already, likely places along the Oregon shore to pull off. Because I was far from the next dam, Bonneville Dam, the shoreline was beachy and easy. I could exit any time, so I kept paddling.

And then the wind, miraculously, died. It just sighed and ceased, leaving the wide Columbia under a high blue sky. I passed a row of windsurfers' beach homes at Rowena, their bright flags and windsocks hanging limp. I shed the life jacket, put the hammer down, and paddled *miles per hour.* At the big bend near Mosier I cut the corner. From the Oregon side I brushed the Washington shore and back to Oregon again while the canoe kept a straight line, slicing west. The calm river reflected bronze cliffs below gold velvet hills, and then the strata of basalt began rising from the river at the angle of a skier's jump-launch, west and up, echoing the upthrust of Cascade Mountains.

At Hood River, the St. Moritz of sailboarding, I passed

beached and hopeless Sunday hordes of windsurfers, one of whom rolled her eyes and good-naturedly flipped me the bird. Kids these days. But the river was mine, and my canoe flew. Steep bluffs near shore hid Mount Hood and Mount Adams from view, but in my mind I could see those two snow-capped sentries that flank the Columbia. The river called Hood tumbled off the east slopes of Oregon Cascades to join the Columbia, and on a plateau above town were the apple and cherry orchards that fill the Hood River packing plants. A row of homes topped the tall bluff of White Salmon, one of the several then-logging towns where my dad attended high school when times were hard.

The river sliced deep into the heart of the Cascades. I had no reason to stop, every reason to keep paddling. Already far beyond anything I'd hoped to reach today, I passed a small peninsula with a full-sized Douglas fir, like a border sign for leaving the brown country and coming into the green country. Hillsides rose thick with fir and leafy undergrowth. The tallest part of the gorge closed in on both sides of the river and I paddled in shadow, dark and warm. The ancient floods had scoured the walls clean, leaving weird cigar-shaped verticals and layered horizontals where the hard stuff was, and the dying light of day made the trees black-green above copper cliffs. Deep through the gash rolled the legendary River Oregon, the river of large poetry, of coffee-table photo books, of raw, unfinished beauty.

Gorgeous. Maybe we see beauty in a chasm like the gorge because it *is* unfinished, so recent on the geologic scale. Elsewhere, water and land have had time to reach agreeable and unspectacular terms with one another, the edges sanded and soft and easy. Here, like the rough Oregon coast where the continent still crumbles into the sea, mountain creeks blitz to abrupt ends, four hundred feet above the river, and crash to the river as waterfalls.

Mileposts along the train tracks ticked off toward sunset— 57, 56, 55—and that's how far I was from Portland, from home.

At milepost 53, wind-poofs erased the reflections off the river. The wind wouldn't have stopped me, but I was exhausted. I'd come thirty-three miles in ten hours. I pulled in at a bulge of woods between the train tracks and the river, where blackberry briers guarded a stand of small firs and vine maples. I cut through stickers, stepped clear of poison oak, and hacked out a clearing just large enough for the tent. Among these new forms of plant life—old friends, old adversaries—I cooked a quiet dinner and watched darkness fall through the limbs.

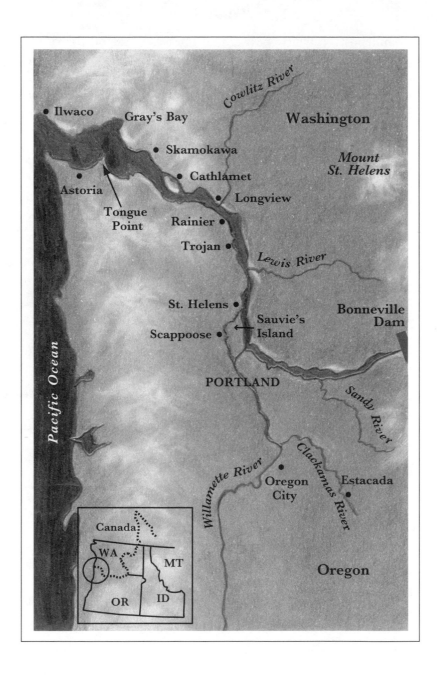

15

THE URBAN WATERWAY
To a Clearing in the Wilderness

A long time ago, when the mountains were people, a stone bridge arched the river and mountains could pass from one side to the other. Coyote, making the world ready, came up the river and found a terrible fight going on. Two brothers we call Mount Hood and Mount Adams were both in love with beautiful Mount St. Helens, who lived toward the sea. The jealous mountains threw fire and rocks at each other across the river. "I'll take care of this," Coyote said. But Hood and Adams kept spouting off. Other great mountains heard about it and began marching with their people from far away, from south and north. Coyote was so mad he smashed the rock bridge across the Chiawana and froze all the mountains where they stood, and where they stand today, the main characters tall and cold white in the Cascade Range. Rubble from the collapsed stone arch made the last angry rapids on the river's way to the sea.

Cold science doubts there was ever a stone arch spanning the Columbia, but the myth of the Bridge of the Gods is easy to read from a red-bluff scarp high above the river's north bank. Just eight hundred years ago, part of the mountain sluffed off and fell to the river. The slide dammed the Columbia hundreds of feet deep and created Cascade Rapids—a barrier to water traffic until Cascade Locks in 1896 let steamships pass.

Bonneville Dam, in 1937, plugged the river just downstream from the rubble and rapids. Like Grand Coulee, Bonneville was a mammoth federal jobs project, but it had nothing to do with irrigation. The purpose of Bonneville Dam was to generate power and to open up river shipping. Once in place, the dam and new federal power lines spread electricity beyond the cities to rural farms and homes, and cheap power lured aluminum smelters, paper mills, and steel mills to the Pacific Northwest. And then came World War II. Henry J. Kaiser, the Allies' miracle worker, built three shipyards in the Portland-Vancouver area. The yards ran flood-lit 24-hour shifts, employed 100,000 men and women, and put out 750 big warships—troop ships, cargo ships, tankers, and cruisers—quicker and cheaper than ever before or since. Righteous purpose and love of country flew high. Everybody knew the Woody Guthrie songs, and there was no edge, no irony, to the words, "Roll On, Columbia, Roll On."

Bonneville's old powerhouse and locks are on the Oregon side, and the spillway is on the far side of Bradford Island. In 1981 the Army Corps of Engineers scoured out the Washington shore to build a second powerhouse, making Bonneville Dam both the oldest and the newest federal power plant on the river. New and larger locks were under construction as I landed on Bradford Island. Ken, a mechanic, drove me in a golf cart from the shop, past vacation rigs in the visitors' parking lot, to the control room. There I was advised against water passage because of turbulence in the fifty-year-old locks. A pickup would be available soon, to lift the canoe around the dam.

Good. Thanks. I would look around in the meantime.

The elevator down to the fish-viewing room opened to a green-carpeted chamber alongside the fish ladder. Broad windows showed a bubbling green cross-section of ladder as fish swam upstream. On this August 27, fat bright chinook salmon, not knowing how beautiful they were, came singly and in pairs. Narrow steelhead swam past in tight squads. The silvers, or coho salmon, were smaller than in my imagination, less hurried than you'd expect from having felt one on a line. In the mix swam jacks—smaller salmon that had spent only a year or two in the ocean and were coming home early.

A regal chinook female nosed the window, delayed, turned tail, and let current sweep her back, as if she might have missed a turn.

Off the viewing room in a windowed cubbyhole—PLEASE DO NOT DISTURB—a woman with glasses sat at a contraption resembling an adding machine, a fish register, clicking off the official count. When I knocked on her door, she opened up and cheerfully shared her count for the day. It was before noon and she had recorded 644 fall chinook, 39 coho, and 401 steelhead. Lucille Worsham had short silver hair and a steel thermos and a joyous round face. "It's a little slow today," she said, "but when it heats up you can get seventy thousand fish on a shift. You need all your fingers, could use your toes."

Her register had subtraction keys, for fish that changed their minds. "This is only about half of it," she said. "There's another counting station, another fish ladder, on the Washington side." She talked and she clicked. She confirmed we were seeing early fall chinook. The sockeye run was finished, and coho just starting. Worsham tallied wild steelhead separately from hatchery steelhead, watching for adipose fins or not. With chinook and coho, you can't always tell wild from hatchery just by looking at them.

A prize chinook, a thirty-pounder, glided by with a hook in his jaw and a leader line trailing. Here came a steelhead with a flesh wound on his flank in the shape of a seal's claws.

A lamprey snaked by on the ladder floor.

"The strangest thing?" she said. "You won't believe this. A deer! I saw four legs coming down the ladder and it was a deer. The deer swam past the window."

On the wall outside Worsham's door were charts displaying the year-by-year fish totals, and this year to date. Numbers for 1990 were running well behind 1989, but the charts showed a sharp peak for all runs in the mid-1980s. More adult salmon returned each year in the mid-1980s than in 1938, the first year of record here and before there were dams upstream. Ocean conditions have a lot to do with the peaks and valleys on the fish-count charts, but the surge in 1986 also followed years of abundant river water through the life cycle of those returning salmon. The last two runs, 1989 and 1990, followed dry years and brought the numbers back down to about average for the fifty-two-year record. These charts certainly didn't read "crisis."

The crisis, of course, is with wild fish. Because the charts make no distinction between native salmon and their hatchery-bred surrogates, a visitor from Iowa might come away baffled about what the fish problem is. Biological diversity. Wild stocks endangered. In the year I came down, not a single wild sockeye made it all the way back up the Columbia, into the Snake, up the Salmon River to Redfish Lake and its native spawning grounds.

A Corpsman named Pat brought a new white pickup to the canoe. "We aim to please," he said. He was a canoer himself. We crossed the spillway and drove to a boat launch on Hamilton Island, a mass of earth scooped from the Washington shore to make room for the second powerhouse. At the launch, a Corps tanker truck spewed steelhead smolts through a foot-wide hose. These fish had been collected high on the Snake and delivered here, seaward of all the dams. Bright silver fish-streaks hit the Columbia in a great confused mass. They swam in excited circles before swift current took over and swept them downstream, tailfirst.

I launched the canoe and dropped to my knees for stability as the river squirreled through a narrow channel below the dam. Sturgeon fishermen lined the rock bank of Hamilton Island, and I shot past a row of small boats in a hogline, their anchor ropes taut and vibrating. Beacon Rock flew by on my right. I was watching the water for pillows and swirls when the blast of an air-horn behind me pierced the world and brought me up straight. I whipped my head around to see a barge closing down on the canoe. I scramble-paddled toward the right bank, but there wasn't time to reach shore. When the barge slid past and the waves came, I was too close to shore. You want to be either on the bank or away from it. Waves deflected off shore into an angry rip with no pattern. There's no defense, only offense, for wild chop. I powered into it, corking from ridge to liquid ridge, and the canoe, the perfect canoe for just this, kept a straight line and swept downstream.

As the water settled, I was still in the gorge but unbothered by wind. I looked up from the widening Columbia to more rock-stacked copper cliffs and basalt columns capped with forest green. Horsetail Falls, Multnomah Falls, Wahkeena Falls, and smaller white laces tumbled off the precipices, and gold lichen and maidenhair fern grew in the canyon slits, where the sun never shines. The old gorge highway—gripping contour where it could, through tunnels and across rock-masonry bridges when it couldn't—snaked the cliffs up to Crown Point, five hundred feet above the river. The Bretz Floods, they say, topped Crown Point and spilled that deep over the Portland flats. It was something to think about.

Now the Columbia, still 130 miles from the Pacific, flowed at sea level. Momentum, not gravity, drove the river. The gatherings of a whole watershed, parts of seven states and Canada, pushed the river and me toward the sea. And somewhere in the dark river below my canoe, those newly freed smolts were flowing out to the world. Their kidneys, gills, and blood chemistry would be changing now as they adapted to salt water ahead. Less than one in two hundred of them would survive the journey that would take them over nine thousand

miles—eight times the length of my own canoe trip—and back
to find the Columbia River again four years later as sleek,
full-grown adults.

The part that gets me is how they know where to go. In
what unfolding chromosome lies that drive to wide ocean, and
back to the same mountain stream where the cycle began?

One time somebody goofed and left a gate open at the
rearing pond at Benson State Park, near the base of Multnomah Falls. Young salmon slipped out into the Columbia
before they could be outplanted to creeks and gravel streams.
Four years later, in September, I happened past Benson State
Park on my bicycle. Freeway traffic had slowed. Trucks and
pickups pulled off and stopped in the westbound lanes. I
crossed from the old highway to the freeway, expecting a
wreck, and found the true horror down at riverside. Adult fall
chinook—long as your leg, thick as your torso—were beaching
themselves into a muddy trickle from the place they'd been
raised. It was awful. These salmon would go nowhere but
home, where they couldn't go. They couldn't possibly spawn.
Here was no gravel, no pure mountain stream. A trucker
picked up one of the brightest salmon in his hands and carried
it away. A fisherman booted a dark female from two inches of
muck, sliced her open and pulled out red-orange strands of eggs
by the thousands. Others of us looked about in wonder, in
despair, at these magnificent fish wriggling in from the river to
join the stench of spent carcasses lining the beach.

I have friends who call the episode of the beached salmon
a good fable, a story with a moral. Hatchery salmon, they insist,
are the enemy of a healthy fishery. Hatchery fish crowd out the
natives, diluting and weakening the gene pool. The correct
thing is not just to release-if-you-catch wild salmon, but also to
kill as many hatchery models as you can. I have friends who
have friends, eco-terrorists, who dynamite returning fish in the
pools below hatcheries.

Others say eco-terrorism is silly, romantic, a sentimental
and nostalgic reaction that sees the world as it might have been

instead of the world as it is. After more than a century of man stirring the Columbia River's fish mix, the fishery is interbred beyond any simple purity suggested by the term "wild salmon." I don't know. Fish biologists don't know. Among the dueling biologists are those who say we can do better, and not just by backing off. My own experience leads me to regard hatchery fish as real fish. Outplanted from hatcheries, spring chinook now run high up the Clackamas River, for example, past that river's dams, where there seemed no hope at all for anadromous fish when I was growing up. And I couldn't watch—nobody could watch—the beaching of those screwed-up salmon at Benson State Park without thinking of that huge homing instinct and hoping good science can help fish like these get it right.

The Columbia widened, its current slowed, and the river carried me to the white sands of low islands lined with sun-bleached driftwood and topped with cottonwoods. The first of these islands lay off Rooster Rock, a monolith known to fur traders as Cock Rock for its stiff reminder of human anatomy, and then renamed when missionaries came into the country. On the island, Sand Island, I was unloading the canoe when a pair of love-stricken nudists came strolling along the beach and deserved to be left alone.

I pushed off again, and soon felt the current slacken and die. The river here is tidal. Not that you can taste salt in it, but the river backs and breathes, ebbs and flows, to echo the same moon pull that washes shores at Seaside, or Waikiki.

The next island, Reed Island, looked so inviting that when I landed I charged without caution into a nettle patch and had to retreat into the river to cool. But then I found flat hard-packed sand to hold tent stakes. I poured boiling water into a plastic pouch that yielded beef Stroganoff, and ate apples and cheese sandwiches. Back up the river, daylight faded on Crown Point and down the cliffs of the gorge. Dusk-piercing lights of

the Royal Chinook Inn, on the Oregon side, promised COLD
BEER, a cruel trick, as an evening breeze licked the river. Cold
beer was close. Right there. But I dithered and finally gave in
to good sense, not daring to cross the choppy Columbia at
night.

You can't have everything. What I had, here, was the quiet
night river and the unseen pull of tide. What a country, this
river. For all the fumblings of man upon nature, for all the
contradictions and things I couldn't know, the river here was
a place of large beauty.

They say some people love rivers, and if you do, you do. As
if a feel for rivers is something you are born with, like blue eyes.
Or maybe a love of rivers is something you come down with,
like a fever. But for me it's more like something to work at. A
love of rivers grows deeper and richer the more you try. Here
on the island was a reward that followed search, followed
engagement and quarrel and making up. It was a peculiar kind
of love, unreligious and not reciprocal, with no more than a
quick illusion that the river might care for me.

The more I know, the smaller I get.

Walls of the gorge fell abruptly the next morning and the
Columbia accepted the Sandy River off the west slope of Oregon Cascades. At the mouth of the Sandy, fall chinook were
moving in, and a row of small boats was anchored gunnel to
gunnel in a hogline.

Fresh from the ocean, these adult salmon will gather now
in deep shaded pools in the Sandy and wait for latecomers to
show up. As they wait, their nourishment comes from deteri-
orating body parts. Skin darkens from silver to brown, mottled
with white fungus and bruise patches. When it's time, about
when the leaves turn, the salmon move swiftly and in swarms
to shallow riffles upstream.

The female builds her nest by bellying loose gravel to make
a depression on the riverbed in the shape of herself. A male

chinook swims in a slow circle around the nest-building female, and he noses off competition from other males. When the nest is ready, the male swims in parallel to the female in her nest, and presses against her. A white cloud of the male's milt drifts over the eggs she drops. River current pushes sand and fine gravel over the fertilized eggs. The female then moves upstream and tail-swishes more gravel over the nest.

The adults die. Some, nearly white, sink to the riverbed. Others thrash about in shallow pools, or flip onto shore to be picked at by raccoons and osprey. The rotting carcasses also feed bugs whose larvae will in turn feed the salmon's own young, come next spring, when the eggs hatch into swim-up fry. The cycle of the salmon continues, its end feeding the beginning.

Ahead lay the low plain of Portland-Vancouver, 1.3 million people living in close proximity. A working-day haze yellowed blue sky at the edges. A whiff of bad eggs, soon gone, came from the paper mill at Camas, and the Reynolds aluminum plant guarded the Oregon shore. I passed chic houseboat colonies, the river sucking at the undersides of Astroturf decks. Swimmers, tanners, and boaters flocked to the river. Lazy sailboats did what they could with a gentle breeze, and ornery speedboats did more, faster and louder, than anybody could want. Waterskiers looped the wide river and landed near bright tents and Perrier parasols on Government Island. The yellowy haze of population was no longer detectable once I was in it, under it, and it occurred to me, as if I didn't live here, that Portland would be a good place to live.

I paddled close to the Oregon shore. A tall levee kept the river in its place, away from low wetlands where the river used to meander and flush. Lewis and Clark paused here for a November night in 1805 and got hardly any sleep at all, wrote Clark, for the "swans, Geese, white & Grey Brant Ducks &c . . . were imensely numerous, and their noise horid." Now

Boeing 737s and DC 10s nosed into and screamed out of Portland International Airport.

On the left came the site of Vanport, which once housed Kaiser shipyard workers. Vanport was erased by the famous flood of Memorial Day, 1948, when the Columbia breached a dike, wiped out $100 million worth of property, and left thirty-three dead. My own memory—a child's dim memory—of the Vanport Flood is strangely at odds with history. Dad drove us to the city to look things over, and the lasting impression is one of great triumph, not disaster. Clearly we were rooting for the river. The floating houses were prefab wartime shacks. Poor people lived there, and it was good riddance, like what you might call today urban renewal. I wouldn't have thought *any-body* died. A bloated cow drifted among the sticks and flotsam. *It just goes to show you,* my dad might have said, and we watched without mourning what a river has every right to do.

Now that all the dams are in place, they say, such a flood couldn't happen. The city of Portland has spread closer to the river and put golf courses, a racetrack, softball diamonds, and soccer fields on reclaimed floodplain.

Great blue herons, from a rookery in tall cottonwoods, looked down on a golfer in white shoes and lime slacks, lining up a putt. Across the river stood pole walls and log blockhouses in replica of Fort Vancouver, where the British ruled Columbiana for thirty years.

Farther up that Vancouver slope—hidden, you'd have to know it's there—is the control center where BPA coordinates the Columbia River power system. The brain of the beast is bunkered into a hillside to withstand earthquake or nuclear blast, stocked and sealed to outlast sixty days of radioactive fallout. Take the elevator down, and the door opens to a Stanley Kubrick movie set with wall-mounted mapboards the size of stretch tennis courts, color-coded for high-voltage and low-voltage power lines, showing the current status of the entire Northwest grid. Lights flash on the mapboards. Blue, yellow, red, green. Buzzers buzz. Computers whirr. Power dispatchers stare at cathode-ray display terminals that sense and remote-control 14,500 miles of transmission lines and 385 power-switching substations. Electricity needs scheduling—yearly, weekly, daily, and then moment-by-moment computerized adjustments, and the moments are measured in nanoseconds—to keep the system pumped up.

Trust these people. Not just power but also irrigation, barge traffic, flood control, the Kettle Falls Sailboat Regatta, flows for fish and wildlife . . . All this gets factored in. The people and computers in the basement here run the river as if its dams were the stops on a massive pipe organ. They're playing the song that we all, without hearing it, dance to every day of our lives.

I'd traveled this way many times before, by car down Marine Drive, by bicycle, and by motorboat. But now I brought the whole river with me and saw it connected to the world. The I-5 freeway bridged the Columbia on its way north to Seattle, south to San Francisco. Past the railroad bridges, I paddled in the shadow of cargo ships lading wood pulp bound for Europe, whole logs bound for Japan, grain headed who knows where. New Hyundais and Hondas shimmered in the heat-squiggles from a lake of asphalt off Terminal 4, and a ten-story Hitachi crane lifted red and green containers the size of boxcars into the hold of *The Evergreen*. I turned the sharp corner at Kelley Point and paddled up the Willamette River toward downtown Portland, still miles away. Here were tankers linked to oil storage tanks, and flying Panamanian and other foreign flags; more Asian car carriers; and a navy destroyer drydocked at Swan Island.

The city is here because this is as far up the river as ocean-going ships can probe. And Portland is called Portland because a pair of founders from Massachusetts and Maine flipped a coin among the stumps, and Boston lost. When Captain John Couch, another of the city's founders, crossed the Columbia

River bar and set up residence at this junction of the Willamette and Columbia Rivers, he knew full well the site's potential for commerce. But what really got Couch was he could shoot ducks from his front porch.

Even today, nature is the hero among Portlanders. Nature makes us different. Salmon and steelhead surge through the heart of the city. Within an hour and a half's drive is year-round skiing, ocean beaches, or virgin timber. The idea of wilderness runs through everyday life as a kind of muffled hum, a constant low-grade emotion, even when we're stuck in town. The eruption of Mount St. Helens gave an enormous boost to Portland's collective psyche by reminding urban frontiersmen that life out here is savage, and we are trailblazers. We are still Captain Couch shooting ducks from his front porch. The myth that sustains us is that we have just emerged to a clearing in the wilderness, the sons and daughters of pioneers, self-selected for rugged individualism.

The people of a city blessed with all the good things nature has can grow smug about who they are, can find complacency in liveability polls, as if we did a lot to deserve it. Paddling through, I was struck by how little man has contributed to the natural beauty of the place. A stark gray seawall separates downtown from the river, and city-center bridges are a series of uninspired connectors, one bank of the Willamette to the other. The freeway runs the east bank, blocking access from that side and marring view from the west. What beauty we have here is in spite of, not because of, the hand of man. And Portland has its environmental problems. Smoke from field and slash burning comes wafting over town when the wind is wrong. The city is outgrowing its water supply, which falls from the west slope of Mount Hood through a series of aging reservoirs, and the backup—wells along the Columbia Slough—is threatened by toxic seep from industrial plants. The sewer system is so overloaded that whenever it rains—or more than a hundred days a year—storm water and raw human sewage spill straight into the Columbia Slough and the Willamette.

Yet Portland today is much more in tune with nature than it was when I was growing up. Restrictions on burning have cleared the summer air. The Willamette River, which used to be an open sewer for all the city's human and industrial waste, is now swimmable. Fish that once couldn't find oxygen in the sludgelike flow are back. Land-use laws and cleaner logging and bottle bills and the recycling ethic have cleaned things up. Bike paths, marine parks, and riverside restaurants bring people to the river as never before in this city. The hopeful thing is that the river can, when we let it, come clean to the heart of urban life.

I checked in at home and loitered about for large parts of two days. But rest was out of reach. The river was still going—another hundred miles from Portland to the sea. I paced the house and made a nuisance of myself. Beached in the city, I slept fitfully and found in familiar surroundings only unexpected change.

The world was different. And the difference was me. Life on the river had opened up a huge gap between how we view ourselves and how we are. A string I hated to pull on, because the more I did the more things unraveled, was rugged individualism. The government's investment in the control of nature can't be subtracted from the world as it is. When we talk about survival now, we're talking about economic survival of a people dependent upon government subsidy for using nature up. The U.S. Forest Service sells logs from National Forests at prices below the cost of replacing them. The Bureau of Reclamation waters land at little cost to farmers. The Army Corps of Engineers subsidizes river shipping, and the Bureau of Land Management gives out mineral and grazing rights as if it were still 1890. BPA pumps out the cheap electricity that keeps the aluminum smelters competitive. Now that we can do with nature what we will, the guts have been sucked from the central metaphor. The taming of the West has come less at the hands of rugged individualists than from the continuing legislative clout of Western senators and a more and more strange-seeming idea, driven by the frontiersman myth, that the river and the land are somehow unlimited, still ours for the taking.

For the symmetry of it, I paddled up the Willamette to Oregon City and the end of the Oregon Trail. Just ten miles from downtown Portland, Willamette Falls drops over a riverwide fault where the natives once fished and urban man still does. Here's where the Territorial government hanged the five Cayuse for the Whitman Massacre, and where the world's first "long distance" electric power lines carried juice from a dynamo at the falls to the streetlights of Portland in 1889. Now the falls are flanked by paper and lumber mills. Along the way to Oregon City I paddle past log booms cabled to the banks, and the wealth of suburbia laid itself out in golf courses and private properties that reached the river with wide green lawns in front of wooded mansions. Saws whined with new construction, out of sight, more people coming into the country.

On the way back from Oregon City, I poked the canoe into the mouth of the Clackamas River, my home stream. The Clackamas ran low in August. I paddled far enough for current to cancel my strokes and put me stationary, paddling but not moving.

Up the Clackamas, just twenty miles by road, maybe thirty by twisting river, River Mill Dam backs the water into a steep canyon and makes a narrow green lake next to Estacada, the mill town my folks moved to from St. Helens when I was five. You could live there and not be too taken with fish and how they get along unless your father, like mine, watched fish very closely. Dad's job as the grade school principal was just a front. The house was on the lake, and the drive to school each morning took us along the potholed lake road. Dad's way of facing the world was to gauge the color and height of the lake each morning. "River's up," he'd say. "River's clearing," or "Still too muddy." He had the clear blue eyes you'd see only in babies or very old men, and he had a great capacity for indirection, for not saying what he meant. I liked him a lot. I understood he carried another person inside him, and that person was always fishing below the dam.

Sometimes you'd see the other person go right inside him as the back screen banged and he came in in hip boots and washed his hands of fish-egg smell and changed to school clothes and caught up with breakfast.

I was the boy and could go fishing with him anytime I wanted. Truth is, I didn't like it much. You'd get up when it was still dark, and cold, and you had to cross under the spillway, inside the gloomy dam. On the other side you had to know where the poison oak was, and if you caught a fish the procedure was usually to release it. Let it go. What was the point?

I've tried to excuse my lack of interest in fish-catching by thinking Dad breathed so deeply of that passion he left none in the air for me. But that's not it. True passion is generous. Surely he wanted as desperately for me to like fish-catching as I yearned to like it, and just didn't. We never talked of such things, so I developed a slow aching failure at not living up to part of what it meant to be a man. This was not a life-scarring issue. There were other ways—in school, playing ball—I could do well the things he admired. But not the core way. Dad's fishing codes were deep and not spoken, and sometimes it was better to go fishing without him.

Once when I was little he was going below the dam for steelhead. Gary Barden and I were heading up Wade Creek for trout. I had a secret. I said to Dad I'd bet him that I'd catch more inches of fish than he did. "Good," he said. A dollar. He liked that. The secret was that Gary and I knew where big fish collected in Wade Creek below Harberts' pond. The fish there were so thick you could wade in and catch one with your bare hands. And I did. It was an ugly fish, all beat up and white-blotchy, but it was huge. I knew Dad wouldn't keep more than one steelhead, so I had him. I also knew my fish was a spawner, but I hadn't thought it through.

I lugged it home, this spring chinook, and triumphantly held it up for Dad. His face got red. Veins stood out on his neck. "It's a spawner!" he said. He put those blue eyes on me in disbelief. "You knothead," he said. *Knothead*, from this man who seldom showed anger, was extremely strong language. As the dollar fluttered to the floor between us, I was cast free to float alone in the galaxy, never to be connected to the world.

But we did share boat time, river time, and if fish-catching didn't grab me, the river part did. The best were those annual trips out over the Columbia River bar in the week before Labor Day. For him it was fishing. For me it was just being there, in the boat, riding the river out to sea and back.

One early summer when I was home from college, Dad and I put the boat in below River Mill Dam, at Carver. We bumped and skipped down the Clackamas to the Willamette, through Portland to the broad Columbia and down to St. Helens, the first family place. We had an 18-horse Johnson on the Birchcraft, and sleeping bags. Poking around, we took two days at it and slept under the stars on a Sauvie Island beach. I don't remember that anything happened. Which is odd. Something always happens on a river. Maybe you never know, while it's happening, what happens. If I was college age, Dad on that trip was the age I am now. I'd like to call him back, and ask him about it. But he wasn't much of a talker. Certainly we were not, or I wasn't, filled with large thoughts about rivers shaping who we were, my dad and me. It was just one of those things you do, a fun trip, taking the water where it was going.

Or maybe that short float on home rivers was a pulse of starlight coursing through empty black space, and you don't see it until long after it happened.

16

THE PULL OF TIDE

So Big and Soon

From Portland the Columbia turns north, accepts the Willamette River and climbs the map to find a dogleg left through
the final barrier—the Coast Range—to the sea. The Coast
Range parallels the Cascades but it's lower and more rounded,
with fir and hemlock and cedar and thick brush that closes in
and makes it hard to hunt, good for deer and Roosevelt elk.
Coast Range peaks won't hold year-round snow, but the
mountains take the first punch of winter storms off the Pacific
and pass them on as slow dark clouds that bunch against the
Cascades and drip over the Willamette Valley. It's not the total
amount of rain but the rain's winter constancy that gets you. A
whole February can go by without a sun-break, without a
glimpse of Mount Hood from the city. Whether it's raining or
not you think it is, and wonder why anyone with a choice
would live here.

The answer to that comes in May, when the roses bloom
and the dogwoods and rhododendrons and azaleas come out.
And then into summer, cool breezes off the Pacific keep the air
moving and clean, for city air, and you wonder why anyone
with a choice would not live here.

In August, now, the river left Portland and split around

Sauvie Island, flat as Holland, with berry fields and pumpkin patches. Chopped corn rows corduroyed the black earth. On the other side of Sauvie Island—three miles away at the island's broadest—lay the Columbia's deep-water channel where the ships come and go, but here in Multnomah Channel were houseboats with flowered decks and rowboats pulled up to dry. Fat white yachts poked their rears to the channel in competition for the silly name prize. Past the houseboats and farms, great blue herons topped the pilings, and a red-tailed hawk on a utility pole ruffed his white chest feathers. A kingfisher swallowed a fish in one neck-stretching gulp, and blackberry vines were alive with birdsong.

I had a touch of Virginia Wyenian frustration that the world now calls this place Sauvie Island. The place I grew up with was Sauvie's Island. That might not look like a big difference, but it was said as all one word—So-vee-ZY-lund—a spongy foreign land across the channel from Scappoose Airport.

Uncle Pat, five years older than my dad, was the flight instructor at Scappoose. When they played semipro ball together, Pat was the shortstop to Dad's second base, and they taught grade school in St. Helens before Dad went in the navy for World War II, Pat into the air force. After the war they came back to St. Helens. Dad taught school again and Pat taught people to fly small planes.

They hunted ducks, and sometimes I got to go along. From the airport, we crossed a fence and slogged through bogs to Pat's duck blind of plywood and cattails. We'd get out there before the sun came up and wade out in hip boots to place rubber decoys in a ducklike attitude on the water. Then hide and be quiet in the duck blind, where there was a bench and a gun rest on the sill of an open window. We lit hand warmers. Pat and Dad passed a flat metal flask between them and sipped from it, and daylight rose over the Columbia River wetlands. Whenever live ducks appeared in the distant sky, Pat honked on the duck call, which was supposed to bring the birds veering toward us but seldom did. Ducks aren't stupid. More often Pat's quacking gave rise to huge fits of giggles. I thought I must be missing what it was all about—these double-barrel shotguns, this camouflage rain gear, and two grown men doubled over in helpless laughter. There was something large here to live up to, but I didn't know what it was. I remember guns blazing and the smell of hot spent shells. "Out of range, I guess," Pat would say, blue smoke issuing from the gun barrels. They must have in fact killed ducks, because I remember plucking ducks, eating ducks, but I can't recall a duck ever falling from the sky.

The Columbia became open river after Sauvie's Island gave out at St. Helens. The stone Columbia County Courthouse, with its bell tower and open-faced clock, faced the river as if St. Helens were still linked to the world by water. Oceangoing ships once called here, but now most of the activity is on Highway 30, a mile away. Downtown has the old rock city hall and boarded-up storefronts and buildings undergoing renovation to capture the Old Town look, with a pizza parlor and a new-old restaurant in the St. Helens Hotel. The docks are built for pleasure boats, not the big ships.

St. Helens is the closest place to rootstock for my dad's restless family. I have a yellowed box score in which the Cody brothers are one-third of the lineup for the St. Helens Papermakers, the local horsehide nine, Pat and Bob batting two and three, Link five. The map calls the narrow island off town Sand Island. We called it The Island. It was farther out in the river then, in the same way doorknobs in the house you grew up in are now surprisingly low. From Estacada we came to St. Helens not just for duck hunting but also for summer cookouts on the island, always for Christmas, and for the stories that give rise to clan in a detribalized people. That feeling of clan is gone now. Five of the six brothers and Pauline didn't live long, their lives shortened by bacon and cream and eggnog. Only Uncle Pat's heart ticks on. The cousins, with smaller or no families, moved off the river and don't bother about where we came from. The last reunion we tried was a strain. The first thing to decide, come to think of it, was where to hold it. Where to gather. We had to think of a place.

Across the river in Washington, in the Cascade Range, Mount St. Helens is shorter than it used to be. Before the eruption, Mount St. Helens had a symmetrical dome, Fuji-like, a vanilla scoop that never lost its snowcap. Now it's a flat-top, gray in August, our newest scape in a land still forming.

There had been warnings. Indian legends told of St. Helens's capacity for tantrum. Geologists heard the volcano's early throat-clearings, and we all watched plumes of ash and steam issue from high vents for months before she blew. And still we didn't believe. When it comes to landscape forming, we think of snail-paced millennial change. We forget that most of what we see on the Columbia is the result of cataclysm, of ice dams bursting and mountains exploding, of titanic clashes between fire and ice. We don't expect anything to happen *now*. When the mountain bulged, in early May, the Forest Service blocked roads to the skirts of Mount St. Helens. But tourists swarmed in, and the owners of vacation cabins threw rocks at the road-blockers. A star on the news shows was the curmudgeonly caretaker of Spirit Lake Lodge, eighty-three-year-old Harry Truman, who vowed to stay put at his beloved lake on the north slope. No goddamned scientist was going to move Harry Truman.

When Mount St. Helens blew, on Sunday morning, May 18, 1980, it lost 1,300 feet of elevation. The northwest slope slid off, buried Spirit Lake Lodge under two stories of steaming mud, and put 100 feet of hot water on top of that. The mud flow sent bungalows and camper trailers down the Toutle River, filled the Cowlitz, and spilled into the Columbia to block ship traffic. Plumes of volcanic ash rose 15 miles into the sky. The blast leveled 40,000 acres of prime timber, which lay dead as jackstraws on a sudden moonscape; no animals, no fish, no birds, just the whirr of helicopters searching for survivors. A month later, 22 dead had been uncovered and 71 were still missing, including Harry Truman, entombed forever under a new layer of land.

In Portland, a fine gray ash drifted down for four days. We drove as little as possible and wore surgical masks to mow the lawn. Ash slid off the roof into gutters, where I collected jelly-jar samples—very dense, this stuff, extremely heavy—and carried it East on a trip, to show children of friends. Here's what a mountain is, when it falls from the sky.

From camp on The Island the next morning I followed the Oregon shore in strong current. A trio of navy battleships steamed up the channel, but their wake was cut off by islands before rollers reached my canoe. I passed the sorry house in Columbia City where Aunt Pauline used to live, and then the Deer Island flats where Uncle Link had his dairy farm until Chevron Chemical bought him out. As the river flowed north, other rivers joined the Columbia. The Lewis and the Cowlitz drained the west slope of the Cascades, across the river. Here on the Oregon side, the pitch of shore was so mild my paddle-stroke dragged sand when I was well off land. Now free from the grip of dams, the Columbia reminded me of its mild beginnings up in Canada. The pace was slow. Soft rain plinked the water. A black beaver so fat he could only waddle, not walk—remember beaver?—spied the canoe and slid quick into water. I braced for a *cha-PLOO* that never came.

The Trojan nuclear power plant billowed white vapor into heavy gray sky. I aimed the canoe into deep water to see the plant at a fuller angle, but water out there was cross-chopped and rough. I slipped the life jacket on and cut back to shore. Below the plant I beached on fine white sand, thinking lunch, and stepped out of the canoe into water sickeningly warm. Perhaps the relative cool of rainy air, not the outflow from the nuclear plant, made the water so bathlike warm. But it curled my toes. I put them right back in the canoe and pushed off.

Trojan, owned and operated by Portland General Electric, began operating in 1976 with promises of cheap, safe, and clean nuclear power. Because of the water needed to cool a reactor and to flash into steam to spin generators, it makes sense for nuclear plants to hug rivers. But here? Just forty miles from Portland, upwind in summer, Trojan sits in an earthquake red zone, directly across the river from Mount St. Helens. Safety wasn't the first consideration in 1976, but nuclear accidents at Three Mile Island and Chernobyl got more and more people interested in what we have here.

Among the horrors that had come to light by the time I paddled past was that Trojan's emergency cooling system had been defective from the start. The Nuclear Regulatory Commission time and again slapped PGE with fines for safety violations. The plant, only fourteen years old, was falling apart. Parts cracked, crumbled, broke. Safety-related down time meant the plant was no longer reliable, and it had never been cheap. Trojan was rated as the worst-performing reactor of its type in the country. Not only that, but its electricity wasn't in local demand. Even while PGE, a large private utility with many other energy sources, was exporting power for profit outside Oregon, the company mounted slick ad campaigns to convince Oregon voters that the Northwest power grid would collapse without Trojan.

(Soon after my trip, in 1992, PGE beat off a pair of ballot initiatives that would have closed Trojan immediately. Months later, with repair costs still rising, PGE decided it would be "uneconomic" to keep Trojan running. The plant shut down for good in January 1993.)

The parts of Trojan you see from the river, and will for the foreseeable future, are the massive concrete cooling tower and the reactor, a bulb-topped building like an observatory. A low metal building, the closest structure to the river, holds four hundred tons of highly radioactive fuel rods. The spent fuel rods lie submerged in a concrete pool, separated from one another to avoid a chain reaction. This pool, like the tanks at Hanford, was designed to store fuel rods only temporarily, until a permanent storage site could be found.

The Columbia turned back on itself. Jetty pilings combed a river flowing backwards, and I paddled hard to reach Rainier at high tide. Rain, like the river, stopped. The wind came up, and I set up camp short of the Rainier-Longview bridge rather than push it past the rocky palisades that defined the Oregon shore ahead. I draped my clothes across bushes to dry. After a swim, I lay in clean sand and second-guessed myself for quitting the river so soon. The wind died. High cirrus clouds laced the blueing sky. The river found its momentum again and flowed to the sea, and I watched it go.

On the far Washington ship channel, the *Ocean Cosmos* cruised out toward the sea. Its wake reached the Oregon shore five minutes later in wide swells that came to the sand in broad white sweeps. Next out went the *Toyota*, a square-stern car carrier riding high, returning empty. The *Melbourne Highway* came up the river. Across the water lay Longview, the longest stretch of deepwater port I had seen anywhere on the Columbia. Steam rose from the mills—Longview Fibre, International Paper, Weyerhaeuser, Reynolds Metals. Conveyer belts ran wood chips from barges to the wharves. At the Weyerhaeuser complex, a crane lifted whole logs into the hold of the *Morning Orchid*, no doubt bound for Japan.

Uncle John—not one of the Codys but my mother's brother, John Charles Hafenbrack—skippered tugs here nearly all his working life. He and his wife, Carrie, met me at Izzy's Pizza in Longview, and we talked about the river.

"Cap Arnold had a big tug," John said. *"The Nadine.* An early diesel, sixty-five-footer, and he always needed a boy. I was ten or twelve. I'd just ride. Maybe I hauled lines across the rafts. The peavey was too heavy for me. One time I fell in the river and came up with the peavey still in my hand. They thought that was something."

John was born in 1913. He's a little guy, always was, wore thick glasses and puffed a fat cigar.

"Long Bell thought they could fill these mills forever, from close, but they started buying logs that came down the Willamette. *The Nadine* towed booms to the mill. They'd give me fifty cents. A dollar. Let me steer the boat. I just liked it. There was always something. One time a ship hit *The Swan* and sunk it. *The Swan* was a dance barge, two stories high, with an orchestra and ornate lattice-type stuff on the upper deck. We tied it off on Sand Island and carried people and musical instruments to St. Helens. Mostly I just rode around. The men who worked the boats were a bunch of hooligans. Jailbirds. Whiskey drinkers."

John glanced at Carrie, who is quite a proper woman. He gave me his river squint, and cackled.

"If you want to know the truth," he said, "we hauled whiskey. The still was on Sauvie's Island. We loaded those five-gallon wooden kegs at night, and if the tide was right we got to Longview before daybreak. One keg for the skipper. I don't know who got the rest of it, or the money. Big shots at Long Bell."

The Hafenbracks moved up and down the Columbia during the Depression, and John was twenty-one when he finished high school. He graduated from Washington State in 1938 and went to work for Equitable Life of New York at an office in Phoenix. And to my mother's everlasting bewilderment, John *wasted* such education and promise. He came back to the river.

"Well, your mother was getting married," John said. "After Betty's wedding, I thought as long as I'm here I'll take a ride on a tugboat. The deckhand—the deckhand!—was making more money than my boss at Equitable Life. Plus it was the trees. Coming back from Phoenix, you see the trees."

Was the river here much different before dams?

"A lot different," he said. "I always dreaded high water. May. June. That was hazardous. If you're bucking high water it catches the tow, and you look for a place to hide. Tie up on a jetty. Going downstream was even worse. The tow could overtake you. You'd be dragging booms—500 feet of line, a boom 750 feet long, two booms abreast. The whole procession would sway back and forth. Dodge a ship. Miss the jetty. One time I scrambled two log rafts off Deer Island. An acre of logs. We had to pick them up one log at a time. All you hear is Vanport," he said, "but down here we had quite a time, too. On Rinearson Slough we tied booms to standing trees on the mainland. One fellow's house was floating around. We towed his house back to its foundation.

"After any big water," John said, "the river channel shifted. This was before depth-finders. You had to feel your way. Run aground. Hang up on a hemlock sinker. This was before radar, too," he said. "I was chugging through fog one day and all of a sudden I was in big waves. I looked up—way up—to the stern lights of a ship right there. Just missed. I was lucky that time. Lots of times. I was always scared. I loved the river, but I was scared of it.

"Now things are better," he said. "Everybody has radar, and the charts are true. The river stays where it is."

Friday, August 31. No wind in the morning. A strong outgoing tide swept the canoe under the Lewis & Clark Bridge and past a long clean beach on the Oregon shore where bank fishermen sat under plastic lean-tos, sipped morning coffee, and watched pole holders jammed into sand. Past a rocky headland the river turned west. I nosed the canoe into quiet sloughs and paddled like an archaeologist past the ruins of a fallen world. Houses slumped to the river at villages that once boomed on logging and fishing. Wildflowers sprouted from sagging docks and mossy foundations. Broken piers rose where canneries once stood, where the back-and-forth wash of river was taking things back. A mink, quick on brown rocks, slid his chestnut-black streak into a hole.

Five brown pelicans cruised upriver in low formation, on the wind. Sea birds! A new smell, a salt smell, came to the river and slid through tall grasses.

The sun rode high in the sky when the tide reversed and the wind kicked up. What I thought was Oregon shore turned out to be Wallace Island, which I reached only by dismounting and towing the canoe through surf across a quarter mile of shallow spit. At the wood line I dropped the food bag against a fallen tree and returned to the canoe for the rest of my gear. When I got back, my food bag was abuzz with wasps. So I left the bag to the wasps and picked another spot, down the wood line, for camp. I had water. And I had a jar of dry-roasted peanuts. Maybe the wasps would settle down in an hour or two, and I could get to my feed.

They didn't.

The next morning I packed everything else and then— wearing pants, a long-sleeved shirt, and a hat pulled low— snuck up on the food bag. When I nabbed it, the wasps rose in a frenzied cloud and raced me to the canoe, where I waved the paddle about, felt for the canoe with my free hand, and shoved off.

Only one wasp stung me, on the left earlobe. But soon my ear was on fire, swelling. An odd itch numbed my chin and neck. I put ashore at Jones Beach and dug out the snakebite kit. A windsurfer, preparing breakfast, agreed to lance my earlobe with the razor. "Hold still," she said. She completed surgery in one sure slash, bloodying her shirt and mine, and we both got woozy as she couldn't get the suction cup to work on my ear. She patched up the slit, and I sat at Jones Beach for an hour to make sure of steady heartbeat and clear vision before pushing off onto glassy morning river.

*   *   *

A six-car ferry poked out of Beaver Slough and headed for Puget Island. So I paddled there too and probed a dairy-island web of sloughs toward the Washington shore, crossing the ship channel to the quiet river town of Cathlamet. From there I took Elochocam Slough, protected from mainstream wind. Blackberries were ripe, and that was lunch. Goat-sized white-tail deer, full-grown, grazed at riverside.

I needled the canoe into a tiny backwater off the slough and came to a never-logged stand of towering trees—hemlock, Douglas fir, and Sitka spruce. How this patch of virgin forest, so close to water, escaped the ax I didn't know, but here was old growth. Here was the difference. Here were trees of mixed ages and heights and species. The dead had fallen at the feet of the live to rot and hold moisture and hide bugs and sprout seedlings from their spongy dead mass. Veils of pale green moss draped from high branches of a gray-scaled spruce that had rooted here before Lewis and Clark came down the river, maybe twice as long ago as that. I walked a slow circle around this spruce. I touched it. A tree may not know much, but it knows place. How strange it would be to know nothing *but* place, to stand here and watch centuries go by, to feel the river's ebb and flow at your roots, big tree, and hold your ground.

Not all old growth forests grew trees this size. The lower elevations and rainier climes held the monster trees. Those went first, leaving stumps you could put the dance band on. When I was growing up in Estacada, the loggers mowed down old growth at higher elevations, tall straight-grained fir and hemlock in the Mount Hood National Forest. A one-log load on a truck was rare. More common were three-log loads pulling in at the mill. I don't remember thinking we would ever run out of woods. The forest stretched from town up the Clackamas River without end, and I knew we were growing more where we cut.

Summers during my college years I worked for the Forest Service. I planted survey stakes, ribboned off timber sales, sifted dirt from rock to see that road-builders were working up to spec, and fought forest fires. Back at school, I explained to my friends the idea of sustained yield. Replant the clear-cuts, stagger those cuts along the length of a logging road, and sixty years later you could come back and start over. Sustained yield. I believed this. I think my supervisors at the Forest Service believed it. Also, I knew, the growing network of logging roads into wilderness helped fight forest fires. Forest management was scientific, modern, farsighted.

Sustained yield is the answer, but we got ahead of it. In the last three decades we marched through old-growth timber faster and faster. Ever-more-efficient computerized mills used fewer sawyers and closed mill towns even while more timber than ever came out of the woods, much of it not even to be milled here but to be exported raw to Japan.

We got ahead of sustained yield, and we didn't understand it very well. Forest management can grow trees to lumber-making size in sixty years, all right, but we can't replace an old growth forest in less time than nature took to do it, over hundreds of years. Clear-cuts, and bulldozing the deadfall and slash into burn piles, disturbed thin soils, fouled streams, and killed fish. New seedlings in the clear-cuts grew fast but not big. The trees were planted all of one vintage, all of one species, and that's not the way a forest works. Trees can be a crop. Forest, once cleared, doesn't come back soon. And now we learn that forest fires, like floods, are an agent of large-scale natural renovation. Nature manages whole ecosystems better than the profit motive has.

You can hardly miss it. Today the second-growth harvest arrives at the Estacada mill in fifteen-log loads, twenty-log loads, pathetic sticks good for little but low-grade two-by-fours. The remaining good wood, the last of the virgin rainforest, is in wilderness areas or locked up by lawsuits related to the Endangered Species Act. The northern spotted owl is the indicator species—the canary in the coal mine—around which the argument rages.

The core of the woods problem is the same as the fish and rivers dilemma. Northwest Man has skidded to the end of that easy road where we can keep taking from nature without putting back. With awareness of vanishing wilderness has come an almost hysterical overreaction. The climate of discourse today encourages a throwing up of hands and giving up on humanity. But the paralyzing environmentalist scream has served a great purpose by raising the alarm while there are still some wilderness forests and wild salmon to save.

From camp at Skamokawa (Ska-MOCK-away) the next morning, I waited for dense fog to lift and then threaded the canoe across the river past mud-shore islands that are islands only when the tide is not high, and then they show only tall grass waving on the river breeze. Colors bled together and I could imagine my ancestors crawling out of the ooze and slime. I didn't know exactly where I was. You could be anywhere, everywhere, on a rising tide of river that filled sloughs and backwater capillaries, and made its last calls before saying good-bye. The Columbia spread to a width of eight miles, salt water in before fresh water out, in a great slow flush. When the wind came up I headed into Knappa Slough, past log booms creaking down their pilings on the tide.

The shoreline was reedy mud shelves, not firm enough to hold a tent. A nip in the air, leaves on the water, reminded me it was September and I was close to summer's end, river's end, trip's end. Afternoon moved to early evening, and I paddled on. Tongue Point stuck out north into the river, protecting a wide bay, and mud shores gave way to a deepwater port. No place to camp. Ahead, waves broke off the tip of Tongue Point. I would have to hit the tide right, and the right tide wasn't now. This close to Astoria, I was pinned down between rough water and rocky shore. I pulled in, rearranged driftwood, moved rocks, chopped roots, and set up the most uncomfortable campsite I had occupied on the entire river.

The hillside above the high-water mark rose nearly vertical, heavily wooded and thick with salal and salmonberry and sword fern. I climbed to the spine and walked the promontory north until trees gave way to view.

Across the wide river was Gray's Bay, where the *Columbia Rediviva* dropped anchor two hundred years ago and claimed the entire unknown watershed for the United States of faraway America. "When we were over the bar, we found this to be a very large river of fresh water, up which we steered," wrote Captain Robert Gray in his log on May 11, 1792. These Bostonians were traders, not poets, not your marvelers of virgin shores. John Boit, a journal-keeper of the crew, set the tone when he observed: "This River in my opinion, wou'd be a fine place for to sett up a Factory. The Indians are very numerous, and appear'd very civill (not even offering to steal). during our short stay we collected 150 otter, 300 Beaver. . . ."

Also along the rocky Washington shore, thirteen years after Gray, November storms and fierce water pinned down the Lewis and Clark expedition for five miserable days. Punished by rain, wind, and cold, blinded by fog, they confused the waves and saltwater taste of the angry river for the Pacific itself. Clark wrote of having arrived at the Pacific—"Ocian in view! O! the joy."—a full week before, in fact, he had seen it.

Weather was kinder to me. I enjoyed high visibility from Tongue Point, and I knew where I was. Just ahead, clinging to the furry south slope, was the steep rivermouth port of Astoria, the first permanent American outpost west of the Mississippi River, the first U.S. post office west of the Rockies. Euro-American settlement began in 1811 as Fort Astor, a remote outpost of John Jacob Astor's Pacific Fur Company. The Americans hacked a clearing in the forest and erected a crude log trading post. News of the War of 1812 didn't reach Fort Astor until 1813. When it did, the Americans panicked and abandoned their two-year-old trading post to Britain's North West Fur Company, which renamed the place Fort George.

The fur trade brought ships off the Pacific, and trappers and Indians came down the river to meet them.

When the fur-bearing species played out and Americans arrived in force, the smells of fresh-cut lumber and fish canneries filled the moist air, and Astoria's dance halls and gaming rooms played to the largest crowds north of San Francisco. Timber and salmon, in turn, played out, and the Columbia River changed from a commercial highway to a commercial barrier. Railroads and automobiles returned Astoria to the condition of its birth and youth: an outpost. Today the big ships bypass Astoria on their way to Longview and Portland. The proudest of the Victorian mansions are museums or bed-and-breakfast places. Astoria is a tourist town. It's come to that.

I wonder at time on the river, at our brief eyeblink of time. Say the history of man on the Columbia River—from Clovis hunters to the *Morning Orchid* now passing out to sea—spans ten thousand years. Robert Gray, Lewis and Clark, David Thompson, and our written history begins only two hundred years ago. The oldest dam is only fifty. If the history of man here were a time line as long as my outstretched arm, the Euro-Americans' "discovery" of the Columbia and its rapid exploitation are all written past the last knuckle. The dams are well out on the fingernail. Trojan nuclear plant you could clip off with no pain, and my voyage of one summer's sun is too little to file.

The world goes by so big and soon. Timed where I am, old enough to have seen the wild river at Celilo Falls and young enough to imagine seeing it again, I can't know if what I saw on the river is right. But time, for the river, seemed to have reached a pivot point as great as when our ancestors diverted streams to water the first crops and built the first waterwheel to grind grain. What got me was how everything—the damage, the work, the people and wildlife, my own family—is connected to how we draw energy from the Columbia. Pluck a strand here and the web vibrates all the way back up the river and plays a tune we will hear far into the future. To imagine a world that spreads another ten thousand years and more ahead of us is to know in your bones that clean waters, ever flowing to the sea, are not just the well-spring of wild salmon but also the source on which the whole web of life, including our own species, will depend.

Astoria is as far as a canoe can go, but it's not quite the end of the river. The fishing village of Warrenton is tucked into the Oregon shore beyond Astoria, and Ilwaco sits inside Cape Disappointment on the Washington side. Jetties stretch ocean-ward to guide the river's exit. From Tongue Point, the ocean is visible only as a place where land is not, as an unbroken line of blue over blue on the horizon.

Here at the mouth is where my first impressions of the big river were formed, on those salmon fishing trips with my dad in a fourteen-foot open boat. Mostly we stayed in the river, trolling plugs or mooching herring between Buoy 10, near the river mouth, and the church at Chinook. But when Dad felt it and conditions were right, we crossed the bar and felt the surge of the whole thing, the river pushing us out, later sucking us back in.

I wonder what he was thinking. These are bad waters, "The Graveyard of the Pacific," where so many ships went down to hazardous currents, freak swells, or the rips at Peacock Spit and Clatsop Spit. Cape Disappointment is home to the U.S. Coast Guard station with the highest rate of emergency rescue missions in the country. And yet here we were, in waters where a sheared prop pin or a plugged gas line could have spelled disaster. The best I can imagine is he *wasn't* thinking. He was all feeling. He knew the river and he could read the weather, and he trusted what he knew. Something in the river drew him out there, and it wasn't just the salmon. It was the place for him to go.

When Dad had his heart attack, he and Mom were on another couple's boat. They had a radio. The Coast Guard arrived within minutes, Mom says, but it was one of those sudden endings where there's nothing anybody could do.

One time we were crabbing on the wet sands of Long Beach, on the ocean side of North Jetty. Low tide left wide depressions, tidal pools, where you could find Dungeness crab. You didn't need a boat or a crab pot. Just pick them up. Check for size, and if it was a male you had a keeper. We walked the beach as a family. Dad in the lead, followed by Mom and Mary Jane, and me, last. I toed a sand dollar and went down as if shot, doubled over in pain, and the family marched on down the beach without me. Nobody looked back. It was acute appendicitis, we found out later, and they operated at Ilwaco hospital as soon as we got there, but the initial attack took away breath and speech, and then surf overdrummed my calls for help. The family walked away. I was surprised. Maybe I was too young to know life could go on without me. My people, moving on, got smaller and smaller. There was no one else on the beach, or in the whole world, and the world was as large as I've ever known it until now.

Labor Day Monday, September 3.

The canoe hovered behind Tongue Point as I waited for slack tide, waited to turn the last corner. According to the tide book, high tide and daybreak would arrive together. But light pinked the eastern clouds and the sea was still rushing in. A wicked whorl off the point could have sucked the canoe like a bug down the drain. Slowly the hole filled and settled, the river stopped, and the air was still.

I rounded the point and paddled hard to beat the river's full force to Astoria. Ships pivoted from their anchor ropes, up-

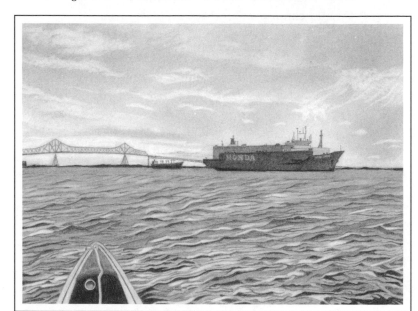

Rounding Tongue Point.

stream to downstream, and the rising sun lit the tall houses of
Astoria tumbling toward the river. The bridge arched the ship
channel near the Oregon shore and crawled low on the water
to Washington, four miles away. Before I reached the bridge,
the river caught up with things and pushed me fast, too fast,
past the legs of Astoria docks. The surge built rollers. A departing trawler complicated the water and forced me away from
shore, and then it was all backpaddle to cut to the inside of the
bridge pier. Scared spitless of missing the narrow opening to
the West Boat Basin, I hit it, and paddled low and small among
large yachts at moorage.

The world wasn't awake yet. I pulled the canoe onto the
dock, just glad the trip was over. The satisfaction of having
come a long way hadn't caught up with me. If I'd been in the
mood for a crowning act, it would have been to fill the canoe
with rocks and sink it to the riverbed. A bright-eyed yachtsman
with a steaming mug of coffee came down the gangplank in

deck shoes and captain's cap. He noticed my odd equipment for this place.

"How long you been on the river?" he asked.

The answer came floating up like a long-submerged log from a forgotten pool. Not eighty-two days, not just a whole summer, but *Since I was little.*

A Note About the Author

Robin Cody is a freelance writer. In 1986 he won the Silver Spur Award for short nonfiction. He is the author of *Ricochet River*, a novel, published by Alfred A. Knopf in 1992. He lives in Portland with his wife, Donna. His daughter, Heidi, graduated from Wesleyan University in 1992 and also lives in Portland.

A Note on the Type

This book was set in a version of Monotype Baskerville, the antecedent of which was a typeface designed by John Baskerville (1706–1775). Baskerville, a writing master in Birmingham, England, began experimenting in about 1750 with type design and punch cutting. His first book, published in 1757 and set throughout in his new types, was a Virgil in royal quarto. It was followed by other famous editions from his press. Baskerville's types, which are distinctive and elegant in design, were a forerunner of what we know today as the "modern" group of typefaces.

Composed by Com Com,
a division of Haddon Craftsmen, Allentown, Pennsylvania

Printed & bound by Arcata Graphics/Martinsburg,
Martinsburg, West Virginia

Maps and illustrations by Heidi Cody

Designed by Cassandra J. Pappas

FALLOUT

Todd Strasser

CANDLEWICK PRESS

Copyright © 2013 by Todd Strasser

Photograph on page 260 courtesy of the author

First edition 2013

Library of Congress Catalog Card Number 2012955123
ISBN 978-0-7636-5534-1

13 14 15 16 17 18 BVG 10 9 8 7 6 5 4 3 2 1

Printed in Berryville, VA, U.S.A.

This book was typeset in Cambria.

Candlewick Press
99 Dover Street
Somerville, Massachusetts 02144

visit us at www.candlewick.com

For My Father

It is insane that two men, sitting on opposite sides of the world, should be able to decide to bring an end to civilization.

— JOHN F. KENNEDY
on the Cuban Missile Crisis,
October 27, 1962

1

I wake to a hand on my shoulder. Dad's voice is urgent.
"Get up, Scott!" The light in the bedroom is on, and I
squint up into his face. Dad's eyes are wide, and he's shaking me hard, not gently, the way he usually does when he
wants to wake me.

"Up! Now!"

I rub my eyes. An inner clock tells me that it's the
middle of the night. My heart starts to race with alarm.
"What . . . ?"

"We're being attacked." He swivels to my little brother
Sparky's bed. "Edward!"

Attacked? As my brain claws toward alertness, I hear
sirens wailing in the distance. Not the melodic bursts

of code directing volunteer firemen to a fire. These are shrill swooping wails.

Sparky groans and tries to roll over. Instead of arguing, Dad scoops him up, blankets and all. "Put me down!" Still half asleep, Sparky kicks as Dad cradles him and turns to me.

"Come on!"

Barefoot, heart heaving with panic, I race after him out onto the cold hall tiles, where we nearly crash into Mom, who's carrying an armful of things she's just gotten from the kitchen.

"Hurry!" Dad barks, and we scurry down the hall. In the dark playroom, he opens the closet and, with a loud clatter, sweeps away whatever toys and games lie on top of the square metal trapdoor. Outside, the sirens continue to blare.

"What's going on?" Sparky cries, awake now.

Mom dumps the things from the kitchen on the floor and pulls him close. "It's okay. Don't be scared."

But now loud banging sounds echo down the hall from the front of the house.

I gasp. "What's that?"

Without answering, Dad yanks the metal trapdoor up and points down into the square of darkness. "Go!"

I can't see a thing. "How?"

Crash! Glass smashes somewhere in the house.

"What's happening?" Sparky wails.

"It's okay," Mom says soothingly. Then to Dad: "Hurry!"

I feel Dad's arms pick me up and lower me into the emptiness. My feet dangle in the dark air. Frightened that he's about to let go, I dig my hands into his arms. "I can't see!"

"Feel the rungs with your feet!" he commands.

I find a cold metal bar with my toes just as footsteps slap into the playroom. It's Janet, our maid who stays over one night a week. She's pulling a light-blue robe closed, and her eyes are moons of terror.

"Go down!" Dad barks at me.

"Richard?" From somewhere in the house, a man's voice calls through the dark.

The metal rungs hurt the bottoms of my bare feet as I lower myself. The dark air in the shelter is cool and damp and smells like mildew. Suddenly boxes and bags of things shower down, bouncing off my head and arms, and falling into the shadows below. I cry out in surprise, even though it doesn't really hurt. Already Mom's feet are on the rungs just above me.

"Hurry!" Dad yells.

"Ow!" Sparky cries, and I wonder if Dad accidentally banged him into something as he tried to lower him through the trapdoor.

One of my feet touches the cold concrete floor; the other steps on a box that collapses with a crunch.

"In there!" a man's voice shouts.

Above me, Mom yells, "Careful, Edward!"

Suddenly there's scratching and grunting overhead. Sparky cries out, and Mom gasps loudly. Something big is plummeting down, and I barely have time to jump out of the way before Mom crashes to the floor with a horrible, crunching thud, Sparky on her chest.

"Mom!" A terrified cry tears through my throat. "Sparky!"

two

"Me could eat horse, Kemo Sabe," Freak O' Nature said in the diction of Tonto, the Lone Ranger's Indian sidekick. Freak O' Nature's real name was Norman Freeman, but his friends called him Freak O' Nature because . . . well, because that's what he was.

It was the last week of fifth grade, and he, Ronnie, and I were lounging on his lawn listening to Freak O' Nature's black transistor radio, which lay on the grass broadcasting the game between the Yankees and the Cleveland Indians. Mickey Mantle, playing for the first time after a month on the disabled list, had just smashed a come-from-behind pinch-hit home run to put the Yanks ahead 9–7.

"Who wants to bet they still lose?" asked Ronnie, wearing a colorful Indian madras short-sleeve shirt that was the current height of style.

"Me hungry," said Freak O' Nature, who sat cross-legged, all sharp, bony angles, with brown hair, freckles, and thin metal wires across his upper and lower teeth from his bite plates.

Lying on my back, feeling the grass tickle my neck and ears, I gazed up at the puffy white clouds in the blue sky. The June sun warmed our faces and arms. In a few days, school would end, and we would have all summer to play baseball and swim and have fun.

On the radio, the Indians' pitcher Gary Bell got Clete Boyer out on a ground ball and Bobby Richardson swinging. But it didn't matter. The Mick was back, and the Yanks were winning.

"Want a Sara Lee cheesecake?" Ronnie asked as he sucked on a stem of clover he'd plucked from the lawn. He was a stocky, muscular kid with black hair greased back along the sides of his head into a ducktail, while the front hung down in a spit curl.

The thought of sweet, creamy cheese filling and graham-cracker crust made my stomach rumble with anticipation. Even though it was only an hour before dinnertime and a sure bet to ruin my appetite, I asked, "How?"

"There's a million of 'em in Linda's garage."

Ronnie might have been exaggerating, but we got the point. The houses in our neighborhood didn't have basements, so people put freezers in their garages and filled them with food.

"You mean, steal it?" I sat up and tugged nervously at the hair behind my ear. I'd never stolen anything . . . except for the stuff it was okay to steal, like cookies from the kitchen when Mom wasn't around and our Halloween candy from the shopping bag Dad hid in his closet so Sparky and I wouldn't eat it all at once—but really, we suspected, so he could eat some of it, too.

"It's not stealing," Ronnie insisted. "We know Linda. Besides, you ever looked in their freezer? It's so full, they'll never notice if one cheesecake is gone."

Linda Lewandowski had four brothers and sisters, so it made sense that there might be more food in the freezer than her mother could keep track of. But even if there'd been enough cheesecakes to fill Yankee Stadium, that still didn't make stealing right.

Freak O' Nature gave me an uncertain look. "What you think, Kemo Scott?"

"What if we get caught?" I asked.

Ronnie plucked another clover from the lawn and sucked on it pensively. "What difference will it make? We could all be dead tomorrow."

3

From above come grunts, banging, and scraping—the sounds of a scuffle. "Richard, let us in!" someone shouts frantically. "Don't let us die!"

Petrified with fear, I crouch on the concrete floor beside Janet, who climbed down after Mom fell. The still forms of Mom and Sparky lie in the dark while Dad clings to the metal rungs and tries to pull the trapdoor closed. But people on the other side are trying to pull it open.

The light's gone on in the playroom, and the shelter brightens each time the trapdoor rises a few inches, then darkens again when Dad manages to yank it down. With each flash of light, I glimpse Mom on her back, one arm stretched out, one leg bent at the knee, the other propped against the wall, Sparky sprawled on top of her.

My brother begins to whimper. Janet draws him off Mom and into her arms. I can't tell if he's hurt, but at least he's moving and making sounds. Unlike Mom, who lies perfectly still.

The trapdoor rises enough to let in the wail of sirens. Someone shouts a curse. Dad's feet are wedged into the metal rungs. His teeth are gritted with exertion as he struggles to close the door. I want to beg him to let the others in. But I don't because this is something I've been scared of ever since he first told me about the shelter, since I realized we were the only family on the block who had one. What if there are dozens of people up there? What if more are coming? What if they all try to squeeze in until those of us at the bottom are crushed to death?

The trapdoor rises. A thin metal tube slides in and swings around as if trying to hit Dad's arms and break his grip. It's a pole from the badminton net.

"Scott, the rope!" Dad shouts.

My eyes meet Janet's. "Do what he says," she tells me.

I look up at Dad. "Where?"

"On the wall!"

We're in a narrow corridor lined with cinder blocks. From a previous visit down here, I know that the wall he's talking about is around the corner, in the shelter itself.

But the small amounts of light seeping in from above don't reach that far. "I can't see!" I yell.

"The light!" Dad shouts. "On the string from the ceiling!"

I scuttle into the pitch-black shelter. Stopping in what I think should be the center of the room, I wave my arms around until I feel a string and pull. A lightbulb bursts on, and in the glare I see the kitty-corner double-decker bunks and wooden shelves lined with food and other supplies. On the wall, a coiled rope is looped over a hook. I grab it. Back out in the narrow corridor, Janet is comforting Sparky, who's staring fearfully up while Dad struggles. Mom still hasn't moved. Something dark is pooling under her head.

A tennis racket slides through the gap between the trapdoor and the closet floor. They're using it as a lever to pry the door open. Dad reaches down and grabs the coil of rope from my hands. Now, in addition to the badminton pole and tennis racket, fingers appear along the edge of the trapdoor. First a few, then more and more, turning white around the fingernails as they strain to pull upward.

The trapdoor starts to rise. The rope falls to the floor beside Mom as Dad tightens his grip on the latch. He grits his teeth and struggles, but the hands from above pull the door higher, and through the gap I see bare feet, pajama-clad legs, the hems of robes . . . then faces peering in — tight lips and clenched teeth like Dad's. The door rises another inch. Dad is being stretched, the skin of his stomach showing between his pajama top and bottoms.

"Uhhh!" he grunts, and lets go.

The trapdoor flies open and light spills in, accompanied by yelps and thuds as the people who were pulling fall backward. The badminton pole and tennis racket tumble down on us with dull thunks. Janet and Sparky cower. Mom doesn't react. Familiar faces crowd around the square opening above. Ronnie and his father. Mr. McGovern and Paula . . .

Clinging to the rungs in the wall, Dad gapes up at them. "There's no room," he protests meekly.

The faces grow determined and grim.

"Go down, Ronnie!" Mr. Shaw shouts.

"But Scott's dad said —"

"Go!" Mr. Shaw yells.

Ronnie's bare foot feels for the top rung. Dad reaches up and swats at it.

"He's stopping me!" Ronnie cries.

Ronnie's feet rise as if he's flying away. They're replaced by bigger feet. Dad swipes at them, but the feet kick back. Legs in blue pajamas force Dad down the rungs.

"You'll kill us all!" he protests.

Ronnie's dad answers with a curse and takes another step down.

"Watch out for Mom!" I cry at Dad, who momentarily freezes when he sees her crumpled below.

Meanwhile, Mr. Shaw and Ronnie are coming down, while others crowd around the trapdoor waiting their turn. Dad hops from the bottom rung, trying not to step on Mom.

"Get her into the shelter!" he yells at Janet as he quickly slides his hands under Mom's shoulders. Janet grabs Mom's ankles, and together they maneuver her around the shield wall. Sparky runs into my arms, his heart beating as fast as a hamster's as we follow Dad and Janet. My last glimpse is of Mr. Shaw helping Ronnie off the rungs while more people climb down. The nightmare is coming true. We're going to be crushed.

four

You never knew what might come out of Ronnie's mouth, but on that June afternoon, our heads filled with baseball and cheesecake, the suggestion that we could all be dead tomorrow was unexpectedly jarring.

"What are you talking about?" Freak O' Nature asked him in a normal voice.

"Nuclear war," I said, since that was the only thing that could result in all three of us being dead by the morning. All year long, the Communist threat had been growing as the Russians spread their influence in Asia and South America and even to a little country called Cuba, which was an island somewhere south of Florida ruled by a

Commie named Castro who had a scruffy beard, wore a green army uniform, and smoked cigars.

"My dad heard the Ruskies are sending ships filled with fighter jets, bombers, and missiles to Cuba," Ronnie said. "And if we try to stop them, it'll be war."

The Russians were evil. Their chubby bald-headed leader, Nikita Khrushchev, had crooked teeth and an ugly gap between the front two, which showed that Russians didn't even believe in orthodontia. And if that didn't make him anti-American enough, there was the time he'd come to the United Nations and banged his shoe on the rostrum, which proved beyond a doubt that the Commies were unpredictable, violent, and crazy enough to blow us all up.

Clover stem squeezed between his lips, Ronnie pushed himself up to his feet and reached down, offering me his hand. "Come on, let's eat."

I felt my stomach tighten at the thought of the proposed criminal enterprise.

"Well?" Ronnie's hand was still out. I grabbed it, just like always.

Freak O' Nature scooped up the transistor radio and sprang to his feet. He was the only kid we knew who could go from sitting Indian style to standing without using his hands, this being one more piece of evidence of his general freak o' naturedness.

We walked along the sidewalk past our neighbors'

homes, each on a quarter acre of property with a front lawn just large enough for a bunch of eleven-year-old boys to play touch football.

As the three of us neared Linda's house, I couldn't help wondering how Ronnie expected to get a cheesecake out of the freezer without one of the numerous Lewandowski children, or Mrs. Lewandowski herself, catching us.

Relief washed through me when the Lewandowskis' garage came into view. "It's closed," I announced, trying not to let on how much better I felt now that I wouldn't have to help Ronnie steal.

"Because they're not home," said Ronnie. "Linda told me she was going to the doctor this afternoon."

The Lewandowskis had a station wagon, and whenever Mrs. Lewandowski took one of her kids somewhere, all the others had to go as well. It was not unusual to see their car weaving erratically down the street, Mrs. Lewandowski steering with her left hand while reaching back to smack one misbehaving child or another with her right.

"So . . . what're we gonna do?" I bit my lower lip nervously.

"Go in there and get us a cheesecake," Ronnie replied, as if the answer were obvious. He stopped at the end of the Lewandowskis' driveway and gazed at the house, which was the color of chocolate pudding.

My queasiness leaped up a notch; intentionally

opening a garage door seemed to imply a greater degree of juvenile delinquency than merely wandering in. I reached behind my ear and took hold of a few more hairs. "You mean, open the garage door?"

"No, Scott, I'm going to walk right through it like that scientist in *4D Man.*"

"Nothing can stop him," Freak O' Nature said in a deep ominous voice, quoting from the TV commercial currently promoting the movie. "A man in the fourth dimension is in . . . de . . . struc . . . ti . . . ble."

By now my reluctance had risen to the level of near-paralysis. "You sure about this?"

"What's the big deal?" Ronnie asked impatiently. "The Lewandowskis are our neighbors. We share stuff all the time."

"But we ask first," I said.

"If they were here, I'd ask." Ronnie took a few steps up the driveway, then stopped and looked back at us. "You guys aren't *chicken,* are you?"

5

Leaving a smudged trail of blood on the concrete floor, Dad and Janet get Mom to a bunk. Ronnie and Mr. Shaw, in their pajamas, stumble into the shelter and look around. Mrs. Shaw, in a pink bathrobe, arrives next. From around the shield wall come shouts of people urging each other to hurry and go down.

Dad spins to face Mr. Shaw. "We're all going to die," he growls as Paula comes in with tears running down her face. "There're already too many. There won't be enough food or water for all of us."

Mr. Shaw and my father face each other for an instant, then march back around the shield wall. Meanwhile

Sparky's still holding on to me, and I can't stop looking at Mom, now cradled in Janet's arms, and wishing she'd move. Ronnie and Paula also stare. Mrs. Shaw pulls both of them to her.

On the other side of the shield wall, Dad and Mr. Shaw shout that there are too many people. Loud grunts and curses follow, as if there's a fight. A man shouts, "My daughter's in there!" In the shelter, Paula cries out, "Daddy!" Her sobs grow louder, and Mrs. Shaw hugs her and says it's going to be okay. But that can't be true. There's a nuclear war and Mom's bleeding and too many people are already in the shelter and more are trying to get in.

The fighting and yelling grow louder. Sparky's grip on me tightens as he pleads, "Make it stop!"

Mr. McGovern staggers around the shield wall with a long red scratch across his cheek. Paula breaks away from Mrs. Shaw, but before she gets to him, there's a sudden bright flash of light as if someone on the other side of the shield wall took a photograph.

A woman's scream pierces the air.

The bulb in the ceiling goes out.

Everything turns dark.

The sirens in the distance stop.

"What happened?" Sparky asks anxiously in the inky void.

Clang! On the other side of the shield wall, the

trapdoor slams shut, and I hear a clank as if a bolt has been thrown.

It is pitch-black in the shelter.

The momentary silence is broken by Paula's sobs, then into the darkness come ragged breaths — Dad's and Mr. Shaw's. From around the shield wall come thuds of fists drumming against the trapdoor. A muffled female voice cries hysterically, "Richard! Richard!"

It's horrible. I cover my ears, but it doesn't help. More thuds and frantic begging join in. "Please!" "For the love of God!" "Don't let us die!"

"I'm scared!" Sparky wails. In the blackness, his sobs join Paula's.

"Don't listen," Mrs. Shaw gasps, as if such a thing might be possible.

Despite the panicked shouts coming from the other side of the trapdoor, there is a strange stillness in the shelter.

"Scott?" Dad says somberly somewhere in the dark.

"Dad?" Ronnie says at the same time his mother says, "Steven?"

"I'm here," Mr. Shaw answers, breathing heavily.

Loud clanks and thumps fill our ears as those left above beat at the trapdoor. But it is made of quarter-inch iron plate. Nothing short of a bazooka could blast through it.

"Make it stop," Sparky pleads.

But it doesn't. There's no getting away from the agonized cries of those who've been locked out. Stomach cramped, heart racing, I fight back tears and wish the banging and shouting would go away.

Now there's a new, more distant sound . . . growing steadily louder like thunder. Then a roar, and one last awful scream that disappears into deafening clatter and crashing. In the dark below, I cower over Sparky and imagine something like a tornado above obliterating everything in its path.

It rumbles over us, followed by a few muffled thumps. And then . . . quiet.

SIX

"Keep an eye out," Ronnie told Freak O' Nature, and continued up the Lewandowskis' driveway. Feeling lightheaded with misgivings, I followed, wondering if Ronnie felt that way, too. He had to know that stealing was wrong. Was a Sara Lee frozen cheesecake really worth this much anxiety?

At the garage door, I glanced back at Freak O' Nature, hoping he would signal that someone was coming and we should abandon this unlawful endeavor. But he wasn't even looking at us. Instead he was staring down at his radio as if watching the words come out.

Ronnie took hold of the garage-door handle. The door creaked upward, revealing a shadowy interior that smelled of car oil and dry grass and was crammed with bicycles, toy carriages, and Hula-Hoops. Without a word, he marched toward the back. The freezer was one of those horizontal models, and a small cloud of chilled white vapor rose into our faces when Ronnie lifted the top. The inner walls were caked white with ice, and it was filled with rectangular packages of chicken pot pies, frozen vegetables, Swanson TV dinners, and the treasure that we sought, Sara Lee frozen cheesecakes. Ronnie picked up a box, covered with a thin film of ice crystals.

And that's when the Lewandowskis' station wagon pulled in.

7

"Turn on a light!" Sparky sobs. Paula's still crying, too. It's impossibly dark.

"Give me a moment," Dad says wearily, his words interrupted by deep breaths.

Above us, there's only silence, as if the world has stopped.

Or disappeared.

"*Please,* Dad?" Sparky implores.

"Yes, Edward," Dad answers in his soft voice. There's a faint rustle in the blackness as he feels around for a light.

"Mom?" I say.

She doesn't answer. I wonder if Janet's still holding her. I'd give anything to hear her reassuring voice.

Paula continues to sob in the dark. It's just her and her dad. Not her mom or brother. My stomach twists. I hate to think of what's happened to them. Our mom may be hurt, but at least she's here.

There's a soft slithering sound like Dad sliding his hands along the wall. "Everybody be still," he says. "There's a flashlight around here somewhere."

Clinks and scratching follow, as if he's touching things.

Crash!

People cry out in surprise. For one terrifying instant, I imagine that the roof of the shelter is caving in, then realize it was just a bunch of things falling from a shelf. Dad curses, then says, "Sorry, everyone."

"You all right?" Mr. Shaw asks.

"Yes."

"Dad, *please* turn on a light," Sparky begs.

"I'm trying, Edward. Believe me, I'm trying." There's frustration in his voice. Things jangle and scrape as he sorts through whatever fell.

"What about the light from before?" Sparky asks.

I don't want Dad to get angry, which he sometimes does when we ask too many questions. So I tell Sparky, "It won't work. There's no electricity anymore."

"Why not?"

There's a clunk and Dad grunts, "Damn it!" as if he banged his head.

"Are you okay?" This time it's Mrs. Shaw who asks.

"Yes." But he sounds even more frustrated. Sometimes when he got this way in the house, I would hide in a closet.

"Why isn't there electricity?" Sparky asks.

"Because the bomb blew everything up," I tell him.

"I didn't hear a bomb," my brother says.

"Be quiet," Dad snaps. "I'm trying to think."

"But I didn't hear a bomb," Sparky whines, his voice breaking. "Just turn on the light."

"Quiet!" Dad bellows.

Sparky starts crying again. Fearing Dad will get angrier and yell even more, I pull my brother tighter to me and shush him the way Mom would. More clinking and scratching follows. Then, finally, a click and a light goes on.

It takes a moment for my eyes to adjust, then I see Dad near the bunks, shining the beam from a long silver flashlight on Mom, whose head is on Janet's lap. My breath catches; there's a big red stain on Janet's robe. Mom's hair is dark and gummy, and in the dim light her skin looks almost gray.

"Mom!" Sparky wails rawly. He bursts out of my grasp and flies toward her, but Dad catches him.

"She's going to be okay," he says, swinging the flashlight beam away. I bite my tongue not to say what I'm thinking, which is that she doesn't look like she's going to be okay. Dad has to wrestle Sparky, who's still struggling to get to Mom. "We have to leave her alone, Edward," he says softly. "We have to let her get better." He holds my little brother gently but firmly.

"Listen to your father," Janet tells him.

"But what's wrong with her?" Sparky asks anxiously, craning to see around Dad.

"Mr. Porter, is there a first-aid kit?" Janet asks.

Dad aims the flashlight at some shelves. "Get it, Scott."

I rise, and that's when I notice Mr. McGovern and Paula near the shield wall. Paula's curled in his arms and weeping miserably. Mr. McGovern hugs her, his eyes glistening.

They're half a family.

It's . . . horrible.

eight

"Run!" Ronnie yelled.

We sprinted around the Lewandowskis' station wagon — past the astonished faces of Mrs. Lewandowski, Linda, and the rest of the brood — and out into the sunlight, where there was no sign of Freak O' Nature. I didn't understand why we were running. Mrs. Lewandowski had seen us. Lest there be any doubt, she now stood at the mouth of the garage and called, "Ronnie? Scott? What's going on?"

Being a dutiful child who'd been taught to answer grown-ups, I began to slow, but Ronnie grunted, "Don't stop!"

So I sped up again.

With the cheesecake box tucked into the crook of his arm like a football, Ronnie led the way. On the sidewalk ahead of us was Freak O' Nature, who'd abandoned his lookout post and was walking home with the transistor radio pressed to his ear. For a moment, I wondered if Ronnie was running after him, angry that Freak O' Nature had gone AWOL. But he ran right past him and kept going.

As I sprinted past Freak O' Nature, he asked, "Where're you going?"

"We got caught!" I gasped.

Ronnie ran another hundred yards and then slowed to a jog. I would have gained on him, but I was winded and slowing as well. Soon we were walking about fifteen yards apart. A stitch had started to cramp in my right side.

"Wait." I gulped in pain. "She saw us. She called our names."

But Ronnie kept going — down the sidewalk . . . across Freak O' Nature's front yard . . . around the side of his house . . . and into the backyard, where he plopped down under a maple tree. I flopped down opposite him, massaging the stitch in my side.

Neither of us spoke. Ronnie sat staring at the Sara Lee cheesecake box in his lap.

A minute later, Freak O' Nature joined us, dropping into an Indian-style position.

"Thanks a lot," Ronnie growled.

"For what?" asked Freak O' Nature.

"I told you to keep an eye out."

"I did."

"For the *Lewandowskis*."

"Oh." Freak O' Nature mulled this over. "Sorry."

"She's probably telling our mothers right now." I imagined Mrs. Lewandowski on the party line, reporting the incident to both our moms at once. "We're dead."

"You could give it back," suggested Freak O' Nature.

"No!" Ronnie clutched the box as if it would shoot right back to the freezer if he let go.

"It's just a stupid cheesecake," I said.

To end the debate, Ronnie tore open the box and peeled back the round tinfoil lid, revealing the light-brown-rimmed yellow cake inside. I wished I felt hungry, but mostly I felt dread. Getting caught stealing surely qualified as a spankable offense.

Prying the cake out, Ronnie gripped the sides and tried to break off a piece, but in its frozen state, it wouldn't even bend. He bared his teeth in the effort, then finally smashed the cake against his knee. It broke sort of in half, and he handed the smaller piece to me and kept the larger for himself.

"What about me?" Freak O' Nature asked.

"You abandoned your post," Ronnie said.

Freak O' Nature didn't reply. He rarely argued with anyone.

The chunk Ronnie had given me bore the indentations of his fingers and was covered with his fingerprints. Ronnie bit into the corner of his piece where the filling met the graham-cracker crust. He held the bite in his mouth for a moment, probably letting the cheesecake soften, and then closed his eyes, a blissful smile appearing on his lips as if to rub in Freak O' Nature's loss.

Somehow, despite all the regret I felt about my participation in this terrible crime, and the apprehension about being punished, my appetite crept back. I found a corner of cake free of Ronnie's fingerprints and took a nibble. The cheesecake was cold and creamy and delicious, and I bit off a little of the nutty brown crust to go along with it. Like a prisoner on death row, I began to savor my last meal.

9

The medical kit is the size of a lunch box, with a red cross on it. Next to it is a green box I've seen once before, in Dad's closet. I know what's in that box, and finding it here catches me by surprise and makes me uncomfortable. I look away and take the first-aid kit to Dad.

He hands me the flashlight. "Keep it aimed on her."

I shine the beam at Mom's face, which is gray with some black-and-blue marks near her ears. As Dad rips open a gauze pad, then gently lifts Mom's head and presses the pad against the wound, my stomach coils with anxiety. Her hair in back is all dark reddish and stuck together. As if Dad knows what I'm thinking, he says, "It looks bad, but head wounds bleed a lot."

"Uh-huh." I agree, mostly because I don't want him to get mad.

"We'll just have to wait until she wakes up," he says, holding the gauze pad in place and pulling a long strip of white tape, which he starts to wrap around her head.

"Mr. Porter?" Janet says.

"Yes?" Dad looks up.

"That's not the way."

Their eyes meet for a moment, and then Dad nods and lets her take over.

Janet takes a small pair of scissors from the first-aid kit and begins to cut the hair away from Mom's wound.

No one speaks. The *snip, snip, snip* of the scissors is the only sound in this little cement box of a room. Maybe there's too much to think about. Paula and her dad must be thinking about Mrs. McGovern and Teddy. Is Ronnie thinking about his collie, Leader? What about the rest of our friends and neighbors, teachers, cousins, and grandparents? Did some of them find shelter in basements and tunnels and the other places with those black-and-yellow Civil Defense Fallout Shelter signs?

Maybe some, but not *everybody.* Not the ones who were on the other side of the trapdoor.

Huddled in the shadows with her husband and Ronnie, Mrs. Shaw quietly begins to sob.

Snip, snip, snip . . . Dark clumps of hair fall to the concrete floor. Janet turns to Dad. "Could I have some water, Mr. Porter?"

With a start, Dad snatches the flashlight from me and shines it up at a large red sausage-shaped metal tank hanging above us. Skinny brown pipes run into it from the ceiling. Rising quickly, he reaches up and turns some valves, then waits as if he's expecting something. Everyone else looks up, too. Paula's cheeks glisten with tears.

"Come on," Dad mutters at the tank, and I feel myself tense.

Seconds pass. He stares intently. "Come on!"

I'm not sure what's supposed to happen, but it's obvious from the way Dad's acting that it's important.

"What is it?" Mr. Shaw asks.

"The water tank. I was supposed to fill it."

"It can't be too late, can it?" asks Mrs. Shaw while Dad shines the flashlight beam on a metal toolbox on the floor near the wall.

"I don't hear water running." He flips the box open, pulls out a hammer, and starts tapping the pipes. *Clank! Clank! Clank!*

Paula buries her face in her father's shoulder. Dad stops and listens, then starts to hit the pipes harder. *CLANK! CLANK! CLANK!*

Sparky covers his ears. "Stop! It's too loud."

Dad listens again. In the glow of the flashlight, the sinews tighten in his neck and his temple pulses.

CLANK! CLANK! CLANK!

Despite the jarring racket, Mom lies perfectly still.

ten

By the time we'd licked the last traces of cheesecake from our fingers, the afternoon was descending toward evening, the shadows growing longer and deeper. The distant train whistle meant fathers were coming home from work. The sweet pleasure of the cheesecake vanished, replaced by the sour taste of dread.

"The Yankees lost," Freak O' Nature said in his normal voice, not affecting any well-known television character, and looked at his watch. "I gotta go in. Are . . . you guys gonna say I had something to do with it?"

Ronnie and I looked at each other and shook our heads. School-yard logic might have dictated that since he'd been part of the crime at the beginning, he was a tiny bit culpable, but spreading the blame probably wouldn't reduce whatever punishment we would face at home.

"Thanks." With a smile of relief and gratitude, Freak O' Nature stood up. Since we were in his backyard, Ronnie and I got up as well. As we started toward our homes, the train whistle blew again, sounding closer.

"I'm gonna get it bad," I said, trying not to step on the unlucky cracks in the sidewalk — a last-ditch effort to keep things from becoming worse.

"We could all be dead tomorrow," Ronnie said.

Either way, I felt doomed.

At the front door, Sparky was waiting with an expression of awe on his face. Even though he got into plenty of trouble himself, nothing thrilled and fascinated him more than when the ax was about to fall on me. Before he could say anything, I raised my hand and said, "I know."

But he had to say it anyway. "You're in big trouble." He grinned with delight.

Mom came out of the kitchen wearing a blue apron and a frown on her face. Then she spoke the words that struck an even greater, or at least more immediate, fear than a Russian attack: "Go to your room until your father gets home."

11

Dad slumps down on the bunk kitty-corner to where Janet sits, still comforting Mom. The tension is gone. Either Dad's tired or he's decided that more banging on pipes won't help. Sparky goes over and settles on his leg. I sit next to him, pressing my shoulder against his arm. In Dad's hands, the flashlight makes a bright bull's-eye against the wall of gray concrete blocks.

"Mr. Porter?" Janet speaks softly.

Dad shines the light back on Mom. Using a bandage and some alcohol from the first-aid kit, Janet wipes her hands, then starts cutting again.

Snip, snip, snip . . .

"Everyone we know," Mrs. Shaw sniffs woefully. "Everyone!"

Mr. McGovern mutters, "It's unbelievable."

There are places I can't stop my thoughts from going to: What about the others who were up there? The ones who didn't get in? Were Paula's mom and brother among them? Freak O' Nature and his family? The Lewandowskis and Sinclairs? Were they all blinded and burned in the heat flash? Poisoned by radiation? Blown apart by the shock wave?

Or are they still out there trying to avoid the fallout floating down out of the sky like poisonous gray snow? Dad said that if you weren't in a shelter, the fallout would be unavoidable. Even if you managed not to get any on you or breathe it in, it would still get into the water and food. At the end of World War II, the United States dropped atom bombs on Hiroshima and Nagasaki in Japan, and hundreds of thousands of Japanese people died from the explosions and the radiation that followed. And those bombs were tiny compared to the hydrogen bombs that the United States and Russia have now.

Thinking of my friends brings a deep, sick, sad sensation. Freak O' Nature, Linda, Puddin' Belly Wright, and Why Can't You Be Like Johnny? could be lying on the ground above us right now, writhing in pain. Shouldn't we go up and look for them? But I know what Dad would say. We'd only be exposing ourselves to the radiation. Then we'd die, too.

Still, how would it feel if it was someone else's bomb shelter and our family were the ones who were locked out? I picture myself crawling through the rubble to the trapdoor, knocking and begging to be let in.

My lungs expand with an involuntary gasp. So far no one's knocked, but what if someone *does*?

Ronnie presses his face against his dad's arm while Mr. Shaw wipes his own eyes with his fingers. Sparky sniffs. Dad stares at the floor. Now I can't stop the tears from coming. In the past when there'd been tears in my eyes, I'd always gone to Mom for comfort. I never wanted Dad to see me cry because that was what girls and little kids did. But what does that matter now?

Janet wraps Mom's head in gauze to keep everything in place. It's so quiet. The loudest sound is Mom's breathing. Dad hardly takes his eyes off her. Every few moments, he reaches over to feel her forehead, pull her robe a little tighter, brush a few hairs away from her face.

"When's she going to wake up?" Sparky asks.

"Don't know," Dad says.

"What if she never wakes up?"

"Let's not think about that."

- - - - - - - -

More time passes. More silence. Dad takes the hammer and raps the pipes again — *Clank! Clank! Clank!* — then pauses to listen.

Still nothing.

He sighs, puts down the hammer, takes some blankets from a shelf, and offers them around. "Try to make yourselves comfortable."

Janet is the only one who says thank you. The Shaws and McGoverns spread the blankets on the cold concrete floor. Both Mrs. Shaw and Paula tuck their knees up against their chests and hug their legs. Paula leans tightly against her dad. After making Mom comfortable on the bunk, Janet sits on the bare concrete floor and wraps her blanket around her shoulders. Soon we are four groups, huddled close to one another in the chilly, damp air.

In science we learned that some people could go a month or more without food by living on stored-up fat and then on muscle. But no one can go much more than four days without water.

It's Sparky who asks the question we're all thinking: "Dad, what will happen if we can't get the water?"

twelve

I went to my room, which I shared with Sparky, whose real name was Edward, but I called him Sparky because his hair grew straight out from his head as if he was always touching something electric.

Wondering how bad the spanking would be, I sat on my bed, tugging at the hair behind my ear, too miserable to look at comics or play with my plastic army men. The paddleball racket was a given. When I was younger, Dad used to spank me, and then Sparky, with his hand, but one day he hurt his wrist and couldn't play tennis for a few weeks, so now he spanked us with the wooden paddle, which hurt like the dickens.

The bedroom door began to open and I tensed, but it was only Sparky. He pretended to look for a toy on his shelf, but I knew he'd really come in to see how I was coping with the stress. He kept glancing at me out of the corner of his eye.

"Dad's really gonna give it to you. You're not supposed to steal."

"Get lost." I picked up *MAD* magazine and pretended to read it. The black and white enemies in "Spy vs. Spy" used the same round black bombs with fizzy fuses that Boris Badenov used against Rocky and Bullwinkle on TV.

"Mom says she doesn't know what she's gonna do with you."

That didn't sound right. Taking the cheesecake was the first bad thing I'd done in months. "No, she didn't."

"Yes, she did," Sparky insisted.

"Liar."

"Nuh-uh. She said, 'I don't know what I'm going to do.' And her eyes got red and watery."

That sounded ominous. Was it possible that even I didn't know how bad what I'd done was? I'd done bad stuff before, like the time Puddin' Belly Wright and I threw dirt bombs at the back of Old Lady Lester's freshly painted garage, or the time I dropped Sparky's brand-new rubber football down the storm drain because he wouldn't share his double-stick cherry ice pop.

But I'd never stolen before. Could stealing mean you'd crossed the line into juvenile delinquency and there was no going back? Could it mean I'd have to be a hood from now on and wear a leather jacket and heavy engineer boots all summer and pretend to be tough even though I knew I wasn't very tough at all? Would I be the only kid on the block who was a hood, and none of my friends would be allowed to play with me? Just thinking about it made me want to cry.

"Go away or you're gonna get hurt," I warned Sparky.

He left and I felt tears of regret slide down my cheeks. Why had I listened to Ronnie?

When the door opened a few moments later, I thought it would be Sparky again, but Dad came in, wearing a dark-green suit. I sniffed loudly, hoping he'd see my red eyes and tear-streaked cheeks and know how remorseful I was and that I'd clearly learned my lesson and therefore really didn't need to be spanked.

The good news was he didn't have the paddle, but that could have been because he wanted to change clothes before he spanked me. Dad never did work around the house in his business clothes. He always changed into dungarees and a sweatshirt first. And that included when he punished us.

I pulled my knees up under my chin and tried to squeeze a few more tears of remorse out of my eyes. Sitting across from me on Sparky's bed, Dad looked serious, his jaw dark with five o'clock shadow, which was something gangsters and men who were desperate or crazy often had on TV.

"You know you're not supposed to steal," he said.

I nodded, blinked hard, and sniffed loudly again. At the same time, I tried to estimate how many swats with the paddle I might get. The last time Dad had spanked me was after I did an experiment to see whether a little rock the size of a nickel could break a window if you threw it really hard from close up. The answer was yes, if a five-inch crack in the glass counted. That got me three swats. But that time Mom hadn't cried or said she didn't know what she was going to do with me. All she did was laugh and say, "Your father is going to love this."

So it stood to reason that the punishment for stealing would be greater — maybe even six or more swats. But it also depended on Dad's mood. If this was one of those days when he came home angry, it could be even worse.

"Why did you do it?" He sounded calm and reasonable, so I felt a little hopeful. The truth was, I didn't know why I'd done it. Hunger had played a part. And Ronnie had said I'd be a chicken if I didn't do it.

"I don't know."

"But you knew it was wrong."

I nodded and felt a tiny bit encouraged; he didn't seem all that angry.

"Do you have anything to say for yourself?" he asked.

"Ronnie said it wouldn't matter because tomorrow the Russians might drop the bomb and we'd all be dead."

To be honest, I didn't think that was such a good excuse, but it was the best I could come up with. At that point, if I'd had to estimate how many swats I was going to get once Dad changed clothes, I would have guessed around five. But Dad didn't move. He blinked, then blinked again. "Stay here," he said, then left the room.

13

"Is there any water at all?" Mrs. Shaw asks. In the dim light, her eyes are glittery.

Dad shakes his head.

"And if we go up there to get some . . . ?"

"We have to wait as long as we can before leaving the shelter," Dad says.

"Maybe it's not as bad as you think," Mr. McGovern suggests.

"A bomb went off close by," Dad says. "We saw the flash and heard the blast winds."

"But we don't *really* know," Paula's dad stresses.

Dad glances at Mom again. On her cheek are a few

streaks of dark dried blood. "I'll check the levels." He takes the flashlight and gets up.

"Can I come?" Sparky asks anxiously.

"No, it could be dangerous."

I put my arm around Sparky's scrawny shoulders. "We'll stay here."

Dad gets a small box labeled FAMILY RADIATION MEASUREMENT KIT. Inside is a tubelike thing about the size of a fountain pen. He goes around the shield wall and into the narrow corridor on the other side.

Without the flashlight, it gets darker in the shelter. We watch the shadows and light in the gap where the shield wall ends and listen as Dad climbs the metal rungs up to the trapdoor.

A few moments later, he returns. "It's four hundred ninety-seven roentgens under the door. That's what's getting *through* a quarter inch of iron plate, which means it's even worse on the other side."

"What does that mean?" asks Mrs. Shaw.

"Anything over fifty roentgens will cause radiation sickness. Anyone who goes out there will be sick within hours and dead within days."

fourteen

When Dad came back into the bedroom, he was still wearing his suit and wasn't carrying the paddle. "We're going to the Lewandowskis."

"Noooo!" I wailed, instantly filled with a different sort of dread; the only thing worse than physical pain was the pain of embarrassment. Now I knew where he'd gone when he left the room — to call Mrs. Lewandowski.

"Yes," Dad said firmly. "I want you to apologize."

"Can't I call?"

"In person." Dad's tone invited no more arguing.

This was the worst, most humiliating thing ever. Not only because I'd have to apologize to Mrs. Lewandowski, but because Linda was pretty and blond . . . and I had a crush on her that was so secret even Russian torturers wouldn't have been able to beat it out of me. Just being near her made me nervous and tongue-tied. The thought of going over there to apologize was unbearable.

"How about you just spank me?" I begged.

Dad's mouth fell open. "Are . . . you serious?"

I nodded. A spanking would hurt more, but once it was over, you forgot about it. But I saw Linda every day in school. If I did what Dad wanted me to do, I was doomed to a lifetime of embarrassment.

15

Dad takes a radio from the shelf and sits down with Sparky and me. He turns the dials. Between gaps of nothing come static and noises like sound bending. He goes back to the static and fiddles around, but all he gets is crackling, scratchy noise.

"What about the Civil Defense channel?" Mr. McGovern asks.

"Tried it." Dad turns the dial. There's nothing. How can this be a war? No explosions. No shots being fired. Not a sound from above.

After he snaps the radio off, it's silent except for Paula's sniffs. It feels like a long time has passed, but it can't be more than an hour or two since Dad picked up Sparky and carried him down the hall to the playroom. Sparky yawns and rubs his eyes. I can't believe he's actually sleepy. Maybe he's too young to really understand what's happened.

So far Ronnie and I have avoided looking at each other. Last night, just a few hours before Dad shook me awake, Ronnie and I had the first fistfight of our lives. It happened on the way back from having birthday cake at Why Can't You Be Like Johnny?'s house, and now I don't know whether to still be angry at him or just try to forget. It seems crazy to be mad at each other now that World War III has started, but I can't help feeling a little sore at him, and I wonder if Ronnie feels sore at me, too.

Sitting with his parents just a few feet away, Ronnie shakes his head as if he's trying to fight drowsiness. Like me, he's probably afraid that something bad may happen while he's asleep.

Sparky yawns again, then lays his head down on Dad's lap. His yawn makes me want to yawn, too, but I cover my mouth and try to fight it.

"Maybe you should get some sleep, Scott," Dad says.

"I don't want to."

"I think you do. It's okay. You need to rest."

Dad slides his arms under Sparky and lifts him to the bunk above Mom's. Then he turns to me. "There's room for both of you."

I climb the bunk ladder, and when my face is level with Dad's, I whisper, "You sure you'll be all right?"

Dad smiles weakly. "Yes."

When I'm on the bunk bed with Sparky, Dad covers us with the scratchy army blanket. He kisses me on the forehead, then tells Ronnie he can use the other upper bunk if he wants and Paula can have the one below it. But Paula doesn't want to leave her dad. Ronnie climbs up to the bunk catty-corner to the one Sparky and I are on. Our eyes meet when he lies down. His mom covers him with a blanket.

The bunk has a small pillow, and I lay my head on it and close my eyes but only pretend to sleep. After a while, I open one eye a tiny bit. Dad must have covered the flashlight with something because it's dimmer in the shelter but not completely dark. The Shaws and McGoverns are sitting on the floor with their backs to the wall. Janet sits by herself.

In the shadows, Dad stands in the middle of the shelter with his ear close to the water tank and taps lightly with his knuckles. A faint, hollow echo comes from inside. Then he lowers his head and looks down . . . I think toward Mom. He kneels and disappears from view.

Quietly I inch to the edge of the bunk and look over. Dad is sitting beside Mom, holding her limp hand in one of his. His other hand covers his eyes. His shoulders tremble, and I know he's hiding tears.

sixteen

Like a prisoner, I was marched through the kitchen where Sparky and Mom had started eating dinner. Sparky stopped in mid-chew and watched as we passed. I could tell he knew where Dad and I were going.

Outside, the air was cool, the moon big and round in the dark sky.

"What am I supposed to say?" I asked.

"What do you think you should say?"

"I'm sorry?"

"And that you promise never to take anything that isn't yours again."

When Dad rang the Lewandowskis' doorbell, the door

opened so quickly that I knew Mrs. Lewandowski had been waiting for us. Behind her stood Linda and three of her four brothers and sisters, all watching curiously. Linda's and my eyes met, and I felt my insides twist into a knot while my face grew hot with shame and remorse.

I apologized to Linda's mother and promised I would never take anything that wasn't mine again. Mrs. Lewandowski said she appreciated it. Then she and Dad nodded at each other as if they'd completed a deal, and my eyes met Linda's for a second time. When she looked away, I knew I was doomed.

As Dad and I walked home through the dark, I couldn't help thinking that even though all my hopes and dreams regarding Linda had been dashed, apologizing wasn't as horrible as I'd imagined it would be.

"That wasn't so bad, was it?" Dad asked.

I almost agreed but then caught myself. If I sounded too happy about apologizing, he might think it wasn't punishment enough and decide to spank me anyway. So I tried to sound unhappy. "It wasn't great. How come you didn't just spank me?"

"Don't you think you're a little too old to get spanked?"

His answer caught me by surprise. I'd never realized there was an age limit for spankings. This was the best news I'd heard in a long time.

Back home, Sparky was taking a bath. While Mom

served Dad and me a slightly cold dinner, she asked how it had gone and Dad said fine, and then she left to make sure Sparky washed behind his ears.

My brother went to bed at eight, but I was allowed to stay up until eight thirty. A small reading lamp on my night table provided just enough light to read *MAD* magazine or its inferior imitator, *Cracked.* After I was in bed, Mom and then Dad would come in and kiss me good night.

That night when Dad came in, I whispered, "What'll happen if the Russians drop the bomb?"

He thought for a moment, and the wrinkles near his eyes deepened. "It'll be the end, I'm afraid."

"Of everything?"

He seemed to hesitate, then nodded. It made me wonder if he thought that since I was now old enough not to be spanked, I was also old enough to hear the truth.

"We'll all be killed?" I asked.

"Well, some people are building bomb shelters. They say that if you can stay belowground and away from the radiation for two weeks, you can probably survive."

"Should we have one?" I asked.

"I've been thinking about it."

It seemed odd that he'd only be "thinking" when it could save our lives.

As if Dad could read my mind, he said, "They're

expensive, Scott, and a lot of people think that because we've reached the point of mutually assured destruction, war no longer makes sense." He sighed. "The problem is, wars almost never make sense — but that never stopped anyone before."

17

My eyes open and it takes a moment to remember where I am, but the sounds of the others breathing in their sleep quickly reminds me. I yawn and stretch, then become aware of dampness around my middle — and the unmistakable smell of urine. My body goes rigid. I've wet the bed, something I haven't done in years. And not only that, but I've done it in front of Ronnie and Paula...

Forget about perishing in a nuclear war; I could die from shame right now — unless I can keep it a secret. If I can somehow get Dad's attention without the others noticing, maybe he can help me figure a way out of this mess. I inch toward the edge of the bunk and look over in the dim light, where my eyes immediately meet Mr. McGovern's. He's sitting against the wall with Paula's head on his thigh while she sleeps. Against the other wall, Mr. and Mrs. Shaw lean into each other with their eyes closed. Janet sits with her head tilted down, her chin on her chest. Dad's directly below me, his head also tilted down. Lying on her back on her bunk, Mom doesn't look like she's moved at all. I inch away from the edge until I feel Sparky behind me.

Wait . . . I touch the front of my pajamas. They're dry. *It was Sparky, not me!* I feel a moment of relief, but then turmoil returns. How can I let the others know it wasn't me without humiliating him?

There's nothing to do except wait for Dad to wake up, but it's chilly on the wet mattress. I curl up for warmth and still shiver. Meanwhile, unwanted thoughts invade my mind: What will happen to us without water? The grown-ups will probably decide that one of them will go out and look for it, even though it may mean getting radiation sickness. What if the water they find is full of radiation and makes us sick, too?

Or what if we find water and stay down here for two weeks, and when we get out, we're the only ones left around here? Dad said we'd have to rebuild. But how could just the nine of us — ten if Mom gets better — do that? We'd need a lot more people.

What if Dad wasn't only talking about rebuilding things like houses and roads, but the human race as well? If Mom gets better, she could have some more babies. And so could Mrs. Shaw. And Janet, who is pretty and slim and a little younger than both Mom and Mrs. Shaw, so maybe she could have a bunch. But that still wouldn't be very many. Could Paula have babies? Maybe not right away, but soon? Like in a couple of years?

Then it hits me. If Paula is going to have babies someday, it's going to have to be with Ronnie or me.

How's *that* going to work? I don't feel like I'm ready to have babies with anyone, but Ronnie probably can't wait. If it was up to him, he'd probably want to start before we even get out of the shelter. There's no doubt in my mind that when it's time for Paula to have babies, Ronnie will be the father. He's stronger and a better athlete and better-looking. I won't stand a chance, which is kind of okay because I never really cared that much for Paula anyway.

But once Ronnie and Paula start having babies, there'll be no one left for me.

I hear a rustle below and peek over the edge. Dad's leaning over Mom's bunk, but I can't see what he's doing.

After a while, he stands up to check on Sparky and me. Our eyes meet and his nose wrinkles. I point at Sparky. Dad nods and then he's still for a moment. His eyes slide away toward the water tank. Is he thinking that if there's no water to drink, then there's none for washing pee-soaked pajamas?

eighteen

Early in July, big sheets of blueprints appeared on our dining-room table. A few days later, Sparky and I followed Dad around the backyard with two men who hammered short wooden stakes into the grass and tied a string that outlined the rectangular boundary where the new addition to our house would go — a new playroom and a bedroom for me.

The next morning, three men with pickaxes, shovels, and a wheelbarrow began digging inside the staked-off area.

By the afternoon, the hole was knee-deep and the size of big kiddie pool. Sparky and I stood on the other side of the string and watched; the men, who were Negroes and wore overalls, stole glances at us. Overalls were not an item of clothing that hung in my father's closet nor, I was pretty certain, in the closets of any of my friends' fathers. Under the overalls the men wore dingy T-shirts with small holes and tears in them.

Each man had his own way of digging. The tall, wiry one with long, sinewy arms slammed the heel of his boot against the top of the shovel to drive the blade down into the soil. Then he would arch back and use his whole body to leverage the dirt into the wheelbarrow. The paunchy man with thick undefined arms would lean against the shovel and wiggle the blade back and forth into the dirt. Then he would jam the handle against his hip and, without moving his feet, swivel toward the wheelbarrow. The third man had broad shoulders that narrowed down to his waist, and muscular arms. He looked like a dark version of the muscle builders in the magazines Dad sometimes read and was strong enough to thrust his shovel straight into the dirt, then bend his knees and toss shovelfuls into the wheelbarrow. Hardly any dirt missed.

Within a few days, the men had dug as deep as their thighs, and the rectangular hole reached to the string on all three sides. Beneath the dark brown topsoil was a layer of lighter soil mixed with sand, and below that appeared to be grayish clay. They used the pickaxes now as well as shovels, and the work went more slowly as they heaved shovelfuls of dirt and clay up onto a canvas tarp at the rim of the hole. It seemed strange that they would be digging so deep for rooms that were supposed to be above the ground.

"Maybe it's an indoor swimming pool," Sparky said.

Could *that* be it? Were they not only building an addition but a surprise swimming pool as well? Having our own pool would be a thousand times better than the pool at the country club. Not only because we'd be able to swim anytime we wanted but because we could have just our friends over instead of sharing with everyone. We could float on rafts, which weren't allowed at the club pool, and private pools had lights, so we could even swim at night.

But the best thing about having our own pool would be doing all the cannonballs we wanted! My friends and I had spent a considerable amount of time the previous summer perfecting cannonballs off the diving board at the club pool. The perfect cannonball resulted in a spout-like splash of water that rocketed straight upward from the point of entry, sometimes even splashing against the bottom of the diving board. Unfortunately, sometimes our splashes veered off at an angle and sprayed the ladies who sunned on the lounges. When that happened, they'd complain to the lifeguards and cannonballs would be banned for the rest of the day.

Seeking confirmation, Sparky and I raced into the

house, where we found Mom sitting at the kitchen table, smoking a cigarette. That was strange. Usually she only smoked on weekend nights when she and Dad had people over for dinner. And when she sat at the kitchen table, she always read a magazine. But it was the middle of the afternoon, there was no magazine, and her gaze slanted up and away into the smoky air.

"Are we getting an indoor swimming pool?" Sparky asked.

Mom scowled and crushed the cigarette out in the ashtray. "What makes you think that?"

"The hole they're digging."

"Your father didn't tell you? It's a bomb shelter."

"What's that?" asked Sparky.

"A place where we can hide in case the Commies drop the H-bomb on us," I said.

"Why?" Sparky was filled with disappointment.

"You'll have to ask your father," Mom said.

Drained of excitement, Sparky and I wandered into the den to wait for Dad to come home from work. The den had a white shag carpet, a white L-shaped couch, and walls covered with whitewashed knotty pine. Dad had made some of the furniture himself using the big DeWalt table saw in the garage. Sparky and I lay down on the carpet. White shag provided excellent ground cover for the wars I staged with my plastic army men, who, hidden in the long white strands, could sneak to within inches of each other before opening fire. The one absolute rule was no eating in the den. Once crumbs got into the shag, they were gone for good unless you went through the long white fibers with a magnifying glass and tweezers. Getting caught eating in the den was almost an automatic spanking.

"Maybe we can get Dad to change his mind," Sparky said.

"Maybe," I said, although I had my doubts. I'd learned a little about nuclear war from duck-and-cover air-raid drills at school, but most of what I knew about the Russians came from the *Rocky and Bullwinkle Show* on TV. Rocky the flying squirrel and his pal Bullwinkle J. Moose were often called upon to foil the sinister plots of Boris Badenov and his girlfriend, Natasha Fatale, who had foreign accents and were no-good spies from a no-good country clearly like Russia.

Americans were a good, peace-loving people. We had a handsome president with a pretty wife, and we wanted to live freely and play baseball and enjoy life. Russia had an ugly leader who most likely wasn't even married and only wanted to destroy America. The Russian people lived in fear of their leaders and probably weren't allowed to play sports.

So it would be too bad if we weren't getting a swimming pool, but maybe a bomb shelter wasn't such a bad thing, either.

19

Sparky and I have no dry clothes to change into, so we sit naked on the lower bunk with a blanket around our shoulders. I feel proud of my little brother for not making a fuss about wetting himself. After a while everyone is awake again, and Dad cranks the ventilator to get more fresh air in the shelter. Janet sits on the edge of Mom's bunk and feels her pulse. People stretch and move around. They glance at Mom and at Sparky and me pressed close together, but no one says anything. Paula wrinkles her nose like she can smell what Sparky did, but then whispers to her father, who speaks in a hushed tone to Dad. They may be whispering for Paula's sake, but everyone knows what they're talking about. Dad gestures at a bucket with a toilet seat on top of it.

"Won't it fill up quickly?" Mrs. Shaw asks.

Dad points at the big metal garbage can next to the toilet bucket. "It goes in here."

Paula starts to cry again. Mr. McGovern hugs her. "It's okay, honey. Everyone's going to have to use it sooner or later."

With her legs squeezed together, Paula leans against him and sobs. I feel bad for her. Maybe everyone will have to use the toilet bucket, but I wouldn't want to be the first, either.

"For Pete's sake," Mrs. Shaw grumbles. I watch in amazement as she pulls up her robe and sits down on the toilet seat. "Don't look," she says, annoyed.

I quickly turn away and hear the hard rattle as her pee strikes the bottom of the empty bucket. Soon it becomes a dribble and then stops. Mrs. Shaw focuses on Dad. "Toilet paper?"

Dad goes to a shelf and gets a roll. "I only stocked enough for four people."

"How could I forget?" Mrs. Shaw snorts. The soft sound of tissue tearing is followed by the rustle of clothes. Then in a gentle voice she says to Paula, "Okay, honey, it's your turn."

Paula sniffs.

"Go on," her father says softly.

"Noooo," Paula wails, as if she's in agony. You can't help feeling bad for her. Dad starts to crank the ventilator again. Only this time it's for the noise.

"Come on, honey," Mrs. Shaw says. "I'll make sure they don't look."

Ronnie glances at me and smirks. But he's being a jerk. Mrs. Shaw stands in front of Paula, and the rest of us look away. When Paula's finished, she comes out from behind Mrs. Shaw with her head bowed and goes back to her dad, eyes downcast.

"Anyone else?" Mrs. Shaw asks. I have to go and now that some of the others have, I figure what's the big deal and maybe it will make Paula feel better. So I say me.

"Well, aren't you the brave one?" Mrs. Shaw says, and I'm not sure whether she means it or is being sarcastic. Since all Sparky and I have to cover us is the blanket, he has to get up with me. Like a four-legged creature, we shuffle over to the toilet bucket. Once again Mrs. Shaw blocks the view and Dad cranks the ventilator. I really do have to go, but I can't with Sparky standing next to me and all these people around. It's as if everything down there is blocked, and in an instant I go from the proud feeling of being brave to feeling completely embarrassed, because even with the ventilator going, the others will be able to tell that nothing is happening. That's when Mrs. Shaw whispers, "Think about waterfalls and garden hoses."

The next thing I know, pee splashes into the bucket, where it mixes with Paula's and Mrs. Shaw's, and I wonder why it was so hard to go before.

Janet goes next, and then one by one, the fathers pee in the bucket, only Dad doesn't crank the ventilator for them. After a while, the only one who hasn't gone is Ronnie. I glance at him, but instead of a smirk, his face is scrunched up as if he's in agony.

Mr. Shaw squeezes his arm. "You better go."

"Shut up," he grunts.

A jolt jumps through me like an electric charge. I've never heard a kid say that to a parent or any grown-up. I wait for Mr. or Mrs. Shaw to scold him, but there's only silence until Ronnie lets out a low moan as if his bladder is about to explode.

A moment later, when I hear a gurgle, I assume Ronnie is going in his pajamas. But Dad quickly looks up at the water tank, and his eyebrows practically leap off his head. It's the sound of running water!

Maybe it's the relief of knowing we have water or the sound of it sloshing through the pipes, but Ronnie races to the toilet bucket and goes.

twenty

When Dad came home from work, Sparky and I followed him into his and Mom's bedroom, where he took off his suit, shirt, and tie, removed his brown leather shoes and placed shoe trees in them. Then he unsnapped the elastic garters around his calves that held up his long, thin socks, and put on dungarees, a gray Fruit of the Loom sweatshirt, white wool socks, and old tennis sneakers.

"Are we getting a bomb shelter?" I asked.

"I'll tell you at dinner," he said, and headed outside. In the summer, Dad often did yard work before dinner. Sparky and I followed him into the backyard, where he stopped to look at the hole.

"How deep will it get?" I asked.

"Pretty deep," Dad said.

"Sure would make a good pool," said Sparky.

"Yes, it would," said Dad.

"A pool would be fun," Sparky said.

"We need a shelter more than we need a pool."

"Couldn't it be a shelter *and* a pool?" Sparky asked.

Just then, Mom called us in. During dinner, Dad told Sparky how there was a chance we might go to war with the Russians.

"Why don't they like us?" my brother asked. "Did we do something bad to them?"

"They don't agree with our form of government."

"What's that?"

Dad tried to explain, but it was hard to go from what a democracy was to why the Russians would want to blow us to smithereens.

"If the Russians win, will we be their prisoners?" I asked.

"Not necessarily," Dad said. "A lot of people think that if there's a war, neither side can win." He must have seen the confused expressions on our faces, because he added, "Both sides have so many bombs that there's a good chance we'll destroy so much of each other's countries that no one will be able to claim victory."

That didn't make sense. Why would anyone go to war if they knew ahead of time that neither side could win? Thus far in the conversation, Mom had remained quiet. Now she slowly shook her head. "Mutually assured destruction. It's ridiculous."

Dad leveled his gaze at her. "I agree, but it's a possibility."

"Don't scare them," Mom said, a bit harshly. The "them" she was referring to was Sparky and me.

"They asked why we're building a shelter—" Dad began to reply.

"Not a shelter, a *bomb* shelter," Mom interjected. "And *we're* not building it—*you* are."

They stared at each other. Then Mom got up and hurried out of the room. Dad let out a sigh. "Finish your dinner, boys." He left to go find Mom.

21

As water races through the pipes and into the tank, I hear someone's throat catch and see Mrs. Shaw hug her husband with relief.

"There was probably an obstruction in the line," says Mr. McGovern. "The water pressure must have forced it loose."

Dad takes a glass from a shelf and fills it, then sniffs tentatively before taking a sip. He grimaces.

"What's wrong?" Mr. Shaw asks. Dad hands him the glass, and Ronnie's dad tries a little, then spits it at the drain in the middle of the floor and wipes his mouth. "*Achh!* It's awful."

"You didn't rinse the system when it was installed?" Mr. McGovern's question sounds critical.

Dad doesn't answer.

"Is that bad?" Mrs. Shaw asks with alarm, directing the question to Mr. McGovern. "Will it hurt us?"

Mr. McGovern pauses thoughtfully. "I don't think so. It won't taste good, but we won't have to drink it forever."

Mrs. Shaw takes the glass from her husband and sips. Her face goes hard. "Well, at least we can wash our hands."

Dad gazes up at the water tank. "Maybe we shouldn't. I'm worried about using it for anything except drinking."

"You don't think there'll be more if this runs out?" Mr. Shaw asks.

Dad shrugs. "I don't know."

"Actually," Mr. McGovern begins, then pauses as if he wants to make sure everyone is listening. "Given the circumstances, I suspect we'll have all the water we'll need."

This comment is met with silence. The grown-ups share the kind of meaningful look that makes kids nervous.

"Why?" Paula looks anxiously at her father, who lets out a reluctant sigh like he doesn't want to give the answer.

But he does. "Because, honey, there probably isn't anyone else left to use it."

Paula begins to sob again.

Dad pours just enough water into a bowl so that we can wash our hands. Then he uses a corner of a towel to gently wipe Mom's face. Sparky and I huddle under the blanket. The sour odor of urine from our wet pajamas mixes with the damp mildew smell of the shelter. I would ask Dad if he'd wash our pajamas, but I know what his answer will be.

He does make a pitcher of Tang. There are only four glasses, so each family shares and Janet gets one for herself. Even with the Tang, the bitter metallic taste from the pipes comes through. By now everyone's a little hungry, and we eat Spam on the bread and broken crackers Mom brought from the kitchen. The Spam tastes spicy and salty, and everyone drinks more Tang. But Dad's being careful. Whether on crackers or bread, we each have about half a sandwich's worth of food and maybe a cupful to drink.

"Herb thinks the water won't be a problem," Mrs. Shaw reminds Dad.

Sitting beside Mom, Dad says, "I don't know how anyone could be certain."

Mr. McGovern exhales noisily, as if he's dealing with

an idiot. "It's a gravity-fed system, Richard. It doesn't depend on electricity or any other kind of power."

"Willing to bet your life on that?" Dad asks sharply, as if he's getting annoyed with Mr. McGovern's attitude. Mr. McGovern exchanges a look with Mr. and Mrs. Shaw, but no one says anything more.

Sparky wriggles under the scratchy blanket. "What about our pajamas?"

Dad shakes his head. "I don't think so, Edward. They won't dry down here, and this could be all the water we'll get."

"Please, Dad?" Sparky whines.

"I said no."

"If they put them back on, won't their body heat eventually dry them?" Mr. Shaw asks.

"Want to try it, boys?" Dad asks us.

Even though Sparky and I are both squirmy and itchy and constantly tugging little bits of blanket from each other, I'd rather be huddling naked with him than put my damp, pee-stinky pajamas back on.

We've eaten and gone to the bathroom, and now there's nothing else to do except sit. Ronnie catches my eye and I know that he wants to talk, but I still don't know how I feel. He may be my best friend, but my scraped elbows and throbbing knee are a reminder of last night's fight. All he's ever done is get me in trouble and make me think about things I don't want to think about. Maybe it's good that I'm sharing the blanket with Sparky, because that means I can't go talk to him.

Dad tries the radio, and again there's nothing but silence and static.

"Did you test it?" Mrs. Shaw asks. "I mean, before?"

Dad doesn't answer, which is kind of an answer in itself. Mrs. Shaw lets out a loud, dramatic sigh of disapproval.

twenty-two

It wasn't long before the hole in the backyard came up to the Negro men's chests. Now two men shoveled, filling a metal bucket, which the third hoisted out of the hole and dumped into the wheelbarrow. The men also began to encounter large rocks, some the size of basketballs, that had to be pried out of the ground and heaved onto the grass beside the hole.

The men always arrived early in the morning and usually stayed until around five o'clock, when a pickup truck would come get them. There wasn't room for all three in the truck cab, so one would sit in front and two would climb into the back. The man who drove the pickup was white.

Each day the men brought metal lunch boxes and thermoses. By now they were used to me and Sparky watching and would sometimes nod at us. And sometimes they would carry on a conversation as if we weren't there.

One day when the sun was like a yellow oven in the sky, sweat dripped from the men's faces. The collars of their T-shirts were dark with moisture, and the skin on their bare arms glistened. They paused often, dabbing the sweat with bandannas and shielding their eyes. I watched the muscular man climb out of the hole and unscrew the cap on his thermos. Only a drop or two came out. The other two leaned on their shovels as if they needed the support. Tracks of sweat lined their faces.

I went into the house. It was hot in the kitchen, and Mom was sitting at the table with a tall glass of iced tea streaked with condensation. She dabbed her forehead with one of Dad's white handkerchiefs.

I gestured to the glass. "I think the men outside could use some."

Mom got up and took three glasses from the kitchen cabinet. "Get some ice."

I took an ice tray from the freezer. Hating the way the frosty metal stuck to my fingertips, I quickly placed the tray in the sink and ran water over it, then pulled the metal lever to crack the ice so Mom could get the pieces out. A few moments later, I carried the glasses outside on a platter.

It was hard to tell whether the men's grins reflected more delight or surprise.

"What's your name, son?" asked the paunchy one.

"Scott," I said.

"Well, Scott, much obliged."

In no time, the glasses were empty. Back in the kitchen, Mom raised her eyebrows. "They asked for more?"

"No, but I think they'll need it."

Mom glanced outside, squinting at the brightness. "That's very thoughtful of you, sweetheart." She started toward the refrigerator, then paused to wipe something out of the corner of her eye.

"You okay?" I asked.

"Yes, Scott." She took out the pitcher of iced tea and put it on the platter, then left the kitchen without another word.

23

After a while, Dad unfolds the card table and invites the others to sit. There are four chairs, and Mr. and Mrs. Shaw and Mr. McGovern sit in three of them. Paula sits on her father's lap. Dad returns to Mom's side.

"You sit with them," Janet says to him. "I'll stay with Mrs. Porter."

Dad hesitates, then gets up, letting Janet take his place. At the table, the grown-ups sit silently in the dim light. Sparky picks at the lint on the scratchy army blanket we're huddled under. Ronnie gnaws at his fingernails.

"You kids want to play a game?" Dad asks.

Paula shakes her head. Ronnie gives me a questioning look. I'm still uncertain about whether to be angry about the fight, and somehow it feels wrong to play games when everything is so serious. But there's nothing else to do, so I lean toward the shelf to get the checkerboard.

"Hey!" Sparky yelps when I accidentally pull some blanket away from him, leaving parts of his naked body exposed to the cool air and others' eyes. He yanks the blanket back, and the next thing I know, I'm completely naked.

By the time my eyes go to Paula, she's looking away, but I have a feeling that's not where she was looking an instant ago. Ronnie grins his jerky grin, which makes me mad at him all over again. I grab the blanket and manage to cover myself, but Sparky grabs it back, and soon we're in a tug-of-war.

"Stop it!" Dad orders, getting up. "I've got an idea."

He holds my damp pajamas under the ventilator while Mr. McGovern turns the crank and blows air on them. After a while, Paula's dad stops to rest, and Mr. Shaw takes over. After two cranks, he's frowning. You can see that it's harder than he expected. His eyes go to his wife.

"Do you have to keep doing that?" Mrs. Shaw asks. "It's cold enough in here."

Dad backs away from the ventilator and hands the pajamas to me. They're cold and still damp.

"Sit on them," Mr. McGovern suggests. "They'll get warmer."

I do what he says, and it's not long before the

pajamas stop feeling cold under my butt. While Paula looks away, I pull on the top and then the bottoms. They're still damp in spots, and when Sparky leans close and sniffs, he wrinkles his nose. But at least now I can get out from under the blanket.

Meanwhile, Ronnie's looking at the checkerboard. Our eyes meet, but I'm still mad at him for grinning when Sparky pulled the blanket off me. If our parents weren't here, I'd tell him he'd have to apologize before I'd play with him. Only knowing Ronnie, he never would.

Sparky and I thumb wrestle. To keep it interesting, I let him win a couple of times, but it gets boring just the same. He's still wrapped in the blanket. I doubt he'd wear his pajamas even if Dad dried them. He's much pickier about things like that than I am. After a while, he says, "Dad, I'm hungry."

"We're all hungry, Edward."

"But, Dad . . . " he whines.

"Let him have something," Mrs. Shaw says.

"There won't be enough food to —" Dad begins, but Mrs. Shaw cuts him short.

"He's a child and he's scared. Food comforts them. We'll worry about running out later."

Dad sighs as if he disagrees but has decided not to argue. It feels strange to hear Mrs. Shaw talk about comfort food, since whenever I ate at their house, she made TV dinners.

While Dad starts to open another can of Spam, Ronnie and Paula share a look. They're also hungry. But I know that they won't say anything because it's our bomb shelter and our food. So it's up to me: "Us, too, Dad."

Ronnie gives me a nod as if he appreciates it, but I look away.

"How long before we've eaten everything?" Mr. McGovern asks.

Dad gestures to the shelf. "That's all we've got."

On the shelf are about two dozen cans of Spam, tuna fish, sardines, some small jars of peanut butter and jelly, bread, and crackers. Even I can see that if we only have one more meal today, and only two small meals for every day to come, it won't last long.

We devour the extra Spam and Tang that Dad gives us. Sparky yawns. "What time is it?"

We don't know. No one was wearing a watch when we were awakened in the middle of the night by the sirens.

"I wonder if it's even noon," says Mr. McGovern.

Everyone is quiet. Are they thinking what I'm thinking? That it feels hopeless? Not even a day has passed, and I'm already bored, dirty, hungry, and smelly in my pee-stinky pajamas. How are we ever going to stay down here for two weeks?

twenty-four

One Saturday just before lunchtime, Sparky came in and asked why the Shaws were in our backyard.

Dad, who'd just come home from tennis and was still wearing his white shorts and shirt, went outside. Mom, Sparky, and I followed. Ronnie's parents were standing beside the hole with their collie, Leader. This was surprising, because even though they only lived one house away and always said hello and acted friendly, my parents and the Shaws never went out together or had dinner with us kids the way we did with other families.

We stood on one side of the hole, and the Shaws stood on the other. Ronnie's parents smiled like they thought something was funny. "That's quite a hole," said Mr. Shaw.

Dad didn't answer.

"What's next?" asked Mr. Shaw.

"Sorry?" Dad said.

Ronnie's dad pointed. "Something's going in there, isn't it?"

"Yes, and over it will go Scott's new bedroom and a playroom," Dad said.

"So what's going in there?" Mr. Shaw asked.

"A shelter," Dad said.

"A bomb shelter," Mom added, annoyed, as if it was silly to pretend it was anything else.

Everyone was quiet, then Mr. Shaw said, "Well, good luck." He and Mrs. Shaw and Leader left.

Back in the house, Dad went to change out of his tennis clothes while Sparky and I set the kitchen table for lunch.

"How come the Shaws wanted to see the hole?" I asked.

"I guess they were curious," Mom answered.

"They never came over before," I said.

"We never had a hole before," Sparky said, as if it was obvious.

Mom laughed.

But when Dad came in, she stopped smiling. Usually at meals our parents would talk or ask us questions about our plans for the day. But that day Mom and Dad were quiet. Sparky kept shooting me puzzled looks, and I'd shrug.

Finally Mom said, "You knew that was going to happen sooner or later."

Dad took a bite of tuna-fish sandwich and gave her the "not in front of the kids" look.

"Don't you think they should know?" Mom asked. "They're part of this, too." She turned to us. "Your friends may say something about the bomb shelter."

"Like what?" I asked.

"They may want to know why we're building it."

"Because of the Russians, right?" I said.

Dad nodded.

"The problem is that not everyone agrees with what we're doing," Mom said.

"Why not?" asked Sparky.

Mom looked at Dad as if it was his job to answer.

"People have different ideas about whether we'll go to war or not," Dad said. "Some think it's likely, and some don't."

"You think it's likely, right?" I asked.

"Well . . ." Dad paused. "I think it's possible."

"And the bomb shelter is for just in case," Sparky said. "Like a spare tire."

"Right," said Dad.

It got quiet again.

"So . . . what's the problem?" I asked.

Mom and Dad looked at each other. I expected Dad to answer, since he was sort of in charge of the bomb shelter. But it was Mom who said, "The problem is that everyone knows about it."

"The threat of war?" I said, confused.

"No, the bomb shelter." Mom looked at me questioningly. "Do you know anyone else who has one?"

"No."

"Your mom's worried that other kids may make fun of you," Dad said.

Sparky made a fist. "Anyone makes fun of me, I'll punch 'em in the face."

"Why would they make fun of us?" I asked.

"Some people think it's silly," Mom said. "They don't believe there'll be a war. And there are other people who think it's silly because if there is a war and everything's destroyed, what would be the point of living?"

"Everyone wants to live," I said.

"Even if there was nothing left?" Mom asked. "No electricity. No jobs. Hardly any food."

"We'd rebuild," Dad said. "Think about what it must have been like when the Pilgrims first got here."

"What a wonderful existence they had," Mom muttered sourly.

"They had Thanksgiving," Sparky said. "After the war, we could have Thanksgiving, too."

Mom's eyes suddenly filled with tears. Her chair scraped loudly as she pushed it back and hurried out of the kitchen.

Dad stared at the empty doorway, then let out a sigh and got up. "Sorry, boys. This is something your mom and I disagree about."

He left Sparky and me at the table. Our parents' voices came down the hall from their bedroom, too faint to make out what they were saying. But we could hear the tone. Mom was upset and angry, and Dad was trying to get her to calm down.

Back in the kitchen, Sparky whispered, "What's so bad about Thanksgiving?"

25

Ronnie catches me looking at the checkers game and raises his eyebrow. I turn away. I may be going crazy with nothing to do, but I'm still not playing with him.

"Come on, you two, let bygones be bygones," Dad says.

I bet he wouldn't say that if he knew what Ronnie said about him.

"Did something happen?" Mr. Shaw asks.

Ronnie and I share another look, neither of us willing to tell.

"They got into a scrape last night," Dad says.

"About?" asks Mr. Shaw.

"You'll have to ask them."

Ronnie's dad studies us.

"Seriously, boys, whatever it was about, how could it matter now?" Dad asks.

"You'd be surprised," I mutter.

"Shut up," Ronnie growls.

"Why don't you tell them?" I dare him.

Ronnie narrows his eyes like he'll kill me if I tell. As if he could do anything with all these grown-ups around. Suddenly it's so stupid, it almost feels funny. I stick my tongue out at him. He blinks, then grins, and sticks his tongue back at me.

Dad and Janet take turns sitting with Mom. When Dad's with her, he holds her hand. Now and then, Janet takes her pulse. I know why they're watching her, but I can't say anything because I don't want to scare Sparky. But I'm scared. I don't want her to die. And what will happen if she does, and we still have to stay down here for two weeks? The idea is so awful, I have to make myself think of other things.

Now that we've stuck our tongues out at each other, it feels dumb to stay angry, so Ronnie and I play checkers. Sparky watches and goes "uh-huh" when he thinks I've made a good move and "nuh-uh" when he doesn't. Normally I'd tell him to get lost, but that would leave him with nothing to do.

The grown-ups start to play cards. I guess they need to find a way to pass the time, too. It's weird because no one knows what time it really is. Is it daytime up there? Night?

Do day and night still exist?

"Two weeks of this?" Mrs. Shaw mutters to no one in particular.

Minutes, hours, countless games of cards and checkers have passed. Sparky wants to take a nap, so Dad puts a towel over the wet spot and helps him up into our bunk. Mr. Shaw lies on some blankets on the floor, and Ronnie squeezes beside his mom on a bunk, just as Paula does with her father. Janet starts to lean her head against the concrete wall, so Dad makes a small bed out of pillows for her on the floor then turns to me.

"You want to sleep?"

I shake my head. Dad and I sit at the card table. My fingers scratch at the red plastic surface, and I can't help thinking about school and my teacher, Mr. Kasman, and, once again, about my friends. . . . I feel a deep sadness like nothing I've ever felt before. Why Can't You Be Like Johnny? . . . Freak O' Nature . . . Linda . . . Can they all be gone? I know what the answer probably is, but it's so hard to believe.

Mr. Shaw starts to snore. The others breathe deeply and steadily. Opposite me, Dad stares at his interlaced fingers.

I whisper, "Do you think it killed everybody up there?"

There's down here and up there. The ones who feel like they're buried are alive, while the ones who aren't buried probably aren't alive. Everything's upside down. Dad gazes at me with sad eyes. "There must have been other people with shelters. People who were less obvious about it." He sounds like he wishes he'd been less obvious, too.

"But they would have dug a hole, right?" I know for certain that Freak O' Nature's and Why Can't You Be Like Johnny?'s and Linda's parents didn't dig holes for bomb shelters, and I have a feeling that if anyone else we knew had, we would have heard about it. It's not fair. Freak O' Nature and Why Can't You Be Like Johnny? never did mean things to anyone and never even *met* a Russian. . . .

My thoughts are interrupted by faint grinding sounds coming from Sparky's direction. He's lying on the bunk, eyes closed as if he's asleep, but his jaw works back and forth.

"Edward?" Dad whispers.

My brother doesn't respond. He's doing it in his sleep.

"He ever do that before?" Dad asks.

I shake my head. Dad watches him for a moment, then glances at Mom.

"She's not going to be okay, is she?" I ask.

With his elbows on the table, Dad brings his clasped hands to his forehead like he's praying. "I don't know, Scott."

But deep down, I think he does.

A slight rustling wakes me. Dad and I have fallen asleep at the table with our heads on our arms. Out of the corner of my eye, I watch Sparky quietly creep down from the bunk. I'd ask him where he's going, but I don't want to wake everyone.

Naked, he heads toward the toilet bucket, so I assume he just has to go. Still sleepy, my heavy eyelids are starting to close when I hear the metallic clink of the big refuse can. Sparky tips open the top and throws his dirty pajamas in.

"Mr. Porter? Mr. Porter!" Janet is sitting up, staring at Mom, who is still lying on her back on the bunk. My first thought is that the worst has happened, but then I see that her eyes are open.

"Don't look." Dad gets up quickly.

"Why not?" I ask.

"Because —" He stops. When Mom hears his voice, her eyes move toward him.

"Gwen?" Dad sounds hopeful and excited.

Her eyes stay on him, but she doesn't move.

The others wake and look. Dad kneels beside Mom. "Gwen?"

No answer.

"What is it?" Mrs. Shaw whispers.

"She's awake." Dad tenderly strokes Mom's cheek. "Can you hear me, sweetheart?"

But Mom's expression remains blank.

The others slowly climb out of the bunks and gather around. Mom's eyes move as she looks at them, but there's no sign of recognition.

"Gwen?" Dad says again.

Her eyes go back to him.

"Gwen, nod if you can hear me."

Mom still doesn't react.

Dad holds a finger up in front of her face and moves it slowly left. Her eyes follow it, but when Dad moves his finger back, her gaze remains directed at the wall.

"Gwen? Honey?" he says again, anxiously.

Her eyes slowly come back to him. But her face is blank. Dad picks up her hand and squeezes it. It looks limp in his. "Sweetheart?" His voice is full of uncertainty.

She doesn't respond. Dad puts her hand down, then turns away and hides his face.

twenty-six

When school began that fall, we had a new teacher and new desks. The teacher was skinny, with hollowed cheeks and a dark shadow over his jaw. He wore a gray suit that looked too big, a thin black tie, and a white shirt. Except for gym, it was the first time we'd ever had a man teacher.

"Welcome to sixth grade," he said. "My name is Mr. Kasman, and we have something in common. This is a new grade for you and a new school for me. If you look inside your desk, you will find a strip of oaktag. Please write your first name in large neat letters and place it on your desk where I can see it."

Our new desks didn't have hinged tops like the old ones. To get things from inside, we had to bend down and squint into them or feel around blindly with our hands. We'd all begun to work on our name cards when the classroom's public-address speaker crackled on: "Hello, students, and welcome back to Willis Road for another exciting year of learning." It was Principal Sharp. "A lot has changed over the summer. We have some new teachers, a new soundproof ceiling, and, as you've probably already noticed, new desks with scratch-proof desktops. After what happened last year, I'm sure you know why we got them. I hope you all have a great first day."

The PA went silent. "What happened last year?" Mr. Kasman asked.

Paula raised her hand.

"Yes, uh . . . " Mr. Kasman squinted at her name card. "Paula?"

"The boys carved things into the desks. Then they couldn't write on them because their pens went through the paper."

Mr. Kasman ran his fingers over the shiny hard surface of a desk in the front row. Then he said, "Please finish your name cards."

I went back to work, but a scratching sound started behind me. With his left arm resting on his desk, Puddin' Belly Wright appeared to be hunched forward, gazing toward the front of the room. But behind his left arm, his right hand was clenched around a bent paper clip, busy scratching at the surface of his new scratch-proof desk.

Puddin' Belly was a big, strong, chubby kid who lived a block away from us and often came around to play fungo baseball and touch football. His real name was Stuart Wright, but his belly bounced and jiggled when he ran, and somehow he'd acquired that nickname. Puddin' Belly would do almost anything if dared, or if even just asked. One morning a few days later, while Mr. Kasman wrote on the blackboard, Ronnie slid him a note. Puddin' Belly read it and raised his hand. "Hey, Mr. Kasman, how come you became a teacher?"

"I'm not a horse," Mr. Kasman said, without pausing from what he was writing.

"Huh?"

"You said 'hey,' and he said he's not a horse," Paula explained.

"Huh?" Puddin' Belly said again.

"Forget it." Mr. Kasman turned from the board. "I became a teacher because I think it's an important job."

"All of the teachers in this school are ladies," said Puddin' Belly. "Except for Mr. Brown, the gym teacher."

"Are you implying that the only teaching job a man should have is gym?" asked Mr. Kasman.

Puddin' Belly wasn't implying anything. He was simply repeating what Ronnie had told him to say. Now that the subject had been broached without Mr. Kasman getting mad, Ronnie must have felt safe to add his two cents. "I think what Stuart means is that men usually don't become teachers."

"My father teaches economics at Hofstra," said Paula.

"That's college," said Ronnie.

"Mr. Kasman?" the PA squawked. It was one of the secretaries. "Can you come down to the office for a moment?"

"Take out your grammar workbooks, and work on pages fourteen and fifteen," Mr. Kasman said, and left.

Ronnie went to the back of the room to sharpen his pencil. The grinding filled our ears. When it stopped, he didn't return to his desk. Instead, he looked up at the new sound-absorbing white cork squares in the ceiling. Holding the pencil at the point, he flicked his wrist. The pencil flew up and stuck, hanging from the ceiling like a thin yellow stalactite.

Ronnie went to the front of the room, took a new pencil from the box on Mr. Kasman's desk, and sharpened it. This time the whole room watched. A moment later, there were two yellow stalactites in the ceiling.

Puddin' Belly flipped his pencil at the ceiling. It bounced off and fell to the floor. Freak O' Nature flipped his pencil. Same result. Eric Flom tried it. Still the same result.

"Stand guard, Scott," Ronnie ordered.

Standing guard was tricky because you had to be in the doorway and watch without being seen by the teacher you were on the lookout for. I'd perfected a method of keeping the door ajar with my foot while sticking just enough of my face out so I could see with one eye. It was nothing any other kid couldn't do, but since I'd been the first to think of it, it had become my role.

By now there was a line of boys at the pencil sharpener and nonstop grinding. Kids asked Ronnie to demonstrate his technique. Soon more pencils were stuck in the ceiling.

Down the hall, Mr. Kasman came around the corner. I backed out of the doorway. "He's coming!"

Everyone hurried to their desks and got to work in their grammar workbooks.

Mr. Kasman came in and sat down and wrote something in his notebook. Then he noticed the empty pencil box.

Then he looked at us.

Then he looked up.

27

The grown-ups sit at the table and talk. The kids sit on the bunks like spectators.

"Maybe she just needs time to recover," Mrs. Shaw says.

"Anyone ever seen anything like this?" Dad asks.

"That depends on what you mean by *this*," Mr. McGovern answers. I think he's talking about his son, Paula's brother, Teddy.

"Mr. Porter?" Janet says from the bunk where she's sitting next to Mom. "She needs to be turned or she'll get bedsores."

"Now?" Dad asks.

"The sooner the better, sir."

One of Mr. McGovern's eyebrows dips. "And you know this because?"

"I was studying to be a nurse, sir."

"You? Where?" Mr. McGovern sounds a little mean.

"Long Island College Hospital of Nursing, sir."

"Never heard of it," Mr. McGovern says dismissively.

For a moment, everyone goes still. I wish I could ask Mr. McGovern why he said that. Then the moment passes, and Dad helps Janet turn Mom onto her side.

That's when we all smell it.

As if the mildew and pee odors aren't bad enough, now there's this. I feel embarrassed for Mom and try not to watch while Dad and Janet remove her soiled clothes and the sheet she was lying on. It all goes into the big refuse can. Dad relents about using water for something other than drinking. For a sponge and towels, Janet tears off the bottom part of her robe. After the rags are used, they also go into the can.

When they're finished, Mom is lying on her side with her bare bottom and legs exposed. Dad takes the sheet from the upper bunk and tears it in half. He and Janet tuck it around Mom, who is as still and quiet as before.

My stomach growls, but I know we need to ration the food, so I keep quiet. Ronnie, me, and Sparky, who's now wearing a little loincloth Janet made for him, have played about a thousand games of checkers. Dad comes over and suggests we switch to Parcheesi. He makes the slightest gesture with his head toward Paula, so I say, "Want to play, Paula?"

With his back to her so she can't see, Dad smiles and nods.

We four kids play Parcheesi, but all I think about is food. Since it's impossible to tell whether it's day or night, people climb into the bunks when they're tired, but now it's more like we take long naps rather than sleep for one extended period. Mr. McGovern snores. Sparky grinds his teeth. Mrs. Shaw talks in her sleep. Once she said, "Ronnie, stop that right now!" and another time it was, "I hate this."

But no one sleeps for long; hunger keeps waking us.

"Is it time to eat, Herr Kapitän?" Mr. McGovern asks.

Sparky looks up curiously. "What's that mean, Dad?"

"He's making a joke," Dad says.

"Well?" Mr. McGovern doesn't sound like he's making a joke.

Dad points at the remaining cans on the shelf. "I only stored enough food for four. Now we're ten. At this rate, we'll use it all up by the end of the first week."

"And you're the one who decides when we eat?" asks Mr. McGovern.

"It's my family's food," Dad points out.

"Maybe it was . . . before what happened," Mr. McGovern says. "But now that we're all in this together, shouldn't it belong to all of us?"

Dad and Mr. McGovern face each other.

"You know," Dad grumbles, "none of us would be alive right now if it wasn't for me. Did it ever occur to you to utter two very simple words like 'thank you'?"

Paula's dad glares. "Thank you, Richard. However, don't forget that if you'd had your way, the rest of us would be dead."

Dad narrows his eyes. "Yes, I tried to keep people out, but only to protect my family. It was horrible and something that's going to haunt me for a long time. But how was I supposed to know how many people were up there? What was I supposed to do? Let everyone in? How'd you like it if there were twenty people in here right now? Or thirty? You might as well be up there."

"I think I'd rather die than know I was responsible for the deaths of others," Mrs. Shaw says.

I've never seen Dad argue or fight with our neighbors before. Except for the disagreements my parents sometimes had, I'm not sure I ever saw grown-ups get cross with one another before.

Now Dad turns to Mr. Shaw. "You want to tell her or should I?"

Mr. Shaw gazes up at the ceiling and lets out a long

breath. "Steph, after I got you and Ronnie down here, I . . . " He trails off and lowers his head.

"He helped me keep the others out," Dad finishes for him. "I couldn't have done it without him."

twenty-eight

Once he'd gone around the room with a yardstick and knocked the pencils out of the ceiling, Mr. Kasman made all the boys stay in for lunch detention.

"What was the point of that?" he asked us.

No one answered.

"Ronnie?" By now Mr. Kasman had figured out who the likely ringleader was.

"It was interesting," Ronnie said.

"How?"

"Just to see if you could do it."

"It appears that most of you figured out you could do it."

"But then we had to figure out if we could keep doing it." Ronnie grinned.

"Was it worth missing recess?"

No one answered.

"Scott?"

I answered honestly. "Well, uh, just this once, yeah."

A couple of guys chuckled. Even Mr. Kasman smirked as if, deep down inside, he understood. Maybe it was good that we had a man teacher, because I had a feeling a woman teacher would never understand. "Okay, but this is the last time, right?"

"Does that mean we can go outside?" asked Ronnie.

"No, it means you'll stay here today, and if it ever happens again, you'll get a week of lunch detentions."

"So we just have to sit here?" asked Freak O' Nature. We'd never had lunch detention before.

"We can talk," said Mr. Kasman. That was strange. Most teachers didn't want to talk to us. They just wanted us to do our work and be quiet. Maybe Mr. Kasman was too new to know that yet.

Ronnie whispered something to Puddin' Belly, who raised his hand. "Are you a beatnik, Mr. Kasman?"

"What's a beatnik?" Mr. Kasman asked.

"They live in Greenwich Village and listen to jazz," said Eric Flom.

Dickie Keller raised his hand. "They play bongos and read poetry."

"And snap their fingers and say 'Cool, man, cool,'" said Freak O' Nature.

"How many of your parents listen to jazz?" Mr. Kasman asked.

A few hands went up around the room.

"Are they beatniks?" our teacher asked.

The kids who'd raised their hands shook their heads.

"Who knows what the word *stereotype* means?"

Silence. If Paula had been there, she probably would have known, but it was only us guys.

Mr. Kasman opened the dictionary. "To stereotype means 'to characterize someone, usually in a negative or unfair way. To make a generalization about them.' So saying that all beatniks listen to jazz and read poetry would be a generalization, but not necessarily in a negative way. But saying that all Russians are evil would be stereotyping them in a pejorative way." Gazing out at a small sea of blank faces he added, "*Pejorative* means negative or unfair."

"But the Russians *are* evil," said Ronnie.

"Dirty Commies," Freak O' Nature said in a low tough-guy voice.

"Why are they dirty?" Mr. Kasman asked.

"They don't believe in God," said Eric Flom. "And the Russian people are starving because the Communists spend all their money on missiles and bombs."

"They take away your freedom," said Dickie Keller.

"You can't vote and there's no freedom of speech and you'll get sent to Siberia if you say something the leaders don't like."

"Why?" asked our teacher.

Everyone went quiet.

"Well, come on," Mr. Kasman said. "Why would they do all those things?"

Dickie raised his arm halfway. "Because . . . they're evil?"

"What if they just have different beliefs?" our teacher asked. "Communism is based on the ideas of a philosopher named Karl Marx, who believed that if all people were equal and were treated equally, they would live in a state of Utopia."

Mr. Kasman must have sensed our confusion because he said, "It's not a state like Rhode Island. It's a state of mind. Marx believed that if no one has more than anyone else and no one is better than anyone else, then everyone will be equally happy."

I raised my hand. "You mean, if no one has anything, then they don't have more than anyone else?"

"In a way."

"What's so great about that?" asked Ronnie.

"Marx thought it was great. I'm not sure I do."

I raised my hand again. "If everyone's equal, who settles arguments?"

A smile grew on Mr. Kasman's lips. "That . . . is a very

good question, Scott. There would still be a ruler and a government, and the government would make those decisions."

"But then everyone wouldn't really be equal," I said.

"Right!" Mr. Kasman seemed pleased I'd figured that out.

I'd been right in class before, but I'm not sure a teacher had ever said so with as much praise. It felt good, and for the first time, I began to understand why Paula raised her hand so much.

Too bad Mom wasn't there to see it.

29

If no one moves or speaks, the loudest sound is the grumbling of our stomachs. That, along with being trapped down here, makes everyone moody and irritable.

"At least give us more to drink," Mr. Shaw says to Dad. "I'd rather have Tang in my stomach than nothing at all."

"What if we run out of water?" Dad replies.

"I told you that won't happen," says Mr. McGovern.

"And I told *you* that we can't know for sure," Dad shoots back sharply.

It seems like Paula's dad doubts almost everything my dad says. Just like he doubted Janet was going to college to learn to be a nurse. Is it because Mr. McGovern teaches college himself? The tension between Dad and the other adults is always just below the surface. When it comes out, Ronnie and I share perplexed looks. Everything is so strange. Our parents getting angry at one another. Mom lying mutely on the bunk. The sadness of Paula being here without her mom and brother.

And wondering all the while what has become of the world on the other side of the trapdoor.

"This was a mistake," Mr. Shaw mutters. "It's over. All we're doing is postponing the inevitable."

"Don't talk that way," Dad says.

"Don't tell me how to talk," Mr. Shaw snaps back.

"Steven, the children." Mrs. Shaw puts a hand on her husband's knee. I wonder if Mr. Shaw will snap at her, too, but he doesn't. What would they be saying if we kids weren't here?

There's still nothing on the radio except bent sound and static.

Mrs. Shaw smirks. "Is there something you don't want to miss, Richard?"

"We're supposed to listen to the Civil Defense channels," Dad replies. "They're supposed to tell us what to do."

"Aren't we doing what we're supposed to do?" Mrs. Shaw asks ironically.

"It *would* be nice to think that someone else has survived," Mr. McGovern adds.

"They have," Dad says. "Lots of people built shelters."

"Lots," Mrs. Shaw echoes, like she's laughing at him.

We hear a soft, low groan. Dad squats down close to Mom. "Gwen?"

She doesn't answer.

He tries her name again and again and touches her face gently, but she doesn't respond. Then he hangs his head.

"She hasn't had anything to drink," Janet says.

Dad nods.

"Is she going to be okay?" Sparky asks anxiously.

"I hope so," Dad answers, but his heart isn't in it.

It doesn't feel as chilly in the shelter as before. Maybe because of our combined body heat or maybe we're just getting used to the chill. But when Dad cranks the ventilator, Mrs. Shaw complains that it's cold.

"Who builds a bomb shelter and doesn't put warm clothes in it?" she asks in a tone Mom sometimes used when the silverware at a restaurant looked dirty.

The question looms over us in the dank, dim air. I brace myself for Dad to get angry, but he doesn't.

"I've been thinking about it, Stephanie," he replies evenly. "Maybe I never got around to putting warm clothes down here and didn't rinse the water tank or test the radio because . . . even though I built this shelter, I never wanted to believe that this could really happen."

"Then why build it in the first place?" Mr. Shaw asks.

Dad throws up his hands. "I was trying to plan for something completely illogical. Why don't you tell me, Steven. How do you apply logic to something that makes no sense?"

Mr. Shaw's forehead furrows. He looks at the floor and doesn't answer.

thirty

Mothers had breasts. When you got hurt, they would press the side of your head against their bosoms, which were sometimes soft and comforting, and sometimes rough if under their blouse they were wearing a bra, which was the thing women wore to hold their breasts in place. Boys and men didn't really have anything that needed to be held in place, except when you played Little League, you were supposed to wear a jock with a protective cup so that you didn't get whacked in the nuts by the ball.

"Watch this," Ronnie said, and crossed the street to where Paula was standing beside her bike, talking to Linda. He went behind Paula, reached for the back of her shirt, pulled something underneath, and then let go. Even across the street, you could hear the snapping sound.

Paula cried out. Her bike crashed to the sidewalk, and she ran home.

Ronnie raced back toward me. "Come on!"

I jumped up and ran after him, suspecting that he'd just done something that would get him in trouble again. At least this time, I could say I had nothing to do with it.

Old Lady Lester's backyard was a good place to hide because she stayed inside all the time. Ronnie and I sat down on the grass.

"What'd you do?" I asked.

"Snapped her bra." Ronnie grinned.

"Why?"

Ronnie stopped grinning. "That's what we're supposed to do. Girls wear bras and boys snap 'em."

"I never heard of anyone doing that before," I said.

"We didn't know any girls who wore bras before."

"My mom wears a bra."

Ronnie looked at me like I was crazy. "You can't snap your mother's bra."

"Why not?" Not that I ever would. But I mostly wanted to hear what kind of reason Ronnie would come up with.

"You just can't." He pulled up a clover and started to suck on it. "Know how to tell how big a woman's breasts are?"

"By looking at them?"

"By how thick their bra strap is."

"Why can't you tell by looking at them?"

"Sometimes you can. Sometimes you can't. It depends on what they're wearing. But you can always tell by the strap. You see a strap like this"—Ronnie spread his thumb and index finger until there was about three inches between them—"and those are really big breasts."

He paused and studied me. I stared down at the grass.

"Ever seen a breast?" he asked. "I mean, for real?"

I felt my face get hot and tugged at some hairs behind my right ear.

He gave me an astonished look. "What about your mom's?"

"She keeps them hidden."

"What about by accident? Like walking into her bedroom when she's getting dressed?"

"We're supposed to knock."

"Haven't you ever forgotten?"

"No."

Ronnie smirked. "You're allowed to forget once in a while."

"You mean . . . on purpose?" I asked, astonished.

He nodded enthusiastically. It was a shocking suggestion. Sneak into your own mother's bedroom to look at her breasts? Only someone as sick as Ronnie would think of something like that.

"You've . . . done that?" I asked.

"Of course. Every kid has."

"I've never heard of anyone doing it."

Ronnie harrumphed. "Just like you've never heard of snapping bras. Come on, you think Freak O' Nature or Johnny is going to tell the whole world he snuck into his mom's bedroom so he could look at her breasts?"

"Then how do you know?" I asked.

"I told you. Every kid does it. The best time is in the morning when she's getting dressed. Or on Saturday nights before she goes out. Moms always take baths and then try on lots of different clothes before they go out, so your chances are pretty good then."

I didn't know what to say. Sneaking looks at your mother's breasts had to be wrong.

"Scott, we could all be dead tomorrow," Ronnie said solemnly. "You want to die without ever seeing a breast?"

31

Mom can sit up if someone helps her. She'll drink and eat if you put water or food to her lips. Janet helps Dad take care of her. Sometimes Dad kneels in front of Mom and talks, but she just sits and stares blankly.

"Would you try?" Dad asks me.

I don't answer because I'm afraid. I'm not even sure what I'm afraid of.

"Come on, Scott," Dad says. "And you, too, Edward."

Sparky bites his lip and shakes his head. He's also scared.

"It's important," Dad says. "Maybe she'll recognize you."

Sparky takes my hand. He's never done that before. We face Mom.

"Say something," Dad says.

"Hi, Mom," Sparky says.

She doesn't react.

"Mom?" I say.

No response.

Sparky starts to sniff, and Dad puts his arms around him. I feel like crying, too. Now I know what I was afraid of — that she wouldn't know us, either.

Ronnie and I sit together on the bunk. Our fight is still on my mind, but most of my anger has passed. He's my best friend. Right now, he's my only friend. Maybe the only friend I'll have for the rest of my life. Before the fight, we'd never hit each other, but we'd disagreed and gotten mad plenty of times. Isn't a fistfight just more of the same?

He presses his fingertips together under his nose like a squirrel eating a nut and sniffs. Then he leans close and whispers in my ear, "Feels like jail."

He's right, with all of us crammed into this tiny room with bare gray concrete walls. I whisper back, "But *they* get more to eat."

Ronnie chuckles. The others frown when they see us whispering. Up till now, everyone's said what they're thinking out loud. And even though Ronnie and I are just talking kid stuff, I have a feeling we shouldn't look like we're sharing secrets.

I hate being hungry. I hate what's happened to my mother. I hate being down here in this smelly, chilly, damp, windowless room, with nothing to do. I hate that everyone has to go to the bathroom in front of everyone else and nobody has any privacy. I hate feeling sad about my friends and everyone else who was up there. I hate that this happened, and I hate whoever made it happen.

Dad says we should exercise. "We need to keep our strength up for what comes next."

"And just what do you think comes next?" asks Mrs. Shaw.

"Rebuilding."

Ronnie's mother rolls her eyes. "You really think life's going back to the way it used to be?"

"There won't be that much destruction outside the blast zone," Dad replies. "I think you'll be surprised."

Mrs. Shaw slowly shakes her head. "What are you going to do for food, Richard? Go to the store? There isn't going to be any food. The animals are dead. The farmers who raised them are dead. There'll be no electricity, no gasoline. If we don't starve, we'll freeze to death. Don't you understand? The world . . . has been destroyed."

"Steph, the kids," Mr. Shaw cautions.

"What difference does it make? They're going to find out soon enough," Mrs. Shaw says scornfully.

Maybe we're supposed to understand that the grown-ups are on edge, but it's still upsetting when they argue. What's even more upsetting is suspecting that Ronnie's mom is right. I tug behind my ear and glance at Sparky, who watches and listens.

"Let me tell you how you're going to spend the rest of your life, Richard," Mrs. Shaw goes on. "You'll be searching for whatever food hasn't been contaminated or gone bad. You'll be looking for clean water. You'll probably wind up migrating south, because without heat, the winters up here won't be survivable. And you want to know what's going to happen when you head south? You're going to run into all the other survivors who've had the same idea. Only then there'll be even less food and water to go around, and—"

"Dad!" Sparky cries out, and runs into his arms. "Is that true?"

"Things will be different from before," Dad says, hugging him and glaring hard at Mrs. Shaw. "But right now we don't know how."

Playing Parcheesi gets boring, so we go back to checkers. Then that gets boring, and we try Go Fish. But eventually we get to the point where we don't want to play any games at all. The boredom is bad because there's nothing to do except wonder and worry about what's going to happen next. The hunger pangs are worse, but sometimes they take my mind off the future. The bare patch behind my ear must be the size of a tennis ball, but I can't stop tugging.

Mom just sits with that blank look like a marionette with the strings cut. Sometimes I wonder if she can think but can't move her arms and legs. But she can move her eyes. Only she hardly ever does.

"I can't stand it," Mr. McGovern says. "I need to eat something."

"We'll never make it if we don't ration," Dad says.

"Then maybe we shouldn't be feeding all these mouths," says Mr. McGovern.

The words hang in the clammy air.

"What do you mean?" Dad asks.

"I think you know."

Again there's silence, as if something serious has happened. Mrs. Shaw's eyes dart from Dad to Mr. McGovern, and it feels like it does in school when a kid does something really bad. Finally, Dad says, "I think you better watch yourself, Herb."

But Mr. McGovern isn't finished. "You didn't come this far just to fail now, did you, Richard? If hunger forces us out of here too soon, it'll all be for naught."

My heart begins to thump. It sounds like Mr. McGovern is suggesting that some people leave. But who?

"We could take a simple vote," he continues. "The majority rules."

"Over my dead body," Dad says.

"You were more than willing to let people die so that you and your family could live. You'll still have your boys."

He's talking about Mom!

Dad is shaking his head in disbelief. "You can't be serious, Herb."

"I can't?" Mr. McGovern laughs bitterly. "I'm talking about survival, Richard. Isn't that what this is all about? Isn't that why you built this shelter? And in this situation, you might as well add 'of the fittest,' because like Stephanie said, that's what it's going to be once we get out of here."

"That's enough!" Dad yells, and starts pacing like a tiger in a cage. My heart beats faster, and my forehead grows hot. Are they going to fight?

Mr. McGovern turns to the Shaws. "Do *you* think it's enough? It's not as if we're guests here anymore. We're all in this together, and we all have an equal say. I think Richard's right about the food. We probably don't have enough to make it until the radiation gets down to a safe level. But with two less mouths to feed, maybe we could."

Two less mouths? Who else is he talking about? He said Dad would still have Sparky and me, and he sure wouldn't be talking about his daughter or the Shaws. . . . *That leaves Janet.*

Just a few months ago, the worst, most scary thing in life was when Dad got angry and came after me with the paddle. After that, the scariest thing was the Russians attacking. Now it's being in this bomb shelter with grown-ups arguing about who should live and die. Forget what Mrs. Shaw said about how hard life will be when we get out of here. What will happen if Mr. McGovern and the Shaws gang up on Dad? They could force Mom and Janet out, and then what would stop them from forcing Dad and Sparky and me out as well? I know Dad's stronger than either Mr. Shaw or Mr. McGovern, and I know what's in the green box on the shelf, but what if they wait until he's asleep? And they could probably make Ronnie fight me, and I'd be sure to lose.

Dad stops his tiger prowl beside Mom's bunk. "I won't hear another word of this. I said over my dead body, and I meant it." He faces Mr. McGovern. "Have you lost your mind, talking like this in front of these children? In front of this woman?" He gestures to Janet. "In front of your own daughter?" He gestures to Paula.

"To quote Charles Darwin, 'It is not the strongest of the species that survives, nor the most intelligent. It's the one that is the most adaptable to change,'" Mr. McGovern shoots back. "It looks to me like we can either adapt to the reality of this situation or starve to death."

"We're not going to die," Dad counters. "As long as we have water, we should be able to survive until the radiation levels go down."

"You hope," Mr. McGovern grouses.

Dad gives him a stern look. "Yes, Herb, I do."

thirty-two

Early each morning, the newspaper boy tossed the paper onto our driveway. Normally Dad would pick it up and read it on the train to the city, where he worked for an insurance company. But lately he went out before breakfast and brought it inside to read with Mom. Sparky and I would come into the kitchen, and they'd be sitting at the table with the paper open, coffee cups in their hands, and serious expressions on their faces.

When I asked what was going on, they either said "nothing" or gave some vague answer about the Russians and Cuba. And Mom would almost always add, "It's nothing you should worry about."

One night when Dad came in to kiss me good night, I asked, "What if the Russians attack when you're not home?"

"You'll have to go into the shelter without me."

"But what'll happen to you?"

"There are lots of shelters in the city. In the basements of buildings and the subway."

"So we could all meet again after the war?"

Dad nodded. "That's the plan."

That was good news because it meant the only times Dad might have a problem was when he was on the train going to and from work. "So if they drop the bomb and you're at work, after the war should we come to the city, or will you come back here?"

Dad ran his tongue over his front teeth and thought. "Things in New York could be pretty chaotic. You should stay out here." He got quiet for a moment. "You and Edward riding your bikes to school every day?"

I looked down at the bedcovers. A few weeks before, Dad had made us promise we would.

"I thought we agreed," he said.

"Sparky quit after the third day, and I don't like riding all the way there alone."

Dad looked off. "Well, I guess I can understand that."

"So what do we do if there's a war and we're at school?"

"Try to get home as fast as you can."

- - - - - - -

The next day after school, I laid a wooden yardstick end over end, marking yards in chalk on the sidewalk in front of our house. When I thought I had enough, I went back and started counting them. "One, two, three."

"Seven, six, eight, twelve," Sparky began spitting out numbers until I forgot where I was. I shook my fist at him. "You want to get hurt?" He backed away and I started over, numbering each yard with chalk. I'd just finished marking off fifty yards when Ronnie and Why Can't You Be Like Johnny? came by.

Ronnie looked at the yardstick and the chalk numbers going up to fifty. Then he saw my stopwatch lying on the grass. He turned to my brother. "What's he up to?"

Sparky shook his head like he wasn't allowed to say, which was what I told him if anyone asked.

Ronnie popped a few Sugar Babies in his mouth and smacked his lips. "Man, these are good." He held the bag out to Sparky. "Want some?"

Five seconds later, Ronnie knew exactly what I was up to: trying to see how long it would take if I had to run all the way home from school.

"Scott, anyone ever tell you you're crazy?" he asked.

"Yeah. You, about a thousand times."

"Make it a thousand and one," Ronnie said. "You're crazy."

"Thanks."

"What's the point?" he asked. "Didn't you see those

pictures of Hiroshima? All those burned-up and deformed people. Why would you want to be around for that?"

"It's better than dying," I said, not because I was really sure that it was, but because it was the only answer I could think of.

"You know about radiation poisoning?" asked Why Can't You Be Like Johnny? He was in the smart class at school and never got into trouble. And he was nice. Not brownnose-teacher's-pet-nice like Paula, but nice and polite in a sincere way that made everybody like him. And if that wasn't bad enough, he was a good athlete who could throw and catch and run really fast. The only thing wrong with Why Can't You Be Like Johnny? was that there was nothing wrong with him.

"A little," I answered.

"What is it?" asked Sparky.

"It's from the radioactive fallout," Why Can't You Be Like Johnny? explained. "After the mushroom cloud, dust and ash float down out of the sky, and it's full of radiation, and when you touch it or breathe it into your lungs, it makes you sick. Your hair falls out and you throw up and—"

"Ahhhhh!" Sparky let out a cry and ran toward the house with his hands over his ears.

"Did I scare him?" asked Why Can't You Be Like Johnny?

"He has this thing about throwing up," I explained. "Even if you just mention it, he starts to cry."

"Sorry, I didn't know," Why Can't You Be Like Johnny? said. And the thing was, he wasn't just saying it. He really was sorry.

Ronnie pointed at the fifty yards I'd marked off. "You gonna try it?"

I gave him the stopwatch, then crouched down like a sprinter, pressing my hands against the rough concrete. "Anytime."

"Ready . . . set . . . go!" Ronnie yelled.

I took off as fast as I could. When I'd passed the fifty-yard line, I stopped and bent over with my hands on my thighs. "How'd I do?" I panted.

Back at the start line, Ronnie shrugged. "How would I know?"

"Didn't you time me?"

Ronnie looked down at the stopwatch. "Is *that* what this is for?"

"Very funny." I walked back to the start line, took the stopwatch, and gave it to Why Can't You Be Like Johnny? "No tricks, okay?"

Why Can't You Be Like Johnny? never played tricks on people. Once again, I crouched down. "Anytime."

"On your mark, get set, go!"

I went.

"Seven point four seconds," Johnny called out after I'd passed the finish line.

Still breathing hard, I took out a piece of paper on which I'd prepared some calculations. There were 2,640 yards in a mile and a half, and divided by 50, it was 52.8. If you multiplied 52.8 by 7.4 seconds, you got 390.72 seconds. "I can make it home in about six and a half minutes," I said.

This was good because there might be things I'd need to do before I went down into the bomb shelter. Like go into my room and get the latest *MAD* magazine if I hadn't finished reading it. And get the Halloween candy if Mom had already bought some. After all, Halloween was less than two weeks away and it would be a shame to see all that candy wasted.

"What about Sparky?" asked Ronnie.

I hadn't thought of that. Sparky was slower than me, but not that much slower. "I think he'll make it in time."

"Can I see that?" Why Can't You Be Like Johnny? gestured for the pencil and paper. I gave it to him and lay back on the grass and looked at the clouds. Today they were thin and wispy, but I was thinking about a mushroom cloud. The only picture I'd ever seen of one had looked dark gray and ominous and was no doubt filled with radioactive fallout.

"You do what we talked about?" Ronnie asked while

Why Can't You Be Like Johnny? was busy scribbling on the paper.

"Huh?"

"What we talked about after I pulled the thing that snapped? And then we ran behind Old Lady Lester's house?"

I shook my head.

Why Can't You Be Like Johnny? looked up from his calculations. "What are you talking about?"

"Nothing," I said.

"You could always look at your father's *Playboys*," Ronnie said.

"I don't think my father has any," I said.

"All fathers have *Playboys*," Ronnie insisted. "Look in his closet. If they're not there, look in his dresser drawer under his shirts."

"Does your father have *Playboys*?" I asked Why Can't You Be Like Johnny?

He shook his head and circled a number on the paper. "I hate to say this, Scott, but it's going to take you a lot longer to run home from school."

"Why?" I asked, unsettled by how he'd stressed *a lot*.

"The fastest man alive can run a mile in about four minutes. Even if he could continue at that same pace for *another* half mile, which is doubtful, it would take *him* six minutes."

"Uh-oh." Ronnie grinned. "You're probably about a

thousand times slower than the fastest man alive. If they drop the bomb while we're at school, you'll never make it home in time."

This was really bad news.

"I'd look for those *Playboy*s if I were you," Ronnie said.

33

The talk of making people leave the shelter has stopped, but it doesn't feel like it's over. A little while ago, after they fed Mom, Dad put his hand on Janet's shoulder as if to reassure her that nothing bad would happen. I guess as long as we're hungry, what Mr. McGovern said will probably be in the backs of everyone's minds.

In the meantime, we have to adapt to less and less privacy. When someone has to go potty, two people hold up a sheet. It's not just for the person who's going, but for the rest of us, so we don't have to watch.

When Sparky and I go, Dad reminds us to use as little toilet paper as possible. The way he says it makes me think he's trying to remind the others as well, because he can't really tell Paula or Ronnie or the other grown-ups what to do. But with ten people, the toilet paper seems to go fast no matter how careful we are.

We quickly get used to the potty noises that made us giggle up there. If a kid in class farted, everyone would laugh and titter. But down here no one cares anymore.

Dad and Janet take Mom to the toilet bucket often in case she has to go. They turn her on her bunk so she doesn't get bedsores. Now and then Dad crouches in front of her and speaks, but he gets no reaction.

Sometimes Sparky sits next to Mom and holds her limp hand. And once in a while, he'll reach for Janet's hand. When he does that, you might catch a frown on Mr. McGovern's face. Ronnie keeps pressing his fingertips under his nose and sniffing. Paula picks her nose but tries to hide it. Mr. Shaw sticks his finger in his ear and rotates it, digging out wax. Maybe they've always done these things in public and I just never noticed, but now there's nothing else to notice. There's no outside, no windows, no TV screens. Nothing to look at but each other. There are a few books and magazines, but if someone uses the flashlight to read them, there's no light for anyone else. We take turns resting on the bunks and sitting on the floor and at the table. We've played about a million games of checkers and Parcheesi and Sorry! and Go Fish. When no one talks, we listen to the groans and cries of empty stomachs.

And I can't help wondering if we've even been down here for three days yet.

thirty-four

Once a week, Janet came to clean our house and babysit Sparky and me so that our parents could go out. She'd sleep on a cot in the laundry room and go home in the morning with a Negro man who drove a dented green car with a cracked windshield. Sometimes when Sparky and I left for school in the morning, the car would be parked in front of our house and the man would be inside it, waiting.

One afternoon back in September, I was playing with my plastic army men on the white shag carpet when Mom called, "Get in the car, kids. We're driving Janet home."

"She's not staying over?" Sparky asked.

"No, your father and I aren't going out tonight."

Mom and Janet got in the front, and Sparky and I sat in the back.

"You'll have to tell me how to get there," Mom said as we backed out of the driveway.

"I'm not exactly sure, Mrs. Porter. Elmore does the driving."

"Oh, I know," Mom said. "I'm that way when Richard drives."

It sounded strange when Mom referred to Dad by his first name. She seemed to know where to go for a while, but then we got to a corner and she stopped and glanced at Janet.

"I think it's a right turn, Mrs. Porter."

It was starting to feel like an adventure. At the next light, Mom asked, "Does this look familiar?"

Janet looked out the window and pulled her lips in. "'Fraid not, Mrs. Porter."

"I wonder if we missed a turn," Mom said. The light changed, and we had to start going again. At an Esso gas station at the next corner, Mom pulled in. "I'll be right back."

While she was in the office, a man in dark-green coveralls strolled past our car. His hands were almost black with grime and grease. When he stopped and squinted at us, Janet looked down. The man took a dirty rag out of his back pocket and wiped his hands. "Everything okay?" he asked me.

I nodded. The man glanced at Janet again and then walked toward a car waiting for gas.

Mom came out of the office and got into the car. "It's a little farther." She started to drive.

"A man asked if everything was okay," Sparky said from the back.

"Why?"

"I think because of Janet."

Janet stared down at her lap again.

"I'm sorry," Mom said.

"It's not your fault, Mrs. Porter."

I wasn't sure if Mom was sorry that Sparky had said it or sorry that the man had asked in the first place.

"Oh, there! There!" Janet suddenly got excited and pointed. "That's the street!"

Mom turned so quickly that the tires screeched, and we all slid to the right. "Aha!" She let out a gasping laugh that sounded like half relief and half surprise that the car didn't wind up on the sidewalk. Lining the street were small brick houses with white shutters. The houses were so close together that there was barely room for a driveway between them. The small yards had low metal fences and gates. In our neighborhood one lawn blended into the next, and no one had a fence. Some Negro boys around my age were playing baseball in the street, and inside a gated yard, some girls were playing teatime with dolls around a small table. The boys eyed us warily as we passed. When my friends and I played on the street, we rarely looked to see who was in the cars that went by.

"There." Janet pointed to the right. "The one with the sunflowers."

Mom pulled to the curb. Parked in the driveway was the dented green car with the cracked windshield. The hood was raised, and tools were scattered on the ground. Tall yellow sunflowers lined the yard. A tricycle lay on the grass.

Janet gathered her things. "Thank you so much for driving me home, Mrs. Porter."

"It was no bother, Janet." Mom looked at the flowers. "How pretty."

"Thank you, Mrs. Porter," Janet said as she got out. "Elmore loves to roast the seeds, but he better pick them quick before the birds get 'em."

The kids in the street were still watching us. It was hard to imagine how they could play when the balls must have constantly rolled under the parked cars that lined the curb.

Then I noticed that two small faces had come to a window in Janet's house. It felt like *High Noon* when the bad men rode into town and everyone peeked from behind curtains.

Mom started back the way we came. When we passed

the Esso station, the man in the dark green coveralls was pumping gas.

"Why did he ask if everything was okay?" Sparky said.

I expected Mom to say she didn't know, but instead she said, "That's just the way some people are, Edward."

"They don't like Negroes sitting in the same car as white people?" I asked.

Mom nodded.

"I thought that was only in the South," I said.

"I think there's a little bit of it everywhere."

35

Dad tries the radio again: nothing.

"Could it mean the Russians won?" Ronnie asks.

"Nobody won," mutters Mr. Shaw. "We destroyed them, and they destroyed us."

"Maybe not," Dad says. "Maybe Kennedy ordered our side not to retaliate."

"What are you talking about?" asks Mr. McGovern.

"There's no sense in destroying everything," says Dad.

Paula's father laughs contemptuously. "Ridiculous. He'd never let the Russians win."

"How do you know?"

"It's obvious you're no student of history, Richard." Mr. McGovern sounds like he thinks he's so smart and

Dad's so dumb. Now I know where Paula gets it. "Great men think of their place in history. They think about what they'll be remembered for. You really believe Kennedy would risk being remembered as the leader of the free world who refused to fight back? As the coward who allowed the Communists to take over? You actually think the president is hiding in a bunker somewhere waiting to surrender?"

I hate the way Mr. McGovern talks to Dad, but what I hate almost as much is how what he says sounds right. When Dad doesn't reply, I wonder if he also thinks Mr. McGovern is right.

"If the Russians did win, would we be their prisoners?" Ronnie asks.

Mr. McGovern snorts. "Just what they need. More mouths to feed. I suppose they'd need men and women for work camps, but they're no strangers to atrocities. Anyone who's familiar with their actions during the war would know that."

Sparky tugs at Dad. "What's he mean?"

"Nothing." Dad shushes him.

"Far from it," says Mr. McGovern.

Dad gets to his feet and steps toward Mr. McGovern, who is sitting with Paula. You can feel everyone grow tense. "That's it, Herb," Dad growls. "If you know what's good for you."

But Mr. McGovern doesn't look afraid. Maybe because

he knows Dad would never do anything in front of Paula and us. I almost wish he would, though.

When Janet isn't helping Mom, she sits alone and hugs her knees, staring at a spot on the floor. She hasn't been mean or done anything bad to anyone. It must be awful for her, knowing Mr. McGovern doesn't want her here.

I go sit next to her. Pulling the blanket around his skinny bare shoulders, Sparky sits on her other side and takes her hand. She sniffs and quietly starts to cry.

Sometimes Mom bought bread at the bakery, and it would still be warm on the inside. Sparky and I would spread butter and jelly on it and eat slice after slice. Sometimes she made a pizza, and we would help her press the dough out flat on the pan and cover it with tomato sauce. Sparky loved the chocolate pudding she made, but he hated the thick, gummy layer on top and would give it to me because I liked to eat it with Cool Whip. Or she'd make chocolate-chip cookies and let us eat the batter, which was always better than the cookies themselves. And at breakfast sometimes she would let us pour heavy cream over our Rice Krispies, then Sparky and I would dump sugar all over it, and it was like eating candy.

All I think about is food. I would eat anything anyone gave me right now. Even spinach.

thirty-six

In school, Dickie Keller said that in some parts of Russia they practiced cannibalism. When I got home, Mom was sitting at the kitchen table smoking a cigarette and reading an article in a magazine about decorating bomb shelters. Sparky was in the den watching TV. Recently, she'd started letting him watch all the TV he wanted. And she said I could go to Ronnie's house, even though I hadn't finished my homework.

On the floor in his room, Ronnie and I played game after game of Nok-Hockey with small wooden hockey sticks and a flat wooden puck the size of a fifty-cent piece. Ronnie won most of the time. After a while the door opened, and Mrs. Shaw came in. Her hair was all poofed up, and she had black stuff around her eyes and bright-red lips like Brigitte Bardot. "Phew!" She pinched her nose and fanned her face. "Somebody better start using deodorant."

When Ronnie lifted his arm to sniff, I saw a dark sweat stain. I felt under my arm. It was as dry as the desert.

"Scotty, your mom called," Mrs. Shaw said. "It's time for dinner."

"He can't go," Ronnie said. "We're in the middle of a huge series. If he goes now, it'll ruin everything."

That was a lie. We weren't playing a series. Ronnie just didn't want me to leave.

"I'll call her back," Mrs. Shaw said. "Maybe you can stay."

"Thanks, Mrs. Shaw."

She left, and Ronnie gave me a knowing smile. "Another game?"

While we played, I wondered how Ronnie had gotten so good at lying. When I told a lie, I really had to work at it. First I had to stop myself from telling the truth. Then I had to think of the lie I wanted to tell. Then I had to think about whether it was believable or not. Then I had to consider what would happen if I got caught. And only after all that would I dare tell it. But Ronnie was a natural. It was almost like he thought of the lie before he thought of the truth. And they were perfect lies, too. Completely believable if you didn't already know.

We were in the middle of the next game when Mrs. Shaw came in again. "Your mom says you can stay for dinner. Fried chicken, okay?"

"Great, thanks."

We must have lost track of time because the next thing I knew, the door opened, and there was Mr. Shaw in a business suit. He took a deep sniff and wrinkled his tanned forehead.

"I believe a shower will be de rigueur before you're permitted to attend tonight's soirée, my son," he said.

Sometimes Ronnie's dad had a strange way of talking, as if even he knew the words sounded funny when he said them. Like it was some kind of inside joke. Now he turned to me. "So, Scott, how about an aperitif while Sport attends to the nether regions?"

I followed him into the den, wondering what half those words meant. Everything in the Shaws' house was new and modern. Instead of white-washed wooden walls, theirs were dark and shiny. Instead of couches made of Naugahyde, which was a kind of plastic imitation leather that stuck to your skin on hot days, theirs were soft and black and made of real leather. In the den, Mr. Shaw opened a cabinet filled with shelves of glimmering glasses. "What'll it be?" he asked himself, and sorted through some bottles. "Ah! Dubonnet!" He took a bottle by the neck. "Hey, Sweet Bumps!" he called cheerfully toward the kitchen. "Wet your whistle?"

"Is the pope Catholic?" Mrs. Shaw called back.

It was like speaking a foreign language using words I knew. I heard the clink of ice in glasses and the splash of liquid. "Be right back," Mr. Shaw said, and left.

A magazine lay open on the black leather ottoman that went with Mr. Shaw's easy chair. With a jolt I realized that it had to be a *Playboy,* because there was a photo of a naked woman. How could it be just lying there, out in the open, in the middle of the Shaws' den?

The magazine was turned away, so the woman was upside down. I wanted to go over and look at her right-side up, but I was afraid that Mr. Shaw would come back and catch me.

Ronnie's dad returned and gave me a glass with ice and some deep red liquid in it. "Cheers."

We clinked glasses, and I took a sip. It tasted cold and sweet and strange. A little piece of lemon rind made it tangy. Mr. Shaw settled into his chair and propped the *Playboy* open on his lap. The cover showed the upper half of a naked woman wearing a tie, her arms crossed over her breasts. "How's that bomb shelter, Scott?"

"Dad says I'm not supposed to talk about it."

Mr. Shaw nodded. "Your parents let you drink wine?"

"No, sir."

Mr. Shaw turned a page in the magazine like it was the most natural thing in the world to give your son's friend wine and look at pictures of naked women while you chatted. "In France, children are offered wine at dinner. By the time they're teenagers, it's a natural part of life. You don't have kids going out on Friday night and getting smashed the way they do here. A much more mature and reasonable approach, don't you think?"

I took another sip and nodded.

"French women go topless at the beach," Mr. Shaw continued. "They're so much more relaxed about the human body. I mean, if a man can go around without a shirt, why can't a woman?"

I didn't know how to answer. Women going around without shirts on? Kids drinking wine? You'd think French people were the strange ones, but Mr. Shaw, sitting there thumbing through his *Playboy,* was implying that we were.

"It's time this country got past its Puritan roots," Ronnie's dad said. "This isn't the sixteen hundreds anymore; we've put men in space and broken the sound barrier. We transmit television wirelessly into people's homes and have X-rays that see through their bodies. But socially and sexually we're still back in the Stone Age."

I was tempted to tell him he was wrong because I'd seen a drawing of a caveman carrying a big club and dragging a woman around by her hair, and nobody did that anymore. By then I'd finished my drink and felt fuzzy and warm, and wished I could be alone in the den and look at the pictures in *Playboy.* Then Ronnie came in with wet hair and wearing shorts and a different shirt and said dinner was ready.

Mrs. Shaw's fried chicken came in a tinfoil tray with whipped potatoes and carrots and peas. The chicken was a little soggy, and the carrots and peas were watery, but I didn't care. They let me feed little bits of chicken to Leader, and almost everything Mr. Shaw said sounded funny and made me giggle. Later I went home, got into my pajamas, brushed my teeth, and went to bed. If Mom or Dad came in to kiss me good night, I didn't hear them.

37

We've run out of toilet paper, mostly because the women use it even when they pee. And we all pee a lot because water is the only thing we have to relieve the gnawing ache of hunger between our tiny meals.

When the air starts to feel stale and even after a deep breath you feel like you need more, it's time to use the ventilator. Dad heaves himself up and starts to crank, but after a few moments, he stops to catch his breath.

He starts again, then stops.

"What's wrong?" I ask.

"Just tired," he answers. "It's hard to keep your strength up."

"Which is *exactly* why we should eat more," Mr. McGovern says.

"Which is why it would be helpful if you took a turn," Dad counters, gesturing at the crank handle.

Mr. McGovern shakes his head. "No, thanks. I'm saving my energy."

That scares me. Is he saving energy so he can take over and kick Mom and Janet out? And then Dad, Sparky, and me after them? Mrs. Shaw gives her husband a nudge, and he reluctantly gets up. But like Dad, after a few cranks, he seems to grow tired. "Ronnie," he says.

Ronnie helps his dad crank. Together they manage to go long enough to fill the shelter with fresh air. But I feel bad. How come Dad didn't ask me to help him?

"We're like animals in a cage," Mrs. Shaw mutters. "I can't stand it."

"If you think we're like animals *now*," says Mr. McGovern, "just wait."

Mrs. Shaw pushes herself to her feet. "I have to wash. I want some water."

"It's for drinking," Dad says.

"I have to wash!" Mrs. Shaw yells. Everyone starts and stiffens. "I can't bear it," she goes on. "I feel like I'm in a dog kennel covered with filth. I'd rather die."

I glance at Mr. Shaw, expecting him to say, "Don't say that," but he just gazes at the water tank.

Mrs. Shaw's balled hands rest on her hips. "Well, Richard?"

Dad pours water into a bowl and hands her a bar of Ivory Snow. Mrs. Shaw stands over the drain in the middle of the floor and takes off her robe and nightgown.

"Don't look," Dad says. But it's impossible not to. Ronnie's mother is naked. She tears some fabric from the bottom of her robe, then dips it in the bowl of water at her feet and starts to scrub her face, neck, arms, breasts, stomach, and legs. Water and lather drip down her body, and she moans with relief as she wipes off the suds, her damp skin glistening in the dim light. Nobody says a word. Of all the eyes watching her, Ronnie's are the widest, and it makes me wonder if he ever did sneak in on her like he said he did.

By the time she finishes, she's shivering, her pale skin rubbed pink and covered with goose bumps. She considers the filmy nightgown, then tosses it aside and pulls on what's left of her robe. "I can't begin to tell you how good that felt," she says. "I feel almost human again. Anyone else want to try?"

I'm not surprised when Sparky jumps up. Shedding his blanket, he rubs the soapy rag over his front and lets Janet do his back. Like a dog being scratched, he closes his eyes as she scrubs and rinses him off, before scampering back to the blanket and huddling beside me, teeth chattering.

After that, one by one the rest of us wash. I used to hate being told to bathe; now, even with cold water, it feels like the best thing in the world.

Finally Dad and Janet lead Mom to the toilet bucket, where she seems to know what to do. Janet whispers something in Dad's ear, and he turns to us. "Don't watch."

This time I don't. Water splashes on the floor. When Janet washes her, Mom lets out a little moan like Mrs. Shaw made.

Maybe she'll be okay after all.

thirty-eight

We were playing fungo in the street in front of Ronnie's house when Puddin' Belly hit a pop-up. In right field (Ronnie's front yard), Freak O' Nature raised his mitt and backed up to catch it. Then he stopped. The ball bounced six feet to his right, but Freak O' Nature was still staring at the sky. Way, way up, three tiny silver jets were streaking across the blue, leaving white contrails. They were so high, we couldn't even hear them. I'd never seen planes that high in the sky before.

"Air force jets," said Why Can't You Be Like Johnny?

"How do you know?" asked Ronnie.

"Commercial flights don't fly that high or close together."

"Think it's war?" Freak O' Nature asked nervously.

"Wouldn't there be sirens?" I asked.

Everyone listened; there were no sirens.

"Should we get in your bomb shelter just in case?" Ronnie said.

Why Can't You Be Like Johnny? turned to Freak O' Nature. "Try your radio."

We listened. Stations were playing music or people were talking.

"Sounds pretty normal," I said.

But we kept listening, as if at any second, the sirens would start or a voice would come on the radio and tell everyone to seek shelter. Finally, Why Can't You Be Like Johnny? suggested we keep playing and check the radio again in a little while. I went back to first base (the storm drain). Johnny was playing second (chalked on the asphalt). Puddin' Belly was in left field (Old Lady Lester's front yard).

Ronnie went to home plate and was about to hit when Paula came by pushing her twin brother, Teddy, in his wheelchair. Teddy had to be strapped in and couldn't talk. His head would roll around, and he'd make strange faces and stick his fingers in his ears. Sometimes Paula would talk to him, but it was hard to tell if he understood. Sparky was afraid of Teddy, and the rest of us felt uncomfortable when he was around.

On the sidewalk, Paula locked the wheelchair's brakes

and sat down on the edge of Old Lady Lester's lawn, right in the middle of left field.

"You can't sit there!" Ronnie called from home plate.

"You don't own the sidewalk!" Paula yelled back.

"Can't you find someplace else?"

"No."

We couldn't risk hitting Teddy with the ball. Why Can't You Be Like Johnny? left second base and sat down on Ronnie's lawn, and the rest of us followed. We stared across the street at Paula and Teddy. Paula stared back.

"Want to throw rocks at her?" suggested Puddin' Belly. That was his standard solution to almost any problem.

Why Can't You Be Like Johnny? shook his head. "Just wait."

"You think if we don't play, she'll get bored and go?" asked Freak O' Nature.

"Don't bet on it," grumbled Ronnie. He and Paula had a strange relationship. They acted like they hated each other but at the same time couldn't stay away from one another.

So we looked at Paula, and she looked at us. Finally Why Can't You Be Like Johnny? went home. Then Freak O' Nature and Puddin' Belly decided to go, too. That left Ronnie and me. I didn't want to go home. Lately Mom was acting really moody, and I never knew what to expect. One minute, she'd yell at you for the littlest thing, and the next, she'd act like she didn't care what you did.

"Sneak into your mom's room yet?" Ronnie asked in a low voice.

"No."

"What about your father's *Playboys*?"

"What do you care?"

Ronnie glanced across the street at Paula, then whispered, "Just hate to think of you dying without ever seeing—"

"I'm not gonna die, remember? I'm the one with the bomb shelter, and I'll be in there for weeks with my mom and get to see everything."

"You might not," Ronnie said. "Might be pretty dark. It's not like you'll have electricity."

Like a dog on the other end of a stick, he wouldn't let go.

"And moms don't really count because you can't do anything with them," he said. "Wouldn't you like to see some you could do something with?"

"Do what?"

"You don't know?" Ronnie asked in that tone that always made me feel like I was stupid.

"Go to hell."

"Keep it down," Ronnie mumbled, and glanced across the street again. "If you could see any pair of breasts in the whole world, whose would you want to see?"

"How would I know?"

"Paula's, right?" he whispered.

The thought had never occurred to me. Paula might have had breasts, but she was also our neighbor and the annoying teacher's pet who always raised her hand in class.

"No," I said.

"Yes, you do."

"No . . . I . . . don't."

Ronnie studied me. "You a homo?"

"A what?"

"A homo. A queer."

"No."

"Sure you are. Any guy who doesn't care about breasts has to be queer."

"No, you don't," I said. "What do breasts have to do with it?"

Across the street, Paula got up and started to push Teddy back home. Maybe she'd decided there was no point in being there if we weren't going to pay attention to her. "You don't even know what queer is," Ronnie sneered.

"Yes, I do."

"No, you don't."

"Do, too."

"Oh, yeah? Then what is it?"

"It's . . . it's you know, when you're, you know, kind of strange and different."

Ronnie's grin grew broader. "You don't know what *queer* means," he sang, like it was a line from a song.

"That's what it means," I insisted.

"No, it doesn't," Ronnie said. "It means you like other guys."

I studied him uncertainly. I liked my friends—most of the time, at least—and they were guys. What was queer about that?

Ronnie saw the confusion on my face. "Queers are guys who have sex with other guys. They're called homos because they're homosexuals."

I smiled. There was no way Ronnie was going to get away with this one. "Guys can't have sex with guys. It's not even possible, stupid."

But Ronnie smiled back. "What rock have you been hiding under?"

It didn't make sense. Men and women had body parts that fit together. Men couldn't have sex with men because they had the same body parts and therefore wouldn't fit.

"So how do they do it?" I asked.

Ronnie shook his head like he knew the answer and didn't want to tell.

"Come on, if you're so smart, let's hear it," I said.

"I would, but if your parents found out, they'd be really mad."

"I swear to God I won't tell them."

"How do I know you'll keep your promise?"

I held out my right pinkie, and Ronnie stopped smiling. A pinkie swear was the most inviolate swear there was. If you broke a pinkie swear, you were branded for life. No one would ever trust you again.

"Come on." I beckoned with my outstretched pinkie.

Ronnie didn't take it.

"See?" I said. "You're such a liar."

39

"I'm hungry." Sparky crosses his arms over his stomach and bends forward like he's in agony. Even before this, he was skinny and bony, but now his ribs poke out, especially where the concave curve of his stomach begins.

"There, there." Janet puts her arm around his shoulders and tries to soothe him. He sits with her almost all the time now.

"Give him something," Mrs. Shaw says to Dad.

"What about my child?" asks Mr. McGovern.

Hunger has turned my stomach into a knot, too, and my own ribs feel tight against my skin, but I don't want to say anything that will make it worse for Dad, who goes over to the shelf. "Sardines?"

Sparky shakes his head.

"Tuna?"

"Okay."

"Why does he get to choose when the rest of us don't?" Mr. McGovern asks.

"If your child was the youngest here, I'd do the same for her," Dad answers.

"But not if she's the second or third youngest?"

"That makes no sense, Richard," Mrs. Shaw says. I hate the way she and Mr. McGovern gang up on Dad. It's still our bomb shelter and our food. Like Dad said, they could have built their own shelters.

"I'm hungry, too," says Ronnie.

"What's left?" asks Mrs. Shaw.

Mr. Shaw hardly talks anymore. Mostly he just stares at the walls and floor. It makes me uncomfortable. He seems like a different person from the one who sat in his den sipping wine and talking about topless women in France.

Dad tells us what remains on the food shelf. "Three cans of Spam, four of tuna, six of sardines, and some peanut butter and jelly."

"No bread?" asks Mrs. Shaw.

Dad shakes his head.

"We could make it last longer," Mr. McGovern says. "For someone hardheaded and logical enough to build this shelter, you've become awfully softhearted, Richard."

Dad glares at him furiously. "You're talking about my wife and this innocent woman, Herb."

"I'm talking about our lives and the lives of our children," Mr. McGovern replies forcefully. "We've already lost enough thanks to this goddamn war. The sooner we use up the food, the sooner we'll be forced to go back up there. And if we go up too soon, we run the risk of radiation sickness. Be rational about it, Richard. It's not going to get any easier once we're up there. Like Stephanie said, we'll be spending every moment trying to survive. There won't be time for anyone who needs help."

"How can you say that?" Dad asks. "I mean, think of your own son."

Mr. McGovern's face darkens. "That . . . is *exactly* why I can say it."

I feel the urge to tug. The spot behind my right ear feels as smooth and hairless as my forehead, but along the edge of the bald spot, I find some hairs to grasp. Mr. McGovern doesn't think we'll be able to take care of Mom once we get out, but why does he want Janet to leave? Because she's a Negro? If he makes her leave, what's to stop him from saying Sparky should go next? After all, he's too young and small to take care of himself.

"So?" Mr. McGovern demands.

Dad gathers himself up. "I said it before and I'll say it again. Over . . . my . . . dead . . . body."

"It won't just be *your* dead body — it will be

everyone's," Mr. McGovern counters, then turns to the Shaws. "Who gave him the right to make decisions for all of us? Because it's his bomb shelter? I'm sorry, but I don't think that matters anymore. We're all in this together now. Are you really comfortable putting your lives in *his* hands? Letting *him* decide how much we eat and drink?"

Mrs. Shaw glances at her husband, who's staring at a wall as if his thoughts are a million miles away. Then she says in a softer, more reasonable tone, "Let the children eat, Richard."

"I never said I wasn't going to," Dad replies icily. He opens a can of tuna and divides it four ways. Normally I could eat my share in one bite, but I separate it into three parts and savor each one slowly.

Sparky gets to lick the inside of the can.

When I finish my three parts, I'm still hungry.

Sometimes, when it's quiet for a long time, I think I hear whispers, as if there's someone else down here. And even though I don't believe in ghosts, I get scared. If I never imagined the whole world being destroyed, what else have I never imagined? Could there be some kind of invisible radioactive creature on the other side of the shield wall? Invisible Godzilla?

I look over at Mom, wishing she would wake up so I could tell her about Invisible Godzilla and she could tell me it's only my imagination. But she just lies there, blank-eyed, so I go over to Janet and hold her hand. If Mr. McGovern and the Shaws say she has to go, I'll say over my dead body, too.

When we run out of rags for washing and the toilet, the men tear off their pajama legs at the knees. We're slowly using up our clothing.

At times the hunger and the feeling of being cooped up in this chilly, smelly dungeon is so bad, I feel like I can't spend another minute down here. Would it be worth risking radiation poisoning to go up and see the sun for a few minutes? Could such a short time up there be *that* bad?

Dad and Mr. McGovern have an argument over how long we've been down here. Dad thinks it's only been five or six days. Mr. McGovern insists it's been eight or nine.

"This is more than a week's worth of beard," Mr. McGovern says, brushing the stubble that mats the lower half of his face. The lower half of Dad's face is similarly darkened, but Mr. Shaw's is only patchy, and I wonder if he could grow a beard even if he wanted to.

"Maybe it's time to check the radiation levels again," Mrs. Shaw says in her nice voice.

Dad starts to get to his feet, then stumbles and has to grab the bunk bed.

"Dad!" Sparky blurts with fright.

"Sorry, just got a little dizzy."

"Hunger," Mr. McGovern grumbles as if it's Dad's fault.

When Dad picks up the flashlight, Sparky whimpers. Janet presses the side of his head to her bosom and comforts him. "He'll just be gone for a moment."

At the shelf lined with supplies, Dad aims the flashlight beam at the green box as if he's thinking about what's inside. Then he takes the Family Radiation Measurement Kit and goes into the corridor on the other side of the shield wall. Once again without the flashlight, it gets darker in the shelter. Then he's back. "A hundred and sixty roentgens."

"Isn't that much better than before?" Mrs. Shaw asks hopefully.

Dad nods grimly. "It's still much too high."

There's nothing on the radio.

"I guess the good news is you're not picking up any stations in Russian," says Mr. McGovern.

"I'd almost feel better if we did," mumbles Mr. Shaw. It feels like it's the first time he's spoken in days.

Ronnie scowls at his dad. "Why?"

"At least we'd know someone was out there," Mr. Shaw replies.

Mr. McGovern, who always has to have the last word, mutters, "Better dead than red."

forty

"Take cover! We're under attack!" We were in the middle of learning ratios when Principal Sharp's voice crackled over the PA system: "Follow your teacher's instructions! Duck and cover! Duck and cover!"

Puddin' Belly Wright ran to the windows. A few weeks earlier, Principal Sharp had told each teacher to select a student to pull down the window shades so we wouldn't be blinded or burned by the nuclear flash. It sounded like an important job, but Mr. Kasman chose Puddin' Belly, who now pulled a shade so hard that the whole thing came crashing down.

"Ahh!" Paula wailed.

"Oh, for Christ's sake," Mr. Kasman sputtered.

Kids dove for the floor.

"Stop!" Mr. Kasman shouted. "It's not an attack. It's just a drill."

"But Principal Sharp said —"

"Be quiet," our teacher ordered. "Do you hear sirens?"

We listened. There were no sirens.

"Why did Principal Sharp say we were under attack?" asked Freak O' Nature.

Instead of answering, Mr. Kasman closed his eyes and squeezed the bridge of his nose with his fingertips as if he was getting a headache.

"Should we still get under our desks?" Ronnie asked.

Our teacher took his hand away from his face. "Sure, go ahead." He sounded like he didn't care.

It wasn't easy. Our new desks came with chairs that were attached. We were crawling around on the floor, trying to get under them, when the PA crackled back on. "Uh, there's been some confusion," said Principal Sharp. "We are not under attack. I repeat, we are not under attack. This is an air-raid drill. I repeat, this is only a drill. Teachers, escort your students into the hallway and await further instructions."

"You heard him," said Mr. Kasman. "Everyone out to the hall."

We wiped our dirty hands on our pants and filed out. Up and down the corridor, kids were pouring from classrooms. Some of the girls were red-eyed and teary, and some boys looked pale and shaken — as if their teachers had believed it was a real attack, too.

"Students, sit with your backs against lockers, your knees pulled up, and your faces buried in your arms," Principal Sharp announced over the loudspeaker.

"Do as he said," instructed Mr. Kasman.

"I have ordered you out into the hall because in the event of a nuclear attack, this will protect you from flying glass and flash burns," Principal Sharp continued. "You will keep your eyes shut and covered to prevent blindness from the flash. No matter where you are, do not look at the blast. Always turn your back to it and look away."

"Always," Mr. Kasman repeated.

41

The hunger pangs have gone from sharp to dull but constant. Everyone's irritable. Ronnie's winning a game of Parcheesi until Sparky rolls a six and knocks one of his pawns back to the start.

"Why'd you do that?" Ronnie asks. "You could have used that roll to get your pawn home."

"I can do that later," Sparky replies.

"Why not now?" Ronnie asks.

"If I don't send your pawn back, you'll win."

"No, I won't," Ronnie says, which is dumb because he wants to win and getting all your pieces home is how you do it.

"Sure you will," I tell him.

"Maybe not," Ronnie says. "Maybe I would have slowed down just to make it interesting."

"So Sparky did that for you," I chip in.

"It wasn't the right move."

"He can make any move he wants," I tell him.

"He would have been better off going home."

"But then you would have won."

"I quit." Ronnie flips a corner of the board, and pawns go rolling everywhere.

That ticks me off. "You're just mad because you thought you were going to win and then Sparky messed you up."

"You're stupid."

"I may be stupid, but even my little brother's smarter than you."

"Oh, yeah? Well, your dad's so dumb, he didn't put enough food or clothes in here."

Silence. Dad winces.

"Ronnie!" Mrs. Shaw snaps, which is a little surprising because she said the same thing about dad a few days ago.

"Well, it's —" Ronnie begins, but doesn't finish. Not that it matters. Everyone knows he was going to say it's true.

I wonder if Dad will get mad, but he bows his head. "He's right. I could've done better. I *should* have. I mean, what was the point of building this shelter and then leaving the job unfinished?"

That's the thing about Dad. Maybe he isn't as smart as Mr. McGovern or as suave as Mr. Shaw, but when he realizes he's wrong, he admits it. Not a lot of parents do that. Kids, either. Mrs. Shaw must feel bad about being so critical of him because now she says, "You did just fine, Richard. If it wasn't for you, none of us would be alive."

"Whoop-dee-do!" Mr. Shaw goes, like he doesn't think being alive is so great.

"Steven!" Mrs. Shaw hushes him, as if instead of being angry at Dad, she's now angry at him.

Mr. Shaw goes back into silent mode, but it's scary to see him act like he's giving up. What if he's right?

forty-two

When the leaves began to fall, Dad bought a lawn sweeper. It had four long brushes on a rotating drum followed by a leaf catcher. You pushed it across the lawn, which made the drum rotate and the brushes turn, sweeping up leaves into the catcher.

I had to sweep the whole lawn, which was hard work. But when I'd dumped a few loads at the curb and had a good-size pile, I was allowed to pour gasoline on the leaves and light them. Fires were great entertainment.

I'd just made a big pile when Freak O' Nature rode up on his bike and told me not to burn them until he came back. A little later, he returned with Ronnie and a jar filled with crickets. I got the red gasoline can from the garage and sprinkled some on the leaves.

"That's all?" Ronnie asked.

"You don't need a lot," I said. "Leaves pretty much burn by themselves."

"Put some more on," Ronnie said, so I did.

"More," he urged.

The leaves glistened and the odor of gasoline was strong in the air. I carried the can far away, then returned, pulling a pack of matches out of my pocket. Normally I'd crouch down and light a few leaves, then wait for the flames to reach the gas. But now there was gas everywhere. It had even started to seep from the leaves and spread onto the street.

Freak O' Nature spun the lid off the jar and dumped the crickets onto the pile. Some started to hop away on the street. Others landed on the gasoline-soaked leaves and seemed stunned.

"Do it!" Ronnie yelled.

I stood back and tossed a lit match toward the pile, but it went out before it hit the leaves. I lit another and tossed it, but the same thing happened. Meanwhile, more crickets were getting away.

"Gimme that." Ronnie grabbed the matches and crouched close to the pile.

Whoomp!

I could have sworn that for an instant Ronnie disappeared in the eight-foot-high ball of flames. The initial burst quickly died down; the crackling leaves burning rapidly, turning bright red and then into ashes. Crickets jumped around frantically in the orange and yellow flames before being immolated. A few even managed to launch themselves, burning, to the pavement, where they kicked once or twice, then lay still, tiny carcasses and smoke.

My friends and I took in the charred devastation. The smoldering heap of gray ash, the wisps of smoke rising like ghosts. All that remained of the crickets were burned carapaces, except for a few dead ones that had managed to hop away before the fire began, only to be poisoned by the gasoline.

"Just like what could happen to us," Ronnie said.

43

When Dad turns the valves, more water gurgles into the tank. "Looks like you were right," he tells Mr. McGovern.

Paula's father nods like he knew he was right all along.

"Then no one else survived," Mr. Shaw mutters.

"Certainly very few," Mr. McGovern agrees.

"How do you know?" asks Mrs. Shaw.

Mr. McGovern explains how water towers are built to hold about a day's worth of water for the population they serve. "So, if we've been down here nine or ten days . . . "

"Or six or seven," says Dad.

"Whatever the number," Mr. McGovern says irritably, "it must mean very few people are using it."

Is it day up there? Night? What day of the week? How many more days do we need to stay down here? Sometimes if I think about it too hard, I feel queasy like after a roller-coaster ride. Mr. McGovern says without knowing day from night that we've become disoriented.

Nobody plays games anymore. It takes too much energy. We sit, or lie down, or sleep. Sometimes someone stands up because they can't sit anymore.

I think about Tootsie Rolls, Milky Ways, Frosted Flakes, Rice Krispies, Pop-Tarts, Premium Saltines, Oreos, Wise Potato Chips, Fritos, peanut butter and jelly sandwiches, milk shakes, hamburgers, Chinese food, spaghetti, pizza, sweet-and-sour meatballs . . .

My stomach churns and cries. Sometimes drinking water helps, but sometimes it doesn't. The air is always stuffy. We take turns cranking the ventilator, but no one has the strength to crank it more than three or four times. So there isn't enough food and barely enough air. But that's not the scariest part of being down here. The scariest part is the way the grown-ups act.

"Check the radiation," Mr. McGovern says. He no longer bothers to ask.

"I just checked it a few hours ago," Dad replies.

"That was yesterday, Richard."

"No, Herb, it was today."

Mr. Shaw sighs. "What does it matter?"

"Anything would be better than being down here," Mr. McGovern says.

"You can leave anytime you like," Dad snaps.

"I'm not the one who should leave." Mr. McGovern's eyes seem full of anger and hatred. Is that what he saved his energy for?

"I told you I won't have that," Dad growls.

"Who made you the commander in chief?" Mr. McGovern turns to Mrs. and Mr. Shaw. "I say we vote on reducing the number of mouths by two. This isn't arbitrary—it's a matter of survival. It's what has to be done if we're going to stay down here long enough to let the danger subside up there."

Janet's eyes go wide. As if my stomach doesn't already hurt enough, now it twists and knots even more.

Is Dad is too tired to argue? When he moves close to the shelves and places his hand near the green box, I feel my heart begin to thump hard and my breaths grow short and fast. He can't be serious. This can't be happening.

But that's what they said about a war with the Russians in the first place.

Mr. McGovern finishes his speech. "All those in favor of reducing the number of mouths by two, raise your hands."

Dad rests his hand on the green box.

Mr. McGovern raises his hand and looks at the Shaws. Neither of them budges.

A scowl darkens Mr. McGovern's face. "Even though we'll die if we have to go up there too soon?"

"I told you before," says Mrs. Shaw. "I'd rather die than be responsible for someone else's death."

"Steven?" Mr. McGovern says.

Mr. Shaw slowly shakes his head. "Up there, down here. What difference does it make?"

forty-four

Despite the duck-and-cover drills and talk about a nuclear war, teachers still had to teach. In current events, Mr. Kasman reminded us that there were other things going on in the world. He wrote "James Meredith" on the board. "Does anyone know who this man is?"

No one answered.

"James Meredith recently became the first colored man ever to enroll in the University of Mississippi," our teacher said.

Paula's hand shot up. "They didn't want to let him in."

"That's right," said Mr. Kasman.

Paula grinned proudly, as if to say, *See how smart I am?* But if she was really so smart, how come she wasn't in the smart-kid class with Why Can't You Be Like Johnny?

"And can you tell us who 'they' are, Paula?" Mr. Kasman asked.

Paula stopped smiling. "Uh, some . . . white people?" she asked more than stated.

"Yes." Mr. Kasman nodded, and Paula looked relieved. But not for long. "You're white, Paula. Would you have been against James Meredith going to the University of Mississippi?"

Paula's eyes darted around nervously. "No . . . "

"Then why do you think those people in Mississippi were against him going?"

Paula didn't answer, and no hands went up. Except for school custodians and cleaning ladies, we hardly ever came into contact with Negro people. I thought about Janet and the three men who'd dug the hole in our backyard.

"Who knows what segregation is?"

Once again, Paula's hand shot up. "It's when white people and Negroes are kept separate."

"Why?" asked Mr. Kasman. It was strange the way he asked us questions instead of just telling us stuff. As if he actually wanted to know what we thought. I couldn't remember a teacher doing that before. Miss Yellnick, my fifth-grade teacher, always acted like the last thing she wanted to know was what we thought. After all, we were kids. How were we supposed to know the answers? But the funny thing was, asking us made us think, whereas half the time when teachers told us stuff, it just went in one ear and out the other.

"In some parts of the South, there are separate restaurants for whites and Negroes," said Mr. Kasman. "There are separate water fountains and bathrooms. Negroes have to ride in the back of public buses."

"Back of the bus," Freak O' Nature rumbled in a deep low voice like the Kingfish's on the TV show *Amos 'n' Andy.* Some kids giggled.

Mr. Kasman ignored him and waited. You could feel discomfort spread through the classroom. What was he waiting for?

"Okay." He seemed to make up his mind. "Here's part of your homework for tonight. I want each of you to write a page answering this question." He turned to the blackboard and wrote: "Why would someone be against letting a Negro go to an all-white university? And do you agree or disagree with that position?"

A bunch of us groaned, but then we always groaned when Mr. Kasman gave us homework.

That night I wrote:

I think people who are against letting a Negro go to an all-white university probably think that

Negroes shouldn't go to college because they were once slaves. I think this is wrong because Negroes are not slaves anymore.

It is wrong for people to be against letting a Negro go to an all-white university because they think that Negroes shouldn't go to college because they were once slaves. I think those people should think about how they would feel if Negroes had made white people slaves instead of the other way around. I don't think white people would like it one bit if they wanted to go to an all-Negro college and weren't allowed. The golden rule says we should do unto others as they would do unto us.

In conclusion, it is wrong for white people to be against letting a Negro go to an all-white university because they think that Negroes shouldn't go to college because they were once slaves.

45

"The refuse can is almost full," Dad says.

"So, what do you suggest, Herr Kapitän?" asks Mr. McGovern, as if he's hoping maybe this could be another reason to reduce the number of mouths by two.

"Oh, am I still in charge?" Dad asks sarcastically.

"Suppose we just put the solid waste in it?" Mrs. Shaw asks.

Dad nods. "That's what I was thinking."

So now liquid waste goes directly into the drain on the floor. The men stand; the women squat. People don't always hold up the blanket for privacy anymore. It takes too much energy. The men just turn their backs and go. Janet and Mrs. Shaw hold the blanket for Paula. Dad and Janet take Mom by the arms and help her to squat. Seeing people go now, I feel the way I used to feel when one of our neighbors' dogs went. What's the big deal?

Why was it ever a big deal?

Out of the blue, Mr. Shaw says, "We're worse than animals. Animals only kill what they need for food. Humans kill for no reason."

Eyes shift as we glance at one another. No one replies.

Dad tries the radio. "There've got to be others. Sooner or later, someone has to start broadcasting."

"Powered by what?" Mr. McGovern sighs like parents do when their kids act stubbornly. "You think the power plants are still standing? And even if they are, you think the people who run them are still alive? And they're just going to go back to work? What's the point? To earn a salary? Who's going to pay them? And even if someone did, what would they do with the money? Go to a store? There's nothing to buy. No one's going back to work, Richard. No one's making anything. They're all too busy just trying to survive."

"The government made contingency plans," Dad counters. "They stored food and gasoline. The army'll get things going again."

Mr. McGovern rolls his eyes. "You've been completely brainwashed. Do you have any idea how much food and fuel it takes to keep this country running? It doesn't matter what the government has stored. Without a constant supply of new coal, oil, and natural gas, whatever they've got won't last more than a month or two. So unless the army is going to start mining and drilling, and processing and refining, and transporting, and running power plants, it can't possibly go back to the way it was."

Nobody argues. Dad has his listening-and-thinking face on.

"And I'll tell you something else," Mr. McGovern continues. "Our power plants and refineries were probably the first things the Russians bombed. Just like their power plants and oil fields were the first things we bombed. And it's not like we can rebuild whatever was damaged; anything that got a direct hit from a nuclear weapon will be radioactive for decades, if not centuries. So to have the energy we need means digging new mines and oil wells, as well as building new power plants. How long do you think *that* will take?"

Dad doesn't answer.

"How long?" asks Sparky.

"Not in our lifetimes," Mr. McGovern answers, still focusing on Dad. "Maybe now you can understand why some of us weren't in a hurry to build bomb shelters."

He makes it sound like it's going to be really awful when we go back up there. Almost like, as horrible as it is down here, we might be better off staying. Meanwhile, Dad turns to Paula's father.

"You know, Herb," he says. "In some ways, you're a very smart guy, but in other ways, you're one of the stupidest people I've ever met."

In the shadows of our dungeon, tension once again begins to spread. I've never heard a grown-up call another grown-up a name before. Certainly not to his face. And not only that, but I never thought Dad would be the one to do it.

At first, Mr. McGovern clenches his teeth. But then he seems to relax and even smiles. "All right, Richard, perhaps you'd like to tell us what makes you say that."

"You fought to get in here because when faced with death, you realized how precious life is," Dad says. "I can't imagine how horrible it must have been to leave your wife and son up there, but you made that choice. We all did, or we wouldn't be down here. None of us really knows what it's going to be like when we get back up there. In the meantime, all we've got to keep us going is hope. But you're so damn intent on proving to everyone how smart you are that you don't seem to care that you're destroying the last bit of hope the rest of us are clinging to. So from now on, keep it to yourself."

But we know who always has to have the last word. "According to Nietzsche," Paula's father replies, " 'In reality, hope is the worst of all evils, because it prolongs man's torments.' "

forty-six

Dad brought home a brown-paper shopping bag with handles made from bamboo and wire.

"What is it?" Sparky asked eagerly.

"I'll show you after dinner," Dad said. That always drove Sparky and me crazy. Maybe it was supposed to teach us patience, but all it really did was make us rush through meals.

To make things worse, Mom served spinach. Except for canned asparagus, there was nothing Sparky and I hated more. But dinner couldn't end until we finished it. I put lots of butter on mine and managed to eat most of it. About halfway through the meal, Sparky got up to go to the bathroom.

He didn't come back.

After a while, Dad said, "Go see what Edward's doing."

As I went down the hall to the bathroom, I heard the toilet flush. Then it flushed again. I knocked.

"Who is it?" Sparky asked.

"Me," I said in a low voice. "What's going on?"

Sparky peeked out, then let me in and locked the door. In the toilet were a million little green pieces of spinach. "I spit it out," he whispered, "but it won't flush."

This was bad. If Mom or Dad found out that Sparky had filled his mouth with spinach and then spit it out, we might not get to see what Dad brought home. I flushed the toilet. The water swirled around and disappeared, then reappeared with most of those little green pieces of spinach still there.

Rap! Rap! The knock on the door made us both jump. "Boys?"

Sparky's eyes went wide.

"Open the door," Dad ordered.

Sparky and I shared a frightened look. As I opened the door, Sparky quickly put down the toilet top and sat. Dad scowled at us. "What's going on?"

"We were just talking," Sparky said.

"With the door locked?" Dad asked.

"It was boy stuff," I said.

Dad frowned. "Well, come on and see what I got."

As we followed Dad down the hall, Sparky rolled his eyes in relief. In the bedroom, Dad took four olive-colored masks out of the shopping bag. Each was about the size of a football with U.S. NONCOMBATANT GAS MASK stenciled in black letters on the outside. They were made of rubber with two clear plastic see-through disks. At one end was a gray canister about the size of a Campbell's soup can. At the other end were straps. Sparky put one on, instinctively knowing that the straps went around the back of his head and the clear plastic disks went where his eyes were. He looked like a green anteater with the gray can for a snout. I followed his example. Dad tightened the straps until the gas masks felt firm on our heads. The air inside quickly became warm and stale.

"What's it for?" I asked, my voice muffled by the mask.

"So you won't breathe in radioactive fallout," Dad said.

Mom came in. When she saw Sparky and me, she frowned.

"They're gas masks, Mom!" Sparky announced with muffled excitement.

Mom crossed her arms and said to Dad, "Scaring them again?"

"We're not scared," Sparky said. But then he turned to me and asked uncertainly. "Are we?"

"I'm not scared," I said, because I didn't want Dad to get into trouble.

"You better take those off," Dad said.

"And go watch TV," added Mom, in a way that indicated that Dad was in trouble anyway.

We went into the den and watched *Sky King*, but I could hear the sounds of an argument coming from Mom and Dad's bedroom. Sparky's eyes were fixed on the TV; I got up and quietly went down the hall to listen.

"The whole town's talking," Mom said. "They stare at me in the store. I can feel their eyes."

"I'm sorry," Dad said. "But I can't sit here and do nothing. Even President Kennedy said we should build a shelter. He's building one at his summer place in Hyannis Port, and we all know there's got to be an enormous shelter in Washington."

"Well, good for him. Meanwhile, Scott's pulling the hair out of his head and is so worried he threw up his dinner."

"What?"

I had to get closer to try to hear what Mom said next. Suddenly the door swung open. Dad looked startled when he saw me. "You . . . were listening?"

I bowed my head in shame.

"You threw up?"

"Ahhhh!" Halfway down the hall, Sparky let out a cry and dashed away. He must have been coming to see what we were talking about.

"I'll take care of him." Mom went past us.

In a low voice, I told Dad that I hadn't thrown up, but that Sparky had been so eager to see what was in the shopping bag that he'd filled his mouth with spinach and spit it out in the toilet. Dad sighed, then reached out and turned my head with his hand. "What's this?"

"I don't know."

"You pull out hair when you're worried?"

I nodded.

"Try not to, okay?"

47

In order to have toilet paper and washcloths, we've torn our nightclothes down to almost nothing. Paula and Janet clutch what remains of their robes tightly when they move around, but Mrs. Shaw can't be bothered and lets her shredded robe hang open, revealing the nakedness beneath. I guess she knows that we're all so hungry, weak, and miserable that no one cares.

"I can't stand it!" Mr. Shaw suddenly pushes himself up. It seems like the first time he's stood up in days, although that probably isn't true. He stumbles toward the gap in the shield wall.

"What are you doing?" Mrs. Shaw gasps.

"I'll take my chances up there."

"Dad!" Ronnie dashes after his father and wraps his arms around one of his legs.

Shock and alarm fill the shelter. For an instant, my dad looks dumbfounded. Then he hoists himself up and grabs Mr. Shaw's arm.

"Let go!" Mr. Shaw tries to yank free.

"You'll kill us all!" Dad warns.

"I can't stay in here anymore!"

"Dad, stop!" Ronnie cries as his father tries to drag him.

"You're scaring him, Steven!" Mrs. Shaw yells.

With Ronnie's arms wrapped around his thigh like a boa constrictor, Mr. Shaw tries to squirm out of Dad's grip in a strange slow-motion dance as if they don't have the strength to move faster. Dad hooks an arm around Mr. Shaw's neck, and they tumble to the shelter floor, a mass of squirming arms and legs.

"Let go!" On the floor, Mr. Shaw tries to wriggle and twist away, but Ronnie's still clamped to his leg, and Dad manages to pin his arms down. Ronnie's crying and Mrs. Shaw is yelling, "Stop it! Stop it!" Mr. Shaw twists his head back and forth and tries to kick with his free leg. "Let me go!"

But Dad has him pinned. "If you open that door now, the radioactive dust that falls in could kill us all."

Her hair a wild mess, Mrs. Shaw kneels and takes her husband's head in her hands. "Stop," she says gently but firmly. "Get ahold of yourself. I understand how you feel. I really do. But you have to think about the rest of us. Ronnie needs you. I need you."

Her words get through. Mr. Shaw goes limp. The back of his head rests on the floor, and he bursts into tears, hiccupping and snorting, his chest heaving.

I've never seen a grown man cry so publically before, and it feels strange and upsetting. Sparky's whimpering. Janet strokes his head reassuringly. Paula's eyes are wide as she clings to her father. We're all so close together; there's nowhere to hide. Ronnie lets go of his father's leg and sits on the floor, wiping his eyes, his face smudged with tears and dirt.

Mrs. Shaw helps her husband to one of the bunks and lies down with him. She kisses his face and whispers in his ear. He slides his arms around her and pulls her close. I feel bad that they can't be alone.

Dad watches Mrs. Shaw caress and soothe her husband. He turns his gaze to Janet hugging Sparky. Then he looks at Mom, lying on her bunk with that blank expression, not the slightest bit aware of what just happened.

Dad doesn't check the radio anymore. But whenever he wakes up from a nap, he goes around the shield wall and tests the radiation levels under the trapdoor.

"A hundred and twenty-seven," he reports.

It's dropped again, but is still high above the safe level. Meanwhile, we're slowly starving to death.

forty-eight

On the TV, President Kennedy wore a dark jacket, white shirt, and thin black tie. He sat at a desk with a dark curtain and an American flag behind him.

The president had a funny way of speaking that had something to do with being from an important Massachusetts family. He said that the Soviets had given false statements about their weapons. The Soviets was another name for the Russians, who were also called Commies, Ruskies, and Reds. The president said that the Soviets were putting two types of weapons on Cuba — medium-range ballistic missiles that could reach Washington and intermediate-range missiles that were capable of reaching Hudson Bay in Canada. Sparky glanced at me with a scowl. Our parents had once gone to Canada for a vacation and came back with Hudson Bay blankets, and I bet he was wondering why the Soviets would want to shoot a missile all the way up there . . . unless they had something against blankets.

The president said the missiles were weapons of mass destruction and that the Soviets were lying about why they were putting them on Cuba. He used a lot of big words, and when he said a quarantine of Cuba was going to be initiated, I wanted to ask Dad what that meant, but I knew he'd tell me to wait until the speech was over.

When the president began talking about the organ of consultation and the Rio Treaty, Sparky started playing with a Slinky. I was tempted to play with my army men, but I watched mostly to see if the president would explain what the Commies had against Hudson Bay and what a quarantine was.

Then Mom came in. I had a feeling that she'd stayed out of the den on purpose to let Dad know that she was against Sparky and me watching the speech, but now she finally gave in to curiosity. She stood with her arms crossed while President Kennedy said that many months of sacrifice and self-discipline lay ahead, and that the cost of freedom was always high and one thing we would never do is surrender. Then he said, "Thank you and good night," and the speech was over.

I looked at Dad. "When he talked about the cost of freedom, he wasn't talking about money, was he?"

Dad sighed and shook his head.

"Maybe we shouldn't go to school tomorrow," I whispered to Dad at bedtime that night. Sparky was already asleep in the other bed.

Dad's forehead wrinkled. "Why?"

"If the Russians attack, we may not have time to get home."

Dad leaned forward and kissed me on the forehead. "Go to school and don't worry so much."

But it was impossible not to.

49

Everyone's sick. The air smells tart and pungent, and there's hardly a moment when someone isn't sitting on the toilet bucket. I feel dizzy and hot with a cramped stomach that's different from the cramps that come from hunger. For the first time in days, I don't think about food or even getting out of the shelter. I just want to stop feeling sick.

By now, the men have torn their pajama tops into rags, but there's still not enough. Dad is the first one to take off his pajama bottoms. Only there isn't any material around for Janet to make him a loincloth the way she did for Sparky.

We nap, wake, sit on the toilet bucket, and lie around feeling too ill and weak to move or talk.

"I wish you'd never built this thing," Mr. Shaw tells Dad.

Finally I wake up and the cramps are gone. Dad hands me a cup of water, and I gulp it down. Most of the others are awake. Somehow they don't look as sick as before.

"It's time," says Mr. McGovern. His jaw is covered by a short, scruffy beard, and the skin that once stretched tightly over his round belly is loose and saggy.

"Let me check—" Dad begins to reach for the radiation kit.

"I don't care anymore," Mr. McGovern says, cutting him short. "I'm going up."

He doesn't sound crazy or desperate like Mr. Shaw did. Instead, he's calm and determined. When he starts to get up, I half expect Dad to try and stop him, but he doesn't. Paula watches without a word.

Mr. McGovern stands in the dim shadows, a grown, naked man with skinny legs and flat feet. "I'll need the light," he says.

Dad picks up the flashlight.

"Can I come?" Sparky asks.

"No."

"Please?"

"Make sure he stays there," Dad tells Janet, and takes out two of the gas masks.

With the masks on, they look like naked men with horse heads. The shelter gets darker when Dad follows Mr. McGovern around the shield wall and into the narrow corridor. We listen to the muffled sounds of Mr. McGovern's grunts and heavy breaths as he starts to climb up the rungs. Then it gets quiet. Then more grunts and heavy breaths. Another quiet period follows.

Finally the bolt beneath the trapdoor slides open with a screech.

My heart speeds up.

Silence.

Then a grunt and a groan as if Mr. McGovern is struggling.

"It's heavy," Dad says, his voice muffled by the mask.

A louder groan follows, along with the clank of metal.

Then more heavy breathing.

We all hear what Mr. McGovern says next: "There's something on the other side blocking it."

A sense of alarm spreads. Mr. and Mrs. Shaw push themselves up and go see. The rest of us follow. Soon we've all squeezed into the narrow corridor watching while Mr. McGovern climbs down the rungs. Dad hands him the flashlight, then turns and looks at us through his mask. Is he going to tell us to go back into the shelter? No. He starts to climb.

Above him is the trapdoor. This is the first time I've seen it since the night we came down here, and back come all the awful memories of the struggle and the desperate cries of those above who didn't get in. Dad was right. Of all the things that have happened, those horrible sounds and haunting pleas are still what I remember most clearly. And somehow, even though I'm only eleven, I know they'll follow me forever.

Dad has to stop partway up the rungs to catch his breath. *Come on,* I think anxiously. *Hurry!*

He starts to climb again, then places his hand against the trapdoor and pushes up. The door rises a fraction of an inch and then falls closed with a loud *clank!* He tries again, straining, and the door rises a tiny bit higher before falling. Dad lowers himself a rung and stares up, catching his breath. Even though he's been weakened by lack of food and exercise, he should have been able to push the trapdoor open.

Mrs. Shaw says what's on all our minds: "We're trapped."

fifty

When Mr. Kasman asked if we'd watched the president on TV, Paula's hand shot up. "He ordered the navy to stop the Russians from giving missiles to Cuba."

"And now what happens?"

I raised my hand. "We wait to see whether the Russian ships will turn back or keep going."

"What will happen if they don't turn back?"

I raised my hand again. "It could be war."

The class grew quiet. Was everyone thinking that the sirens might start at any moment? That right at this very second, Khrushchev could be ordering an attack? That Russian bombers might already be on their way and missiles could be blasting off?

Dickie Keller raised his hand. "My father says we should bomb them before they bomb us."

"But what if they don't really intend to attack us?" asked Mr. Kasman.

Eric Flom raised his hand. "Then why are they putting missiles on Cuba?"

"Some people think it's because we have missiles in Turkey aimed at them."

"We do?" Freak O' Nature asked in his normal voice, sounding surprised.

Mr. Kasman pulled down a map of Europe and eastern Asia and used a wooden pointer. "Turkey is almost the same distance to Moscow as Cuba is to Washington."

Dickie Keller raised his hand. "Why did we put missiles there?"

"I'd guess for the same reason that the Russians are putting missiles on Cuba," Mr. Kasman answered.

"To attack them?" Eric Flom asked, reflecting the confusion many of us felt. Could this really be true? On TV, President Kennedy had said we wanted peace, not war, and that we would never attack Russia unless they attacked us first.

"Does that change the way you think about the situation?" Mr. Kasman asked.

Maybe it was still too early in the morning. Or maybe this information was too confusing, but we sat there like bumps on a log. The room would have been completely silent were it not for a faint scratching sound. Mr. Kasman frowned, then stepped quietly toward the back. We all turned to watch.

Puddin' Belly Wright's head lay on his arm as if he were asleep, but he wasn't. He was busy scratching his initials into the scratch-proof desktop with a paper clip. Mr. Kasman tiptoed close and craned his neck. After a moment, Puddin' Belly must have sensed that it was too quiet. He straightened up with an astonished expression when he realized that we were all watching him, then quickly placed his forearm over his handiwork.

"Move your arm, Stuart."

Puddin' Belly slid it away, revealing the initials SW scratched nearly a quarter of an inch into the new desktop. Everybody held their breath and waited for Mr. Kasman to send him to the office, where Principal Sharp would probably suspend him and make his parents pay for a new desk.

"Looks like you've been working pretty hard, Stuart," said our teacher. "Imagine what would happen if you applied all that energy to your schoolwork."

Puddin' Belly hung his head remorsefully.

Mr. Kasman patted him on the shoulder. "Think about it, okay?"

51

"We're not trapped," Dad says as he climbs down the rungs.

"How can you say that?" Mr. McGovern demands.

"The door moved. We just have to get whatever's on top of it off."

"And how, if I may ask, do you plan to do that?" Paula's dad asks.

"Give me a moment, okay?" Dad grumbles.

"Lot of good *that* will do us," Mr. McGovern mutters.

Sparky kicks Mr. McGovern in the leg. My brother's not strong enough to hurt him with his bare foot, but Mr. McGovern jumps and looks surprised.

"Edward!" Dad snaps.

But I think, *Good for you, Sparky.*

Are we doomed to slowly starve to death in this dark, damp, smelly dungeon?

Dad goes back into the shelter and sweeps the flashlight around until it stops on the bunk bed next to the one where Mom lies. "Steven, could you give me a hand?" he asks.

"To do what?" Mr. Shaw replies.

"Take the bunk apart and put it back together on the other side," Dad says. "Then we can stand on it and push open the trapdoor."

It sounds like a lot of work, and I'm surprised when Mr. Shaw, who acts like everything is so hopeless, agrees to help.

Dismantling the bunk takes time. Dad gets tired and has to rest. Mr. Shaw takes over for a while, and then Mrs. Shaw, and even Mr. McGovern. Parts have to be unscrewed, then moved around the shield wall and put back together. With the extra activity, the air gets stale faster, so Dad assigns Ronnie and me to crank the ventilator. They need to use the flashlight, so when they're working on the other side of the shield wall, the rest of us are in near-dark.

"We should eat what's left," says Mr. McGovern,

panting as he finishes assembling part of the bunk. "There's no point in rationing anymore."

It takes a moment to realize what he means: if we really are trapped down here, rationing what food is left isn't going to make a difference. My heart rises into my throat, and I try to swallow it down. Imagine running out of food, then growing weaker and weaker until no one has the strength to crank the ventilator. . . .

"It could still take a while to get out," Dad cautions.

"You men should eat," suggests Mrs. Shaw. "It will help give you the strength you'll need to get this done."

"I feel terrible doing this," Dad says a little later, running his finger around the inside of the peanut butter jar to get every last smudge. But the strange thing is, it isn't so hard to watch. I've been hungry for so long that I've almost gotten used to it. What's more upsetting is knowing that after this there'll be no more food no matter what happens.

"You're doing it for our sake," Mrs. Shaw reminds him.

It doesn't take long for the men to finish what little food is left, but rather than get back to work, they yawn and say they have to rest first.

So we wait while they nap. But it's hard because now the clock is ticking. The food's gone. If we don't get out soon, we'll really begin to starve.

fifty-two

We continued to do normal stuff at school, but it felt like a shadow hung over everything. You couldn't forget about the Russians for long. A teacher would pull down a shade, and you'd think about how Puddin' Belly was supposed to do that if we were attacked. Or a kid would slam a locker, and everyone in the hall would jump.

On the news, they talked about the Russian ships sailing toward Cuba and the American blockade around the island. The moment of confrontation was nearing.

At dinnertime, Sparky and I went into the kitchen and found Mom sitting at the table, gazing out at the backyard.

"Where's Dad?" Sparky asked.

"Working late."

"Because there might be a war?" I asked.

Mom puffed on her cigarette. "I don't know."

"Is there any news?" I asked.

She blinked, and I could see that she wasn't certain what I meant.

"About the Russians?" I added.

"I haven't been listening."

That seemed strange. Why wasn't she following the news like everyone else?

"What's for dinner?" Sparky asked. Mom glanced at the kitchen clock, then got up and looked in the refrigerator. She said dinner would be ready soon and we should go watch TV.

While Sparky watched and Mom cooked, I snuck into my parents' bedroom. Inside the top drawer of Dad's dresser was a felt-lined tray with compartments for cuff links, tie tacks, and tie bars. Dad had a miniature gold tennis-racket tie bar and a silver one that was a pair of crossed skis. Another compartment held the small brass stays he inserted into his shirt collars so that they would keep their shape all day.

The next drawer contained Dad's shirts, each one folded over a piece of cardboard and held in place by a paper band. The mixed scents of Dad's body smell and chemicals from the dry cleaner wafted up as I slid my hands under the stacks of shirts and felt around. The drawer below that one contained underwear — white V-necked T-shirts and boxers. The bottom drawer was for sweaters.

I tried his closet next. Here amid the hanging suits and slacks, the scent of feet and leather filled my nostrils. Two shelves held shoes, each pair kept in its proper shape by wooden shoe trees. A small chest of drawers contained Dad's wool socks, tennis clothes, and sweatshirts. I slid my hands under the contents. Nothing. So Ronnie was wrong. Not every father hid *Playboy* in his dresser drawers.

Now I looked up. Above the rod where Dad's suits hung was a shelf, and from the floor I could see the corners of things like boxes and maybe a book. I climbed up on the chest of drawers. The shelf was still mostly out of reach, but if I stretched on my tiptoes, there was one green box I was able to work toward the edge until it tipped and fell into my hands. It was the size of a cereal box but heavy, and I was lucky that it didn't slip through my fingers and crash to the floor.

The box had the shiny, slick feel of newness. Still standing on the chest of drawers, I opened it curiously.

Inside was a gun.

Other than on a policeman's belt, it was the first real gun I'd ever seen. The metal had a vague sheen of oil, and I was afraid to touch it, afraid that it might go off accidentally in my hands.

Then Mom called: "Scott? Edward? Dinner!"

I inched the box back up on the shelf. There was only one reason why Dad would have a gun: for war.

In the kitchen, instead of setting the table, Mom had placed two plates of spaghetti and meatballs on a tray, along with napkins, forks, and glasses of milk.

She said, "They're for you and Edward. Go eat in the den."

"Dad said we're not allowed."

"I say you can," Mom said.

I carried the tray into the den, where Sparky was watching *Quick Draw McGraw,* and placed the food between us.

Sparky touched the spaghetti with his fork, then stared at the TV. I felt my insides tighten anxiously. Dad had a gun. Mom was letting us eat in the den. Could there be any clearer signs that the end of the world was approaching?

53

We sit in near-dark in the shelter and listen while the men work on the other side of the shield wall. Sparky has taken up permanent residence on Janet's lap.

"What's the first thing you'll do when you get out?" Mrs. Shaw asks.

Sparky: "Everything."

Paula: "Take a bath."

Ronnie: "Eat something good."

Me: "Take a bath *and* eat something good."

Ronnie's mom says, "What about you, Janet?"

"Look for my children, Mrs. Shaw."

Ronnie's mom utters a little "Oh!" of surprise. "I'm so sorry."

As if there weren't already a million reasons to feel bad, now I feel even worse. The two small faces at the window the day Mom drove Janet home . . . All the time we've been together down here, she never said a word. Sparky snuggles closer to her. "If you can't find them, you can be my other mommy."

Janet starts to cry.

The fathers' voices come around the shield wall. "Move it a little to the right." "Can you shine the light on this?" "Anyone see the screwdriver?"

Finally Dad calls, "I think we're ready."

We go into the corridor to find the bunk bed rebuilt under the trapdoor. Standing on the floor, Mr. McGovern is holding the flashlight on Dad and Mr. Shaw, both wearing masks and squatting naked on the top bunk under the trapdoor. Dad presses his back against it. He reminds me of that statue in New York City of Atlas holding up the world, only Atlas was all muscles and Dad looks so skinny. Next to him, Mr. Shaw lies on his back with his feet against the door.

They grit their teeth and push and strain. The bunk bed creaks; the trapdoor rises slowly. The creaking grows louder.

The trapdoor rises a tiny bit more.

Crack! The sound of splintering wood explodes into our ears.

"Stop!" Mr. Shaw gasps.

Clank! The trapdoor slams down.

Atop the bunk, both fathers breathe hard for a moment, then Dad asks, "What happened?"

"The board under us cracked," says Mr. Shaw.

"Of course," Mr. McGovern says, as if he's just realized something. "You're pushing up on a metal door, but at the same time you're pushing down on a wooden board. This is never going to work."

fifty-four

The Russian ships were getting closer to the quarantine line set up by the United States Navy. There was going to be a showdown. Would one side back down, or would there be war?

My stomach was in a nonstop knot, and I would catch myself at my school desk with my hands clenched and my toes curled up in my shoes. At lunch, the spaghetti and meatballs looked slimy, and I hardly had any appetite anyway. On the way home from school, I asked Ronnie if he wanted to play Nok-Hockey again.

"Why?" He asked.

"Don't you want a rematch?"

"I killed you last time."

"You won't this time."

Ronnie gave me an uncertain look.

"Scared I'll win?" I challenged him.

He snorted. "Fat chance."

We went to his house, where he beat me eleven games to one.

"Can I eat over?" I asked. "We could watch TV."

The Shaws were the only family I knew with a color television set. In the den, Ronnie and I watched *The Jetsons*, but what I really wanted to do was look in a *Playboy* before we went to war, only I was afraid Ronnie would make fun of me. When *The Jetsons* ended, Ronnie glanced toward the kitchen, where his mom had started dinner, and then went to the liquor cabinet and poured some Dubonnet into a glass. "We'll share," he whispered.

We each drank some, and then Ronnie went to the bathroom to wash the glass. As soon as he left the den, I lifted the bottle of Dubonnet to my lips and took a big gulp. The wine warmed my throat and my empty stomach, and I felt myself relax. The anxiety of war became one step removed.

Ronnie and I watched more TV. A little while later, Mr. Shaw came into the den wearing a suit and smelling of cigarettes and the train. He looked serious. "Any news?"

We shook our heads.

Ronnie's dad took off his jacket and rolled up his

sleeves. "How about a little something to take the edge off, gentlemen?"

Ronnie and I shared an uncertain look.

"Come on, boys, you wouldn't let a man drink alone at a time like this, would you?"

It wasn't long before I had a glass filled with ice and more Dubonnet. Ronnie shot me a smirk as if he thought we were getting away with something. Little did he know.

We sipped our drinks. When I closed my eyes, I felt like I was on the deck of a boat in swaying seas.

"That bomb shelter might come in handy after all, Scott," Mr. Shaw said. For once he wasn't joking.

"You really think we could go to war, Dad?" Ronnie asked.

"It's hard to imagine," Mr. Shaw said gravely. "I mean, the sheer insanity of it. No one can win."

"What if the Russians don't care about winning?" Ronnie asked.

Mr. Shaw sighed and shook his head.

From the kitchen, Mrs. Shaw called, "Dinner's ready. I called your mom, Scotty. She said it was okay."

Mr. Shaw got up. "Shall we?"

I stood up, and the room suddenly rocked.

55

"It's hopeless," mumbles Mr. Shaw.

We're all back in the shelter. Mom's on her bunk. The rest of us sit on chairs or on the floor.

"Is it, Dad?" Sparky asks.

"I need to think," Dad says.

"About what?" Mr. McGovern demands. "How stupid it was to build this shelter in the first place? How much better it would have been if we'd just died when we had the chance?"

"*Shut up!*" Dad shouts so loudly, we all jump. This time, Paula's father does what Dad says.

I'm scared sick. The shelter seems dimmer than usual until Dad replaces the batteries in the flashlight and it's brighter again.

"Well, at least you made sure to have enough batteries," Mr. McGovern says bitterly.

"Buried alive," Mr. Shaw mutters.

Sparky lets out a frightened whimper and hugs Janet tightly.

"There's a way," Dad says a little while later.

"Oh, give it up already, will you?" Mr. McGovern growls.

"What's your idea?" asks Mrs. Shaw.

"We have to reinforce the bunk bed."

"It won't work," Mr. McGovern says.

Dad turns to Mr. Shaw as if asking if he'll help, but Ronnie's dad lowers his head.

They don't think it can be done. And if they won't help, it's hopeless. Dad can't do it alone. My insides churn. How can they just give up and let us die down here?

It's Janet who speaks up. "I'll help you, Mr. Porter. I want to find my children."

Her eyes meet Dad's, and he blinks slowly and hard as if to fight back tears. Is it because he's grateful that she's offered to help? Or is it sadness because it's hard to imagine how her children could still be alive?

"Thank you," Dad says.

They begin by moving Mom from her bunk to some pillows on the floor and making her comfortable. Then Dad turns toward the bunk she was lying on and says, "We have to take this one apart and use the pieces to reinforce the other one." But his shoulders stoop, as if just the thought of all that work is too much. "We're going to need more hands."

None of the other grown-ups reply.

I clear my throat. "I'll help."

"Me, too," says Sparky.

Dad gives us a weak smile as if he doesn't think we can make much of a difference. You can tell by the way he looks at Mr. Shaw that he's hoping he'll try again, but Ronnie's father sits besides his wife with his knees pulled up under his chin and doesn't respond.

"What good will giving up do?" Dad asks.

Ronnie's dad looks up at him, and then back down without answering.

"Seriously, Steven," Dad persists.

"I don't know what's on the other side of that trapdoor, but whatever it is, it's too heavy," Mr. Shaw finally says. "We tried, Richard. Before the board cracked."

Dad stands still, his face tilted upward in thought. Is he considering giving up, too?

He looks at Sparky and me. "I'm going to keep trying. Come on, boys."

I realize I've been holding my breath. When I push

myself up, dizziness causes my vision to narrow, and I have to bend over with my hands on my knees and my head as low as it will go.

When I straighten up, everyone's staring.

"You okay?" Dad whispers.

I nod. He gives me a screwdriver and shows me which screws to take out of Mom's bunk bed. I do what I'm told, but I don't say what I'm really wondering: Is he just trying to keep us busy so we won't think about what's ahead?

fifty-six

"Whoa!" In the Shaws' den, Ronnie's father caught me by the arm. "Steady, sailor."

Holding my elbow, he led me into the kitchen, where four aluminum trays were set with little compartments that kept the meat from touching the potatoes and vegetables. Mrs. Shaw pointed to a chair. "You're there, Scotty."

I went to sit but missed the chair and nearly fell over. Mrs. Shaw frowned and looked at her husband.

"Cheap drunk," said Mr. Shaw.

Mrs. Shaw's eyes widened. "Steven, you didn't."

"Couldn't have been more than a thimbleful," Mr. Shaw said. "He just needs to get something in his stomach."

We began to eat. I tried to cut into the meat, but it was really tough.

"Ahem, Scott." Mr. Shaw cleared his throat. "Your knife's upside down."

"Oh." I turned the knife and started again. That's when the Salisbury steak shot off my tray and landed in the middle of the table like a small brown island on a sea of white.

"Let's try a sharper knife." Mr. Shaw went to a drawer and got one with a black handle. "Careful with this one, okay? We'd like to send you home with all ten fingers."

Ronnie made a funny noise, as if muffling a laugh. I decided to try the corn, but most of the kernels fell off the fork before they got to my mouth.

"Care to spoon-feed your friend, Ronnie?" Mrs. Shaw suggested.

"Why doesn't he just go home?" Ronnie sounded like I'd become an embarrassment. His parents had a conversation with their eyes.

Mr. Shaw turned to me. "Try the mashed potatoes, Scott."

It would have been impolite not to, but as soon as I felt that mealy sensation in my mouth, I spit them back onto the tray.

Ronnie muttered, "Jesus Christ."

"Sorry," I apologized. "I forgot that I hate mashed potatoes."

"*Now* will you send him home?" Ronnie begged his parents. "Or are you scared you'll get into trouble because he's drunk?"

"He's not drunk," Mrs. Shaw replied.

"Oh, really?" Ronnie asked in a fresh way that would have definitely gotten me spanked. "What would you call it?"

57

I can't loosen the bunk-bed screws. Are they *that* tight, or have I just grown too weak? I'm so scared that we're never going to get out, but I keep it to myself because I don't want to make things worse. Paula quietly weeps and clings to her dad. Sparky tried to help but gave up and now huddles with Janet, his eyes nervous and darting.

Ronnie takes the screwdriver and tries, but he can't get the screws loose, either. Dad struggles with them for a while, then gives up and sits down beside Janet, Sparky, and me. He gazes away, slowly kneading the muscles in his forearms. "I'm sorry, Janet."

She places her hand on his shoulder. "Take a rest and try again, Mr. Porter," she gently urges him. "For your children. For mine."

Dad lets out a deep sigh, then picks up the screwdriver and tries again.

A hand gently shakes me awake. It's Dad. He's finally gotten one of the bunk boards loose and needs help carrying it around the shield wall.

I yawn and get up, and we carry the board into the narrow corridor. Dad looks up at the bunk, and once again his shoulders sag as if he's not sure he has the strength to lift the board up there. We lean against the cinder blocks. Everyone else is on the other side of the shield wall. Dad puts his arms around me, and I slide mine around his waist and press my cheek against his cool skin. I think he must be a good father. There may have been a lot of things he didn't think of, and a lot of times he got mad and spanked Sparky and me, but he was never mean.

And he always tried his best.

When we go back into the shelter, it feels like no one's moved. Dad starts to unscrew another bunk board but spends more time resting than working. Janet kneads his shoulders and whispers encouragement. When he's finally ready to move the second board, he asks her to help. The three of us pick it up and take a few steps, but the board slips out of our hands and hits the floor with a loud *clack!* Everyone jumps.

"Listen," Dad says, breathing hard. "We can't do this without the rest of you." He pauses as if just the act of talking takes an effort. "If you folks just want to sit here and wait for the end, I can't stop you. But I want to keep trying."

No one moves. The air is stale. The ventilator should probably be cranked.

"You're wasting your time," says Mr. McGovern. "Whatever's on top of the door is too heavy."

"No one's going to come and save us, Herb," Dad answers. "This is our only chance."

No one moves.

We sit. Dad hugs Sparky and me to him. I touch Sparky's arm and nod over at Janet. He may only be nine, but he knows what I'm thinking. He takes her hand.

What a good little brother he is.

In the dim light, Ronnie sits between his parents, holding their hands. Mr. McGovern has his arm around Paula. Everyone's quiet — lost in thought, I guess. My thoughts go to my friends. I think about playing fungo and touch football and throwing dirt bombs and burning leaves. How could they do this to kids? We never had anything against Russian kids, and it's hard to believe they had anything against us.

What'd we do to deserve this?

"May I say something, Mr. Porter?" Janet's voice squeezes through the gloom.

"Yes, of course, Janet."

She addresses everyone. "Mr. and Mrs. Shaw, Mr. McGovern, if we die in here, you'll go to your graves knowing what happened to your children."

Heads rise as they exchange quizzical looks.

"As awful as this is, you'll have that peace of mind," Janet continues. "Without your help, I will never know what happened to mine."

Silence.

"Please," Janet urges them. "I am asking you to put yourself in my place."

Silence.

fifty-eight

"The Yankees sure are something, huh?" Mr. Shaw said after dinner. "Four World Series in seven years."

"Yeah." I'd managed to eat most of the steak and corn. The euphoric feeling brought on by the wine was gradually giving way to throbbing in my skull.

"Maybe this'll be the Giants' year to win it all, too."

"Definitely," I said. "Tittle's great."

"He your favorite player?"

"No, Sam Huff."

"A fine linebacker," Mr. Shaw agreed. "Your dad taking you to any games this fall?"

I started to shake my head, but that made it hurt more. Dad was a football fan, but we'd never gone to a game.

"Ronnie and I go a lot," Mr. Shaw said. "Have a great time, don't we, Sport?"

Ronnie nodded morosely.

"Maybe you'd like to come with us to a game?"

"You mean, if there isn't a war?" I asked.

"That's right," Mr. Shaw said patiently. "We'll only go to the game if we haven't gone to war. Would you like that, Scott?"

"Sure, that would be great," I said.

Ronnie's dad smiled. "Okay, let's plan on it."

When it was time to go, Ronnie got his jacket.

"Where are you going?" I asked.

"With you."

"Because I'm drunk?" I asked.

Mr. Shaw rubs my head. "You're not drunk, Scott. Now, run along."

It was dark and chilly outside. Ronnie kicked a stone down the sidewalk. "Don't tell your parents, okay?"

"That I'm going to a football game?"

"No, dummy, about the wine." He held up his pinkie. "Swear?"

I had to think about it. I guess I knew they were using the Giants to get me to not tell, but the truth was, except for my head hurting, no harm had been done. I didn't know why I'd taken that big gulp of Dubonnet, but they hadn't made me, and I didn't want to get the Shaws into trouble or to make Ronnie angry with me.

I hooked my pinkie to his. "Swear."

"Okay." He nodded grimly and patted me on the back. "See you tomorrow."

59

No one's spoken since Janet made her plea for their help to find her children. I know they must feel as bad as I do, but right now we're so weak, and fortifying the broken bunk bed under the trapdoor seems like such a huge task. Maybe if we just rest awhile . . .

But minutes pass and no one moves.

It's Sparky who finally speaks up. "I'll try again, Janet."

Of course, there's nothing he can do, but somehow, hearing him say it gets the others to reconsider. Eventually, everyone, even Mr. McGovern, agrees to try. It takes a while, but we manage to get the boards up on top of the bunk under the trapdoor. Dad wants to use some of the posts from the other bunk bed to make this one stronger, and Mr. McGovern suggests angling them in a way that Dad didn't think of.

Sometimes it feels like we're working in slow motion, but finally we're ready.

Then Dad climbs up and says something that really surprises me: "Ronnie and Scott, I want you to help. There's only room for two adults up here. But I think we can squeeze two boys in place of one adult and still have room for me."

As frightening as it all is, it makes me feel good that Dad wants me to help. That he thinks Ronnie and me together will be stronger than Mr. Shaw.

We slowly climb up on the reinforced bunk bed, and all three of us put on gas masks. Feeling a crazy mixture of fright and hope, I lie on my back next to Ronnie with our feet against the underside of the cold trapdoor while Dad wedges his back against it. "I hate to say it, boys, but our lives depend on this."

What if I'm not strong enough?

What if no one would be strong enough?

"One, two, three . . . push!"

We grimace and push as hard as we can. It's difficult to breathe with the masks on, and the clear plastic disks quickly fog from exertion. The trapdoor feels like it weighs a ton. Something really heavy must be on top of it.

Dad grunts. My heart thuds so hard, I can feel the pulse thumping in my ears. The door rises slightly.

"It's working!" Mrs. Shaw's voice reaches my ears. "Keep going!"

"You can do it!" Sparky yells.

The trapdoor rises a little more. Bright light begins to seep in.

"A post!" Dad croaks, and Mr. Shaw quickly jams one into the gap between the trapdoor and the closet floor above.

"Stop pushing," Dad gasps.

Ronnie and I go limp, panting and exhausted from the effort. The light seeping in around the trapdoor feels unnaturally bright, and we have to squint.

With the light comes cold air. Dad studies the instruments from the radiation kit. "Fifty-five roentgens. That's close enough."

When he yanks off his mask, it catches me off-guard. It almost seems reckless.

"Come on, boys," he urges.

Ronnie and I pull off our masks, and cool, fresh air fills our lungs. It feels amazing.

But with it comes a smell.

Like rotten meat.

The others smell it. Noses wrinkle, eyes wince. Dad's face falls. "Everyone into the other room," he orders grimly.

Janet leads Sparky back around the shield wall. Ronnie and I climb down and follow. Only the dads stay behind.

In the shelter, Ronnie, Paula, and I sit together, listening to every sound and whisper that comes around the shield wall. Wood scrapes and men grunt.

"Can you turn that post sideways?"

"Wedge it in as far as it will go."

"There's a hammer in the toolbox," Dad says.

Mr. McGovern comes back into the shelter. He seems full of energy, and I wonder whether it's from excitement or if he really has been saving it up like he said he was. He gets the hammer and goes back through the gap, and soon we hear banging.

"That should work."

"What about this piece?"

"Can you jam it in that way?"

A long silence follows. Those of us in the shelter exchange uncertain glances.

"Dad?" I call.

"Just a second," he calls back. Then to the other fathers: "Ready?"

We hear grunts and heaving noises. Wood creaks. Metal hinges squeak. . . .

There's a slithering sound as if something is sliding off the trapdoor.

The narrow corridor on the other side of the shield

wall fills with light. Different light. Natural light. Sparky jumps to his feet and dashes out.

The rest of us follow.

Above us, the trapdoor is open. Dad's standing on top of the bunk bed, his body half out of the shelter, his pale skin bathed in light. It's cold, and the rotten meat smell is awful. Mr. McGovern and Mr. Shaw are standing on the floor below.

"How is it?" Mr. McGovern asks somberly.

Something in Dad's throat catches. "It's . . . okay . . . I guess."

sixty

It was Why Can't You Be Like Johnny?'s birthday. Earlier
in the day, a U.S. Air Force spy plane was shot down over
Cuba, and now the U.S. Armed Forces were being mobi-
lized. Preparations for war had begun.

The Sinclairs canceled the birthday party but invited
Ronnie, Freak O' Nature, and me over for cake because
we lived so close. Dad said it was okay to go. This was
the first time we'd been allowed in the Sinclairs' house
since the Pee Steam Incident of the previous summer.
Why Can't You Be Like Johnny?'s bedroom was upstairs
and had its own porch, and one night we'd brought sleeping bags over and slept on the porch under the stars. It
was chilly in the morning, and Ronnie said that instead

of using the bathroom, we should pee over the railing because when it was cold, your pee had steam. Why Can't You Be Like Johnny? said it wasn't cold enough for pee steam, and Ronnie said, "Wanna bet?"

I was surprised that Why Can't You Be Like Johnny? took the bet, but I guess he was determined to prove Ronnie wrong. We stood at the railing and peed down onto the flower beds. Of course, Why Can't You Be Like Johnny? was right because he was always right. Then Ronnie laughed and said he'd known all along that it wasn't cold enough for pee steam and he'd really just wanted to see if he could get us all to pee off the porch.

Unfortunately, Mrs. Sinclair was in the kitchen making breakfast when she looked out the window and saw four glittering gold streams cascading down onto her rosebushes. We were immediately sent home.

"How come she changed her mind?" Freak O' Nature asked while he, Ronnie, and I walked over for birthday cake.

"Maybe she figures we could all be dead tomorrow, so what does it matter?" Ronnie said.

Mrs. Sinclair let us in with a narrow-eyed look as if warning that if we did anything wrong this time, we would be banned from her house forever. The funny thing about the Sinclairs was that they weren't all brains like Why Can't You Be Like Johnny? Mr. Sinclair owned a plumbing company and spent most evenings watching TV. And a few months before, Why Can't You Be Like Johnny?'s eight-year-old sister, Barbara, had swallowed a safety pin and had to go to the hospital.

Mrs. Sinclair served a cake with a rocket ship made of icing, and we sang "Happy Birthday," only under his breath, Ronnie sang:

"Happy birthday to you.
You live in a zoo.
You look like a monkey,
And you smell like one, too!"

I was afraid Mrs. Sinclair had heard him, but she smiled while she cut the rocket cake, so it looked like we were in the clear.

Then Mr. Sinclair brought out a long box wrapped in birthday paper, and Why Can't You Be Like Johnny? got excited because inside was a telescope, and he said we should all go up to his porch and look through it. As we headed upstairs, Mrs. Sinclair once again gave Ronnie, Freak O' Nature, and me that look that said we were dead if we got into any mischief.

Out on the porch, Why Can't You Be Like Johnny? set up the telescope. I felt my insides corkscrew when I imagined looking through it and seeing Russian missiles streaking our way.

He aimed the telescope at the moon. "That big white

spot is Copernicus crater. And that round dark area right above it? That's called the Mare Imbrium. It's Latin for 'the Sea of Rains.'"

"It rains on the moon?" said Freak O' Nature.

"It was a sea of lava," explained Why Can't You Be Like Johnny? "A long time ago, a huge asteroid hit the surface and made a hole so deep that lava came out."

"What's an asteroid?" Freak O' Nature asked.

"It's like a shooting star," said Johnny. "Only it's just a big space rock. People used to think they were stars because they glowed when they burned up in the atmosphere."

I looked up into the dark. A tiny, starlike dot was moving slowly across the night sky. "Like that?" I pointed.

"Oh, my gosh!" Johnny gasped excitedly. "It's *Echo*! The communications satellite."

"You can see it?" Ronnie asked, dubiously.

"It's a giant silver balloon," said Johnny. "This is unreal!"

What was unreal was seeing Johnny get so excited. He never acted like this.

"How do you know it's not a shooting star?" asked Freak O' Nature.

"They streak across the sky and are gone in an instant," said Johnny.

"And how do you know it's not *Sputnik*?" asked Ronnie. *Sputnik* was a Russian satellite.

"You can't see *Sputnik*," said Why Can't You Be Like Johnny? "Here, everyone look."

We took turns looking at *Echo* through the telescope. It still looked like a bright dot, only bigger.

"You know that the Ruskies sent *Sputnik* into space to prove they had a rocket strong enough to launch a nuclear bomb at us?" said Ronnie, looking at me. "Think your bomb shelter can stand up to that, Scott?"

"Pretty soon it won't even matter," said Johnny as we watched *Echo* creep across the star-speckled sky. "Now that we can put men in space, they're going to build laser cannons that can destroy a whole city with a single blast."

I didn't know whether laser cannons were something Johnny had read about in his Tom Swift books or something real, and I didn't want to ask because I was afraid I'd look dumb. Besides, what difference would it make? Why did they need laser cannons when they already had nuclear bombs that could destroy everything? All I knew was that for an instant, while looking at *Echo*, I'd managed to forget about war, but now it had all come rushing back.

High above us, *Echo* gradually dimmed and vanished into the dark.

"Where'd it go?" asked Freak O' Nature.

"Into Earth's shadow," said Johnny.

We watched the sky for something else exciting to come along, but nothing did. Behind us, Ronnie was peering through the telescope. Only it was pointed across the street.

"What are you doing?" asked Johnny.

"Nothing," Ronnie answered.

Why Can't You Be Like Johnny? aimed the telescope at the moon again and showed us some mountains and craters. Then Mrs. Sinclair came out and said it was time to go.

Outside the Sinclairs' house, Freak O' Nature went one way, and Ronnie and I went the other. Bugs zoomed crazily around the streetlights, kind of like missiles.

"Guess what I saw tonight?" Ronnie asked.

"The moon and that *Echo* satellite."

"How about Paula's bedroom?"

"How?"

"With the telescope, dummy. Right into her window. Want to know what I saw?"

I stopped under a streetlight and squinted at him. Here we were possibly on the brink of World War III, and all he could think about was looking in a girl's bedroom. My jaw tightened, and I suddenly felt angry. Maybe because I was so scared and he was acting like he wasn't. "No," I said.

Ronnie put his hands on his hips. "Sure, you do."

"No . . . I . . . don't."

61

Dad looks down from the trapdoor with a pained expression. "Steven, could you climb up here? Herb, would you get everyone back into the shelter, and then come up and join us?"

"But, Dad—" Sparky starts.

"You'll all be out soon," Dad promises. "You just have to wait a little longer."

Mr. McGovern herds us back around the shield wall. His eyes look glittery. In a quavering voice, he says, "Stephanie, make sure the kids stay put."

Janet and Mrs. Shaw stand guard by the shield wall to make sure we don't try to sneak back into the corridor.

You'd think they'd be ecstatic that we can finally get out, but they're both quiet and sad.

"Why can't we go?" Sparky asks.

"Soon, I promise." Mrs. Shaw strokes his head reassuringly.

Sparky looks up into Janet's face. She nods.

Ronnie leans so close, his lips practically touch my ear. "You know what was on top of the door?" he whispers.

"Uh-huh."

Paula's face scrunches up as if she might start to cry. Ronnie reaches out, hesitates, then places his hand on her arm. I watch their eyes meet. "We'll all get out soon," he says, sounding just like my father.

But every second we wait feels like forever. Cold air fills the shelter, and we start to shiver. Finally Dad calls down, "Scott?"

I go into the corridor and squint in the light coming through the square above. Dad's up there, out of the shelter, wearing dungarees and a sweatshirt. "It won't be long," he says, dropping down a box of Ritz crackers and a package of Oreo cookies. "Here's something to keep you busy. They're okay to eat."

Back in the shelter, everyone eats ravenously. Stale crackers and cookies never tasted so good.

sixty-two

"Why not?" Ronnie asked.

Trouble swirled around me like those bugs around the streetlight. It was times like this when I wished Ronnie wasn't my best friend. I needed a friend I could admit I was scared to without having to worry that he'd make fun of me. "Because we might be on the verge of nuclear war. Doesn't that bother you?"

Ronnie shrugged. "Okay, forget it. I'm not gonna tell you what I saw."

"Suit yourself," I said.

Ronnie narrowed his eyes. "Come on, admit it—you're dying to know."

"No, I'm really not," I said, feeling anger and fear and resentment percolating inside me. "And you want to know why? Because we could all be killed tonight. And if we're not, you're gonna come up with some scheme to look through Paula's window again, and I'm gonna get in a ton of trouble. And you're not gonna get in any trouble because you never get punished for anything."

"You are the biggest baby I ever saw," Ronnie taunted. "You don't know anything, and you're afraid to find out. Go be a coward in your dumb bomb shelter. Want to know something? My dad thinks your dad's an idiot. Because there's never gonna be a war because everyone knows the world would be destroyed and no one would win. Only an idiot would be stupid enough to build a bomb shelter."

"Well, your father's stupid for giving kids wine and reading *Playboy* in front of them and never making you do any chores," I shot back. "And your mom's stupid because she dresses like a movie star even though she's just a mother, and she gives you TV dinners instead of real meals because she's too lazy to cook."

"Coward," Ronnie said.

"Spoiled brat," I said.

"Homo."

I balled my hands into fists and swung as hard as I could, hitting him on the arm. It must have hurt a little, but not enough. Ronnie tackled me, and we slammed to the street and rolled around, swinging our fists wildly. I knew I was going to lose, but it didn't matter. I just wanted to hit him as hard as I could. I wanted to make him pay for calling my father an idiot and for not being scared and not doing chores and for always getting me into trouble and having a home filled with so many temptations.

Even when Ronnie pinned me on my back, I still kicked and tried to hit him. If it hadn't been for him, I wouldn't have stolen that cheesecake or drunk too much Dubonnet or had to think about my mother's breasts and queers. I was sure that behind our backs his father made fun of my father, and that his mother was one of the ladies who stared at my mother in the supermarket.

"Break it up. Come on, boys, that's enough." Dad's voice came through the dark.

I felt Ronnie's weight rise off me and saw Dad pulling him by the arm. I pushed myself to my feet. My right elbow stung where the skin had been scraped, and my knee throbbed where I'd banged it on the street.

"What's this about?" Dad asked.

Ronnie and I glared at each other but said nothing. Except for his shirt hanging out and one knee of his pants being torn, he didn't look like he'd even been in a fight.

"Come on, what's the story?" Dad asked.

We were silent. I knew that if I told what happened, I'd be labeled a tattletale and a sissy. Dad probably knew it, too.

"Okay, Ronnie, you better go home." He let go, and Ronnie headed toward his house.

Dad and I started up our driveway, but I limped.

"You okay?" he asked.

"Yeah."

"Want to tell me what happened?"

I shook my head.

"A boy thing, huh?" He smiled slightly, almost as if he was proud.

"Yeah."

Mom cleaned my elbow and knee with Mercurochrome, which stung even more than scraping them had in the first place. She was annoyed when I said I couldn't tell her what had happened and Dad said it was my private business. I had a feeling they were going to have an argument.

I went to bed wondering if Ronnie was right and there wouldn't be a war after all. I wondered what would happen tomorrow when I saw him at the bus stop. Would he tell everyone we'd had a fight? Would he say he won or that it had been broken up before either of us could win?

Dad came in and sat on the side of my bed. "How're you feeling?" he whispered.

I shrugged. It hurt, but not as much as you'd imagine a fight would. "Mom was pretty mad," I said.

"She's been upset about a lot of things lately." Dad seemed sad. "It's a hard time for everyone."

"You think there's going to be a war?"

"No one knows," he answered.

"That's what the fight was about, kind of."

He looked surprised. "Seriously?"

"Ronnie said something bad about you because of the bomb shelter."

Dad let his breath out and slowly nodded. "Maybe they're right. Maybe it was a mistake. I was just trying to protect us."

"I think you did the right thing, Dad."

One of his eyebrows rose. "Even though you got into a fight about it?"

I shrugged. "Ronnie's a jerk."

"But he's your best friend."

"Yeah."

A sad knowing smile crept onto Dad's lips. "Kind of like your mom and me."

63

Dad throws down clothes. Sparky and I find our own things, and the others put on whatever comes closest to fitting. Mrs. Shaw and Janet dress Mom.

A few minutes later, Dad and Mr. Shaw climb back down into the shelter.

"Can we go up?" Sparky asks.

"In a moment." Dad eases Mom to her feet. It's so strange the way she doesn't know us but knows to walk when he leads her. In the narrow corridor, Janet and Mrs. Shaw work with Dad to get her onto the bunk bed. Above them, Mr. McGovern reaches down to help her out.

Paula and Sparky go next.

Then Mrs. Shaw and Janet.

Then Ronnie.

Dad looks down from above. "Your turn, Scott."

I climb up on the bunk bed toward the light and the bad smell. It's slow going because I'm weak and have to pause and rest, but I'm eager and scared, too. Finally I poke my head out. Even though I'm in the playroom closet, it's so bright that I have to squint. The playroom windows have been blasted out, leaving jagged ridges of glass in the frames. The floor is covered with broken glass, small branches, leaves, and toys. The rotten meat smell is strong, and I don't have to ask what the large lumps are that lie under bedsheets here and there. My insides tighten, and the awful thoughts of what it must have been like for those above gnaws at me.

"Don't look," Dad says. "Go outside."

Behind me, Mr. Shaw climbs out of the shelter and hands Dad the flashlight, first-aid kit, the green box, and some other things. Then he and Dad close the trapdoor.

Out in the backyard, the air is cold and fresh. The trees have been stripped bare, and all that remains are stubby, leafless limbs and trunks missing bark on the side that faced the blast. Window screens, tree branches, roof shingles, and sheets of newspapers lie on the ground among the dead leaves and patches of scorched brown grass. The sun is in the west, so for the first time in weeks, we have a sense of what time it is. The air is still, and the sky is mostly blue, with a few feathery clouds here and there.

Up here in the light, it's a shock to see how thin and gaunt everyone's gotten. Dad and Mr. McGovern look strange with their short beards. We move slowly and keep looking upward as if trying to adjust to not having a ceiling overhead. Squinting in the angled sunlight, we hug ourselves, not just because we're chilled.

We're outside.

It's so quiet that we can hear Sparky's teeth chatter.

We're alive.

Squawking and honking comes from overhead. A *V* of black-and-white Canada geese flies high above us.

"From up north," Mr. McGovern says.

"Look." Mr. Shaw points behind us. In the distance a thin column of white smoke rises almost straight up into the air.

"Other people," Dad says.

We're not the only ones.

But now Dad's looking back into the playroom with a stricken expression. He closes his eyes as if he wishes he couldn't see.

Mrs. Shaw takes his arm. "It's horrible, but we all couldn't have survived, Richard."

It's strange that she's the one who says it. Dad nods slowly as if he knows she's right, but it still doesn't make him feel better. He turns to Mr. Shaw and Mr. McGovern. "We have to give them a proper burial."

The others agree. Paula tugs at her father's hand as if there's something he needs to do. "Daddy?"

"Yes, honey, in a second," Mr. McGovern says, and steps closer to Dad. "Steven, I . . ." He trails off and swivels his head at Janet, who looks away. Paula's father turns back to Dad. "I'm sorry. We all made mistakes. . . . Would you watch Paula for me? There are things I need to do."

Dad nods. Mr. McGovern heads off, around our house, toward his own.

Mr. Shaw extends his hand. "Thank you, Richard."

They shake.

"See you in the morning?" Dad asks, tilting his head toward our playroom.

"Yes, definitely."

Mrs. Shaw gives Dad a hug, and Ronnie shakes his hand, then looks at me and moves his lips as if to say, *See you later.* He joins his parents, and they walk across Old Lady Lester's backyard toward their home.

Dad turns to Janet. "It's going to be dark soon. If you can wait until tomorrow, I promise that as soon as we finish what we have to do here, we'll help you look for your children."

"Thank you, Mr. Porter," Janet answers.

When Dad turns to me next and places his hands on

my shoulders, it catches me by surprise. He turns me to face him. "Scott, I'm proud of you. It was terrible down there, and you conducted yourself like a man."

I don't know what to say. Dad smiles and says we should go inside, where he'll make a fire and heat water so we can wash and cook some food. He leads Mom toward the house. Janet and Paula go with him, and I begin to follow, then stop and look back.

Amid the broken branches, torn shingles, and ripped screens, Sparky's on his toes with his arms spread out, spinning around and around on the scorched grass, laughing.

I can't help but smile. What a kid.

AUTHOR'S NOTE

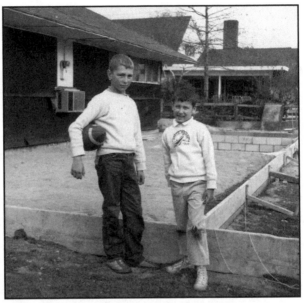

The author, age twelve, with his younger brother, Leigh, standing in front of their family's new below-ground bomb shelter, 1962. A playroom and bedroom would soon be built over the shelter.

The one-story ranch house looks smaller than I remember. The white pine in the front yard that I used to climb as a boy looms a dozen feet higher than the roof. The locust tree I helped my father plant fifty years ago is now almost as tall as the pine. The front lawn, which once felt so expansive, now looks hardly large enough for a game of tag.

The home's current owner invites me in. The slate floor in the living room has been replaced with carpeting, and the kitchen has been modernized. As we walk down the hall toward the back of the house, I am flooded with memories — the games my brother and I played, the fights, the chases, the nooks and crannies we hid in for hide-and-seek.

At the back of the house, where the playroom once was, there is now a short hall and two smaller bedrooms. We go into the first bedroom — decorated in pink, a color virtually nonexistent in the male-dominated home of my childhood — and the owner opens a closet door. He clears away some shoes and dolls from the carpeted floor. "Listen." He raps the carpet with his knuckles, producing a dull, echoing clang. "We never had it removed."

He means the metal trapdoor. He can't show it to me without pulling up the carpet, but it evokes a memory just the same — of the Cuban Missile Crisis and the years after, when the threat of nuclear war had diminished, and the trapdoor practically vanished under toys and balls and other sports equipment.

The trapdoor has been permanently sealed. No one will ever open it and climb down, as I did as a teenager to show my friends the shelter. Instead there is an outside entrance to the shelter now, and, as the owner leads me out to the backyard, he asks me about the stories the neighbors told him when he and his family moved in twenty years ago.

Is it true that before he had the shelter built, my father had a twelve-foot fence erected around the property so that no one would be able to see in? No, I tell him, that's not true. Besides, building a fence would have only invited questions and scrutiny.

Was it true that building the shelter took every spare cent my family had, and as a result we had to forgo vacations, dinners out, and other leisure activities? While I was not privy to my family's finances as a child, it's doubtful. I recall that we vacationed on Cape Cod and skied in Vermont, and we went to Chinese and Italian restaurants.

In the backyard, except for one large weeping willow, the trees I remember are gone. Here concrete steps lead to a subterranean wooden door. Before we descend, the owner tells me the story of having this entrance built: after inspecting the shelter from the inside, the contractor estimated that the job of digging the new outside entrance would take no more than three or four days. At first the digging went quickly, but when the workers started to break through the cinder-block concrete wall, they found something unexpected—an interior lining of quarter-inch-thick iron plating.

A welder had to be brought in to cut through the iron with an acetylene torch, and when this was done, there was yet another surprise—on the other side of the iron plating was a second wall of cinder blocks.

"Your father really wanted to protect you," the owner says as he leads me down the entrance steps.

I wish I could say that once inside the shelter, old, forgotten memories were unearthed, but almost everything down there is different now. The bunks and wooden shelves of supplies are gone, replaced with metal file cabinets. The overhead water tank has been removed, and a dehumidifier hums in one corner. The steel ventilator still pokes out of the wall, but the crank is missing.

Holding a flashlight, the owner leads me around the shield wall and into the narrow corridor beneath the trapdoor. The rungs in the wall are still there, shrouded in spiderwebs. The owner offers an unnecessary apology for the webs, saying he rarely comes down to the shelter anymore, and it has been many years since he's looked on this side of the shield wall.

Later, we leave the shelter and I thank him for allowing me to visit. I get in my car, drive past a few houses, and stop at the top of the hill for which the street is named. Lining the curb are the houses of my childhood friends and neighbors, a few unchanged, but others almost unrecognizable thanks to redesign and renovation. Here my thoughts are once again filled with the memories—of baseball and football games we played on this street, of the Good Humor Man's ringing bells and how we'd all run home to beg our mothers for quarters for ice cream, of playing in piles of leaves, splashing in puddles, and building snowmen. Ours were truly innocent childhoods.

People say that the era of post–World War II American innocence died on November 22, 1963, with the assassination of President John F. Kennedy. But I wonder if perhaps that innocence began to fade earlier than that, with the Cold War nuclear arms race and the threat of mutually assured destruction. Certainly that was the first time my friends and I became aware that there were countries thousands of miles away, on the other sides of vast oceans, that wanted to destroy us. Countries populated by people we didn't know, had never met, and had no reason to dislike.

As history shows, the Cuban Missile Crisis was averted and no bombs fell. The American people were led to believe that Soviet premier Nikita Khrushchev backed down and ordered the ships carrying missiles and other weapons to return to Russia. In actuality, though, the crisis was forestalled when President Kennedy secretly agreed to Khrushchev's demand to remove all American nuclear missiles located in Turkey — on the condition that this information not be made public. Thus, what was presented to our country as a military triumph was at best a draw, if not a defeat.

Why is it that since the dawn of civilization, we have persisted in following a pattern where mere handfuls of influential men manage to convince or force great masses of peaceful human beings to fear and hate one another enough to go to war? Has the result ever been anything other than misery, death, and destruction?

More than fifty years have passed since that week in October of 1962 when the world came the closest it's ever been to complete annihilation. And yet we are still at war.

Will we never learn?

ACKNOWLEDGMENTS

My heartfelt thanks to:

Stephen Barbara, for getting behind this book and steering it to the wonderful folks at Candlewick.

Karen Lotz, for taking a leap of faith on a partial manuscript from an author she'd never worked with before.

And finally, the magnificent Kaylan Adair, whose long, thoughtful, elegantly phrased editorial letters were precious gifts.